DUTCH AND INDIGENOUS COMMUNITIES IN SEVENTEENTH-CENTURY NORTHEASTERN NORTH AMERICA

DUTCH AND INDIGENOUS COMMUNITIES IN SEVENTEENTH-CENTURY NORTHEASTERN NORTH AMERICA

What Archaeology, History, and Indigenous Oral Traditions
Teach Us about Their Intercultural Relationships

Edited by

Lucianne Lavin

Cover Image: L. F. Tantillo. *Curiosity of the Magua. Mohawk warriors approach the ship of Arent Van Curler*, 1650. Oil on canvas. 26" x 38". © L. F. Tantillo

Published by State University of New York Press, Albany

For information, contact State University of New York Press, Albany, NY
www.sunypress.edu

Library of Congress Cataloging-in-Publication Data

Names: Lavin, Lucianne, editor.
Title: Dutch and indigenous communities in seventeenth-century northeastern
  North America : what archaeology, history, and indigenous oral traditions teach
  us about their intercultural relationships / Lucianne Lavin.
Description: Albany : State University of New York, [2021] | Includes
  bibliographical references and index.
Identifiers: LCCN 2020048642 (print) | LCCN 2020048643 (ebook) | ISBN
  9781438483160 (pbk. : alk. paper) | 9781438483177 (hardcover : alk. paper) |
  ISBN 9781438483184 (ebook)
Subjects: LCSH: New Netherland—History. | Indians of North America—Northeastern
  States—History—17th century. | Indians of North America—Northeastern States—
  Government relations. | Dutch—New York (State)—History—17th century. |
  Dutch—New England—History—17th century. | Excavations (Archaeology)—
  Northeastern States. | Ethnohistory—Northeastern States.
Classification: LCC F122.1 .D87 2021 (print) | LCC F122.1 (ebook) | DDC
  974/.02—dc23
LC record available at https://lccn.loc.gov/2020048642
LC ebook record available at https://lccn.loc.gov/2020048643

10 9 8 7 6 5 4 3 2 1

*This book is dedicated to the Institute for
American Indian Studies Museum and Research Center
(Washington, Connecticut) and its staff, whose strong ethic
of research and public education initiated, encouraged,
and affected its production.*

Contents

Abbreviations

ASG   Archive of the States-General (in *NA*).

DRCHNY John Brodhead, Edmund O'Callaghan, and Berthold Fernow, ed., *Documents Relative to the Colonial History of the State of New York*, 15 vols. Albany: Weed, Parsons and Company, 1853–83.

FOCM   Charles T. Gehring, trans. and ed., *Fort Orange Court Minutes, 1652–1660*. Syracuse, NY: New Netherland Document Series, vol. 16, part 2, 1990.

HNAI   Bruce Trigger, ed., *Handbook of North American Indians*, vol. 15, *Northeast*. Washington, DC: Smithsonian Institution, 1978.

JMOC   Charles T. Gehring and William A. Starna, trans. and ed., *A Journey into Mohawk and Oneida Country, 1634–1635: The Journal of Harmen Meyndertsz van den Bogaert*. Syracuse, NY: Syracuse University Press, 1988.

NNN   John Franklin Jameson, ed., *Narratives of New Netherland, 1609–1664*. New York: Charles Scribner's Sons, 1909.

NYCM   New York Colonial Manuscripts (in NYSA).

NYHM   Arnold J. F. van Laer, trans. and ed., *Register of the Provincial Secretary, 1638–1642*. New York Historical Manuscripts: Dutch, vol. 1. Baltimore: Genealogical Publishing, 1974.

        Arnold J. F. van Laer, trans. and ed., *Register of the Provincial Secretary, 1642–1647*. New York Historical Manuscripts: Dutch, vol. 2. Baltimore: Genealogical Publishing, 1974.

Arnold J. F. van Laer, trans. and ed., *Register of the Provincial Secretary, 1648–1660.* New York Historical Manuscripts: Dutch, vol. 3. Baltimore: Genealogical Publishing, 1974.

Arnold J. F. van Laer, trans. and ed., *Council Minutes, 1638–1649.* New York Historical Manuscripts: Dutch, vol. 4. Baltimore: Genealogical Publishing, 1974.

Charles T. Gehring, trans. and ed., *Council Minutes, 1652–1654.* New York Historical Manuscripts: Dutch, vol. 5. Baltimore: Genealogical Publishing, 1983.

Charles T. Gehring, trans. and ed., *Council Minutes, 1655–1656.* New York Historical Manuscripts: Dutch, vol. 6. Syracuse, NY: Syracuse University Press, 1995.

Charles T. Gehring, trans. and ed., *Correspondence, 1647–1653.* New York Historical Manuscripts: Dutch, vol. 11. Syracuse, NY: Syracuse University, Press, 2000.

Charles T. Gehring, trans. and ed., *Correspondence, 1654–1658.* New York Historical Manuscripts: Dutch, vol. 12. Syracuse, NY: Syracuse University, Press, 2003.

NYHS   New York Historical Society, New York.

NYSA   New York State Archives, Albany.

NYSL   New York State Library, Albany.

ORA   Oudrechterlijke archieven van het Kwartier van Veluwe, deel II Het platteland in het Gelders Archief.

VWIS   Verspreide West-indische Stukken.

VOC   Verenigde Oostindische Compagnie, or the Dutch East India Company.

WIC   West India Company.

Introduction

The purpose of this book is to introduce its readers to the significant impact of Dutch traders *and* settlers on the early history of Northeastern North America, and their extensive and intensive relationships with its Indigenous peoples. Few people know that New Netherland extended well beyond the Hudson River Valley, westward into present-day New Jersey and Delaware and eastward to Cape Cod. Even fewer realize that Dutch settlers accompanied the Dutch traders. New Netherland was not just a loose linking of Dutch trading posts. Dutch colonists founded villages and towns along Long Island Sound, the mid-Atlantic coast, and up the valleys of the Connecticut, Housatonic, Hudson, and Delaware Rivers. Their daily routines brought them into frequent contact with their Native American neighbors. Although altercations and violence did occur, in general the relationships resulted in Dutch-Indigenous interdependence that enhanced living standards and promoted goodwill within both communities.

Unfortunately, little of this substantial history has found its way into local history books and the public school systems, especially in what was once eastern and western New Netherland (i.e., southern New England and the Delaware River Valley, respectively). Consequently, in 2016 I decided to organize a public conference on this theme. The result was the 11th Annual Native American-Archaeology Round Table, held on October 29, 2016 and hosted by the Institute for American Indian Studies Museum and Research Center in Washington, Connecticut (IAIS).[1]

Entitled "Early Encounters: Dutch-Indigenous Relations in Seventeenth-Century Northeastern North America," it included nine presentations on various aspects of New Netherland by ten well-known experts in Dutch and Native American histories. Many of the audience were educators, who urged publication of the papers. I concurred, because the Dutch-Indigenous histories they discussed deserve a more prominent position in future history

1

books, museum exhibits, and in school curriculum and instruction than they have previously enjoyed. The end result is this book. It consists of ten chapters, most of which are revisions of the papers presented at the 2016 IAIS Round Table conference. Chapters 1–6 discuss Dutch involvement in New York, specifically, the Hudson and Mohawk Valleys.

Chapter 1, *Henry Hudson Goes Ashore on Castle Hill* by Shirley W. Dunn, introduces the reader to the English sea captain and explorer Henry/Hendrick Hudson, sailing for the Dutch in 1609 in search of a northwestern passage to China and the "spice islands" of the East Indies. Instead of the South Pacific, Hudson sailed into New York Bay and up the river that now bears his name. Hudson's encounters with Native American communities along his route are the first documented Dutch-Indian relationships in what eventually becomes New Netherland. Dunn addresses the following questions: Where exactly did Hudson make this landfall? Whom did he meet, and what happened during that historic meeting?

Chapter 2, *Sources Relating to Dutch-Indian Relations* by Charles T. Gehring, sets the stage for subsequent chapters by providing an overview of the founding and history of New Netherland. It introduces readers to the Dutch people and answers the following questions: Who were the Dutch? Why did they come to the New World? What did they do after they got here? What do we know about Dutch-Indian relations? The chapter begins with the acquisition of the Low Countries by the Habsburg Empire in the fifteenth and sixteenth centuries, the revolt of the seventeen provinces against the empire, and the formation of the United Provinces of the Netherlands from the original provinces to create a new nation and world leader in maritime trade. Gehring discusses the opening of the New World fur trade at the beginning of the seventeenth century, the exchange of shell beads (*sewant, wampum*) in Long Island Sound for beaver pelts on the upper Hudson, and the resulting violent competition that the trade engendered. He demonstrates how Dutch–Native American relations became crucial to the economic survival of New Netherland. Continuing through to the midcentury, Gehring shows how four seventeenth-century Indian wars—Kieft's War, the Peach War, and the two subsequent Esopus wars and their aftermath—led to a reconfiguration of the Dutch settlements and new economic endeavors. Chapter 2 concludes with an examination of the seventeenth-century Dutch primary sources available for acquiring descriptions of the Native American population in New Netherland through Dutch eyes, particularly those of Harmen Meyndertsz van den Bogaert, Adriaen van der Donck, and Arent van Curler.

Chapter 3, *Declarations of Interdependence: The Nature of Dutch-Native Relations in New Netherland, 1624–1664* by Stephen T. Staggs, introduces the reader to the early Dutch settlers in New Netherland and their diverse and sustained relationships with their Native American neighbors. Staggs uses original Dutch-language records from New Netherland to show that cultural adaptation, accommodation, and transculturation occurred within both Dutch and Indigenous communities.[2] Sharing new foods, tools, and ideas and providing labor, military assistance, and political support created bonds of mutual dependence between the Dutch colonists and Indigenous tribal communities that often bordered on what Staggs describes as "familiarity." Cross-cultural physical intimacies and marriages transpired, as the Dutch "welcomed Indians into their homes and families."[3]

Chapter 4, *Building Forts and Alliances: Archaeology at Freeman and Massapeag, Two Native American Sites* by Anne-Marie Cantwell and Diana diZerega Wall, uses archaeological data to help address the nature of Dutch-Indigenous relationships in upstate New York and on western Long Island. Cantwell and Wall focus on two seventeenth-century fortified Native American archaeological sites that indicate Dutch influence. The Freeman site contained the cultural remains of the Mohawk palisaded village of Kaghnuwage, located in the present Mohawk Valley town of Root, New York—homelands of the Iroquois-speaking Mohawk. Fort Massapeag was a palisaded trading post with an adjacent wampum manufacturing site located in present-day Massapequa, Long Island—the homelands of Munsee Algonquian-speaking communities. Cantwell and Wall argue that, although occupied by very different tribal peoples for very different reasons, both sites symbolize status and political power, and that Dutch-Indigenous interdependence in economic endeavors, military defense, and international politics in both regions created strong political alliances, of which these palisaded sites are material symbols.

Chapter 5, *Mohawk and Dutch Relations in the Mohawk Valley—Alliance, Diplomacy, and Families from 1600 to the Two Row Treaty Renewal Campaign* by Paul Gorgen, presents an Indigenous perspective of colonial relationships with Dutch settlers in the Mohawk Valley. A member of the Kanatsiohareke Mohawk Community whose ancestry includes both Mohawk and Dutch lineages from seventeenth-century Schenectady, Gorgen uses Haudenosaunee (Iroquois) oral history as well as New Netherland primary source documents to provide a distinctive description of Mohawk-Dutch interactions and interdependence, occurring on both political and personal levels that continued well beyond the political entity of New Netherland.

Importantly, he demonstrates that all Mohawk-Dutch relations were founded on the concept of an equal partnership, which was originally confirmed by an early seventeenth-century trade agreement known as the Two Row Wampum Treaty. A significant portion of the chapter deals with the legacy of the Dutch-Mohawk alliance, which has extended into the present century.

Chapter 6, *The Dutch and the Wiechquaeskeck: Shifting Alliances in the Seventeenth Century* by Marshall Joseph Becker, discusses Dutch-Indigenous relations in southern New York, southwestern Connecticut, and northeastern New Jersey. Becker focuses on the Wiechquaeskeck, a major tribe whose homelands once included present Westchester County and Manhattan Island in New York and southwestern Connecticut. Today, the tribe is virtually unknown to academics as well as to the general public. Becker explains why this is so in his narration of the tribe's relationships with the Dutch, the English, and other Indigenous communities on the regional landscape. The Wiechquaeskeck survival strategy during subsequent social and economic upheavals was migration. Using primary sources—especially land transactions—and buffer zone theory, Becker determines where they emigrated and who they eventually became.

Chapters 7–10 introduce the reader to the eastern portion of New Netherland, namely, southern New England. **Chapter 7**, *Early Seventeenth-Century Trade in Southern New England* by Kevin A. McBride, combines the use of early historic documents and recent archaeological site information to provide new insights into Dutch-Pequot trade relationships in southeastern New England ca. 1614 to 1637. Recent excavations at five Pequot War era (1636–37) Pequot settlements directed by McBride unearthed thought-provoking finds that included over 450 trade items. They and the primary documents are helping to reveal the nature, extent, and mechanics of European (especially Dutch) trade with the Pequot tribe that "significantly altered Native lifeways"[4] in early seventeenth-century Connecticut.

Chapter 8, *Roduins: A Dutch Fort in Branford, Connecticut* by John Pfeiffer, details the exciting discovery and excavation of an early European contact period archaeological site in present-day Branford, Connecticut, which the author interprets as an early seventeenth-century Dutch fort. Pfeiffer describes the various artifacts and features recovered from this remarkable archaeological site, which include both Native American and European items, and the remnants of a semisubterranean wattle and daub structure enclosed by a ditch and berm palisade. Primary documents housed in America and in Holland are used to explain the Dutch rise as a major mercantile power and the raisons d'être for their involvement with New

World explorations. (It was not just the fur trade.) The documents suggest that the Dutch settlement of Roduins may predate the Dutch trading post House of Good Hope.

Chapter 9, *The Fresh River and the New Netherland Settlement, "House of Good Hope"* by Richard Manack, relates the story of Connecticut's first well-documented, permanent European settlement, which is little known even to state residents.[5] The House of Good Hope (Huys de Goede Hoop) was a Dutch settlement founded in 1633 by the Dutch West India Company (WIC) on the Connecticut River at present-day Hartford. It consisted of a trading post and a *bouwerie*—a circa twenty-five-acre farmstead tended by Dutch settlers. An important part of this story was the Dutch's intense involvement in the fur and wampum trade with Indigenous trading partners along the Connecticut River and southern New England coast. Using primary Dutch and English documents, Manack demonstrates how the WIC emphasis on this trade, originally lucrative, eventually caused problems with the English and with and among the Pequots and local tribal peoples. The disagreements detrimentally affected the Dutch farming settlement at Hartford, and effectively caused the demise of the House of Good Hope and the loss of most of eastern New Netherland by 1653.

Chapter 10, *Dutch–Native American Relationships in Eastern New Netherland (That's Connecticut, Folks!)* by Lucianne Lavin, reflects on the little-known fact that the first Europeans to settle in what is now western Connecticut and western Massachusetts were the Dutch. It describes how Dutch traders and farmers carried on mutually satisfying relationships with their Indigenous neighbors before and after the advent of English colonists in the region. Unlike their English counterparts in this region, the Dutch recognized the sovereignty of Native American nations and treated their trading partners and neighbors as political equals. They were less judgmental and more tolerant of Indigenous cultures, actively accommodating their Native neighbors, even when both communities were laboring under English rule. For their part, the local Native American communities provided economic and military support to the Dutch, all of which illustrates an interdependence and mutual accommodation in Dutch-Indigenous relationships in eastern New Netherlands similar to that described by Staggs in chapter 3 for the Hudson Valley. The various ways Dutch relationships changed Indigenous community lifeways and the Indigenous-Indigenous sociopolitical landscape in eastern New Netherland is also enumerated.

In summary, the chapters in this book demonstrate a strong Dutch presence in Northeastern North America as traders and as settlers from the early stages of European visitation. In some regions, that presence lingered through the centuries, occasionally to the present day. In the Northeast, seventeenth-century American history evolved from the actions and interactions of numerous Native American tribes with each other as well as with the Dutch and English, and from relationships of the Dutch with the English. Dealings with the French in present-day Canada and with the Swedes in the lower Delaware Valley contributed to those regional histories. The facts demand that we view American history not through the traditional lens of an Anglo-American past, but as a "conjoined history"[6] created by the interrelations and interdependence of diverse ethnic groups through time.

Lucianne Lavin
February 9, 2018

Acknowledgments

Sharon Clapp kindly reviewed an earlier version of this manuscript. Many thanks to historical artist Len Tantillo for generously allowing the use of his beautiful painting, *Curiosity of the Magua. Mohawk warriors approach the ship of Arent Van Curler, 1650*, on the front cover of this book.

Notes

1. The Institute for American Indian Studies Museum and Research Center (IAIS) is a private, nonprofit museum and educational and research center located on thirteen acres of woodland in the Litchfield Hills of northwestern Connecticut. Founded in 1975 as the American Indian Archaeological Institute, the Institute's main focus originally was archaeology and research. Because of the vast knowledge and information gained from six Indigenous people on staff, the Institute's focus soon included preservation, education, and Native American studies. In 1990 the Institute's name was changed to its present designation to encompass those additional focal points. IAIS is dedicated to the study of the histories and cultures of Indigenous peoples throughout the Western Hemisphere, particularly those of Northeastern North America. Its facilities include a museum/visitors center, a research building that houses all collections not currently on display, and outdoor exhibits featuring a Native American medicinal plant garden and a replicated Algonkian village with several house structures, dugout canoe, central firepit, food drying racks, and a Native vegetable garden. The Institute also maintains several nature trails with signage that

identifies the various trees and plants and their traditional economic and medicinal uses by local Indigenous communities.

2. For a discussion of adaptation and transculturation within both Euro-American and Indigenous communities in Connecticut, see Lucianne Lavin, *Connecticut's Indigenous Peoples: What Archaeology, History, and Oral Traditions Teach Us about Their Communities and Cultures* (New Haven, CT: Yale Peabody Museum of Natural History and Yale University Press, 2013), 311–315.

3. Stephen T. Staggs, chapter 3, this volume.

4. Kevin A. McBride, abstract to a PowerPoint presentation entitled "War and Trade in Eastern New Netherland," presented at the 11th Annual Native American–Archaeology Round Table, "Early Encounters: Dutch-Indigenous Relations in 17th Century Northeastern North America," October 29, 2016.

5. The Dutch settlement at Saybrook Point in present Old Saybrook appears to have been occupied at an earlier date, but there are few references to it in the published literature. See Lucianne Lavin, "Dutch-Native American Relationships in Eastern New Netherland (That's Connecticut, Folks!),"chapter 10, this volume.

6. An apt term borrowed from Anne-Marie Cantwell and Diana Wall, "Building Forts and Alliances: Archaeology at Freeman and Massapeag, Two Native American Sites," chapter 4, this volume.

1.

Henry Hudson Goes Ashore on Castle Hill

SHIRLEY W. DUNN

After passing through what is now called New York Harbor in 1609, Hendrick Hudson and his crew began to sail up the river today known by Hudson's name. An Englishman sailing for the Dutch, Captain Hudson was seeking a northwest trade route to the East Indies (figure 1.1). Instead, he introduced his employers to new trading partners and the lucrative North American fur trade.

First Documented European Contact with Mohican Peoples

Near present-day Catskill, Hudson met friendly Mohican Indians (also called Mahicans) and called them "a loving people."[1] Trusting in the good intentions of the resident Mohicans around him, Captain Hudson bravely accepted an invitation to visit a Mohican village that was situated beside the River of the Mountains, that is, the Hudson River. The Mohican village was at the location of the present-day village of Castleton, New York.

Hudson had observed unknown Native populations while on previous voyages that he had made in hopes of finding a northern route to establish trade on the opposite side of the earth.[2] While many Indigenous people were hostile, on this river in sight of the mountains the Native Americans were friendly. Therefore, with a Native chief as his guide, possibly from the

9

Figure 1.1. Portrait drawing (apocryphal) of Henry Hudson (*Appleton's' Cyclopædia of American Biography*, vol. 3, 1892, p. 296).

Catskill area population, Hudson left his ship and went ashore at a dramatic hill that is behind today's Castleton Village.

Hudson was welcomed at the Indian village east of the river at this location. To the Natives' disappointment, he returned to his ship instead of staying for the night among them. According to Donald S. Johnson in his book *Charting the Sea of Darkness*, Hudson's notes of the day's visit were later copied by "John [*sic*] de Laet" in his book *Nieuwe Werelt*, which was published in 1625.[3] Hudson's accounts provided the following well-known recital of his visit to the Mohicans. Hudson wrote:

> I sailed to the shore in one of their canoes, with an old man, who was the chief of a tribe consisting of 40 men and 17 women; these I saw there in a house well constructed of oak bark, and circular in shape, so that it had the appearance of being well built, with an arched roof [meaning having a rounded rooftop; see figure 1.2, Adrian Block's map, for an illustration of houses]. It contained a great quantity of maize or Indian corn, and beans of the last year's growth, and there lay near the house for the purpose of drying, enough to load three ships, besides what was growing in the fields. On our coming into the house, two

mats were spread out to sit upon, and immediately some food was served in well made red wooden bowls; two men were also dispatched at once with bows and arrows in quest of game, who soon after brought in a pair of pigeons which they had shot. They likewise killed a fat dog, and skinned it in great haste with shells which they had got out of the water. They supposed that I would remain with them for the night, but I returned after a short time on board the ship. The land is the finest for cultivation that I ever in my life set foot upon, and it also abounds in trees of every description. The natives are a very good people, for when they saw that I would not remain, they supposed that I was afraid of their bows, and taking the arrows, they broke them in pieces, and threw them into the fire.

Figure 1.2. The map above was made by Adriaen Block in 1614. Just beyond the large capital "E," at top left, a few Mahican (Mohican) houses are shown. These were built in the manner described by Henry Hudson. Note the word MAHICANS below the trees and houses. Some nearby houses are shown as rectangles, each representing part of the village population (Algemeen Rijksarchief, The Hague, The Netherlands).

A second version of Hudson's visit to the Indians exists, which may pre-date the previous well-known account that is quoted above. The alternate account reads as follows:

> On the evening of the 15th he [Hudson] arrived opposite the mountains which lie from the river side, where he found a very loving people and very old men, and the day following, reached the spot hereafter to be honored by his own illustrious name. One day more wafts him up between Schodac and Castleton, and here he landed and passed a day with the natives, greeted with all sorts of barbarous hospitality; the land the finest for cultivation he ever set foot upon; the natives so kind and gentle that when they found that he left them—poor children of nature—because he was afraid of their weapons—they broke their arrows in pieces and threw them in the fire.[4]

In his book *History of the Seventeen Towns of Rensselaer County*, historian A. J. Weise noted that tradition adds to this historic record that the place where Hudson was thus entertained was on Castle Hill, an eminence east of the village of Castleton, whereon was the house of the Indian chief referred to in de Laet's history.[5] Because of the degrees of latitude given with Hudson's notes, however, Weise separated himself from the tradition that Hudson visited the site. Weise next wrote that he believed Hudson's ship was actually farther south than Castleton. According to Weise, who was writing in 1881, as the southern boundary line of Rensselaer County was located at 42'27" north latitude, Hudson's visit on the east side of the river "would rather indicate that it was nearer the city of Hudson, in Columbia County, which was at latitude 42'14".

Castle Hill: The Documentary and Archaeological Evidence

Such a conclusion was clearly a wrong assumption by Weise. The purpose of this chapter is to present information about Henry Hudson's 1609 visit at Castle Hill, well north of the later county line. Fortunately, there is evidence for accepting the present-day Castleton area on the east shore of the Hudson River as the location of Hudson's visit. The Mohicans there were some of the "loving people" first met by Hudson and his crew near present-day Catskill. They were friends, not a threat to Captain Hudson.

According to the surviving first map of the Hudson River—supposedly drawn by the Dutch sea captain Adrian Block in 1614—a large Mohican settlement was located at Castle Hill in the early 1600s (figure 1.2).

In addition, a Mohican population was situated in the area on the eastern hill behind present Castleton according to local tradition.[6] In recent years, the population who welcomed Hudson has been somewhat forgotten. Block's map of 1614, however, includes simple drawings of a few Native houses in that location, just far enough from the river's shore to avoid floods. The houses shown at the Castleton site were rectangular, with arched roofs as described by Henry Hudson in his account (see figure 1.2). There are other references to the Mohican population. For example, in the *Rensselaer County Atlas* of 1880 appeared the following statement: "Proceeding slowly and cautiously the vessel arrived on the 18th of September opposite the site of the village of Castleton."[7] The same book said that Castleton "takes its name from an eminent Indian Castle or Chief Wigwam, which once occupied the crest of the hill back of the village known as Castle Hill."[8] Dutch settlers later replaced the Mohicans. Castleton was named a town in 1827 and was incorporated in 1888.

Additional vital proof of the Native presence comes from archaeology. According to a modern village resident who attended school there as a boy, he was one of several children who dug in the dirt around the tennis court at their local school on the hill. They often found Indian relics in the dirt brought from the yards of nearby houses. A local adult amateur archaeologist probing the hillside over the years also found many Native American objects. Some of those artifacts have been sent to the Mohican tribal reservation, which is now located in Bowler, Wisconsin.

Discussion

Hendrick Hudson visited parts of a very large village of Mohicans on the knoll east of present Castleton in 1609. The Mohicans later moved, as they are then shown on another early seventeenth-century map archived at the Library of Congress, near two dots at the top of this early map (figure 1.3). They were reportedly by then eight miles from the Dutch trading post of Fort Orange, which the West India Company constructed in 1624. It is interesting to note familiar sites such as Kinderhook and Claverack on this map. For lack of a more specific word, the early Dutch called all recognizable Indian villages "castles." As a result, the earlier hill site of the

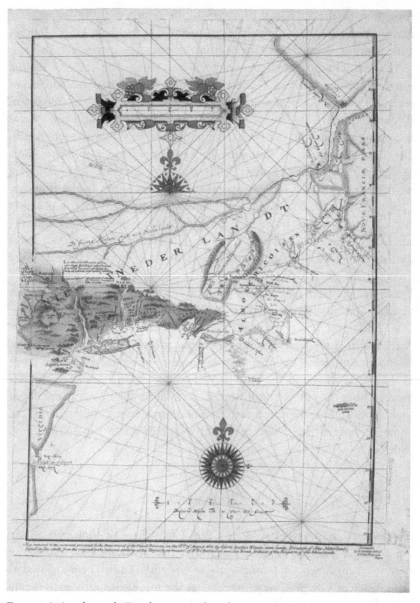

Figure 1.3. Another early Dutch map, attributed to Joan Vinckeboons (?1639), entitled "Pascaert van Nieuw Nederlandt Virginia, ende Nieuw-Engelandt verthonendt alles wat van die landin by See, oft by land is ondect oft Bekent" (Library of Congress, Geography and Map Division).

Mohican settlement received the Dutch name of Castle Town, shortened later to Castleton. A community of modern homes now lines the roads.[9]

However, according to early local tradition and memories of his visit to the Indian town, Hudson's first visit was made on the side of the hill beside the Hudson River. The site overlooked the river from the knoll east of present Castleton, and presumably extended down the bank to the river. In later years, when the Dutch colonists appeared, they began to settle along the river and gradually moved inland.

Notes

1. J. H. French, *Gazetteer of New York* (Syracuse, NY: R. Pearsall Smith, 1860), 559.

2. Timothy Paulson and Hubert de Leeuw, *Coming to Terms with Early New Netherland–New York History: 1609, Henry Hudson Revisited* (Albany, NY: New Netherland Company, 2014). See also Charles Gehring, "Sources Relating to Dutch-Indian Relations," chapter 2, this volume, for a discussion of Hudson's four voyages.

3. Donald S. Johnson, *Charting the Sea of Darkness: The Four Voyages of Henry Hudson* (Camden, ME: International Marine Publishing, 1992), 49–52.

4. French, *Gazetteer*, 559. Footnote 13 states that the quote is originally from *Everett's Address*, given at the inauguration of Dudley Observatory, and to see their page 54.

5. A. J. Weise, *History of the Seventeen Towns of Rensselaer County* (Troy, NY: Francis and Tucker, 1881; rep. 1975), 69, n. 2.

6. See, for example, Weise, *History*, 69, and Nathaniel Bartlett Sylvester, *History of Rensselaer Co., New York* (https://archive.org/search.php?query=creator%3A%22Sylvester%2C+Nathaniel+Bartlett%2C+1825-1894%22Philadelphia: Everts & Peck, 1880), 407.

7. Sylvester, *History*, https://archive.org/search.php?query=creator%3A%22Sylvester%2C+Nathaniel+Bartlett%2C+1825-1894%22398.

8. Sylvester, *History*, 407.

9. Sylvester, *History*, 407, note, and French, *Gazetteer*, 559, n. 13. https://archive.org/search.php?query=creator%3A%22Sylvester%2C+Nathaniel+Bartlett%2C+1825-1894%22.

2.

Sources Relating to Dutch-Indian Relations

CHARLES T. GEHRING

In the 1640s three Dutchmen found themselves in a world in total contrast to their homeland. Surrounded by mountains, in a heavily wooded landscape, populated by people speaking languages they couldn't understand, it must have been an exciting adventure. The three young men were Harmen Meyndertsz van den Bogaert, Arent van Curler, and Adriaen Cornelissen van der Donck. They all began their careers in the New World working in close contact with Native Americans on the upper Hudson in an area now called Albany. Their lives would all come to an abrupt end, involving Indians in one way or another.

The United Provinces of the Netherlands

All three had just left the Netherlands during the final years of the Eighty Years' War with Spain (1568–1648). Several generations of children would grow up in the Low Countries knowing nothing but marauding armies, cities under siege, famine, and pestilence. It is ironic in a way that many people probably avoided coming to an unfamiliar and potentially dangerous environment in the New World, not realizing that New Netherland could be much more agreeable than the turmoil of Europe.

The war with Spain was actually an eighty-year revolt against the Habsburg Empire. How the Dutch became part of this empire is too complex to relate here; however, in short it happened in the following manner: during the fifteenth and sixteenth centuries, the dukes of Burgundy acquired the Low Countries through a succession of dynastic marriages, purchases, and bequests. When Mary, daughter of Charles the Bold, Duke of Burgundy, married Maximillian Habsburg, the Low Countries became part of an empire that circled the globe.[1]

As a part of the Habsburg Empire, the Low Countries became one of the most prosperous regions of Europe. Although the industriousness of its population was a contributing factor, its strategic location was unique for commercial activity. Not only were they neighbors to all the countries bordering the North Sea, but they were midway between the Baltic and Mediterranean worlds, as well as the terminus to three major river systems—the Rhine, Maas, and Scheldt—all watersheds of major areas of Germany and France. As a result of this strategic location, there developed a merchant class that would soon control most of the Baltic and Mediterranean carrying trade and send commercial fleets around the world.

For centuries, the Baltic trade or *moeder negotie* (the mother trade), as the Dutch called it, was the focus of their commercial activity. As a part of the Habsburg Empire, goods flowed into the Netherlands from all over the world. There they were warehoused, often reprocessed or refined, and shipped on to the Baltic in exchange for grain and timber—both commodities in much demand in the Netherlands itself as well as in the Mediterranean region. Portugal, for example, shipped spices into the Netherlands from the Far East and salt from the Iberian Peninsula. While England and the Baltic region were a ready market for the spices, the salt was consumed by the flourishing Dutch herring industry.[2] However, this lucrative commercial balance was disrupted in 1568 when the Low Countries revolted against their master, the Habsburg Empire.

The revolt was the result of several actions taken by Philip II, King of Spain. In 1556 he inherited the Low Countries upon the abdication of his father, Charles V, king of Spain and emperor of the Holy Roman Empire.[3] Charles was born and brought up by the Flemish nobility in Ghent. His affection for the Low Countries came from the heart. On the other hand, his son Philip was born in Spain and had no love for these cold and damp holdings on the northern edge of the Empire. Although the wealth of the Low Countries had been financing Habsburg entanglements for generations, in return for various local rights and privileges, Philip considered them a mere fatted cow to be exploited. Rather than negotiate for financial support, he attempted to implement a central control and authority to the detriment of local privileges.

As galling as this political issue was to the local population, Philip also struck an emotional chord. As a devout Catholic, he considered the reformed religious movement in the North as a disease to be stamped out before it spread. His solution was the establishment of the Inquisition in the Low Countries to suppress the Protestant heresy. Thousands of nonpenitents were persecuted, thousands were hanged. Thus, Philip's attempt to establish a central control to provide economic and human resources for his political agenda, and his inability to view his subjects in the Low Countries as anything more than hostile heretics, fueled a revolt from which would arise a new country, a new people, and a new global commercial empire.[4]

The first phase of this long war lasted from 1568 until 1609. During this time tens of thousands of Protestant refugees fled north to the newly proclaimed United Provinces of the Netherlands.[5] A massive exodus of wealth, talent, and human energy occurred in 1585 when Spanish troops captured Antwerp. This action led to the blockade of the Scheldt River by the Dutch rebels, denying Antwerp access to the sea. Amsterdam, already a thriving commercial center, grew dramatically, while Antwerp declined in importance and economic power.

When the Netherlands began its long struggle with the political empire, it also disconnected itself from the commercial empire. Friendly waters around the globe had become hostile. Dutch merchants were forced to develop their own markets, and establish and maintain their own overseas trade routes. Although the United Provinces were fighting for their independence from an oppressive master, they were also struggling for their economic survival.[6]

The Dutch responded to this challenge by establishing their own markets and trade routes from the New World to the Far East. The search for salt to support their lucrative herring industry led them into the Caribbean, where they clashed with Spanish interests along the coast of Venezuela. The loss of their access to the Portuguese spice trade in Indonesia when Portugal united with Spain in 1580 led the Dutch directly to the Far East, where they eventually gained control of a large part of the spice markets.[7]

By 1602 competition in the spice trade among Dutch commercial interests had become so fierce that it led to the formation of the Verenigde Oostindische Compagnie (VOC) or the Dutch East India Company. Chartered by the States General—the ruling body of the United Provinces—it gave the competing cartels the opportunity to participate as shareholders in a monopoly. Rather than having many private interests competing with one another to everyone's detriment, the VOC would fix prices by monopolistic control, maximizing profits to the benefit of all. Portuguese commercial interests in the Far East were soon under intense pressure from the VOC. By the mid-seventeenth century, Portuguese trading interests in the spice islands of the Indonesian archipelago, Ceylon, Formosa, and Japan had been replaced by the VOC.[8]

Although the Dutch were enjoying great success acquiring Portuguese possessions during the revolt and establishing a commercial empire in the Far East, the trading fleets still had to pass through hostile waters. Heavily armed ships reduced cargo space, decreasing profits; potential loss to hostile forces increased marine insurance premiums. Armed convoys also ate away at profits. All of these detrimental forces to successful trade drove both the English and the Dutch to search for safer routes to the north. The lure of this theoretical route was driven by the ancient notion of symmetry in nature: if the world's land masses allowed for a southern route to China, there should also be a northern route.[9] English attempts by Martin Frobisher and John Davis, and by Dutch mariners such as Willem Barentsz and Jacob Van Heemskerck, all failed. It is in this context that Henry Hudson ended up sailing west while searching for the legendary northern route to the East.[10]

In 1607 and 1608 Hudson made two northern voyages in the employ of the English Moscovy Company. Both failed to discover the "passage to Cathay." His experience and enthusiasm, however, attracted the attention of the VOC. Hudson was given command of the Dutch-built ship *Halve Maen* with instructions to sail northeast in the wake of Barentsz. After encountering adverse weather conditions and dangerous ice floes his nearly mutinous crew forced him to sail to safer waters. Contrary to his contract with the VOC, Hudson turned his ship about and headed south by southwest.[11]

When Hudson sailed along the coast of North America from Delaware Bay to New York Harbor in 1609, he was unaware that he was defining the future limits of a significant Dutch possession in the New World. The VOC had hired Hudson to find another route to the Far East, one that was possibly shorter and one that was certainly safer. Hudson failed to find either the eastern or western passage, but did succeed in opening up an area of North America to the Dutch (figure 2.1).

Shortly after Hudson's explorations, various commercial operations in the Netherlands were licensed by the States General to trade with the Natives in the major waterways from Maine to Virginia. One of the most active trader-explorers in these early years was Adriaen Courtsen Block. Sailing for Lutheran merchants out of Amsterdam, Block made three voyages

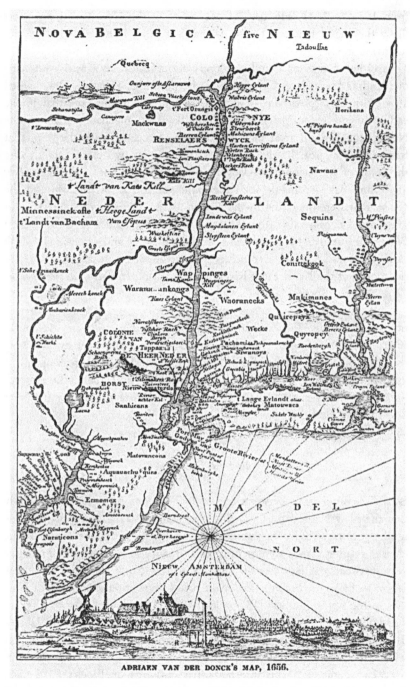

Figure 2.1. Adriaen van der Donck's map of New Netherland, 1656 (public domain).

from 1611 to 1613. His base of operations in the New World was most likely the island between Rhode Island and Long Island that still carries his name today.

Other names of Dutch explorers also became associated with various landmarks, such as Cape May at the mouth of Delaware Bay, named after Cornelis Jacobsz May of Hoorn. It is interesting to note that in the early years of bloodthirsty competition between merchant cartels in the Netherlands, certain areas may have become associated with the ships that frequented the area. In any case, it is curious that two place names along the coast of Massachusetts—*Vos Haven* or "Fox Harbor" and *Craen Baij* or "Crane Bay"—coincide with the names of two ships, the *Vos* and the *Craen*, that were operating in the area in 1611–12 under the command of Jan Cornelisz May, also from Hoorn. These place names are recorded on Block's "Figurative Map" of 1614. Although foxes and cranes existed all along the coast, it is not a coincidence that further north, approximately at the mouth of the Kennebunk River, is the notation *Het Schip de Schilpadde*, "The Ship the Turtle."

Block's initial voyage was apparently a follow-up to Hudson's explorations. Whereas Hudson had approached Manhattan from the south, Block was attempting to find the entrance to Hudson's river by following the coast of New England. According to Johannes de Laet's reading of his journal, Block sailed into every river and stream from Cape Cod westward, indicating clearly that he had the specific intention of finding the river described by Hudson.[12]

New Netherland

By 1614 competition between traders had become so violent and bloody that the New Netherland Company was chartered as a monopoly to trade in the region in order to stabilize the situation. Under the terms of the charter, trading cartels were permitted to finance four voyages within three years between the latitudes 40 and 45 degrees (from Barnegat Bay, New Jersey, to Eastport, Maine). The main base of operations became Fort Nassau on the upper Hudson, 135 miles north of Manhattan Island. The fort was built on Castle Island, now mostly occupied by the port of Albany. The interior was a fifty-eight-foot square surrounded by a moat eight feet wide. The moat and breastworks protected a trading house thirty-eight feet by twenty-eight feet. This information is indicated on Block's 1614 map, including its location on the island. Fort Nassau served as a focal point for trading activities in an area that was to become the most lucrative fur-trading operation in the Northeast.[13]

Expeditions were sent from this post into the interior in search of exploitable mineral deposits and other natural resources. One such expedition in 1615 turned near misfortune into a wealth of new and useful geographical information. Sometime during the year a man named Kleyntie, accompanied by two compatriots, ventured westward into unexplored country, where they were captured by Indians and held for ransom. The following year they were rescued in the Delaware River Valley by the Dutch trader Cornelis Hendricksen. Their adventures from Fort Nassau to their point of capture, along the Schoharie watershed near the source of the Delaware River, and their eventual ransoming in the Delaware Valley, gave Kleyntie insights into the configurations of the various waterways within New Netherland. The 1616 map, upon which Kleyntie's expedition is recorded, shows awareness of the source of the Delaware River extending far to the north into territory supplying furs to Fort Nassau. Dutch knowledge of the course of the various waterways within New Netherland is important for understanding later concerns of allowing a foreign power access to the Delaware River.

When the New Netherland Company's charter expired in 1618, the territory was once again opened to cutthroat trading practices. As if to define the moment, Fort Nassau was washed away by a spring freshet the year before, forcing traders to operate seasonally aboard ship or from tents on shore. During this period of unregulated trading several events occurred worth mentioning. The following incident in the Connecticut River Valley was reported in a Dutch chronicle of contemporary events:

> The Sickenanes are located to the north between the Brownists and the Hollanders. The chief of this nation recently made an agreement with Pieter Barentsz to trade with no one but him. Jaques Elckes had held him prisoner on his yacht in 1622. A large ransom had to be paid or he intended to cut off his head. He paid out one hundred forty fathoms of zeewan, which are small beads that they make themselves and value as jewels. For this reason, he now trusts no one else but this one.[14]

Assuming that the above report is accurate, this incident demonstrates that unscrupulous traders were employing brutal tactics to deprive the Natives of *sewant* or wampum. Jaques Elckes aka Jacob Eelkens was also indirectly involved in another attempt to extort sewant—possibly in the same year. In an interrogatory sworn before a notary, it was revealed how Hans Jorisz Hontom had held a Mohawk sachem hostage aboard his ship. After ransom was paid, Hontom cut out the male organs of the chief, causing his death. Jacob Eelkens was supercargo aboard Hontom's ship. Although we do not know for certain whether Eelkens condoned this action, we do know that he had previously threatened to remove another part of a sachem's anatomy in the Connecticut River Valley. Putting the brutality of these trading practices aside, it is important to note that, already in 1622, the Dutch traders had recognized the value of sewant, which was being produced by the Pequots. If these two incidents occurred in the same trading season of 1622, then it is quite likely that Hontom and Eelkens had been busy acquiring sewant from the Pequots to take up the Hudson for use in acquiring furs from the Mohawks.[15] Sewant became so essential in trading operations that it became known as the "source and mother of the fur trade." The Dutch had developed the ideal trading relationship in New Netherland—an exchange of European hardware for Pequot sewant for Mohawk furs.[16]

The chaotic situation created by private traders was not resolved until 1621 when the West India Company was chartered as a trading monopoly. As a joint-stock company, it was similar in organization to the VOC. The WIC's area of operations extended from the west coast of Africa westward across the Atlantic and Pacific to the eastern reaches of the Indonesian archipelago. New Netherland was only one of its many trading interests, which included the gold coast of Africa, Brazil with its wealth of sugar and dyewood, and the salt-rich Caribbean islands. Although the WIC was founded in June 1621, it took almost two years for it to raise enough capital to finance its first attempt to take possession of its holdings in North America.[17]

The first colonists brought over in 1624 were mostly Walloons settled at outposts on the three major river systems in New Netherland: the Connecticut (Verse, or Fresh, Rivier), the Hudson (Noort, or North, Rivier), and the Delaware (Suyt, or South, Rivier). Their settlements in the proximity of the three trading posts were to serve as agricultural support communities. Nut Island (presently Governors Island) was to serve as a point of assembly for transferring cargo from coastal-trading vessels to oceangoing ships, a similar role played by the island of Texel in the Netherlands.[18]

In 1625 the WIC directors sent over Willem Verhulst as director of New Netherland, with instructions to strengthen the trading posts and their related settlements. However, he was also ordered to strengthen the post on High Island (Burlington) in the Delaware the most, and to make it the center of New Netherland. The directors of the WIC were apparently looking for a location deep in Indian country with an ice-free port, unlike Fort Orange. The directors had obviously been misinformed about High Island, as in the winter of 1634 Indians coming from the west were able to cross the river on the ice approximately where the present Franklin Bridge crosses to Camden. In the end, it was not the decision of poorly informed directors but an incident at Fort Orange on the upper Hudson that determined the location of the center of New Netherland.[19]

In 1626, only two years after Fort Orange (present-day Albany) was laid out, the local commander, Daniel van Crieckenbeeck, became involved in a war between the Mohawks and the Mahicans. When he and six of his soldiers accompanied a Mahican war party for an attack on the Mohawks, they were surprised a short distance from the fort. Crieckenbeeck and three of his soldiers were killed, together with an untold number of Mahicans. The Mohawks were outraged that the Dutch, who had instructions to remain neutral in such conflicts, would betray them in this manner. Fortunately, Crieckenbeeck's disobedience coincided with the arrival of Peter Minuit as the new director of the colony. It was also fortunate that someone as reliable and trusted as Pieter Barentsz was available. He was the same trader who had gained the confidence of the Pequots after the incident with Jacob Eelkens in 1622.[20]

Barentsz was immediately dispatched to Mohawk country to discuss the unfortunate incident near Fort Orange. He was able to convince the Mohawks that it had been an unauthorized initiative on Crieckenbeeck's part and assured them that it would not happen again. Upon hearing the news of the disaster to the north, Minuit sailed immediately to Fort Orange. He had been in the colony the previous year as a volunteer, with the assignment of exploring New Netherland from one end to the other for exploitable resources.

Minuit knew the land and the Indians better than anyone else at the time. He saw the dangers in the situation and realized that the outlying support communities were in peril of attack. Minuit resolved the problem by purchasing Manhattan Island and moving all the outlying families to this central location. Apparently, the Mohawks agreed with Barentsz to allow trading personnel to remain at Fort Orange, but they insisted that the eighteen families be removed with the veiled threat that they could no longer guarantee their safety. At this time, even the families from the Connecticut River and High Island were withdrawn. Instead of retaining a presence at the post on High Island, it was moved to a new location on the eastern shore of the Delaware River (present Gloucester, New Jersey) and named Fort Nassau.[21]

For the first five years, the Company supplied New Netherland only with enough settlers to develop agricultural support farms at the various trading posts, and later on Manhattan. Although there was a genuine fear among certain directors that colonization would adversely affect profits, it is also the case that the Company was concentrating most of its attention on Africa and Brazil. In 1624, shortly after capitalization was attained, the WIC sent an expedition of twenty-six ships and thirty-three hundred men for the capture of Bahia in Brazil; few resources were left for New Netherland. Initial gains in Bahia were soon reversed the following year by a Portuguese relief squadron; however, the market potential of Brazilian sugar was still the WIC's main interest in the New World. The euphoria following Piet Hein's capture of the Spanish silver fleet in 1628 resulted in an even larger and more determined commitment toward the capture of Brazil—all to the detriment of New Netherland.[22]

Harmen Meyndertsz van den Bogaert

Among the three young Dutch adventurers, the first to arrive in New Netherland was Harmen Meyndertsz van den Bogaert. He stepped ashore at New Amsterdam from the *Eendracht* in 1630 at the age of eighteen. Shortly after his arrival at Fort Orange as an employee of the WIC, Harmen was sent on a mission into the Mohawk Valley. His objective was to find out why the supply of furs coming down the river was dropping off. Without the profit from furs, the WIC would have found it difficult to justify maintaining trading posts in New Netherland. Furs were at a premium as most fur-bearing animals had been hunted out in northwestern Europe. This paucity of furs coincided with the height of the Little Ice Age, which produced colder than average temperatures.[23] Fur apparel was not only popular for warmth but also made a fashion statement. *Castor* (beaver) hats were the most sought-after head gear. This is evident in the numerous winter scenes depicted in Dutch genre paintings, even in advertising art such as the gentlemen on the Dutch Masters cigar box. Of all the fur-bearing animals available, the beaver was deemed the most suitable.

Unlike the French *coureur de bois*, who would go into the outback to negotiate for furs, the Dutch let the Indians come to them at the trading posts where transactions were made. To make the transporting of them over long distances possible they were eviscerated, scraped clean of fat, and attached to boards to dry. After removing them from the boards, the Indians carried them in packs to Fort Orange, where they were exchanged for manufactured goods they were not able to produce themselves, such as axes, awls, knives, scissors, mirrors, mouth-harps, duffels (a coarse woolen cloth); also, sewant, which became a form of currency in New Netherland. Baked sweet goods were also prized by the Indians. This led to an increase in bakers during the trading season from June to September, which prompted regulations against baking only for the Indian trade.

Once the furs were assembled at Fort Orange they were shipped downriver to Manhattan, where they were loaded onto oceangoing ships. When they reached Europe, they were sold to wholesalers who made them available to various fur processors who turned them into coats, clothing decorations, or hats. Many furs were first sent to Russia where a process called "combing" had been developed to remove the soft interior fur below the long guard hairs without damaging the hide or exterior hairs. The soft interior hair was then bought back by the Dutch to produce felt for making hats. A step in this felting process called "carroting" required the application of mercuric nitrate, which was quite toxic. It could eventually lead to insanity, giving rise to the expression "mad as a hatter." When the flow in this pipeline was reduced to a trickle, Harmen and two compatriots at Fort Orange were commissioned to investigate its cause.[24]

Adriaen Cornelissen van der Donck

Both the Mohawks and the Mahicans proved to be quite an attraction to the young Dutchmen. Adriaen van der Donck was no exception. A law student at Leiden University, Adriaen has been described as the most intelligent person to settle in New Netherland (figure 2.2). Although he was hired by Kiliaen van Rensselaer to serve as a law enforcement officer on his patroonship, Adriaen was evidently more interested in the Indians. Shortly after his arrival in 1641 he moved his residence from the *Bijeenwoningh*, or community, which was developing north of the fort, farther north to a place closer to the Indians. This was done much to the displeasure of the patroon in Amsterdam, who ordered that he move back to the center of the settlement where a law enforcement officer was expected to be. During

Figure 2.2. Generally accepted portrait of Adriaen Cornelissen van der Donck (public domain).

this period, he apparently acquired facility in several Native languages and closely observed Native customs—both of which would be useful during future Indian contact and for his later writings about New Netherland.[25]

After serving out his three-year term of employment at Rensselaerswijck, Adriaen moved downriver to the Manhattan area. This change in scenery was prompted by his service to Director Willem Kieft during treaty negotiations in 1645 at the end of a war with Indians on the Manhattan rim. Kieft demonstrated his gratitude by granting Adriaen twenty-four thousand acres of land in the southwest corner of what is now Westchester County. As a large landowner, he assumed the title of *Jonckher* or "squire" on his estate, which he named Colendonck. We know the place today as Yonkers.[26]

Adriaen's proximity to the center of power on Manhattan brought him into the arena of WIC politics, which would dominate the rest of his life. His prominent position in the community as a major landowner soon promoted him to the role of leader of the settlers, who were protesting the narrow policies of the for-profit-only Company. His opposition to Company policy eventually brought him into conflict with both directors Kieft and Stuyvesant. So fervent were his beliefs in the rights of the settlers that he brought his complaint directly to the States General, the governing body of the United Provinces of the Netherlands.[27]

The States General had originally chartered the West India Company in 1621 as a stock company. Its formation coincided with the end of the twelve years' truce with Spain. The Company's primary mission was to carry on the war with Spain in the Atlantic—secondary was the exploitation of natural resources. Similar in structure to the East India Company, the WIC could declare war within its sphere of influence and conclude peace, all accomplished with its own army and navy. It was basically the privatization of foreign policy. When the WIC found it difficult to attract people to serve in remote outposts such as New Netherland, it also resorted to privatization.

Protracted debate in the WIC concerning colonization resulted in a concession called the "Freedom and Exemptions," which promoted privatization of colonization rather than expending WIC capital. A faction of the WIC favored privatization in order to develop agricultural support communities for the trading operations, while an opposing faction was satisfied with Company control over all aspects of maintaining trading posts. This privatization of colonization allowed an investor or group of investors to negotiate with the Natives for a tract of land upon which he was obligated to settle fifty colonists within four years at his own expense. In return, the patroon was granted the rights of high, middle, and low jurisdiction. In addition, he would hold the land as a perpetual fief of inheritance with the right to dispose of the colony by last will and testament. Of all the patroonships registered from Sable Island near Nova Scotia to the island of Fernando do Noronho in the South Atlantic only Rensselaerswijck on the upper Hudson experienced any degree of success. The other proposed patroonships either failed to be capitalized or were repurchased by the WIC. The antipatroon faction among the directors of the Company were so hostile and suspicious of the system that there was little chance for success.[28]

Arent van Curler

However, one of the directors of the WIC, Samuel Blommaert, was so committed to this form of colonization that he secretly supported Sweden's attempt to establish a trading operation with agricultural support communities in the New World. In fact, Blommaert knew the right man for the job. He was Peter Minuit, former director of New Netherland and promoter of the patroonship plan of colonization. He was out of a job because of pressure from the antipatroon faction. He knew the geography of New Netherland better than anyone at the time. He also knew where the Dutch were weakest and proceeded in 1638 to establish a Swedish trading operation on the west bank of the Delaware River, now present-day Wilmington, Delaware. On his way over aboard the *Kalmar Nyckel*, he had to put into port at Texel in the Netherlands because of a storm. While at anchor, Kiliaen van Rensselaer made contact with Minuit. As a WIC director, he would have known Minuit as director of New Netherland from 1626 to 1631 and especially as an advocate of privatizing colonization. Kiliaen took advantage of the situation by requesting Minuit to take aboard six men whom he had employed for service on his patroonship. One of the six was Arent van Curler. Arent eventually made his way from the Delaware River to Rensselaerswijck with his five companions. A few months later, Minuit was lost at sea on his return to Sweden, but New Sweden survived as a thorn in Stuyvesant's side.[29]

Arent was Kiliaen van Rensselaer's grand-nephew. Kiliaen thought highly of the eighteen year old's potential, but first sent him to Rensselaerswijck to be assistant to Jacob Planck, his business manager. He explained to Arent that "one has to be servant before one can be master."[30] He proved that Kiliaen had a good eye for talent by rising rapidly in the patroonship's administration, from bookkeeper to secretary, and eventually to manager.

If Arent had a flaw, it was spending too much time in the woods with the Indians when he should have been sending back reports and accounts to the patroon in Amsterdam. As a living space, he chose an area north of Fort Orange where he could be in close contact with Indians coming in from both the north and the west. The area was called the "Flatts." On this site, he had a 120-foot *schuurhuys*, or combination house-barn, and a thirty-foot house for farmhands built. Shortly after the death of the patroon in 1643, he acquired a six-year lease to the land to raise a family.[31]

Dutchmen and Indians

In the early 1640s all three Dutchmen would have been living in the area near Fort Orange, and most likely met frequently in one of the many taverns. They were probably eager to exchange firsthand experiences with the Indians of the area. Harmen could have related his 1634–35 mission into the Mohawk Valley to investigate why the traffic in furs had decreased so radically (figure 2.3). After enduring many hardships traveling through knee-deep snow and freezing conditions in December and January, he finally reached an Oneida village southeast of Oneida Lake. Here he and his companions met with several Onondaga sachems to discuss the fur trade. Suspicions were confirmed that the French were involved in the fall-off of the fur trade. Eventually, a new price structure was agreed upon and the furs began to flow down the valley again.[32]

Adriaen and Arent both could have compared notes on their acquisition of the various Indian languages in the area, especially Mohawk, and their customs and rituals. A wealth of information regarding the Indians, both Mohawks and Mahicans, was probably exchanged when Harmen was in their company. Unfortunately, this relationship was not to last long. The first casualty was Harmen Meyndertsz van den Bogaert.

About ten years after his mission in the Mohawk Valley, Harmen was appointed *commies* of Fort Orange. In this position, he was commander of the fort and in charge of the trade goods warehoused in the fort. He was probably given this important command on the strength of his knowledge of the Indians and the fur trade coming down the Mohawk Valley. However, in late 1647 the course of his life changed dramatically when he was accused of sodomy with his Negro servant, Tobias.

Figure 2.3. Painting of *Winter in the Valley of the Mohawk* by L. F. Tantillo.

In an attempt to escape prosecution and capital punishment, he fled back up the Valley to where he had been in council with the Onondaga sachems twelve years before. He was tracked down by Hans Vos, an employee of Rensselaerswijck. During a shootout, the longhouse in which Harmen was hiding, and which held a winter's storage of furs and corn, caught fire. Vos captured him alive and brought him back to Fort Orange to face justice before Director General Stuyvesant. However, while awaiting trial until after the river was clear of ice, the fort was destroyed by a sudden thaw and ice floe. During the turmoil, Harmen managed to escape. This time he fled eastward across the river. Before making it to the other side the ice gave way and he drowned. The Indians were compensated for their loss of the longhouse and its contents from the proceeds of the sale of Harmen's real estate on Manhattan.

Next in line was Adriaen van der Donck. Although he had gone back to the Netherlands to submit a complaint concerning actions of the WIC directly to the States General, he found himself trapped by the outbreak of the first Anglo-Dutch War in 1652.[33] Before the war, he had argued for political reform, the recall of Stuyvesant, and the chartering of New Amsterdam as a municipality. At first, all his arguments and proposals received a positive response; however, the war had darkened the mood for any reform and caused the decision to recall Stuyvesant to be reversed, but it allowed the chartering of New Amsterdam.

Unable to return to his estate in New Netherland because of an English blockade of the coast, he kept himself busy working on his magnum opus, *A Description of New Netherland*. The book is a catalogue of the flora and fauna, rivers and mountains, animals, and foodstuffs, with a long section on the manners and customs of the Indians. It was published in the Netherlands shortly after Adriaen was allowed to return to Colendonck. The book is so positive about the potential of the country that it must have been an inspiration to many people to emigrate to the New World. Adriaen would have been delighted to hear newly arrived settlers praise his book as the reason for their coming to New Netherland. Unfortunately, it is quite likely that he never held a copy of it in his hand.[34]

The end of the war with England in 1654 was celebrated with bonfires and days of thanksgiving. The prospect of a period of peace gave the WIC the opportunity to settle old scores. The loss of Brazil in the same year to the Portuguese forced the WIC to shift its commercial activities farther to the north. New Netherland and the Dutch islands in the Caribbean had the potential to develop a symbiotic relationship under the leadership of Stuyvesant.

New Netherland had the resources to exchange wheat, timber, and bricks for building purposes in exchange for salt and horses from the islands. It was in this context that the WIC ordered the elimination of New Sweden.[35]

Since 1638, with the arrival of Minuit, the Swedish colony had grown into a competitor of the Dutch in the South River region of New Netherland. Up until the arrival of Stuyvesant in 1647, the Dutch and Swedes were able to coexist, viewing the English as their common enemy. However, Stuyvesant wanted total control of the Delaware River, which led directly into fur trading country west of Rensselaerswijck. If control of this river fell into the hands of the English, the Dutch would lose their advantage in the fur trade. Stuyvesant began a chess game with the Swedes in 1651 when he moved Fort Nassau (just below Camden, New Jersey) to the west side of the river (New Castle, Delaware) several miles below the Swedish trading post, Fort Christina (Wilmington, Delaware). He named it Fort Casimir, after an ancestral family figure. The Swedes countered by establishing a trading post on the east side (Salem, New Jersey) below Fort Casimir called Fort Elfsborgh. The last straw was the Swedish capture of Fort Casimir in 1654 on Trinity Sunday. The Swedes renamed the trading post Fort Trefaldighet, Fort Trinity.[36]

The final move on the Delaware was made in the fall of 1655. Under orders from the WIC, Stuyvesant led a naval force of seven ships and 340 soldiers to New Sweden. Both Swedish forts were quickly taken by the Dutch without resistance. Stuyvesant's smooth operation soon turned into chaos when rumors began to spread that the Swedes had instigated Indians to attack Manhattan while it was relatively unguarded. It is unknown whether the Swedes were involved in the so-called Peach War, but two things are known: that the Indians attacked Manhattan, Staten Island, and Pavonia, ostensibly looking for "Northern Indians," and the rumors of possible Swedish complicity caused the Dutch soldiers to inflict severe damage throughout New Sweden in a riotous fury. Another casualty was Adriaen van der Donck.[37]

All that we know about Adriaen's last days is that he was back in New Netherland from his extended stay in the Netherlands and that in the months following the so-called Peach War he is referred to twice, only in the past tense. The assumption is that he was killed by Indians during the turmoil associated with the attack on Manhattan in September 1655. He was only thirty-seven.

Unlike Harmen and Adriaen, Arent van Curler lived to see the arrival of the English in 1664. Following the end of the first Anglo-Dutch War in 1654, New Netherland experienced rapid growth. The loss of Brazil in the same year allowed the directors of the WIC to devote more resources to this once neglected possession. The final ten years of Stuyvesant's leadership witnessed increased population growth and diversification of economic interests. As the fur trade fell off in the late 1650s, more interest was paid to developing an export trade in wheat and involvement in the tobacco trade. It was most likely these signs of a growing viable presence between New England and the English tobacco colonies of Maryland and Virginia that attracted the attention of the English crown. As the English profited more from duties on shipments of tobacco, the more the Dutch presence in the Delaware became a concern. The Dutch were in an ideal location to provide a market for the English tobacco farmers, in the process circumventing duties to English coffers. It was time for England to establish hegemony along the Atlantic coast.[38]

Since arriving in New Netherland in 1638, Arent van Curler had become a prominent farmer at the "Flatts." Although it was located north of the village and fort on ideal alluvial soil along the river, it did not seem to be enough for him.[39] Several missions to the Mohawks for the renewal of trade agreements had introduced him to an even better location. While traveling to the Mohawk settlements in the Mohawk Valley, he would have followed the route through the woods to the river. There he would have found a large expanse of alluvial soil suitable for a concentration of farms. After petitioning Stuyvesant several times for permission to negotiate with the Mohawks for the land and to receive a proper patent, he was eventually granted land upon which to resettle fourteen families from Rensselaerswijck on farms.[40] Arent's agricultural venture was called Schenectady, "beyond the woods" in the Mohawk language.[41]

Van Curler's new agricultural settlement gave him proximity to the Mohawks, which would develop into an authentic friendship. Although Schenectady was excluded from the fur trade according to the agreement with Stuyvesant, Arent would grow in stature among the Mohawks as their trusted spokesman. His name alone represented respected authority to the point that well after the English takeover and Arent's death, Mohawks would address New York provincial governors simply as Corlaer or Cora. In a way, this friendship contributed to Arent's death.

After the English takeover of New Netherland in 1664, concern about a French attack on the Mohawks, Schenectady, and Albany grew. Van Curler communicated with both governors Alexandre de Prouville de Tracy of Canada and Francis Lovelace of New York in an attempt to mitigate the situation. Although Van Curler appeared to be caught in the middle, he may also have been attempting to establish a Dutch-Mohawk trade route along the Lake Champlain corridor to Quebec. We do not know his exact motive for being in a canoe with a Mohawk family (husband, wife, and baby) and two other Dutchmen, heading north along the west coast of this lake. All that we know is that Governor Tracy had invited him to Quebec for a visit. Ultimately, he was probably trying to find a way to protect the Mohawks, and especially his settlement of Schenectady, from a French attack.[42]

Just before sundown, while paddling along the west shore of the lake, Van Curler left the shoreline and struck out across open water from one point of land to another. Today the body of water between the two points is known as Corlaer Bay.[43] Suddenly a strong wind arose, which created waves high enough to swamp the canoe. Already overloaded with five adults and a large quantity of gifts and trade goods, the canoe rolled over. The Mohawks stripped off their clothing, preparing to swim for it. While struggling to stay afloat among the high waves, the baby was lost, one of the Dutchmen—a baker from Pomerania—also went under, and Arent van Curler, who didn't know how to swim, was never seen again.[44]

As painful and sudden as the final moments for all three Dutchmen must have been, they all left something of value behind as contributions to our knowledge of Dutch/Indian relations. As William Starna, coauthor of the translation of Harmen Meyndertsz van den Bogaert's journal, states in the preface, without it "we would be deprived of the earliest known description of the Lower Iroquois and their environment, including detailed accounts of their settlements, healing rituals, systems of protocol, language, and subsistence practices. It stands as a unique and compelling document."[45] Fortunately, Adriaen van der Donck was able to complete his *Description of New Netherland* before meeting his fate.

In the final words of his book, van der Donck foresees a bright future for his adopted country: "In conclusion, a territory like New Netherland, so suitable for commerce, as we have seen, which from its own resources produces assorted goods and requisites and has a surplus for supplying to others, must it not, given appropriate initiatives and direction, eventually prosper?"[46] Russell Shorto succinctly observes in his foreword to the new translation that "its depictions of North America at mid-seventeenth century are intoxicating even—especially—today. It is a raw and rough classic, a window into what once was and is now lost forever. And it is a work of ironic prophecy, for all that Van der Donck predicted would come to pass, but it would happen under the auspices not of the Dutch but of the

English."[47] The work's extensive description of the manners and customs of Indians is considered one of the most reliable available.

Arent van Curler left behind a legend based on his relationship with the Mohawks (figure 2.4). According to Trelease, whether it was because of his honesty as a trading agent for the patroon or "some other quality which no longer stands out, he won their confidence and retained it for the rest of his life." His influence over the Mohawks was unrivaled until years later with the appearance of William Johnson.[48] And, last but not least, Arent van Curler is still celebrated today in Nijkerk, his hometown in the Netherlands, and in New York as the founder of Schenectady.

Een Wilde, SYCHNECTA genaamt, van de MOHAWK uyt NOORD-AMERICA, te zien geweest in Blaauw Jan 1764.

Figure 2.4. An etching of a Mohawk Indian named Sychnecta on exhibit in Amsterdam in 1764 (public domain).

Notes

1. For a history of the formation of the Netherlands as a nation and state, see Jonathan I. Israel, *The Dutch Republic: Its Rise, Greatness, and Fall 1477–1806* (Oxford: Clarendon Press, 1995); and, for cultural history, see Simon Schama, *The Embarrassment of Riches: An Interpretation of Dutch Culture in the Golden Age* (Berkeley: University of California Press, 1988).

2. During the Middle Ages, the Dutch developed a preservation method that gave them an advantage over competitors. By immediately gutting the herring, except for digestive pouches and pancreas, and preserving them in a brine solution, Dutch herring boats could remain at sea longer in order to maximize their catches. This method required large quantities of quality salt.

3. Upon abdication, Charles V conferred his titles of emperor of the Holy Roman Empire on his brother Ferdinand, and king of Spain on his son Philip.

4. For works on the Dutch revolt, see Pieter Geyl, *The Revolt of the Netherlands, 1555–1609* (London: Williams and Northgate, 1932; paperback by Cassell History, 1988); Geoffrey Parker, *The Dutch Revolt* (Ithaca: Cornell University Press, 1977).

5. Originally, there were seventeen provinces in the Low Countries. The seven breakaway provinces making up the United Provinces consisted of Holland, Zeeland, Utrecht, Friesland, Groningen, Gelderland, and Overijssel. The remaining ten provinces stayed under Spanish control for the duration of the war and now make up what is now the country of Belgium.

6. Charles R. Boxer, *The Dutch Seaborne Empire, 1600–1800* (London: Hutchinson and Co., 1965); D. W. Davies, *Primer of Dutch Seventeenth Century Overseas Trade* (The Hague: Martinus Nijhoff, 1961); Jonathan I. Israel, *Dutch Primacy in World Trade, 1583–1740* (Oxford: Oxford University Press, 1989).

7. A major factor in the Dutch ability to compete on such a large scale was the development of a new ship design near the end of the sixteenth century. Called a *fluyt* or flute, it had a large cargo capacity. A simplified rigging allowed it to be sailed by a crew 50 percent smaller than ships of equal tonnage. It had a comparatively shallow draft, allowing it to sail in 29½ feet of water. Interchangeable parts made it possible to turn *fluyts* out quickly and economically by an assembly-line process. These parts could also be stockpiled at repair facilities around the globe. However, by sacrificing cannon for cargo space the lightly armed vessels needed to sail in convoys, protected by warships. Otherwise, they could be easy prey for pirates or other enemies of the Netherlands.

8. The VOC was formed as a joint-stock trading venture. Chartered by the States General of the United Provinces of the Netherlands, the VOC had a trading monopoly from the Cape of Good Hope eastward to the Strait of Magellan; it was most of the world except for the Atlantic region. It had the power to raise its own armies and navies, make alliances with local sovereigns within its sphere of operations, and, if necessary, it had the power to make war and peace in defense

of its interests. Company shares were traded on the Amsterdam stock exchange; investors represented a broad spectrum of society, from prosperous merchants to barmaids. Within one month of announcing its intentions, the VOC was able to raise six and a half million guilders in operating capital. The company was governed by a board of directors, seventeen in number, who represented the interests of the six chambers centered at Amsterdam, Middelburg, Delft, Rotterdam, Hoorn, and Enkhuizen. The monopoly was granted for twenty-one years and was an immediate success. For a history of the VOC, see Femme S. Gaastra, *De geschiedenis van de VOC* (Zutphen: Walburg Pers, 1991).

9. For information on the classical concept of the shape of the world, see A. Torayah Sharaf, *A Short History of Geographical Discovery* (London: George G. Harrap and Co., 1967).

10. Explorers were attracted to the idea of a northwest passage by legends such as *Fretum trium fratrum per quod Lusitani ad Orientem et ad Indos et ad Moluccas navigare conati sunt* (Strait of the Three Brothers through which the Portuguese attempted to sail to the Orient and the Indies and the Moluccas), which enticed navigators with the promise of a passage from the Atlantic to the Pacific at 40 degrees. See Samuel Eliot Morison, *The European Discovery of America: The Northern Voyages* (Oxford: Oxford University Press, 1971), for a discussion of the various explorations and tales surrounding the northwest passage. Willem Barentsz (after whom the Barents Sea is named) accompanied an expedition in 1596 to discover a passage along the northern coast of Siberia to the Far East. When the Dutch ship was frozen in the ice at Nova Zembla, Barentsz and his crew were forced to spend the winter there under extreme hardship. Barentsz died as he and the remainder of the crew were preparing to return to the Netherlands. After more incredible adventures and hardships, the crew eventually made its way back to Amsterdam to tell the tale. See *Reizen van Willem Barents, Jacob van Heemskerck, Jan Cornelisz Rijp en anderen naar het noorden, 1594–1597,* ed. S. P. L'Honoré Naber ('s-Gravenhage: Martinus Nijhoff, 1917) for the journal and drawings of Gerrit de Veer, a survivor of Barnetsz' crew.

11. See Henry Hudson's Voyages from *Purchas His Pilgrimes* by Samuel Purchas (originally printed in London, 1625; reprinted in facsimile form by Readex Microprint Corp., 1966) for the accounts of Hudson's four voyages. For a thorough analysis of Hudson's service with the VOC, see *Henry Hudson's Reize onder Nederlandsche vlag van Amsterdam naar Nova Zembla, Amerika en terug naar Dartmouth in Engeland, 1609,* ed. S. P. L'Honoré Naber ('s-Gravenhage: Martinus Nijhoff, 1921). For a detailed analysis of Hudson's four voyages, consult Donald S. Johnson, *Charting the Sea of Darkness: The Four Voyages of Henry Hudson* (Camden, ME: International Marine, 1993); also consult www.ianchadwick.com/Hudson.

12. Johannes de Laet, *Beschrijvinghe van West-Indien* (Leyden: Elzevier, 1630), 101–104.

13. For documents relating to the New Netherland Company, see Simon Hart, *The Prehistory of the New Netherland Company: Amsterdam Notarial Records of the First Dutch Voyages to the Hudson* (Amsterdam: City of Amsterdam Press, 1959).

14. See "Wassenaer's Historisch Verhael" in *Narratives of New Netherland, 1609–1664*, ed. J. Franklin Jameson (New York: Charles Scribner's Sons, 1909), 86. For another translation made from the original, see Nicholaes van Wassenaer, *Historisch verhael alden ghedenck-weerdichste geschiedenisse, die hier en daer in Europa, als in Duytsch-lant, Vranckrijck, Enghelant, Spaengien, Hungaryen, Polen, Sevenberghen, Wallachien, Modavie, Turchyen en Neder-lant, van den beginne des jaar 1621 . . . (tot Octobri des jaers 1632) voorgevallen syn.* (published in twenty-one semiannual parts at Amsterdam), vol. 4, 39.

15. See Charles T. Gehring and William A. Starna, "Dutch and Indians in the Hudson Valley: The Early Period," in the *Hudson Valley Regional Review*, September 1992, for the full text of the interrogatory and the consequences of Hontom's actions.

16. For a discussion of the Pequot as power brokers in the sewant trade and their relationship to the Dutch, see Kevin McBride, "The Source and Mother of the Fur Trade: Native-Dutch Relations in Eastern New Netherland," in *Enduring Traditions: The Native Peoples of New England*, ed. Laurie Lee Weinstein (Westport, CT: Bergin and Garvey, 1994).

17. The West India Company was modeled after the East India Company, except that it was administered by nineteen directors instead of seventeen. See endnote 8 for a description of the VOC. See H. J. den Heijer, *De Geschiedenis van de WIC* (Zutphen: Walburg Pers, 1994; rev. 2002), for a comprehensive history of the stock company responsible for the maintenance of New Netherland.

18. See E. B. O'Callaghan, *Documentary History of the State of New York* (Albany: Weed, Parsons & Co., 1850), 3:49–51, for the settlement of the Walloons as told by Catelina Trico.

19. See *Documents Relating to New Netherland, 1624–1626*, trans. and ed. A. J. F. van Laer (San Marino, CA: Henry E. Huntington Library and Art Gallery, 1924), for the instructions to Verhulst as director and other related documents.

20. Wassenaer, *Historisch*, 84–85.

21. C. A. Weslager, *Dutch Explorers, Traders and Settlers in the Delaware Valley, 1609–1664* (Philadelphia: University of Pennsylvania Press, 1961).

22. See Heijer, *De Geschiedenis*, for WIC interests in Africa and Brazil. See also Johannes Postma and Victor Enthoven, eds., *Riches from Atlantic Commerce: Dutch Transatlantic Trade and Shipping, 1584–1817* (Leiden: Brill, 2003), and Jonathan I. Israel, *Dutch Primacy in World Trade, 1585–1740* (Oxford: Clarendon Press, 1990).

23. See Geoffrey Parker, *Global Crisis: War, Climate Change, and Catastrophe in the Seventeenth Century* (New Haven: Yale University Press, 2013), for the effects of the "Little Ice Age."

24. Allen W. Trelease, *Indian Affairs in Colonial New York: The Seventeenth Century* (Ithaca: Cornell University Press, 1960); Thomas Elliot Norton, *The Fur Trade in Colonial New York, 1686–1776* (Madison: University of Wisconsin Press, 1974).

25. A. J. F. van Laer, trans. and ed., *Van Rensselaer Bowier Manuscripts* (Albany: University of the State of New York, 1908).

26. E. B. O'Callaghan, *History of New Netherland or New York under the Dutch* (New York: D. Appleton & Company, 1848), 1:382–383, for reference to Van der Donck's estate.

27. See Jaap Jacobs, *New Netherland: A Dutch Colony in Seventeenth-Century America* (Boston: Brill, 2005), 144–148.

28. For a discussion relating to whether to promote colonization or maintain a trading post structure, see Van Cleaf Bachman, *Peltries or Plantations: The Economic Policies of the Dutch West India Company in New Netherland, 1623–1639* (Baltimore: Johns Hopkins University Press, 1969). See also Charles T. Gehring, *Privatizing Colonization: The Patroonship of Rensselaerswijck*, www.newnetherlandinstitute.org/research/essays-and-articles/#annals.

29. See C. A. Weslager, *A Man and His Ship: Peter Minuit and the Kalmar Nyckel* (Wilmington, DE: Middle Atlantic Press, 1990), for details of Minuit and the settlement of New Sweden on the Delaware.

30. van Laer, *Van Rensselaer*, 410.

31. See "Online Exhibit" by William Greer, *Arent van Curler and the Flatts* at www.newnetherlandinstitute.org/history, under History.

32. Charles T. Gehring and William A. Starna, trans. and ed., *A Journey into Mohawk and Oneida Country 1634–1635: The Journal of Harmen Meyndertsz van den Bogaert* (Syracuse: Syracuse University Press, rev. ed., 2013).

33. When Oliver Cromwell came to power in England in 1648, he sought ways to improve his country's commercial interests around the world at the expense of the Dutch. His weapon was the institution of a navigation act, which cut into the lucrative Dutch carrying trade. According to the act, only English ships or ships of the country of origin were allowed to transport goods to England. Dutch success at sea depended on the principle of freedom to trade anywhere at sea without penalty. This act led to the first Anglo-Dutch War, which lasted from 1652 to 1654.

34. Adriaen van der Donck, *A Description of New Netherland*, trans. Diederik Willem Goedhuys, ed. Charles T. Gehring and William A. Starna with a foreword by Russell Shorto (Lincoln: University of Nebraska Press, 2008).

35. Charles T. Gehring, trans. and ed., *New York Historical Manuscripts: Dutch Council Minutes, 1652–1654* (Baltimore: Genealogical Publishing, 1983).

36. C. A. Weslager, *New Sweden on the Delaware 1638–1655* (Wilmington, DE: Middle Atlantic Press, 1988); Stellan Dahlgren and Hans Norman, *The Rise and Fall of New Sweden: Governor Johan Risingh's Journal, 1654–1655, in Its Historical Context* (Uppsala: Almquist and Wiksell International, 1988).

37. Gehring, *New York Historical Manuscripts*, 36–47.

38. Christian J. Koot, *Empire at the Periphery: British Colonists, Anglo-Dutch Trade, and the Development of the British Atlantic, 1621–1713* (New York: NYU Press, 2011).

39. SeeError! Hyperlink reference not valid. for information about his farm.

40. Trelease, *Indian Affairs*, 136.

41. See Thomas E. Burke Jr., *Mohawk Frontier: The Dutch Community of Schenectady, New York 1661–1710* (Ithaca: Cornell University Press, 1991), for the formation of Van Curler's settlement on the Mohawk River.

42. See Burke, *Mohawk Frontier*.

43. The bay is on the New York side of Lake Champlain just south of the Port Kent ferry route to Burlington, Vermont. Port Douglass is located at the westernmost interior curve of the bay.

44. A. J. F. Van Laer, "Documents Relating to Arent van Curler's Death," in *The Dutch Settlers Society Yearbook* 3 (1927–28): 30–34.

45. Gehring and Starna, *A Journey*, xvi.

46. Van der Donck, *A Description*, 142.

47. Van der Donck, *A Description*, xv.

48. Trelease, *Indian Affairs*, 115–116. Johnson (1715–74) was appointed superintendent of Indian affairs in 1756. His residences at Fort Johnson near Amsterdam and Johnson Hall in Johnstown, both in Mohawk country, gave him the proximity to develop a relationship with the Natives as strong as that of Arent van Curler.

3.

Declarations of Interdependence

The Nature of Dutch–Native Relations in New Netherland, 1624–1664

STEPHEN T. STAGGS

After urging the members of the States-General to give New Netherlanders a greater voice in governing the colony of New Netherland, the lawyer and councilor Adriaen van der Donck prepared to return to New Amsterdam in spring 1652. However, the outbreak of a naval war with England in May prevented his immediate return. With time on his hands, Van der Donck decided to continue promoting New Netherland in the Dutch Republic by writing a detailed description of the colony. When he sat down and put quill to paper, he decided to also address the questions of potential colonists, including why Europeans had come to "this beautiful land" in the first place. The answer, according to Van der Donck, was the beaver.[1]

The beaver had, in fact, initially been the centerpiece of Indian–Dutch relations. Henry Hudson's report of plentiful furs and friendly Indians along the upper part of the North (Hudson) River sparked widespread interest because beaver felt hats were the rage in northern Europe. However, the traditional suppliers, Russia and Poland, could not meet the increasing demand. Within a few years' independent traders were sending ships to the North River to exploit this new market. Then, in 1614, the States-General provided a three-year monopoly over the trade on the North River to the

New Netherland Company, whose representatives constructed Fort Nassau, a small, fortified trading post on Castle Island near the mouth of the Norman's Kill (figure 3.1).

From 1614 to 1618 resident traders exchanged iron axes, brass kettles, knives, awls, small brass bells, woolen broadcloth, simple monochrome and polychrome glass beads, and ivory combs for the furs and food that the Mahicans and Mohawks brought to the fort. The European objects secured by the Mahicans and Mohawks were then incorporated and often modified to meet traditional needs. Iron axes, for example, were scored and processed into traditional tools such as celts, knives, and scrapers. However, it would not be until the subsequent period (1624–40), during which time settlers became a more permanent feature, that Indians and New Netherlanders would come into increasing contact with one another.[2] Using the original Dutch-language records of the government of New Netherland, this chapter evaluates the nature of the relationships that developed between the Indians and colonists in and around the Dutch colony of New Netherland between 1624 and 1664 as a result of those contacts (figure 3.2).

Figure 3.1. Fort Nassau: The first recorded European structure in New York state, 1614 (Len F. Tantillo, *The Trading House*).

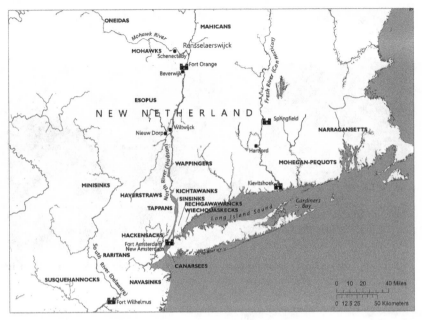

Figure 3.2. Northeastern North America in the seventeenth century (drawn by Jason VanHorn).

Dutch Declarations

In summer 1624 the Dutch West India Company (WIC) began establishing fortified settlements: Fort Wilhelmus on the lower parts of the Delaware River, Fort Orange on the Upper Hudson, Fort Amsterdam on the Lower Hudson, and Kievitshoek (Plover's Corner)—present-day Old Saybrook—at the mouth of the Connecticut River. For the colonists inhabiting those settlements, treating Indians fairly was a matter of survival. And they could neither afford to offend the various groups of Delaware, Mahicans, and other Algonquian speakers on whose territories they were living nor the Iroquois-speaking Mohawks, who were the principal supplier of pelts to the Dutch merchants and settlers who depended on the fur trade to supplement their incomes (figure 3.3). By 1628, however, the few Dutch colonists who had settled in the colony were struggling to survive. Of the four initial settlements, only New Amsterdam on the island of Manhattan and Fort Orange on the upper Hudson remained. To make matters worse, the fur trade, which was initially promising, had become stagnant.[3]

Figure 3.3. Mohawk warriors approach the ship of Arent van Curler, 1650 (Len F. Tantillo, *Curiosity of the Magua*).

Events in Europe and in neighboring New England did not bode well for the survival of the colony either. King Charles of England signed a peace treaty with Spain in 1632, ending English support for the Dutch Republic, disputing Dutch claims to the lands along the Hudson River, and proclaiming that those lands belonged to England by right of discovery. Four years later English settlers built a settlement at Hartford on the Connecticut River and, in 1638, established a trading post at Springfield farther upriver to compete with Dutch fur traders at Huys de Hoop (House of Hope) and Fort Orange (figure 3.4). The establishment of the settlement at Hartford and the trading post at Springfield signaled the hostile intent of the English. It also redirected furs away from Dutch traders and threatened to cut off Dutch access to the *sewant*—a southern New England Narragansett Algonquin name for a particular type of loose polished shell beads—being produced by the Narragansetts, Pequots, and other Indigenous communities who lived along Long Island Sound.

What's more, the leaders of the Massachusetts Bay colony had, in 1636–37, directed a brutal campaign that virtually destroyed the Pequots, leaving the sewant trade in southeastern New England in the hands of the Narragansett, who were allies of the English.[4] This was a significant turn of affairs for New Netherlanders who relied on the flow of sewant from the Pequots and Narragansetts as it was not only "the source and mother of the

Figure 3.4. The first permanent settlement in New York (Len F. Tantillo, *Fort Orange, 1635*).

beaver trade," but also the common currency of the colony, more valuable than *stivers* and used to trade for tobacco, wood, and other commodities, pay salaries and taxes, and purchase lands.[5] From 1624 to 1640, then, the colonists of New Netherland were struggling to survive and found themselves dependent on Indians for provisions, directions, instructions on where to cultivate and how to clear the land, protection, and, most importantly, beaver pelts.

The WIC, which had maintained a monopoly on the fur trade since 1621, responded by opening the trade to all free Dutch citizens in January 1639. As a result, the volume of trade between the Mohawks and the Dutch increased dramatically (figure 3.5). The Mohawks also began to see a difference in the quality and quantity of merchandise offered by the Dutch. Most of what the Mohawks received—kettles, axes, knives, awls, beads, wampum, and woolen cloth—usually came in exchange for furs. The Dutch settlers, for their part, used the furs to obtain food, guide services, or other necessities. The colonists also relied on imports from the Republic for many commodities, including textiles; however, imports from the Republic had to be paid by the export of pelts or tobacco.[6]

The opening of the fur trade in 1639 thus provides a window into the importance of furs to the survival of New Netherlanders as they repeatedly ignored legislation passed by the Council of New Netherland to regulate the fur trade. Private traders and settlers either traveled with cloth, good sewant, and other articles of trade into Susquehannock and Iroquois country, or intercepted Indians in the woods near Fort Orange in order to acquire beaver skins at a cheaper rate.[7] In the eyes of those sitting on the Council, too many people were practicing no other vocation other than waiting daily in the woods in order to trade peltries with the Indians. Therefore, the Council members decreed, "no Christian nor savage is allowed, either outside or within the settlement, to directly or indirectly draw to him, call, nor lure any savages coming from the countryside with peltries, by giving them gifts."[8]

Meanwhile, the director general or governor of the colony, Petrus Stuyvesant, was fielding complaints from the principal traders in and around Fort Orange and a request from the *predikant* (preacher) in New Amsterdam, *Dominee* (Reverend) Henricus Selijns. The traders decried the exorbitant amount of annual gifts given to Indian brokers while Selijns requested to be paid in beaver skins.[9] The fact that Selijns sought payment in beaver skins and that such exorbitant gifts were yearly given to Indian brokers to facilitate the fur trade underscores the importance and value of the furs that the Mohawks and other Indians exchanged with New Netherlanders.

Figure 3.5. Mohawk hunters return to their longhouses, circa 1625 (Len F. Tantillo, *Winter in the Valley of the Mohawk*).

It also highlights the fact that Dutch authorities had not only learned the importance of ceremony and reciprocal gift exchange in cementing political and economic ties among Indian groups such as the Mohawks, but had also adopted those practices when dealing with their Indian neighbors.[10]

The records of the government of New Netherland bear this out repeatedly. When, for example, the colony's Council members had, by 1647, still failed to provide the cloth and several hundred fathoms of sewant that had been promised to the various Delaware groups living near New Amsterdam at the conclusion of five years of back and forth hostilities between some New Netherlanders and Delawares in 1645, the most prominent citizens of New Amsterdam repeatedly visited the Council to express their concerns that the Indians are restless and dissatisfied and that they dread a new war if the "Indians are not made content by presents."[11] The Council members decided to offer them this gift once and for all as "a renewal and continuation of the ancient alliance and friendship" and told the Delaware that they were "not responsible for the last war which the old Sackima [Willem Kieft] who has gone away may have caused and that we have no desire for new trouble and war, but wish to live with them in peaceful alliance and as good neighbors, in token and in confirmation of which we offer them this gift."[12]

Kieft's successor, Petrus Stuyvesant, continued exchanging gifts to cement political and economic relationships with his Indian neighbors and secure the release of Christians. During the conflicts with the Esopus Indians, for example, the leaders of the new village of Esopus convinced Stuyvesant to send four pieces of duffel, some guns, powder, lead, and other small wares in May 1663 in order to pacify the Indians.[13] Later that spring Stuyvesant and his Council gave twenty guilders worth of sewant to an Indian woman who, along with Oratam, sachem of the Hackensack, Hans de Wilt, Kastangh, Memmesame, Meninger, and Mamarikickan, leaders of the Minisinks, brought in the son of Jan Lootman Backer, a settler in the Esopus.[14] Certainly, the political and military authorities in New Netherland not only adopted the practice of reciprocal gift exchange in their relations with the Indians, they also relied on their Native neighbors to help them secure their imprisoned compatriots.

New Netherlanders also turned to their Indian neighbors when they found themselves struggling to turn the Eastern Woodlands into farmland and, as a result, failing to produce enough grain. *Dominee* Michaëlius testified to the support that the surrounding Indians provided the inhabitants of New Amsterdam, informing the members of the Classis of Amsterdam that "the savages also bring some things [goods to us]."[15] The first secretary of New Netherland, Isaac de Rasière, reinforced this message in 1628 when he informed a WIC director that the Indians on Manhattan provided the colonists with canoes to paddle and fish, corn, cornbread, and porridge to eat (figure 3.6). In return, female colonists provided the Indians with cheese. Thirty-three years later New Netherlanders were still purchasing Indian corn, fish, and venison from various retailers in New Amsterdam.[16]

Colonists also asked Indians to teach them to hunt turkeys. According to de Rasière, turkeys ran so hard and fast that they would reach the woods where the settlers could not see them.[17] During their trip into Mohawk and Oneida country, it appears that the Dutch traders Harmen Meyndertsz Vanden Bogaert, Jeronimus de la Croix, and Willem Thomasz also received some turkey hunting lessons from a Mohawk leader named Ateryóhtu.[18] During their excursions New Netherlanders relied on Indians for directions and provisions as well. On their return journey from Mohawk and Oneida country, for example, Van den Bogaert, De la Croix, and Thomasz received directions to Fort Orange from the Indians because they "knew the paths better than we."[19] While sailing along the Atlantic coast north of New Amsterdam, the prominent New Netherland merchant Govert Loockermans and his crew purchased two geese at Krommegou (Crooked Coast—present-

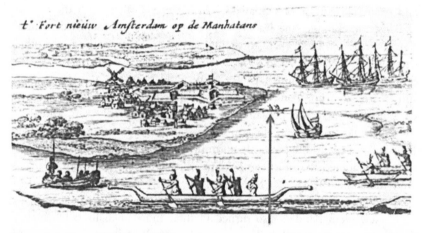

t' Fort nieuw Amsterdam op de Manhatans

Figure 3.6. Two colonists paddling a dugout canoe toward the shores of Manhattan from the engraving *t' Fort Nieuw Amsterdam op de Manhattans*, published in *Beschryvinghe van Virginia, Nieuw Nederlandt, Nieuw Engelandt . . .* (Amsterdam: Joost Hartgers, 1651).

day Gardiners Bay) from an Indian leader named Rochbon and a half a deer from an Indian at Pakatoc (Pakeketock).[20] The settlers living along the South River and in and around Beverwijck, Rensselaerswijck, and the Esopus also relied on Indians to provide them with turkeys, deer, fish, and grain. However, when the Indians did not bring foodstuffs settlers could find themselves begging the governor to send them food.[21]

This did not mean that the Dutch did not clear any land for cultivation, but when they did they often looked to their Indian neighbors for instruction. New Netherlanders adopted the Indian practice of burning down forest areas and received advice from Indians regarding which areas to clear.[22] For example, when Adriaen van der Donck once found himself standing with an Indian near a young wood that Van der Donck was clearing for cultivation, the Indian told Van der Donck that the piece of land in question had "very good soil and bears grain abundantly, which I well know because it is only twenty-five or twenty-six years ago that we planted grain there and now it has become wood again."[23] Those colonists who did successfully clear the woodlands found themselves turning to Indian laborers to work in their fields and receiving advice on how to tend their cornfields.[24] The Esopus Indians also advised the "Christians" living in and around Fort Esopus on how to improve their crop since the corn was spoiling in the fields. The Esopus Indians instructed the settlers to plow their fields and hunt the crows on a daily basis for the crows were doing great damage to the corn.[25]

Corn was, in fact, an essential element in the diet of both Indians and New Netherlanders. However, the colonists did not produce enough corn and so relied on their Indian neighbors for provision. Corn was, for example, one of the forms with which Indians were instructed to pay the tribute that the leaders of New Netherland demanded in 1639 to defray the costs of protecting Indians through the construction of fortifications and the payment of soldiers and sailors.[26]

In fact, the corn trade was so essential that the government of New Netherland saw fit to regulate the value of corn as well as the amount of corn (twelve *schepels*, or nine bushels) colonists could trade with the Indians for one coat of duffels. Anyone caught violating this ordinance would be punished with a fine as colonists like Abraham Planck, Cornelis Lambersz, and George Rapalje and his wife found out the following year.[27] Then, in 1640, the government of New Netherland ordered colonists to either herd or fence in their livestock because they were uprooting Indian corn hills. The author of the ordinance warned that if this ordinance was not heeded "corn would be dear in the autumn and our good people [will] suffer want [and] the *savages* be induced to remove and conceive a hatred against our nation and thus out of mischief inflict some injury or other upon us."[28]

In October of that same year the patroon David de Vries took a trip to Tappan in order to exchange cloth for corn. However, when he arrived he discovered that a WIC *sloep* (a small boat) had already docked and the WIC officials were demanding a contribution of corn from some Christian Indians who refused to give them their corn. After the WIC *sloep* disembarked, the Indians informed him that he (a Dutchman) must really be a "mean fellow" to come, without being called, and inhabit Indian land and then expect to be given corn for nothing. Despite the fact that they did not have a great surplus, the Indians were willing to exchange some of their corn with him since he was willing to give some cloth in return.[29] According to the author of the *Breeden-Raedt aende Vereenichde Nederlandsche Provintien*, these same Indians also reminded De Vries that they had provided enough corn and other food for the colonists to survive two very harsh winters when the settlement was in its infancy.[30]

The importance of the corn trade in New Netherland is also underscored by the fact that the Council of Twelve Men—a group of men who, in 1641, were selected to advise Kieft on governmental affairs—chose to maintain the trade with their Delaware neighbors despite the outrage that the "scandalous murder" of Claes Swits by a Delaware Indian caused among many colonists.[31] Indeed, the colonists living in New Sweden relied on the Delaware as well as the Susquehannocks to supply them with corn and furs.[32] In order to feed themselves, colonists also stole corn from the Indians at various times of the year. For example, in the dead of winter, in January 1643, Roelant Hackwaert was arrested for digging up and stealing corn that Indians had stored for themselves in some pits about a pistol shot from the wagon path at Marechhawieck.[33] Four years later Barent and Hans Jansz confessed that they had, with Cornelis Melyn's consent, paddled a canoe to Long Island and stole and destroyed some of the Indians' corn.[34]

Canoes were another aspect of Indian life adopted by New Netherlanders. In the background of his engraving of New Amsterdam circa 1626–28, for example, Joost Hartgers depicted two colonists paddling a dugout canoe toward the shores of Manhattan (figure 3.6).[35] In the records from the government of New Netherland, there are a number of examples of colonists using canoes. A few notable examples include the testimony of Van den Bogaert who, in 1647, reported to Governor Kieft that the "lusty" Raritans stole a canoe from his party.[36] Eight years later Director-General Stuyvesant and his Council prohibited colonists from crossing over the Hudson River by boat, canoe, or any other vessel.[37] Colonists on the upper Hudson were using canoes as well. In 1658, for example, the former manager of Rensselaerswijck, Arent van Curler, appeared in court demanding restitution of his canoe, which the defendant, the Beverwijck mason Jan Cornelisz (Gauw/Vijselaer), had taken from the banks of the Hudson. According to Cornelisz's testimony, he had, without knowing it, taken Van Curler's canoe because there were two canoes along the shore.[38]

Of course, colonists needed Indians to permit them to travel, inhabit, and cultivate these lands in the first place, which representatives of the Delaware and Mohawks were quick to remind New Netherlanders. In 1643 a group of Delaware reminded David de Vries that they "had given you [the Dutch] land, which you inhabit; nevertheless, we remain masters of that [the land], which we still have reserved for ourselves."[39] During a meeting at the patroon's house in Rensselaerswijck circa 1648, some Mohawk representatives informed Brant van Slichtenhorst, the newly appointed director of the colony of Rensselaerswijck, of this reality. After being entertained for many days, much to Van Slichtenhorst's obvious annoyance, the Mohawks reminded him that they "fight for us" and had "allowed the Christians to live there, because they should convenience them [the Mohawks] with everything, and otherwise the Christians might just as well cross the great water again."[40]

During this same period (1640–52), New Netherlanders increasingly spread out along the upper and lower Hudson, which meant that lands had to be purchased from the Indians. In 1640 and 1645 WIC officials purchased lands on Long Island and then, in 1649, purchased a large tract of land from Wiechquaskeck leaders in what is now Westchester County.[41] The need to purchase land and the corresponding need to have "neighboring tribes as allies and not adversaries resulted in a shift from trade-based to politically-based relationships."[42] On the upper Hudson, this meant it was essential for the Dutch to maintain their alliance with the Mohawks who controlled much of the fur trade, outnumbered the Dutch, and claimed all Mahican land west of the Hudson by right of conquest.[43]

Such alliances were mutually beneficial as both Indians and New Netherlanders relied on one another for military support, intelligence, and mediation when relationships turned sour and open warfare broke out in the colonial Hudson Valley, most notably during Kieft's War (1639–43), the Peach War (1655), the First Esopus War (1659–60), and the Second Esopus War (1663–64). However, the number of soldiers garrisoned in the colony was low due to the WIC's difficult financial situation.[44] As a result, the directors and councilors of New Netherland relied on their Indian allies for military support. During Kieft's administration (1638–47), for example, the councilors gave Witaneywen a WIC yacht in spring 1645 and instructed him to take forty-seven of his armed Shinnecock warriors to "the place where he is to put ashore" and, once his spies have discovered the enemy, "defeat them with all his force," whereupon he was to return to New Amsterdam with the yacht to receive his reward.[45]

The practice of securing Indian military assistance continued during Stuyvesant's administration (1647–64). When conflict broke out between Esopus settlers and Indians, for example, Stuyvesant employed the assistance of Long Island Indians against the Esopus Indians.[46] Then, after conflict broke out again in 1663, the councilors of New Netherland deemed it necessary to augment colonial forces so they commissioned Pieter Wolphertsz van Couwenhoven as lieutenant of a troop of Natives and colonial volunteers.[47]

It also appears that Dutch soldiers also adopted Indian military tactics. In spring 1660, for example, Ensign Dirck Smith and his officers decided to employ the same guerrilla tactics that the Esopus used against the Dutch, lying in ambush in the rocks with forty-five men at a distance of about two to three shots from the fort. Smith and his troops lay hidden for three to four hours, but were discovered by about fifteen Esopus warriors armed with guns, at which point Smith and his troops immediately broke loose and shot at them, imprisoning one Indian and wounding and killing another.[48]

It is also quite clear that New Netherlanders relied on their Indian neighbors for a certain amount of military intelligence as well. During the conflicts with the Esopus Indians, settlers and WIC officials were repeatedly informed of Esopus plans vis-à-vis the Dutch. For example, on July 29, 1659 a Mohawk named Amires informed Sergeant Andries Lourisz that the Esopus hated the Dutch and were prepared to go to war. A young Indian and a female Indian also informed the settlers in the Esopus that the Esopus Indians were planning on killing the Dutch settlers. During the Second Esopus War, Stuyvesant and his councilors received numerous reports from their Indian allies.[49] In September a Hackensack Indian, known as Pieter van Hackensack by the Dutch—which, given the name change, likely suggests he was a convert to the Reformed faith—entered Fort Amsterdam (figure 3.7) to inform the Council that thirty Esopus Indians had been defeated along with some women and children and the Christian prisoners recaptured, news that, if confirmed, would result in Pieter receiving a new coat.[50] However, the Esopus threat was not over and Stuyvesant and his councilors

Figure 3.7. Arent van Curler's bark passes Fort Amsterdam, Manhattan, 1650 (Len F. Tantillo, *Fort Amsterdam*).

continued receiving military intelligence from, among others, Oratam and Karstangh, two Hackensack Indians.[51]

Dutch officials also relied on their Indian allies to assist in peace negotiations. During the conflicts with the various Delaware groups surrounding New Amsterdam, Governor Kieft and his Council asked Mohawk and Mahican ambassadors to assist as mediators in the peace negotiations. Thus, when the articles of peace were concluded in the open air in Fort Amsterdam on August 30, 1645, not only were Oratam, sachem of the Hackensack, Sessekennick and Willem, sachems of the Tappan and Rechgawawancks, and the inhabitants of New Amsterdam, including Governor Kieft and his Council, present, but also Aepjen, a Mahican sachem representing the Sinsinks, Wappingers, Wiechquaeskecks, and Kichtawanks, and Agheroense, a Mohawk ambassador.[52]

During the conflicts with the Esopus Indians, Dutch officials turned to their Indian allies to broker peace once again. In September 1659 Vice-Director Johannes La Montagne sent Mohawk and Mahican delegates from Fort Orange to the Esopus with gifts in order to procure an armistice from the Esopus Indians.[53] In response, the Esopus sent several of their own allies to the *stadhuis* (city hall) in New Amsterdam in order to mediate with Stuyvesant and the Council members on their behalf. However, Stuyvesant and the Council members insisted that the Esopus send their own sachems to meet with them.[54] This demand would still not be met when, on May 24, 1660, Mahican leaders, including Aepjen, appeared before the Council with the intent of securing a peace between the Dutch, Esopus, and Mahicans.

The next Indians through the *stadhuis* door were Hackensack and Haverstraw sachems, a group that most likely included Oratam. This time Stuyvesant and the Council commissioned Claes Jansz de Ruyter to accompany these sachems to the Esopus to receive their proposals for peace.[55] However, a lasting peace with the Esopus was not secured despite the ongoing efforts of the Mohawks in the winter and spring of 1661. Following the attack on the Dutch settlements of Nieuw Dorp and Wiltwijck on June 7, 1663, the Council employed Mohawks to recover those of "the Christian nation" who had fallen into the hands of "the barbarians," and asked Oratam to inform the Esopus that the Dutch were interested in securing a peace.[56] Over the course of that winter Oratam appeared before Stuyvesant and the Council members on three separate occasions, keeping them abreast of his negotiations with the Esopus on their behalf.[57]

The following spring Oratam again appeared before the Council, this time with Navasink, Wappinger, Wiechquaeskeck, and Kichtawank leaders who brought a Dutch child that they had purchased from the Esopus for thirty-one fathoms of sewant. They also informed the Council members that they had also delivered six imprisoned "Christians" to Lieutenant Van Couwenhoven, one of whom was an important female servant, which they had done as a mark of their desire for peace. Beyond the gifts of sewant, brandy, and duffels given to the various Indian leaders, Stuyvesant and the Council gave Oratam an imprisoned Indian woman and two Indian children as well as his own sheet of cloth for his trouble (and assistance).[58]

Native Declarations

Between 1652 and 1664 Native peoples found themselves increasingly reliant upon their New Netherland neighbors, who were becoming a more permanent part of the landscape as many new settlements were established in the colony. In Iroquoia, the peace treaty that had been signed with the French in 1653 did not last. Indeed, by 1658 the Mohawks faced renewed warfare with the French on their northern borders, the Susquehannocks on their southern border, and New England Algonquin-speaking peoples on their eastern borders. Faced with these numerous challenges, the Mohawk turned to their Dutch allies to assist them with their negotiations.[59] However, the Mohawk were not the only Indians who needed the Dutch as a trading partner and strategic ally. The Mahicans, Esopus, Kichtawanks, Wappingers, Wiechquaeskecks, Hackensacks, Navasinks, and Minisinks as well as various Indian groups living on Long Island looked to the Dutch for protection and peace as well.[60]

The appearances and requests of Native leaders before the governor and Council of New Netherland between 1652 and 1664 not only underscore the increasing reliance of Natives upon the Dutch for military support but also for material goods.[61] According to the archaeological record, most of the Native traditional technologies and materials such as ceramics and stone, bone, and antler tools had disappeared from Mohawk villages by 1660. Furthermore, the tendency to adapt and reuse European materials also decreased as items such as axes, knives, and kettles became more and more readily available. "As European ceramics and bottle glass begin to appear in Native refuse along with white clay pipe stems, nails, broken gun parts and the bones of domestic animals," the archaeologist James Bradley writes, "Native archaeological sites do not look that different from the sites of the more rural Dutch homes."[62]

The written record reinforces this conclusion and reveals the extent to which Indians relied upon their European neighbors for a whole host of material goods. Land deeds from this period reveal that sewant, woolen cloth, blankets, needles, awls, coats, mirrors, kettles, guns, lead, gunpowder, axes, adzes,[63] knives, brandy, beer, tobacco, and pipes were among the goods Indians valued. One of the more interesting land deeds during this period was an accord struck between the Dutch and Navasinks. The Navasink leaders demanded four thousand guilders, one hundred fathoms of black sewant, sixty guns (large and small), sixty pieces of lead, sixty hatchets, sixty adzes, sixty knives, sixty needles and awls, sixty tobacco pipes, sixty kettles, sixty mirrors, sixty children's coats, sixty pairs of socks, sixty stockings, twelve cloth jackets, four blankets (one green, one white, and two red), three rolls of tobacco, two pieces of duffel, two ankers of brandy, and gunpowder in exchange for some of their unsold lands.[64] A number of these items also appear on a 1654 ordinance that imposed duties on "*wiltse cargasoenen*" (savage cargoes or trade goods), which also sheds light on the sort of goods preferred by the Indians living in and around New Netherland. *Wiltse cargasoenen* included duffels, woolen cloth, Indian coats, kettles, blankets, salt, beer, brandy, French and Spanish wines, and distilled spirits. They were, according to the authors of the ordinance, also among the cargoes that not only produced the most profits but also caused the least amount of trouble for the community.[65]

Another 1654 ordinance also reveals that some Indians, both men and women, found it more convenient to cross the East River on the ferry of Manhattan rather than paddling their own canoes (figure 3.8). They could also find rest and drink in the ferry house that was constructed on the Long Island shore by the master carpenter Egbert van Borsum, who from 1654 held the lease on the ferry and ran a tavern in the ferry house.[66] In fact, it was during this period (1652–64) that alcohol played a more significant role in the relationships between Indians and colonists.

The fact that ordinances and warnings against the selling of strong liquor to the Indians were persistently renewed makes it clear that the liquor traffic persisted throughout the period because not only did it bring

Figure 3.8. Dutch settlers cross the Hudson River near Fort Orange, 1643 (Len F. Tantillo, *The Ferry*).

more customers and profits to the many tavern keepers throughout New Netherland, Indians—like many colonists—enjoyed the opportunity to drink. Many Dutch tavern keepers were happy to oblige despite the threat of penalties that ranged from five hundred guilders for the first offense to a double fine, arbitrary corporal punishment, banishment, and liability for all damages caused by the sale for the second offense. The promise of greater profits, especially during the trading season, was too much for many New Netherlanders to resist.

Familiarity and Intimacy

The incidents surrounding the sale of liquor to Indians that are recorded in the court records also suggest that the interdependent relations between Indians and New Netherlanders led to more familiar interactions. Since New Netherland taverns were typically located in someone's home, New Netherlanders found themselves drinking and relaxing in the company of Indians, or, as in the case of the New Netherlander Michel Tadens, smoking a pipe in one's kitchen in the company of an Indian acquaintance to whom you had given a shot of brandy.[67]

The familiar nature of Indian–Dutch relations is highlighted by the fact that Indians and New Netherlanders not only drank together, rode the ferry together, and fought alongside one another, but also learned each other's language, visited each other, appeared in court together, and had intercourse and children with one another. According to the records of the government of New Netherland and Adriaen van der Donck, there were at least twenty-nine New Netherlanders who, having conversed in the Indian languages over an extended period, could understand and communicate in them.[68] The fact that there were New Netherlanders who had learned Indian languages suggests that interactions between the Indians and colonists of New Netherland were complicated, intensive, and long lasting.[69] The records also make it quite clear that Indians and colonists spent time in each other's homes and villages (figure 3.9). The Beverwijck preacher, Johannes Megapolensis, for example, testified to this: "They sleep by us, too, in our chambers before our beds. I have had eight at once lying and sleeping upon the floor near my bed."[70]

The paths between Indians and New Netherlanders were certainly not one-way streets. New Netherlanders entered Indian villages and homes

Figure 3.9. Mahican traders approach a Dutch farm along the Hudson River in 1635 (Len F. Tantillo, *Visitors at Dusk*).

as well. During the conflicts with the Esopus, for example, there were at least three diplomatic missions sent to Esopus villages between 1659 and 1663.[71]

Relations between New Netherlanders and Indians were also physically intimate despite ordinances against adultery with the "Gentiles" having already been established in 1638.[72] In fact, Megapolensis complained, "our Dutchmen run after them [Mohawk women] very much."[73] Some of those Dutchmen are identified in the records. Arent van Curler, for example, business manager of Rensselaerswijck from 1642 to 1644, and, in 1662, founder of the village of Schenectady, had a daughter with a Mohawk woman. Though the girl grew up with her mother and belonged to her mother's kin, the sources suggest that Van Curler maintained contact with her since the people of Beverwijck were well aware of her existence and knew exactly where she lived nine years after Van Curler's death.[74] Van Curler's neighbor, Cornelis Theunisz van Slyck, had at least three children with a Mohawk woman. The three children, Martin, Jacques, and Hilletie, spent their early years with their Mohawk mother, but eventually settled in Schenectady where Martin died at an early age. However, Jacques and Hilletie lived there for several decades and married Dutch colonists.[75]

Physical relationships between New Netherlanders and Indians also developed further down the Hudson River and along the South River. In February 1660 *Commies* La Montagne at Fort Orange received a letter informing him that Jacob Theunisz, the *schout bij nacht* in Beverwijck who conducted community-wide surveillance at night, had indeed arrived in order to secure the freedom of Evert Pels's son, Hendrick, who had been taken captive by the Esopus Indians, but that it did not appear that this was going to happen. The Esopus Indians had sent word to Ensign Smith that the young man was living with an Indian who had become pregnant. According to the Esopus Indians, the young man did not want to leave this woman who, it appeared, he had married. In Smith's opinion, Dutch officials should stop wasting their time, energy, and resources in trying to secure his freedom because the boy was difficult to deal with and the Indians were untrustworthy.[76]

Conclusion

Although Dutch-Native relations were certainly contested and marred by violence at times, the stories of Oratam, Michel Tadens, Arent van Curler, Hilletie van Slijck, and Hendrick Pels, among others, indicate that the relations between New Netherlanders and Indians were also marked, to a great degree, by interdependence and familiarity. The records of the government of New Netherland indicate that Indians allowed Europeans to settle on the land and taught colonists how to survive in what for them was a new environment. Indians taught New Netherlanders how to clear the land; where and how to plant, fertilize, harvest, store, and cook maize; how to fish the local waters; how to hunt turkeys; how to use guerrilla tactics in woodland warfare; and how to construct and use canoes and snowshoes. They also taught New Netherlanders that gift giving was a central element of Indian relationships; provided military support and mediation with their Indian enemies; provided labor and court testimonies; introduced them to sewant; and welcomed them into their homes and families. In other words, Indians in and around New Netherland successfully converted their Dutch neighbors to certain aspects of their way of life. New Netherlanders were, to a certain extent, also successful in converting Indians to certain features of their way of life. New Netherlanders provided their Indian neighbors with military support and mediation with their enemies, protection, transportation, justice, and trade goods, introduced them to new religious ideas, and welcomed Indians into their homes and families.

Abbreviations

ASG   Archive of the States-General (in NA)

DRCHNY   John Brodhead, Edmund O'Callaghan, and Berthold Fernow, ed., *Documents Relative to the Colonial History of the State of New York*, 15 vols. (Albany: Weed, Parsons and Company, 1853–83)

FOCM   Charles T. Gehring, trans. and ed., *Fort Orange Court Minutes, 1652–1660* (New Netherland Document Series, vol. 16, part 2) (Syracuse: Syracuse University Press, 1990)

HNAI   Bruce Trigger, ed., *Handbook of North American Indians*, vol. 15, Northeast (Washington, DC: Smithsonian Institution, 1978)

JMOC   Charles T. Gehring and William A. Starna, trans. and ed., *A Journey into Mohawk and Oneida Country, 1634–1635: The Journal of Harmen Meyndertsz van den Bogaert* (Syracuse: Syracuse University Press, 1988)

NA   Nationaal Archief, Den Haag

NNN   John Franklin Jameson, ed., *Narratives of New Netherland, 1609–1664* (New York: Charles Scribner's Sons, 1909)

NYCM   New York Colonial Manuscripts (in NYSA)

NYHM   Arnold J. F. van Laer, trans. and ed., *Register of the Provincial Secretary, 1642–1647* (New York Historical Manuscripts: Dutch, vol. 2) (Baltimore: Genealogical Publishing, 1974). Arnold J. F. van Laer, trans. and ed., *Council Minutes, 1638–1649* (New York Historical Manuscripts: Dutch, vol. 4) (Baltimore: Genealogical Publishing, 1974)

NYSA   New York State Archives, Albany

VWIS   Verspreide West-indische Stukken

Acknowledgments

Blessed are You, King of the Universe, for providing the direction, support, and encouragement through a great many institutions and individuals that helped me bring this chapter to fruition. The History Department and Graduate College at Western Michigan University provided various kinds of academic and financial support. I also received funding and support from the New York State Archives Partnership Trust and the New Netherland Institute. Without this funding or the indefatigable support I received from the archivists and librarians in Albany, I would not have been able to complete my research. I am also grateful to the Consulate General of the Kingdom of the Netherlands in New York who funded the presentation of this research at the Omohundro Institute of Early American History and Culture's twenty-second annual conference.

I would also like to thank José António Brandão and James Palmitessa, my faithful advisers at Western Michigan University, as well as John Saillant, Janny Venema, and Mark Meuwese for their support and feedback. Their contributions improved this chapter immeasurably. In addition, Dr. Martinus Bakker's instruction in the Dutch language proved most invaluable. I also wish to thank Professor Lucianne Lavin for inviting me to present a portion of this work at the Institute for American Indian Studies' Eleventh Annual Native American Roundtable. I am also indebted to Jason VanHorn, for the historically accurate map he drew for this chapter, and Len Tantillo, who graciously gave me permission to use images of his beautiful historical paintings, which so strikingly illustrate the places mentioned and assertions made in this chapter. To my parents, siblings, in-laws, friends, neighbors, and the Fulbright "Crew," thank you for your encouragement and support. Finally, I wish to acknowledge my wife, Lori, and our daughters, Emma and Kate. Thank you will never seem like enough.

Notes on Usage

This work is based on a variety of original Dutch sources located in archives on both sides of the Atlantic. Where I quote from Dutch-language documents that have appeared in published translation, I have relied on the existing translation unless otherwise noted. All other translations from the Dutch are mine. The original Dutch sources from the New York State Archives have been given the English titles assigned by Edmund O'Callaghan in the *Calendar of Historical Manuscripts in the Office of the Secretary of State, Albany, N.Y.* and *Documents Relative to the Colonial History of the State of New York.*

Unless explicitly stated otherwise, all the dates are in the New Style, since the new Gregorian calendar was in use in Holland, Zeeland, and New Netherland.

In the rest of the Dutch Republic as well as England and the English colonies, the Julian calendar style or Old Style was used. Throughout the seventeenth century, Old Style dates were ten days behind those in the New Style.

Notes

1. Adriaen van der Donck, *Beschryvinge van Nieuw-Nederlandt* (Evert Nieuwenhof, 1st ed. Amsterdam, 1655. 2nd ed. Amsterdam, 1656), 82; Ada van Gastel, "Ethnic Pluralism in Early American Literature: Incorporating Dutch-American Texts into the Canon," in *Early American Literature and Culture: Essays Honoring Harrison T. Mesorole,* ed. Kathryn Zabelle Derounian-Stodola (Newark: University of Delaware Press, 1992), 114–115; Jaap Jacobs, *Een zegenrijk gewest Nieuw-Nederland in de zeventiende eeuw* (Amsterdam: Prometheus-Bert Bakker, 1999), 180.

2. Simon Hart, *The Prehistory of the New Netherland Company* (Amsterdam: City of Amsterdam Press, 1959), 7–16, 19–21, 23–28, 31–33, 35–69, 73–74, 76, 78, 80–86, 90–92, 97–98; Allen W. Trelease, *Indian Affairs in Colonial New York: The Seventeenth Century* (Ithaca: Cornell University Press, 1960; reprint, Lincoln: University of Nebraska Press, 1997), 30–34; Donald Lenig, "Of Dutchmen, Beaver Hats and Iroquois," in *Current Perspectives in Northeastern Archaeology: Essays in Honor of William A. Ritchie,* no. 17, ed. by Robert E. Funk and Charles F. Haye III (Rochester: State of New York Archaeological Association, Researches and Transactions, 1977), 73, 77; Oliver Rink, *Holland on the Hudson: An Economic and Social History of Dutch New York* (Ithaca: Cornell University Press, 1986), 32–46; Daniel Richter, *The Ordeal of the Longhouse: The Peoples of the Iroquois League in the Era of European Colonization* (Chapel Hill: University of North Carolina Press, 1992), 76–90; Margriet de Roever, "Merchandises for New Netherland: A Look at Dutch Articles for Barter with the Native American Population," in *'One Man's Trash Is Another Man's Treasure': De metamorfose van het Europese gebruiksvoorwerp in de Nieuwe Wereld,* ed. Alexandra van Dongen (Rotterdam: Exhibit Catalog, Museum Boymans-van Beuningen, 1995), 77–82; Jan Baart, "Combs," in van Dongen, *One Man's Trash,* 175–187; Laurier Turgeon, "French Fishers, Fur Traders, and Amerindians during the Sixteenth Century: History and Archaeology," *William and Mary Quarterly,* 3rd ser., vol. 55 (1998): 585–610; Jacobs, *Een zegenrijk gewest,* 55–60; Paul Otto, *Dutch–Munsee Encounter: The Struggle for Sovereignty in the Hudson Valley* (New York: Berghahn Books, 2006), 51–77; James Bradley, *Before Albany: An Archaeology of Native-Dutch Relations in the Capital Region, 1600–1664* (Albany: State University of New York/State Education Department, 2007), 34–35, 39, 44, 47, 49, 83; Susannah Shaw Romney, *New Netherland Connections: Intimate Networks and Atlantic Ties in Seventeenth-Century America* (Chapel Hill: University of North Carolina Press, 2014), 135–136.

3. Charles Gehring and William A. Starna, trans. and ed., *A Journey into Mohawk and Oneida Country, 1634–1635: The Journal of Harmen Meyndertsz van den Bogaert* (Syracuse: Syracuse University Press, 1988), 1, 13, 15; Trelease, *Indian Affairs*, 54; Rink, *Holland on the Hudson*, 102–103; Richter, *Ordeal of the Longhouse*, 90–93; Jacobs, *Een zegenrijk gewest*, 187; Russell Shorto, *The Island at the Center of the World: The Epic Story of Dutch Manhattan and the Forgotten Colony That Shaped America* (New York: Doubleday Press, 2004), 46–47; Otto, *Dutch–Munsee Encounter*, 78–79, 81–84; Bradley, *Before Albany*, 58–60; Mark Meuwese, *Brothers in Arms, Partners in Trade: Dutch–Indigenous Alliances in the Atlantic World 1595–1674* (Leiden: Brill, 2011), 270; Romney, *New Netherland Connections*, 130, 136–137.

4. Bradley, *Before Albany*, 61, 76–77; Shorto, *Island at the Center of the World*, 69–72; Trelease, *Indian Affairs*, 55–56; Francis Jennings, *The Invasion of America: Indians, Colonists, and the Cant of Conquest* (New York: W. W. Norton, 1975), 188–227; Richter, *Ordeal of the Longhouse*, 84–85; Jacobs, *Een zegenrijk gewest*, 178; Jacobs, *New Netherland*, 195; William S. Simmons, "Narragansett," in *HNAI*, 190. The Narragansetts were an Eastern Algonquian speaking people who occupied lands that included the southern part of what is now Kent County, Rhode Island, Dutch and Conanicut Islands, most of what are now Washington County, Rhode Island, and the area between Weekapaug and the Pawcatuck River, which was fought for and won from the Pequots.

5. "Resolution. To extract tribute from the Indians in maize, furs, and wampum, and in case of unwillingness, to employ proper means to remove their reluctance," NYSA, NYCM 4: 49 (September 15, 1639); "Letter. Directors to Stuyvesant," NYSA, NYCM 13: 1(2) (February 13, 1659); "Letter. Stuyvesant to the directors at Amsterdam," NYSA, NYCM 13: 96(6) (April 23, 1660); "Minute. Engagement of Mr. Luyck at a salary of 1,000 guilders ($400) a year in wampum," NYSA, NYCM 10²: 273 (August 16, 1663); "Order. To Paulus van der Beecq, to deliver good stringed wampum to the burgomasters in payment of the excise tax," NYSA, NYCM 8: 581 (May 15, 1657); Richter, *Ordeal of the Longhouse*, 85; Jacobs, *Een zegenrijk gewest*, 177; Otto, *Dutch–Munsee Encounter*, 59; Bradley, *Before Albany*, 76–77; Romney, *New Netherland Connections*, 133, 137. In 1639 the Council of New Netherland demanded tribute payment from the Indians living in and around New Amsterdam in the form of corn, furs, and wampum. A stiver was one-twentieth part of a guilder.

6. Arnold J. F. van Laer, trans. and ed., *Documents Relating to New Netherland, 1624–1626* (San Marino, CA: Henry Huntington Library and Art Gallery, 1924), 232; Rink, *Holland on the Hudson*, 136–173; Bradley, *Before Albany*, 61, 74, 79; Jacobs, *Een zegenrijk gewest*, 49, 177, 197, 204, 227; William A. Starna, "Indian-Dutch Frontiers," *De Halve Maen* 64 (2) (1991): 24; Lois M. Feister, "Indian-Dutch Relations in the Upper Hudson Valley: A Study of Baptism Records in the Dutch Reformed Church, Albany, New York," *Man in the Northeast* 24 (1982): 90; Romney, *New Netherland Connections*, 136, 145.

7. "Protest. Fiscal van der Huyghens, against Govert Lockermans trading with the Indians at the South River," NYSA, NYCM 2: 105 (May 23–24, 1644); "Ordinance. Forbidding all persons trading in the interior, ordering them to remain at the usual trading posts," NYSA, NYCM 4: 296 (June 18, 1647); "Ordinance. Against runners trading in the Mohawk or Seneca's country," NYSA, NYCM 5: 68–69 (September 30, 1652); "Ordinance. Renewing the ordinance against trading up the North or South River, without a permit," NYSA, NYCM 9: 317 (June 21, 1660); "Ordinance. Director and council of Rensselaerswyck, forbidding trade in the woods with Indians," NYSA, NYCM 9: 591–592 (March 21, 1661); "Approval of said ordinance by the director-general and council of New Netherland," NYSA, NYCM 9: 593 (April 25, 1661); "Instructions to the aforesaid deputies," NYSA, NYCM 6: 56–57 (June 10, 1655); "Order. To publish an ordinance against boslopers, or runners among Indians," NYSA, NYCM 6: 60 (June 21, 1655); "Approval of the ordinance enacted at Fort Orange against runners who follow Indians in the woods to secure their furs," NYSA, NYCM 6: 66–67 (July 27, 1655); "Ordinance. Against runners purchasing furs of Indians in the woods, and against selling liquor to Indians," NYSA, NYCM 10[1]: 185 (July 21, 1660); "Ordinance. Renewing and enforcing the preceding," NYSA, NYCM 10[1]: 186–188 (August 5, 1662).

8. "Ordinance. Further regulating the Indian trade," NYSA, NYCM 10[1]: 195 (August 12, 1662).

9. "Letter. Vice-director La Montagne to director Stuyvesant," NYSA, NYCM 13: 114(1a) (June 15, 1660); "Petition. Rev. Henricus Selyns referred to above," NYSA, NYCM 10[3]: 33 (February 7, 1664).

10. José António Brandão, "*Your Fyre Shall Burn No More*": *Iroquois Policy toward New France and Its Native Allies to 1701* (Lincoln: University of Nebraska Press, 1997), 48–49, 106; Matthew Dennis, *Cultivating a Landscape of Peace: Iroquois-European Encounters in Seventeenth-Century America* (Ithaca: Cornell University Press, 1993), 154–179, 213–271. For other works addressing gift giving among Indian societies, see Neal Salisbury, *Manitou and Providence: Indians, Europeans, and the Making of New England, 1500–1643* (New York: Oxford University Press, 1982), 35–36, 44–49, 53; James Axtell, *The Invasion Within: The Contest of Cultures in Colonial North America* (New York: Oxford University Press, 1985), 79, 88–89; Otto, *Dutch–Munsee Encounter*, 15–16, 37, 41–42, 44, 46–47, 54, 59, 61, 87, 92, 97–98, 100, 113, 115, 121–122, 126, 129n35, 137–138, 142, 144, 146, 149–150, 152, 164, 172–174, 195.

11. A fathom was a linear measure equal to six feet. Scholars often refer to the hostilities between various New Netherlanders and Delawares as Kieft's War. For an overview that places these hostilities in political context, see Jacobs, *Een zegenrijk gewest*, 133–138.

12. "Propositions submitted by the director-general to the council," NYSA, NYCM 4: 328–329 (August 26, 1647); *NYHM* 4: 428–431. For more examples

of gift giving under Kieft's administration, see also "Minute. Of the appearance of Gauwarowe, sachem of Matinneconck," NYSA, NYCM 4: 187 (April 15, 1644); "Resolution. To employ Witaneywen, sachem of Mochgonnekonck on Long Island, with twenty-seven warriors, who offered their services, to attack a party of hostile Indians," NYSA, NYCM 4: 222–223 (May 24, 29, 1645).

13. "Minute. Directing that a present be sent to the Esopus Indians," NYSA, NYCM 10²: 92 (May 10, 1663).

14. "Proposals of Hackingsack, Staten Island, and Minissink Indians, with answers," NYSA, NYCM 10³: 89–90 (March 6, 1664); Ives Goddard, "Delaware," in *HNAI*, 213. The Minisinks were a Munsee-speaking group that occupied lands on the headwaters of the Delaware River above the Delaware Water Gap. A guilder was a monetary unit of the Dutch Republic, consisting of twenty *stivers*. Twenty guilders was worth $8. For more examples of gift giving during Stuyvesant's administration, see "Letter. Director-general to the council, on a claim now made by Indians for payment of certain lands in Flatbush," NYSA, NYCM 5: 43 (June 17, 1652); "Minute. Of the return of fourteen Christians (men, women, and children) by Pennekeck, chief of Achkinkeshacky, and of presents made him in consequence," NYSA, NYCM 6: 108 (October 18, 1655).

15. Albert Eekhof, trans., *Jonas Michaëlius: Founder of the Church in New Netherland: His Life and Work* (Leiden: A. W. Sijthoff, 1926), 124, 136.

16. NA, VWIS, 1.05.06, inv. nr. 2, 1–3, 6; "Order. Authorizing the burgomasters of New Amsterdam, to adopt measures to prevent the monopoly by retailers of Indian corn, fish, and venison brought to market," NYSA, NYCM 9: 835 (October 13, 1661). See also Romney, *New Netherland Connections,* 171.

17. NA, VWIS, 1.05.06, inv. nr. 2, 1–3, 6.

18. *JMOC,* xix, 4–5, 32–33.

19. *JMOC,* 22.

20. "Declaration. Andries Luycassen and others," NYSA, NYCM 3: 20 (September 28, 1648).

21. Johannes Megapolensis, *Een kort Ontwerp vande Mahakuase Indianen, haer landt, tale, stature, Dracht, godes-dienst ende magistrature* (t'Alkmaer: Ijsbrant Jansz. Van Houten, 1644), 3; "Proposals made to the Esopus Indians and their answers," NYSA, NYCM 12: 91(1–5) (October 15, 1658); "Letter. Ensign Smith to director Stuyvesant," NYSA, NYCM 13: 80 (March 29, 1660); "Letter. Ensign Smith to director Stuyvesant," NYSA, NYCM 13: 112(b) (May 30, 1660). See also Romney, *New Netherland Connections,* 151.

22. Jacobs, *Een zegenrijk gewest,* 197.

23. Van der Donck, *Beschryvinge van Nieuw-Nederlandt,* 15–16; Ada van Gastel, trans. and ed., "Van der Donck's Description of the Indians," *William and Mary Quarterly,* 3rd ser., 47 (1990), 411–412, 414; Michel-Rolph Trouillot, *Silencing the Past* (Boston: Beacon Press, 1995), 73. In 1841 Jeremiah Johnson translated Van der Donck's *Beschryvinge van Nieuw-Nederlandt,* which is, according

to Ada van Gastel, one of the most important extant sources on Indian–Dutch relations as it contains thirty pages describing the Indians of New Netherland. However, Johnson's translation deleted words, phrases, clauses, sentences, and five chapters, which misrepresented Van der Donck's text and reversed its meaning. For example, Johnson translated the aforementioned passage this way, "It has happened when I have been out with the natives . . . that we have come to a piece of young woodland. When I have told them, in conversation, that they would do well to clear off such land, because it would bear good corn, that they said, 'it is but twenty years since we planted corn there, and now it is woods again.'" Johnson's translation, which remained the only English translation available to historians until Van Gastel produced her additions and corrections in 1990, assumed that European technology and knowledge was certainly more advanced than that of the Indians. In the mind of Johnson, it must have been unthinkable for an Indian to instruct a European because such an idea ran counter to the ontology of his time; namely, that Europe had a superior civilization to the indigenous civilizations of North America. This is an example of what Michel-Rolph Trouillot has called "silencing the past."

24. "Notice. To all persons employing Indians, to pay them for their labor, on pain of being fined," NYSA, NYCM 4: 417 (September 28, 1648); "Declaration. Certain Katskill Indians as to the origin of the collision with Indians at the Esopus," NYSA, NYCM 13: 1(a) (October 14, 1659). Thomas Chambers, for example, hired nine Esopus Indians to cut down the corn in his field.

25. "Proposals of the Esopus Indians," NYSA, NYCM 13: 29(1) (September 4, 1659). These same Esopus also offered to help the colonists capture the horses that had left them.

26. "Resolution. To extract tribute from the Indians in maize, furs, and wampum, and in case of unwillingness, to employ proper means to remove their reluctance," NYSA, NYCM 4: 49 (September 15, 1639). See also Romney, *New Netherland Connections*, 137, 153.

27. "Ordinance. Fixing twelve *schepels* (nine bushels) of maize as the price of a coat or cloak of duffels to the Indians," NYSA, NYCM 4: 50 (September 22, 1639); "Court Proceedings. Fiscal vs. Abraham Planc," NYSA, NYCM 4: 79 (October 25, 1640); "Court Proceedings. Fiscal vs. Abraham Planc, Cornelis Lambersen Cool, and George Rapalje," NYSA, NYCM 4: 79 (November 1, 1640). A *schepel* was a dry measure equal to 0.764 bushel of wheat. Although they claimed to have traded ten to eleven *schepels* of corn with the Indians, Planck, Lambersz, and the Rapaljes were brought before the court for violating the ordinance.

28. *NYHM* 4: 73. The italicized word is the author's translation of the Dutch word "*wilden*," which Van Laer translated as "Indians."

29. David Pietersz de Vries, *Korte Historiael ende Journaels Aenteykeninge van verscheyden voyagiens in de vier delen des werelts-ronde, als Europa, Africa, ende*

America gedaen, ed. H. T. Colebrander (The Hague: Nijhoff, 1911), 246–247; Jacobs, *Een zegenrijk gewest*, 134. A patroon was a Dutch landholder with manorial rights to a large tract of land.

30. *Breeden-Raedt aende Vereenichde Nederlandsche Provintien [. . .] gemaeckt ende gestalt uyt diverse ware en waerachtige memorien* (Antwerp: I. A. G. W. C., 1649), 19.

31. *DRCHNY* 1: 414–415.

32. "Testimony of divers persons that brandy is sold openly throughout the South River to Indians," NYSA, NYCM 9: 159 (April 9, 1660); NYSA, NYCM 9: 191 (April 8, 1660); Meuwese, *Brothers in Arms*, 279.

33. "Deposition. Geertje Nannincx and Roelant Hackwaert respecting some pits of Indian corn at Marechkawieck," NYSA, NYCM 4: 158 (January 27, 1643); Goddard, "Delaware," in *HNAI*, 214. The Marechkawieck were Indians in Brooklyn who are sometimes grouped together with the Canarsee and Nayack and referred to as the Canarsee. For another example of colonists stealing corn from Indians, see "Declaration. Respecting the circumstances attending the killing of Dirck Straatemaker and his wife by Indians, at Pavonia," NYSA, NYCM 2: 57a–b (May 18, 1643).

34. "Declaration. Barent and Hans Jansen," NYSA, NYCM 2: 160 (July 23, 1647); *NYHM* 2: 441.

35. Roderic H. Blackburn and Ruth Piwonka, *Remembrance of Patria: Dutch Arts and Culture in Colonial America, 1609–1776* (Albany: Albany Institute of History and Art, 1988), 45.

36. *NYHM* 2: 409. For more examples of Dutch soldiers using canoes, see "Declaration. Jan Warrensen and Hans Nielsen, soldiers, respecting an attack made by Indians at the colonie of Achter Col," NYSA, NYCM 2: 85 (October 30, 1643); "Ordinance. Director and council of Rensselaerswyck, forbidding trade in the woods with Indians," NYSA, NYCM 9: 592 (March 21, 1661).

37. "Ordinance. Forbidding all persons going across the river," NYSA, NYCM 6: 107 (October 18, 1655).

38. *FOCM*, 364–365; Janny Venema, *Beverwijck: A Dutch Village on the American Frontier, 1652–1664* (Albany: State University of New York Press, 2003), 451. Having heard both parties, the members of the court of Fort Orange condemned Cornelisz to return the canoe or another as good as his within twenty-four hours and to pay the costs of the suit. For another example of colonists suing each other in order to recover their canoes, see also "Complaint. Jacob Kip against John de Sweet, of Flushing, for recovery of a canoe," NYSA, NYCM 9: 859 (October 20, 1661).

39. *Breeden-Raedt*, 16.

40. Venema, *Beverwijck*, 43.

41. "Instructions to secretary Van Tienhoven to proceed to Martin Gerritsen Bay, on Long Island," NYSA, NYCM 4: 62 (May 13, 1640); NYSA,

NYCM GG: 52, 222; "Letter. Directors to Stuyvesant," NYSA, NYCM 11: 29(5) (March 21, 1651); "Letter. Directors to Stuyvesant," NYSA, NYCM 11: 53(7, 18) (April 4, 1652); "Indian deed to Cornelis van Werckhoven for New Utrecht, L. I.," NYSA, NYCM 11: 74a (1–2) (November 22, 1652); "Indian deed to Cornelis van Werckhoven for the land called Naiecq," NYSA, NYCM 11: 74b(1–2) (December 1, 1652). In 1652 WIC officials deemed it necessary to negotiate for as much land from the Indians as possible in order to obviate what they considered to be dangerous dealings of private parties who were purchasing lands from Indians without first consulting them. Lubbert van Dincklagen and Govert Loockermans, among others, had, in fact, purchased a sizeable amount of land from the Raritans on the *kil* opposite Staten Island without a conveyance. Meanwhile, the Utrecht magistrate, Cornelis van Werckhoven, was purchasing lands for Nieuw Utrecht and Nyack on Long Island.

42. Bradley, *Before Albany*, 131.

43. Bradley, *Before Albany*, 86, 107; Dean R. Snow, "Mohawk Demography and the Effects of Exogenous Epidemics on American Indian Populations," *Journal of American Anthropology* 15 (1996): 164; Rink, *Holland on the Hudson*, 144; Shirley Dunn, *The Mohicans and Their Land, 1609–1730* (Fleischmanns, NY: Purple Mountain Press, 1994), 112–114; Richter, *Ordeal of the Longhouse*, 96–104.

44. "Letter. Stuyvesant to the directors at Amsterdam," NYSA, NYCM 13: 32(1b) (September 17, 1659); Jacobs, *Een zegenrijk gewest*, 74–75.

45. *NYHM* 4: 265. For other examples of reliance upon Indian allies for military support during Kieft's administration, see also "Articles of peace between the Dutch and the Indians of Achkinkenshacky, Tappaen, Rechgawawanc, Kichtawanc, and Sintsick," NYSA, NYCM 4: 166 (April 22, 1643); "Resolutions of the Eight Men to renew the war against the Indians, except those of Long Island," NYSA, NYCM 4: 176 (September 15, 1643).

46. "Letter. Directors to Stuyvesant," NYSA, NYCM 12: 69(2) (December 22, 1657); "Letter. Directors to Stuyvesant," NYSA, NYCM 12: 80(1b) (May 20, 1658). For other examples of reliance upon Indian allies for military support during Stuyvesant's administration, see also "Proposition. Indians of Long Island on the part of Tackpaasa, requesting a continuance of the peace with their tribe," NYSA, NYCM 12: 170–171 (November 27, 1655); "Minute. Acceptance of an offer by the Indians of the East, and of Long Island, to march against those of Esopus," NYSA, NYCM 10²: 199 (July 20, 1663); "Proposals of the chief of the Menissing Indians and the answer thereto," NYSA, NYCM 10²: 299–300 (September 20, 1663).

47. "Instructions for Captain Cregier," NYSA, NYCM 10²: 171–173 (June 30, 1663); "Commission. Peter Wolphertsen van Couwenhoven to be lieutenant of a troop of Indians and volunteers," NYSA, NYCM 10²: 228a (July 6, 1663).

48. "Letter. Ensign Smith to secretary Van Ruyven," NYSA, NYCM 13: 92 (April 9, 1660); "Letter. Ensign Smith to director Stuyvesant," NYSA, NYCM 13: 111 (May 1660).

49. "Letter. Andries Lourissen to director Stuyvesant," NYSA, NYCM 13: 22 (August 4, 1659). For examples of the reports received by Stuyvesant and the council members from various Delaware Indians during summer 1663, see "Proposals communicated to Oratam, sachem of Hackinkesacky, and Mattanou, sachem of Nayack, and their answers," NYSA, NYCM 10²: 163–166 (June 27, 1663); "Notice. That the Esopus Indians are on a war expedition, and warning all persons to be on their guard," NYSA, NYCM 10²: 167 (June 27, 1663); "Proposal of the chief of the Hackensack Indians to sell a portion of their land behind the Kill van Kol; effort of the Esopus Indians to engage the Minisinks on their side," NYSA, NYCM 10²: 229 (July 20, 1663); "Minute. Attendance of the chief of the Wickquaeskeck Indians, to notify the council that his people had fled to Haerlem, on a report that the Esopus Indians were about to attack them," NYSA, NYCM 10²: 247–248 (July 26, 1663); "Minute. Information furnished of an intended massacre of the Dutch on the North River," NYSA, NYCM 10²: 280a (August 30, 1663); "Minute. Information furnished to the wife of Michiel Jansen by an Indian of an intended attack in order to take only Dutch prisoners," NYSA, NYCM 10²: 280b (August 30, 1663); "Information furnished by Oratam, chief of the Hackingsacks, respecting the Esopus Indians," NYSA, NYCM 10²: 280c (August 30, 1663); "Information brought by a Hackingsack Indian of the defeat of the Esopus Indians, and of the recapture of the Christian prisoners," NYSA, NYCM 10²: 294 (September 10, 1663).

50. "Information brought by a Hackingsack Indian of the defeat of the Esopus Indians, and of the recapture of the Christian prisoners," NYSA, NYCM 10²: 294 (September 10, 1663). The indigenous names of those Indians who had become familiar through trade or diplomatic relations are frequently recorded in the records of the government of New Netherland. However, the records of the Dutch Reformed churches reveal that those Indians baptized into the Reformed faith were given Christian names. For example, when a forty-year-old Mohawk "Gentile called Swongora among his people" was baptized in the Reformed Dutch Church of Albany on July 11, 1690, he was given the name David. For other examples, see the *Records of the Reformed Dutch Church of Albany, New York, 1683–1809* in *Yearbooks from the Holland Society of New York* (New York: Holland Society of New York, 1904), 51.

51. For examples of military intelligence provided to Stuyvesant and the council members by various Delaware Indians, see "Minute. Proceedings of the council on receipt of intelligence that the River Indians were about to make a descent on the Dutch settlements at Hoboken, Ahasimus, and the Manhattans," NYSA, NYCM 10²: 343–344 (October 15, 1663); "Instruction.

Peter Wolfertsen van Couwenhoven to ascertain and prevent the movements of the Esopus and Wapping or Highland Indians," NYSA, NYCM 10[2]: 345–346 (October 16, 1663); "Declaration of a Hackingsack Indian, as to the intention of the Nevesinck chief to sell his lands to the English of Gravesend," NYSA, NYCM 10[3]: 65 (February 16, 1664); "Proposals of the chiefs of the Kichtawas, Wappingers, Wighquaeskecks, Hackingsacks, and Newesinghs, with the answers," NYSA, NYCM 10[3]: 135 (March 24, 1664); "Proposals of Hackingsack, Staten Island Indians, and answer," NYSA, NYCM 10[3]: 89 (March 6, 1664); "Report, by Peter W. van Couwenhoven, of information communicated to him respecting intrigues of the English with the Esopus and Wappinger Indians against the Dutch," NYSA, NYCM 10[3]: 121–124 (March 20, 1664); "Information of English intrigues with the Esopus Indians," NYSA, NYCM 10[3]: 296 (August 27, 1664).

52. "Articles of peace concluded, in the presence of the Mohawk ambassador in Fort Amsterdam, in the open air, between the Dutch and the Indians," NYSA, NYCM 4: 232 (August 30, 1645); Meuwese, *Brothers in Arms*, 264; William A. Starna, *From Homeland to New Land: A History of the Mahican Indians, 1600–1830* (Lincoln: University of Nebraska Press, 2013), 127.

53. "Report of the rising of the Esopus Indians, and a collision between them and the settlers," NYSA, NYCM 13: 37(2) (September 22, 1659); "Letter. Vice-director La Montagne to Stuyvesant," NYSA, NYCM 13: 38 (September 26, 1659); "Letter. Vice-director La Montagne to Ensign Smith," NYSA, NYCM 13: 48 (October 21, 1659); Starna, *From Homeland to New Land*, 133.

54. For examples of Indians mediating with Stuyvesant and the council members on behalf of the Esopus, see "Treaty of peace renewed with the chiefs of Marsepingh and Rechkawick, Hackinkasacky, the Highlands, Najeck, Staten Island, Rumachenanck alias Haverstraw, and Wiechquaeskeck," NYSA, NYCM 8: 119a–c (March 6, 1660); "Minute. Of the interview of Goethels, chief warrior of Wappingh, sent by Esopus Indians to the director and council, to conclude a peace," NYSA, NYCM 9: 125 (March 15, 1660); "Letter. Magistrates of Fort Orange and Rensselaerswyck to Ensign Smith, enclosing proposals of the Katskill and Mahican Indians, and requesting safe pass for their delegates," NYSA, NYCM 13: 94 (April 21, 1660); "Letter. Ensign Smith to Stuyvesant," NYSA, NYCM 13: 97 (April 24, 1660); "Conference between the director and council and the chiefs of Hackinckesacky, Najack, Wieckquaeskeck, Haverstraw, and the Wappings; peace concluded with the Wappings," NYSA, NYCM 9: 252–254 (May 18, 1660). See also Starna, *From Homeland to New Land*, 133–138.

55. "Conference between the director and council and three Mahican chiefs who solicit that peace be made with the Esopus Indians; declined," NYSA, NYCM 9: 257–259 (May 24, 1660); "Letter. Director Stuyvesant to Ensign Smith," NYSA, NYCM 13: 110 (May 25, 1660); "Conference between the director and council and the chiefs of Hackinckesack and Haverstraw; armistice granted the Esopus Indians," NYSA, NYCM 9: 278–279 (June 3, 1660); "Commission.

Claes Jansen Ruyter to accompany the above chiefs to the Esopus to receive proposals of the Esopus Indians," NYSA, NYCM 9: 280–282 (June 3, 1660); "Instructions to Claes Jansen Ruyter," NYSA, NYCM 9: 283 (June 3, 1660).

56. "Proposals made by the Mohawk chiefs at Fort Orange and the answer thereto," NYSA, NYCM 14: 8 (January 22, 1661); "Letter. Vice-director and magistrates [of Fort Orange] to director Stuyvesant," NYSA, NYCM 14: 11 (January 29, 1661); "Resolution. To make war against the Esopus Indians and to employ the Mohawks in recovering the Christians in their hands," NYSA, NYCM 10²: 131 (June 17, 1663); Meuwese, *Brothers in Arms*, 272. On June 27, 1663, Stuyvesant and his council accepted help from the Mohawks and Mahicans in their negotiations with the Esopus, sending the Dutch interpreter, Jan Dareth, along with a Mahican leader named Skiwias and three Mohawks, including Canaqueese, a Mohawk born of a Dutch father who was known as Smits Jan by the Dutch and the Flemish Bastard by the Jesuits.

57. "Minute. Information communicated by Oratam, chief of the Hackingsacks, that the Wappinger and Esopus Indians are on their way to conclude peace," NYSA, NYCM 10²: 430 (December 10, 1663); "Conference with the chiefs of Hackingkeshacky and Nyacks, respecting a continuance of the armistice with the Esopus Indians," NYSA, NYCM 10²: 445–448 (December 28–29, 1663); "Proposals of Oratam and the Hackingsack and Staten Island Indians, and answer," NYSA, NYCM 10³: 88–89 (February 23, 1664).

58. "Proposals of Hackingsack, Staten Island, and Minissink Indians, with answers," NYSA, NYCM 10³: 89–90 (March 6, 1664); "Proposals of the chiefs of the Kichtawans, Wappingers, Wighquaeskecks, Hackingsacks, and Newesinghs, with the answers," NYSA, NYCM 10³: 133–134 (March 24, 1664).

59. *FOCM*, 400–402, 453–454; Trelease, *Indian Affairs*, 121–122; Brandão, *Iroquois Policy*, 89–90, 100–114; Venema, *Beverwijck*, 158–159; 203–204; Bradley, *Before Albany*, 134–136; Meuwese, *Brothers in Arms*, 269–270; Mark Meuwese, "From Intercolonial Messenger to 'Christian Indian': The Flemish Bastard and the Mohawk Struggle for Independence from New France and Colonial New York in the Eastern Great Lakes Borderland, 1647–1687," in *Lines Drawn upon the Water: First Nations and the Great Lakes Borders and Borderlands*, ed. Karl Scott Hele (Waterloo: Wilfrid Laurier University Press, 2008), 53–54.

60. For examples, see "Letter. Magistrates of Fort Orange and Rensselaerswyck to Ensign Smith," NYSA, NYCM 13: 94 (April 21, 1660); "Proposals of the Katskil sachems on behalf of the Esopus Indians," NYSA, NYCM 13: 95a (April 21, 1660); "Proposals between the Mahican and Katskil sachems," NYSA, NYCM 13: 95b (April 21, 1660); "Conference between the director and council and Tapousagh, chief of the Long Island Indians, who asks aid against Ninnegret, chief of the Narrycanse tribe," NYSA, NYCM 9: 397–399 (September 2, 1660); *Proceedings of the New York State Historical Association* (New York: New York State Historical Association, 1906), 78; *Collections of the*

Massachusetts Historical Society, vol. 9 (Boston: Hall and Hiller, 1804), 82; "Minute. Permission to the Indians of Wickquaeskeck to fish near Haerlem," NYSA, NYCM 10^2: 390 (November 15, 1663); "Proposals made to the Esopus Indians and their answers," NYSA, NYCM 12: 91(1–5) (October 15, 1658); Meuwese, *Brothers in Arms,* 283; "Proposals of the chiefs of the Kichtawas, Wappingers, Wighquaeskecks, Hackingsacks, and Newesinghs, with the answers," NYSA, NYCM 10^3: 133–135 (March 24, 1664); "Minute. Attendance of Tapausagh, chief of the Long Island Indians, and Rompsicka, on the council, to inform them that they had been summoned to Flushing, and there required to sell all their lands to the English, &c.," NYSA, NYCM 10^3: 7–8 (January 7, 1664); "Proposals offered by the Minesink Indians on renewing peace with the Dutch," NYSA, NYCM 10^2: 261–263 (August 15, 1663); "Proposals of the chief of the Menissing Indians and the answer thereto," NYSA, NYCM 10^2: 299–300 (September 20, 1663); "Minute. Attendance of Oratam, chief of Hackingsacky and others, to explain the circumstances attending the murder of Mattys Roelofsen, gunner, by a Wappinger Indian," NYSA, NYCM 10^3: 211–212 (April 26, 1664). The Minisink leader who appeared before Stuyvesant on September 20, 1663 informed him that the Minisinks would attack the newest palisaded Esopus village and destroy the surrounding cornfields if the Dutch would give him a new coat, forty-four duffels, and protection for his people. Although the Dutch text reads "*het nieuwe Esopusse fort,*" referring to a new fort among the Esopus Indians, the author has translated this into a "new palisaded village" because the Esopus did not build forts. Rather, they built palisaded or fortified villages in order to protect themselves from their enemies, including the Dutch.

61. Bradley, *Before Albany,* 172; Romney, *New Netherland Connections,* 167–168.

62. Bradley, *Before Albany,* 172.

63. An adze is a wood-working tool with a sharp cutting edge.

64. "Indian deed for a tract of land on the west side of the North River beginning at the great rock above Wiehaecken, thence in a straight line inland to above the island Sickakes, and thence along the Kil van Col unto Constable's Hook, from the said hook back to the place of beginning, with all the islands, kills, creeks, and valleys included therein," NYSA, NYCM 8: 707–710 (January 30, 1658); "Indian deed to Andries Herbertsen and Rutger Jacobsen of Beverwijck, for an island nearly opposite Bethlehem, called Pachonakelick by the Indians, and Long, or Mahikanders Island, by the Dutch," NYSA, NYCM 8: 553–554 (February 8, 1661); "Proclamation of the above armistice [between the Dutch and the Esopus Indians], and pass to two Indians," NYSA, NYCM 10^2: 449–450a (December 26, 1663). An *anker* was a liquid measurement equal to around 37.84 liters or 10.25 gallons.

65. "Ordinance. Imposing duties on duffels, and other Indian goods, wine, brandy, beer, and salt, in lieu of one percent on all imports in general," NYSA,

NYCM 5: 204–206 (January 28, 1654); "Answer to the above. Remitting one-fourth of the present duties," NYSA, NYCM 5: 309–312.

66. "Ordinance. Regulating the ferry," NYSA, NYCM 5: 291 (July 1, 1654); Jacobs, *Een zegenrijk gewest*, 281; Eugene L. Armbruster, *The Ferry Road on Long Island* (New York: G. Quattlander, 1919), 8; Romney, *New Netherland Connections*, 149.

67. "Ordinance. Against selling strong liquor to the Indians," NYSA, NYCM 4: 239c (November 21, 1645); "Court Proceedings. Fiscal vs. Maria de Truy, for selling beer to Indians," NYSA, NYCM 4: 252b (April 26, 1646); "Ordinance. Against selling strong drink to the Indians," NYSA, NYCM 4: 297a (July 1, 1647); "Sentence. Of David Wessels, for selling brandy to Indians," NYSA, NYCM 5: 342 (August 28, 1654); *FOCM*, 128, 166, 194; "Ordinance. Against selling strong liquor to the Indians," NYSA, NYCM 5: 343c–344a (August 28, 1654); "Indictment. Sander Toursen and his wife, for selling brandy to Indians of Mochgeyckkonck," NYSA, NYCM 6: 355b (April 2, 1656); "Sentence. [Of Sander Toursen and his wife]," NYSA, NYCM 6: 356 (April 2, 1656); *FOCM*, 251; "Indictment. Michel Tadens, an inhabitant of Pearl Street, New Amsterdam, for furnishing liquor to Indians," NYSA, NYCM 8: 85–86 (July 25, 1656); "Sentence. Michel Tadens, to be fined 500 guilders; imprisoned until paid, and to be afterwards banished from the province," NYSA, NYCM 8: 113–114 (August 3, 1656); "Letter. Magistrates [of Beverwijck] to director Stuyvesant," NYSA, NYCM 8: 147 (August 14, 1656); "Complaint. Fiscal against Nicolas Lange Velthuysen, for selling liquor to Indians, &c.," NYSA, NYCM 8: 183 (September 13, 1656); "Order. The aforesaid Lange Velthuysen to prepare to quit the country in the first sailing ship," NYSA, NYCM 8: 184 (September 13, 1656); "Pardon. Nicolas Lange Velthuysen," NYSA, NYCM 8: 187 (September 19, 1656); "Ordinance. Against furnishing liquor to Indians, or exporting wine, beer, or other liquors, without a permit," NYSA, NYCM 8: 249b–251a (October 26, 1656); "Complaint. The fiscal against Jacob Stevensen Kuyper and his wife, for selling liquor to the Indians," NYSA, NYCM 8: 289–290 (December 6, 1656); "Letter. Jacob Jansen to director Stuyvesant," NYSA, NYCM 12: 75 (April 9, 1658); "Declaration. Hendrick d'Raat and Jan Broersen that brandy has been sold openly to the Indians on the South River," NYSA, NYCM 9: 191 (April 8, 1660); "Testimony of diverse persons that brandy is sold openly throughout the South River to Indians," NYSA, NYCM 9: 159 (April 9, 1660); "Indictment. Jan Juriaens Becker, for selling liquor to Indians," NYSA, NYCM 9: 151 (April 12, 1660); "Answer of Jan Juriaens Becker thereto," NYSA, NYCM 9: 155–158 (April 12, 1660); "Sentence. Jan Juriaens Becker for selling liquor to Indians; fined 500 guilders, to be degraded from his office of clerk to the church, to remove from the South River and pay costs of suit," NYSA, NYCM 9: 181–182 (April 26, 1660); "Order. Remitting the find imposed on Becker," NYSA, NYCM 9: 192 (May 3, 1660); "Ordinance.

Against selling liquor to Indians," NYSA, NYCM 9: 349–350 (July 21, 1660); "Proceedings against Albert Albertsen for continuing to reside on his farm at a distance from New Utrecht," NYSA, NYCM 9: 781 (September 15, 1661); "Complaint against Jacob van Couwenhoven for an attempt to convey spirituous liquors to the Neversinke," NYSA, NYCM 10[1]: 125–126, 134 (May 4, 1662); "Minute. Rejecting the prayer of a petition of Juriaen Teunissen to keep a tavern at the north side of the mouth of the Esopus Kill," NYSA, NYCM 10[1]: 153 (June 15, 1662); "Prosecution of Maria de Truy, wife of Jan Peeck, for selling brandy to Indians," NYSA, NYCM 10[2]: 451 (December 30, 1663); "Complaint. Fiscal against Maria de Truy, wife of Jan Peeck, for selling liquor to Indians," NYSA, NYCM 10[3]: 1 (January 3, 1664); "Complaint of an Indian from Tappaan against Jacob Wolfertsen van Couwenhoven, for not giving up his gun, pawned for liquor, on his desire to redeem it," NYSA, NYCM 10[3]: 65 (February 16, 1664); "Declaration of two Indians as to where they obtained brandy," NYSA, NYCM 10: 272 (July 14, 1664); Bradley, *Before Albany*, 136; Jacobs, *Een zegenrijk gewest*, 213, 363; Venema, *Beverwijck*, 14, 93, 166, 168, 307, 310, 313–314. It most likely was no coincidence that Unsickan, the "Indian from Tappaan," went to Jacob van Couwenhoven's house in New Amsterdam in order to obtain 3.5 quarts of brandy. Unsickan probably met Jacob's brother, Pieter Wolphertsz, when he was sent to the Tappan in fall 1663 in order to obtain information concerning the movements of the Esopus and Wappinger. It just so happened that Pieter was also a brewer in New Amsterdam and, in summer 1663, was the one put in charge of a troop of Indians during the conflict with the Esopus.

68. "Appointment of Cornelis van Tienhoven to be provincial secretary," NYSA, NYCM 4: 10 (June 3, 1638); "Declaration. Jan Evertsen Bout and Claes Jansen," NYSA, NYCM 2: 142d (March 7, 1645); "Declaration. Ponkes, of Marechkawieck," NYSA, NYCM 2: 142f (March 9, 1645); "Resolution to send secretary Van Tienhoven, and one or two of the village of Heemsteede, who understand the Indian language, to the east end of Long Island," NYSA, NYCM 4: 327b (August 23, 1647); Van der Donck, *Beschryvinghe van Nieuw-Nederlant*, 94; "Proposition. Indians of Long Island on the part of Tackpaasa, requesting a continuance of the peace with their tribe," NYSA, NYCM 6: 170–171 (November 27, 1655); "Appointment. Claes Jansen Ruyter to be an Indian interpreter," NYSA, NYCM 9: 112 (March 1, 1660); "Treaty of peace renewed with the chiefs of Marsepingh and Rechkawick, Hackinkasacky, the Highlands, Najeck, Staten Island, Rumachenanck alias Haverstraw, and Wiechquaeskeck," NYSA, NYCM 9: 119a (March 6, 1660); "Information furnished by Oratam, chief of the Hackingsacks, respecting the Esopus Indians," NYSA, NYCM 10[2]: 280b (August 30, 1663); "Instructions to Mr. Verbraack and serjeant Harmen Martens van den Bosch, sent with lieutenant Couwenhoven," NYSA, NYCM 10[2]: 347–348 (October 16, 1663); "Instructions. Lieutenant Van Couwenhoven, serjt. Peter

Ebel, and Harmen Douwesen, all three well-versed in the Indian language, to ascertain the disposition of the Wappinger and Esopus Indians towards a peace," NYSA, NYCM 10²: 393 (November 21, 1663); "Land deal between the Dutch and the Newesing Indians," NYSA, NYCM 10²: 449–450a (December 26, 1663); "Report, by Peter W. van Couwenhoven, of information communicated to him respecting the intrigues of the English with the Esopus and Wappinger Indians against the Dutch," NYSA, NYCM 10³: 121, 123–124 (March 20, 1664); "Resolution to dispatch lieutenant Couwenhoven to the Wappingers to inquire into the truth of the above statement," NYSA, NYCM 10³: 122 (March 20, 1664); Willem Frijhoff, *Wegen van Evert Willemsz: Een Hollands weeskind op zoek naar zichzelf* (Nijmegen: SUN, 1995), 627–628; Ives Goddard, "The Use of Pidgins and Jargons on the East Coast of North America," in *The Language Encounter in the Americas, 1492–1800*, European Expansion and Global Interaction, vol. 1, ed. Edward G. Gray and Norman Fiering (New York: Berghahn Books, 2000), 63–64; Jacobs, *Een zegenrijk gewest*, 190, 327; Meuwese, *Brothers in Arms*, 56; Daniel K. Richter, "Cultural Brokers and Intercultural Politics: New York–Iroquois Relations, 1664–1701," *Journal of American History* 75 (1988): 46, 52–53; Romney, *New Netherland Connections*, 147; Venema, *Beverwijck*, 166–167. On the linguistic attitudes and communication strategies of the Dutch and Indians in New Netherland, see Lois M. Feister, "Linguistic Communication between the Dutch and Indians in New Netherland," in *Neighbors and Intruders: An Ethnohistorical Exploration of the Indians of Hudson's River*, National Museum of Man Mercury Series, Canadian Ethnology Service, no. 39, ed. Laurence M. Hauptman and Jack Campisi (Ottawa: National Museum of Canada, 1978), 185–190; Sarah G. Thomason, "On Interpreting 'The Indian Interpreter,'" *Language in Society* 9 (1980): 182–186; Nancy L. Hagedorn, "'A Friend to Go between Them': The Interpreter as Cultural Broker during Anglo-Iroquois Councils, 1740–1770," *Ethnohistory* 35 (1988): 60– 80; Anthony F. Buccini, "*Swannekens Ende Wilden*: Linguistic Attitudes and Communication Strategies among the Dutch and Indians in New Netherland," in *The Low Countries and the New World(s): Travel, Discovery, Early Relations*, ed. Johanna C. Prins, Bettina Brandt, Timothy Stevens, and Thomas F. Shannon (Lanham, MD: University Press of America, 2000), 11–28. According to Buccini, the Dutch who learned to speak Indian languages were actually speaking Pidgin Delaware (23).

69. See also Venema, *Beverwijck*, 166; Romney, *New Netherland Connections*, 188–190. For a different interpretation of Indian–Dutch relations, see Nan A. Rothschild, "De sociale afstand tussen Nederlandse kolonisten en inheemse Amerikanen," in van Dongen, *One Man's Trash*, 189–190, 193; Jacobs, *Een zegenrijk gewest*, 271; Andrew Brink, *Invading Paradise: Esopus Settlers at War with Natives, 1659, 1663* (Philadelphia: Xlibris Corporation, 2003), 13–14, 23–24, 221–223; Donna Merwick, *The Shame and the Sorrow: Dutch–Amerindian Encounters in New Netherland* (Philadelphia: University of Pennsylvania Press, 2006), 52.

70. *NNN*, 175.

71. "Letter. Andries Laurens to director Stuyvesant," NYSA, NYCM 13: 12(a–b) (May 24, 1659); "Letter. Thomas Chambers and other officers of the militia to director Stuyvesant," NYSA, NYCM 15[1]: 2 (January 15, 1663); "Report. Claes Jansen Ruyter, of the result of his visit to the Esopus Indians," NYSA, NYCM 9: 660 (June 16, 1660); "Instructions for lieutenant Van Couwenhoven, sent to renew peace with the Wappingers, and to endeavor to procure the release of the Christian prisoners," NYSA, NYCM 10[2]: 255 (August 9, 1663); "Journal of a voyage to the Newesings, by capt. Martin Cregier and others," NYSA, NYCM 10[2]: 431–434 (December 12, 1663).

72. "Ordinance against private individuals trading in furs . . . and finally warning all against fighting, adultery, mutiny, thieving, false swearing, slander, and other immoralities," NYSA, NYCM 4: 3a (April 15, 1638). On cross-cultural sexual relationships in New Netherland, see Romney, *New Netherland Connections*, 178–182. In the end, Romney asserts that "too much proximity brought conflict, not intimacy" between Natives and New Netherlanders (189).

73. *NNN*, 174.

74. Charlotte Wilcoxen, "Arent van Curler's Children," *The New York Genealogical and Biographical Record* 110 (1979): 82–84; Venema, *Beverwijck*, 169–179; Bradley, *Before Albany*, 93; Janny Venema, *Kiliaen van Rensselaer (1586–1643): Designing a New World* (Hilversum: Uitgeverij Verloren 2010), 261; Romney, *New Netherland Connections*, 181.

75. Tom Arne Midtrød, "The Flemish Bastard and the Former Indians: Métis and Identity in Seventeenth-Century New York," *American Indian Quarterly* 34 (1) (Winter 2010), 88; Venema, *Beverwijck*, 170–171; Meuwese, *Brothers in Arms*, 263.

76. "Letter. Ensign Smith to vice-director La Montagne," NYSA, NYCM 13: 71(a–b) (February 24, 1660); Venema, *Beverwijck*, 122. Later that year Stuyvesant informed the directors in Amsterdam that a certain Dutchman known as Jacob Mijn Vriend, who had been sent to the South River by certain colonists who had provided him with some money to trade among the Indians for a year, had been living with the Susquehannock and had begun a relationship with an Indian with whom he had several children. In his letter, Stuyvesant expressed uncertainty over the status of Jacob's relationship with the Susquehannock woman. He was not certain whether Jacob had married the Susquehannock woman or had made her his concubine. "Letter. Stuyvesant to the directors at Amsterdam," NYSA, NYCM 13: 116(10b) (June 25, 1660).

4.

Building Forts and Alliances

Archaeology at Freeman and Massapeag, Two Native American Sites

ANNE-MARIE CANTWELL AND DIANA DIZEREGA WALL

In considering intercultural relationships in the Dutch colony of New Netherland, we focus on two Native mid-seventeenth-century archaeological sites: Fort Massapeag in Munsee Algonquian Country and Freeman in Mohawk Iroquois Country. In both cases, the Dutch were involved in some way with their construction. Looking at New Netherland from the perspective of these two Native American sites, what we see are the entangled lives, shifting political dynamics, and necessary political alliances of some of the peoples in and around New Netherland as the colony itself shifted from an extractive colony with a focus on the fur trade to a settler one.

Although both these sites are fortified, the fortifications were built by very different peoples for very different purposes. Freeman is a palisaded village, or "castle" as the Europeans called them, while Massapeag is an intermittently occupied, palisaded trading post with an adjacent wampum manufactory. We argue that these fortifications were also extremely potent symbols of status and political power.[1] Why, then, at midcentury, were the Dutch, who had problems maintaining their own fortifications, involved in helping build such structures for these two particular Native peoples?[2]

And, what exactly were the roles that Natives and Dutch played in these endeavors? They seem to be different, though significant, in each case. But we argue that in building these fortifications, all the participants were at the same time building much-needed alliances.

These two sites, Massapeag and Freeman, lead us to think about not just Dutch history or just Native history, but instead about a conjoined history, one that tells about those sometimes violent and turbulent times when the lives of these very different peoples were entwined, when they needed each other and had to make alliances with each other. To be sure, in many ways the Indians and Dutch led very separate lives and had very different interests, but not in all ways. Here, we discuss several of those entanglements and cooperative ventures. We are not talking about friendship. Many probably just plain didn't like, trust, or even understand each

Figure 4.1. Circa 1685 Visscher map of New Netherland (Library of Congress, Geography and Map Division) overlain with the locations of Fort Orange, Fort Amsterdam, and the Freeman and Fort Massapeag archaeological sites.

other, although others certainly may have. Rather, the leaders were probably simply looking to advance their own interests and those of their peoples.

Briefly, the Mohawk are an Iroquoian-speaking people who historically lived in the Mohawk Valley in central New York. Their society was highly organized and they lived in large, densely populated villages. These villages were often fortified and surrounded by large fields of corn, beans, and squash. Over the years, they continued to play a major role in the fur trade with the Dutch. The Munsee (sometimes referred to as the Delaware or the Lenape) were, at that time, a coastal and riverine Algonquian-speaking people, part of a larger Delaware group who lived in small, loosely structured, independent villages, with a mixed economy of hunting, fishing, and planting small gardens of corn, beans, and squash. In the early years of the colony, they were involved in the fur trade, but the beaver was soon hunted out of their territory.[3]

A Treaty Is Signed and Broken

August 30, 1645, was a day of alliances and entanglements in New Netherland. This was the day of the signing of the treaty that ended Kieft's War, a bloody conflict made up of attacks and counterattacks between the Europeans and the Algonquians that ravaged the coastal region, named for the unpopular Willem Kieft, director of New Netherland. Finally, the brutal war was over and a peace treaty was signed "under the blue canopy of heaven" at Fort Amsterdam in what is now New York City. The signing took place in the presence of a large part of the community of New Amsterdam, a number of Mohawk dignitaries and spokesmen, including Sisiadego, who had helped mediate the treaty, and representatives from several Algonquian groups who had fought in the war, including Tackapausha, a Long Island leader from a powerful family. At the signing, the Algonquians and the Dutch agreed to a firm peace that neither side would ever break. Like so many peace treaties, this one was soon broken.[4]

In August 1647, Kieft, who had been recalled to the patria, drowned when the ship on which he was traveling was wrecked off the coast of Wales. He was replaced by Petrus Stuyvesant, who was in 1646 appointed director general of New Netherland, Curacao, Bonaire, Aruba, and other Dutch colonies in the West Indies. There continued to be some minor clashes between various groups, Dutch vs. Native or Native vs. Native, over time.[5] Then in

September 1655, while Stuyvesant was on an expedition against the Swedish forces in the Delaware, New Amsterdam was attacked by a large group of Natives from several nations. This conflict, sometimes known as the Peach War, started early in the morning of September 15 when eighty-four canoes carrying at least five hundred men from various Native communities landed in the city. They were later joined by two hundred other warriors. That was the start of what turned out to be a short-lived but bloody conflict that ravaged the area around New Amsterdam including Staten Island, Pavonia in New Jersey, and northern Manhattan.[6]

During all of this, Tackapausha, now chief sachem of the western Long Island Indians, continued to keep the peace and often came to Fort Amsterdam or sent an emissary with gifts of wampum, the shell beads that had both ritual and economic importance. In fact, on November 27, 1655, two months after the end of the Peach War, seven Long Island Natives came to the fort. They told Stuyvesant that Tackapausha offered "absolute friendship" and reminded Stuyvesant of Kieft's War and "that there were people killed on both sides . . . but that such must be forgiven and forgotten." Further, they pointed out that there were no Long Island Indians among those who had attacked New Amsterdam two months earlier. They added that Tackapausha "has done no harm to the Dutch nation, not even to the value of a dog, and he still intended to continue doing so" and assured Stuyvesant that all he had to do was summon Tackapausha's people and "they would be ready at all times" to help.[7]

In the aftermath of the Peach War, both Stuyvesant and Tackapausha must have needed allies. Tackapausha was boxed in between the English and their Indian allies to his east and the Dutch to his west and, in addition, he did not trust some of the mainland Indians. Accordingly, he threw in his lot with the Dutch, visited Stuyvesant, sent emissaries, and gave presents and offers of help. And Stuyvesant himself also needed Native allies to help the colony in conflicts with *other* Indian groups *and* with the English.

Perhaps in response to Tackapausha's diplomatic overtures and maybe to ensure his future cooperation, Stuyvesant in March 1656 promised that in six months he would build a "house or fort" stocked with "Indian trade or commodities" in western Long Island. And Tackapausha vowed that he would live in peace with all the Dutch and English within the jurisdiction of New Netherland.[8] We know Tackapausha kept his part of that bargain, but it was never certain whether Stuyvesant had given Tackapausha the promised trading post he wanted; the documents do not say. But a site found on Long Island provides evidence that he very well may have done so.

Fort Massapeag

In the 1930s, almost three centuries after Stuyvesant promised that trading post, Ralph Solecki, a teenager from Queens, and two friends, C. Carlyle Smith and Matthew Schreiner, excavated some remains of a site that was known locally as Fort Massapeag on Fort Neck in Massapequa, Long Island. The area around the site was about to be destroyed by a large suburban development. In fact, parts of the site had already been plundered by looters, some using shovels, others using potato hooks, as they hunted for treasure. Solecki and his friends were interested in archaeology and, joined by some local citizens, had been trying to excavate sites before development destroyed them. There was no institutional or governmental support for local archaeology then, so they tested the site on their own time, using their own money, and discovered what very well could be the remains of this promised, but so far legendary, trading fort. Then came World War II. After the war, Solecki went on to become a professional archaeologist, teaching at Columbia University and working on important Neanderthal sites in Iraq and Syria. But he always maintained an interest in local archaeology. In the 1990s, he went back to consider the site he and his friends had dug over a half century before. He did an incredible job of research and analysis, including tracking down finds made by local collectors decades before, and showed that Fort Massapeag was probably the promised trading post.[9]

In talking about fortifications at Fort Massapeag and elsewhere, we draw upon a highly specialized vocabulary to describe those aspects of fortifications that are relevant to the two sites we discuss in this chapter. An *enceinte* is a defensive enclosure that can be made up of many components, including a palisade or curtain wall, bastions, ditches, and embankments. *Curtains* are walls such as palisades that protect defenders from attack while they are using their weapons. Furthermore, they provide a screen that hides the defenders' activities and strength (or weakness) from their attackers. *Bastions* are the projecting parts of a fortification, built at an angle to the line of the curtain wall, so as to allow defensive fire in several directions. *Ditches* are self-explanatory and they and *embankments* (built up mounds of earth) together impede the movements of those attacking. Of course there have to be entranceways into and out of the enclosure, and they are often screened or baffled; *screens* and *baffles*, in their simplest form, consist of segments of wall that overlap defenses (i.e., ditches, palisades) to form an indirect and flanked entrance passage to slow down and endanger those attempting to enter the fort.[10]

Fort Massapeag was a mid-seventeenth-century quadrangular earth-work, one hundred feet square. Its enceinte was made up of a continuous line of curtain wall (in this case, a palisade of red pine), outlined in part by an encircling ditch and an inner embankment, with two bastions. At Fort Massapeag, the northeastern bastion measured fifteen feet, five inches wide and sixteen feet, eight inches long and the southeastern one was fourteen feet wide and eighteen feet long. Since the ditch was not present at the southeast bastion, which faces the bay, nor at the northeast corner, facing a probable contemporary village, Solecki suggested these might be entranceways, although there is no evidence of a baffle or screen in either location. In addition, there was no sign that the fort had burned as there was at Freeman, the other site to be discussed, and Solecki suggested that it was likely abandoned and just rotted away.[11]

Reportedly, there was an Indian village with household refuse as well as a cemetery in the vicinity, both possibly contemporary with the fort, but if so both were destroyed by development and little is known about them other than scattered finds that Solecki managed to track down. Although some think the fort might have served as a refuge for women and children in case of attack, a seventeenth-century English colonist, Daniel Denton, claimed that Native women and children usually hid in swamps or on islands in times of conflict. And, of course, small refuges like this fort could be death traps for those crowded within them.[12]

Fort Massapeag is too small to be a fortified living place, and besides there was no household trash found inside it. Solecki argued that it was a fortified trading post, where Natives manufactured wampum outside its walls and where wampum and furs were safely stored inside until an itinerant Dutch trader came to trade with the Massapeag, collect the wampum, and perhaps meet with other groups as well. In addition, he made the point that the Dutch had to be involved, one way or another, in the fort's con-struction, and we would have to agree. At the fort, he discovered clinched nails—nails that had been driven through the pieces of wood being fastened, with the protruding tip of the nail then being bent over and pounded flat into the wood. Clinching increases the holding power of a nail enormously and was used, at that time, in European nautical construction. But this was not a Native practice. Its presence also indicates that iron hammers were used. Solecki reasoned that this in turn implies the use of sawn boards, suggesting a European-trained carpenter. But of course we don't know if the actual construction of the fort was performed by Dutch, enslaved African, or Indian labor, or some combination of all three. Members of all of these groups are known to have engaged in construction projects.

The date of the fort is also significant. Although forts of all kinds are found throughout the Midwest, Southeast, and Iroquoia in the Northeast, dating to centuries prior to the European arrivals, they are not common either on Long Island or in southern New England. In many cases where palisades were built by Native peoples in other parts of the country before the European arrivals, the palisade posts were placed in a "continuous dug trench, into which blunt ended . . . posts were set. Earth from a surrounding exterior borrow ditch was heaped at the base of the post for helping support."[13] But this was not the case here. There was no evidence of such a trench and, more significantly, the posts were sharpened with iron axes of European origin, and presumably driven or twisted into the ground.

Adjacent to the fort, Solecki and his friends found a shell midden that was made up largely of debris from wampum manufacture. These shell beads, made from local hard-shell clams and whelks, were used for ritual, trade, tribute, and even as gifts to Stuyvesant. The Dutch also used them as currency. By now, when the beaver had been hunted out of the area, making wampum or selling land was the coastal Munsee's best entree into the new economy.

Solecki found midcentury Dutch trade items at the site, but no English ones, indicating that the fort was short-lived, abandoned by the mid-1660s, before the English takeover of New Netherland. Trade goods found included nails and spikes, a few glass beads, an antler-handled knife with an iron blade, and fragments of European glass and ceramics. They also included a brass mouth harp stamped with an "R." Mouth harps were very popular with both Natives and Europeans. In fact, when Jasper Danckaerts and Peter Sluyter went to Brooklyn in 1679, they were surprised by how well the Indians there played them. Many were of iron but by midcentury mouth harps made of brass and stamped with an "R" (like the one at Massapeag) started appearing at some Native sites as well as at Dutch sites both here in New Netherland and in the Dutch Republic. Some argue that these were all made by a single craftsman in Amsterdam between 1640 and 1680. In addition, Solecki reports finding clay smoking pipes.[14]

Also found were Native goods including ceramics, a wooden mortar, and copper and brass arrow points made from European metals as well as the debris from wampum-making. Solecki argued that there was little evidence of stone debitage, the debris from making stone tools, and this could be because it was the time when Natives were no longer making stone arrow points but had switched to making them from European metals. He sees this as "a joining of the old and new traditions" on Long Island.[15] These copper and brass points were not trade items in their own right. They, and other weapons like them, were carefully crafted by Indian armorers throughout the Northeast from metals recycled from kettles they had acquired in exchange for furs and other commodities. In fact, Native peoples on Staten Island who were friendly with David De Vries, a prominent figure in New Netherland, asked him for his "copper kettle, in order to make darts for their arrows."[16]

Although European guns and metal trade goods such as knives, kettles, and axes were highly valued by Indians for their practical and prestige qualities, anthropologists James Bradley and George Hamell argue that it was the metals themselves, copper and brass, that were important. This was not just because they were useful but also because they fit into traditional value systems. Native copper had been important in Indian beliefs for thousands of years, long before the Europeans came. It had mythical origins and was associated with exchanges with extremely powerful spiritual beings and other world Grandfathers, such as horned serpents. These gifts from the spirit world could assure long life, physical and spiritual well-being, and success in hunting, warfare, and courtship. Native peoples wanted copper not just because it was useful but also because its power was so intimately related to the very concept of life itself. These copper and brass points show the complexity of the trading relationships between the two peoples involved, the sometimes creative misunderstandings, and the ways in which Native peoples adapted both the Dutch and European material culture into their own Native systems of belief and technology.[17]

The fort's location was ideal for a trading post. It faced a salt meadow (now an athletic field) with strategic access to the Great South Bay and from there by canoe or yacht to the Long Island coast and New York harbor. While it functioned, the fort must have been important in coastal New Netherland and nearby New England. It was a place where Indians could nurture social and political relationships as well as economic ones with each other and with their Dutch allies. They could share a pipe or play a mouth harp. These relationships, we argue, were not only important then for the participants, but are important for us now in understanding the complexities of those times.[18] The fort also, we argue, must have served as a material symbol to everyone—Dutch, English, African, and Indian alike—of the alliance between Stuyvesant and Tackapausha, one that went beyond trade, and one that both would call upon in the difficult years ahead. Visible and prominent in the landscape, the fort was a product of this alliance.

Kaghnuwage: The Freeman Site

Also midcentury, Mohawk leaders came to Fort Orange, in what is now Albany, to ask the Europeans for help in building their fortified villages. On June 16, 1657, Sisiadego, who was present at Fort Amsterdam for the signing of the peace treaty that ended Kieft's War, along with other Mohawk leaders representing the three Mohawk castles, met with Johannes La Montagne, vice-director of Fort Orange and Beverwijck. Among other things, they asked "as old friends that we [the Dutch] should accommodate them with some horses to haul logs out of the woods to repair their castles."[19]

Two years later, in September 1659, a group of Mohawk sachems, whose names were not recorded, came to Fort Orange. There, before the courts of Fort Orange and Rensselaerswijck, they renewed their friendship, offered gifts, expressed their concerns about a number of pressing issues, and ended by arguing that the Dutch, as good allies, should help them. They pointed out that the French helped "their Indians" and then added, "Do the same for us and help us repair our Castles." They went on to ask that the Dutch send thirty men and horses and sleds "to cut and draw wood for their castles to repair them."[20]

The Dutch magistrates then had a series of meetings among themselves to consider these requests and finally decided to send representatives to Kaghnuwage, the easternmost castle. There they would "enter into a further covenant" with the Mohawk, answer their many propositions, and offer them gifts of wampum, "75 pounds of [gun]powder, 100 pounds of lead, 15 axes and two beavers' worth of knives."[21]

And so, on September 24, 1659, a historic meeting was held at Kaghnuwage with sachems from all three Mohawk castles and seventeen Dutch dignitaries. This was an extraordinary event for both the Mohawk and the Dutch. Going into Mohawk country is not what the Dutch court usually did, nor did many Dutch. In fact, this could have been only the third or fourth official visit in the history of the colony.[22] Its account, written by the Dutch after the event, reports that the Dutch, calling the Mohawk "brothers," affirmed their friendship and offered strings of wampum after each of their responses to the earlier Mohawk requests. This is the response that concerns us: the Dutch spokesman said, "Brothers, we see that you are very busy cutting wood to build your fort. The brothers have asked us for horses to haul it out. That is not feasible for horses, because the hills here are so high and steep, and the Dutch cannot carry it out as they become sick merely from marching to this place. . . . How then, could they in addition carry palisades? But as the brothers sometimes break their axes in cutting wood, we give the brothers these axes," and he handed over fifteen iron axes as well as the knives, gunpowder, and lead. Given the tensions of the time, the gunpowder was a particularly valuable and welcome gift.[23] And that is as far as the documents go.

Archaeology fills in some of the gaps in this account. This extraordinary conference, archaeologists believe, took place at what is now known as the Freeman archaeological site, located in present-day Montgomery County in upstate New York. The artifacts found there suggest a midcentury date, which would make it the easternmost castle, the one closest to Fort Orange at that time. Its location, on a high and defensible hilltop, also seems to fit with the Dutch complaint of their difficult march to Kaghnuwage. Some sporadic collecting had been done at Freeman over the years, but in the mid-1960s, a ranch house was going to be built on the site. And so Kingston Larner, a local physician and avocational archaeologist, sometimes with the help of Dick Barker, a former chair of the English Department at Brooklyn College, both members of the Van Epps-Hartley Chapter of the New York State Archaeological Association, did a phenomenal job and excavated whatever they could before the bulldozers came. Like Massapeag, this was a rescue operation. Among the artifacts salvaged from the site were both Native-made goods and midcentury European trade goods. The latter included iron axes and knives, perhaps some of those presented by the Dutch at the September 1659 conference, as well as a brass mouth harp stamped with an "R," similar to the one found at Massapeag, along with funnel-shaped clay smoking pipes that were made in Amsterdam specifically for the Indian trade, gun parts, and a whole lot more.[24]

The Dutch account of that conference mentioned that the Mohawk were busy building their new fortifications. The Mohawk were probably in the midst of moving from their previous eastern castle, which has been identified as the Printup archaeological site. Mohawks moved their villages every ten or so years, when they had exhausted the wood supply for fuel and repair of their palisades, in cases of an insect infestation, or if the soil had lost its fertility. We might add that constructing a new settlement or simply maintaining an old one required considerable effort. Some have estimated that an average-sized Iroquoian village required approximately twenty thousand poles for the construction and maintenance of longhouses and palisades.[25]

Larner discovered part of a straight palisade wall with what appeared to be a corner bastion. Because the salvage excavations were necessarily limited, we do not know how much of Freeman was enclosed by a palisade or how many bastions there were. With the limited evidence we have, the bastion and straight wall seem to be unusual among the Mohawk for this period, but we are unsure if that novelty is an artifact of the way sites had been dug. Unfortunately, many Mohawk sites have been heavily looted over the years and excavations at others, because of constraints of time and money, were limited to living areas, and have not included the attendant fortifications. We do know that earlier, in the sixteenth century, Mohawk sites such as Garoga, a palisaded village in Fulton County, New York, were what the English would call a "promontory fort" and the French call an *éperon barré*. Garoga was located on a high, steep-sided ridge with a curtain made up of several rows of palisades along the one accessible side of the fortified village while the other sides were defended by very steep natural slopes. At the later Caughnawaga site, where the Freeman community eventually migrated, that village was enclosed by a rectangular, straight-walled palisade with no bastions. It is the only Mohawk site to have been completely excavated.[26]

This brings up the problem of bastions. As mentioned above, a bastion is an external projection from a curtain allowing defenders a clear line of fire. It changes a curtain from being a passive defense to an active offense. Some have argued that bastions and straight-walled palisades were new to the Northeast, were associated with the appearance of firearms, and, therefore, their introduction was influenced by the presence of Europeans and their fortifications. The bastions at Massapeag and Freeman were not of the same design as those at, for example, Fort Orange or Fort Amsterdam, though the purpose they served, both defensive and offensive, was likely the same. Unfortunately, since so few Mohawk villages have been extensively excavated, we don't really know when the Mohawk began to build them or how they were designed. But was the bastion at Freeman built with Dutch advice?[27]

We ourselves are not altogether convinced that the concept of a bastion was introduced to Iroquoia by the Europeans. For us, the evidence for European influence in the construction of the palisade is clear at Massapeag but is much murkier at Freeman. It is certainly possible that the construction of the straight walled palisade and bastion or bastions at Freeman was influenced by European advice or by observation of European forts. After all, Dutch New Netherlander Adrian van der Donck in the seventeenth century wrote that the Mohawk did not know about curtains and bastions, but it is not clear how much of Iroquoia he had observed.[28] And Jean de Brebeuf described the French telling the Huron to the north of Iroquoia to make their forts square so "that, by means of four little towers [or bastions] at the four corners, four Frenchmen might easily with their . . . muskets defend a whole village."[29]

Despite Van der Donck's observation, the palisade design at Freeman could have been influenced by Mohawk or other Native peoples' own observations of Native fortifications with bastions in other parts of eastern North America that were either Indigenously designed or influenced by Europeans. Certainly, straight-walled palisades with bastions were common features in the midcontinental and Southeastern North American landscapes long before European arrivals, beginning at least as early as the eleventh century, and their numbers increased over time.[30] Furthermore, the Boland site, which is on the fringes of Iroquoia in the upper Susquehanna drainage and which dates to the end of the eleventh century, has a straight-walled palisade and may have had bastions as well. And, of course, all these early palisades with bastions were prominent in eastern North America when the weapon of choice was still the bow and arrow, long before the arrival of gunpowder.[31]

Surely generations of Iroquois, a people who traveled widely in their economic, political, and military pursuits, could have seen or heard of them and remembered them in oral traditions. The Iroquois were not isolated, far from it; their military tacticians could easily have been influenced by other Native groups or by their own cultural memory. So we think it best to withhold judgment on exactly who influenced the Mohawk in the building of bastions.[32]

The Dutch embassy to Kaghnuwage came at a time when the Mohawk were building their new castle, and although the Dutch apparently did not give them horses to help haul the posts, they did give them iron axes to help them in their labors and lead and gunpowder to help them in their wars. But whether or not, along with their gifts, they also gave them advice on building straight walls and bastions we just do not know. But in any case, the issue is not just about building fortifications, we argue—it is also about building political alliances at a critical time.

War on the Esopus

The conference in Kaghnuwage was interrupted by the arrival of an African messenger with a letter from La Montagne, informing the Dutch magistrates that violence had broken out on the Esopus in the Hudson Valley between the European settlers there and the Esopus Indians, a violence that marked the beginning of the First Esopus War. Stuyvesant was certainly aware of the possibility of this outbreak. He knew back in August that trouble was brewing. Like Sisiadego and Tackapausha, he needed allies in a politically unstable world. The Mohawk were anxious about their troubled relationships with the French and the French Indian allies, and they wanted Dutch support as well. When the Dutch magistrates at the conference told their newly reconfirmed allies and brothers, the Mohawk, the news of the events at Esopus, the latter, in turn, swore that they would side with the Dutch and tell the Esopus or any Indian who fought against the Dutch that "they would kick them with the foot and say to them, 'You beasts, you hogs, go away from here; we want to have nothing to do with you.' "[33]

Soon after this conference, the Mohawk volunteered to send a messenger with wampum, which they got from the Dutch, to the Esopus Indians, warning them to do no harm to the Dutch.[34] But war began anyway and Stuyvesant had trouble getting Europeans to volunteer to fight. Reportedly, he enlisted his house servants, presumably enslaved Africans.[35] He even wrote to the vice director of Curacao, asking for enslaved Africans who might be able to pursue fleeing Esopus or help carry the soldiers' baggage.[36] Tackapausha, however, sent several dozen men to fight along with the Dutch to help his ally. And when that peace treaty was signed on July 15, 1660, it specified that, in the event that any hostile act was committed against Tackapausha and the Massapequa Indians, Stuyvesant "would consider it his duty to assist them"—exactly what Tackapausha wanted.[37]

Then came the Second Esopus War, which started in 1663. The Mohawk again tried to intervene but to no avail, although they did ransom La Montagne's daughter, one of the prisoners the Esopus had captured. Stuyvesant again had trouble getting Europeans to fight. Again Tackapausha agreed to help out with about forty troops, though he bargained beforehand about gifts, booty for his men, and the length of their military service. His troops fought along with Captain Martin Cregier's contingent of enslaved Africans, colonists, and soldiers. The war ended the following spring and on May 15, 1664, the Esopus signed a peace treaty with the Dutch that included the Massapequa, who were, as far as Tackapausha was concerned, on equal footing. He sent his younger brother, Chopeycannows (who had fought in the war), and twenty other Massapequas to witness the treaty signing.[38]

That victory, though sweet, was short-lived, and the peace that Stuyvesant, Tackapausha, and Sisiadego all wanted and worked for did not last. On

September 6 of that same year, 1664, Petrus Stuyvesant transferred the colony over to the English commander and governor designate, Richard Nicolls. Two years later, in October 1666, the French, led by the Marquis de Tracy, came down from Canada and burned the Mohawk settlements, including Kaghnuwage, the Freeman site, which De Tracy refers to as "Andaraque." The archaeology at Freeman shows clear signs of that burning. Writing of De Tracy's raid, the French Jesuit François Le Mercier recounted that the Mohawk knew of their coming and abandoned their castles but "in the distance could be seen the Barbarians, loudly hooting on the mountains and discharging many wasted shots at our soldiers." Le Mercier's account also mentioned that the "last" Mohawk village that they encountered and burned was surrounded by a triple palisade twenty feet high with four bastions. If by the "last" village he meant the westernmost, that would mean he was not talking about Kaghnuwage, the Freeman site, which was the easternmost, and would imply that bastioned palisades were common in the Mohawk Valley at that time. The account of the raid concludes: "So our people were forced to content themselves, after erecting the Cross, saying Mass, and chanting the Te Deum on that spot, with setting fire to the palisades and cabins, and consuming the entire supply of Indian corn, beans, and other produce of the country, which was found there. Then they turned back to the other villages and wrought the same havoc there, as well as in all the outlying fields."[39]

The Aftermath

What happened after that? These Indian groups did not fade away into the sunset. In fact, despite disease, changing ecosystems, inundations of European settlers, land dispossession, and later migrations for some, they maintained their ties to their seventeenth-century homelands. Many Algonquians moved west to new homelands in Oklahoma and Canada. Others stayed in the area.

When renovations began on the Main Building of Ellis Island in preparation for the opening of the Museum of Immigration in the 1980s, archaeologists discovered human remains and a Native American midden. Using morphological criteria, the human remains were identified as precolonial Native Americans. After these initial discoveries, representatives of the Delaware, of which the Munsee are a part, traveled from Oklahoma and Canada, where they now live, back to their homeland in New York to bless the bones of their ancestors before those bones were analyzed. Some years later, in 2003, they and other Delaware reburied the remains of their ancestors in a private ceremony in a quiet spot behind the Museum of Immigration. Today, standing near their graves on Ellis Island, a visitor can see lower Manhattan, where Fort Amsterdam once stood.[40]

Many Mohawk moved to Canada at the end of the seventeenth century, but some retained a presence in New York. In the twentieth century, many worked in high steel and came down from Canada to New York City to build the skyscrapers that define the city's skyline. After our nightmare of September 11, 2001, many rushed to join the rescue and cleanup operations of the Twin Towers that their fathers and uncles had helped build in the 1970s. This was important to them and a very emotional endeavor. Many sought traditional spiritual healing at a tobacco-burning ceremony at the nearby National Museum of the American Indian–New York, the George Gustave Heye Center, which today sits atop where Fort Amsterdam once stood. Some went on to work on the Freedom Tower, One World Trade Center. And it was a Mohawk ironworker that bolted in place a steel column that made the Freedom Tower the tallest building in New York.[41]

Over the next few centuries, the Dutch and other Europeans in what had been New Amsterdam were joined by millions of people from all over the globe as the city became an international capital. But the descendants of the original settlers still maintained a presence there. Recently, that presence has been acknowledged by members of the modern-day Collegiate Churches of New York City. The church's founding dates back to 1628 in New Amsterdam as the first Reformed Dutch Church in America. The first church services were held in a loft above a grain mill outside the walls of Fort Amsterdam and were conducted by the first pastor, Reverend Jonas Michaelius. Since then, the church has grown, with many ministries throughout the modern city, and has held services and events that focus on the church's colonial past, especially on its relationships with Native peoples.[42]

On November 27, 2009, the church held a Healing Turtle Island ceremony in front of the National Museum of the American Indian, the site of the former Fort Amsterdam where Sisiadego and Tackapausha had met centuries before "under the blue canopy of heaven." It was the day after Thanksgiving and marked the first Native American Heritage Day, as signed into law that June by President Barack Obama. Many Munsee, Lenape, and Delaware, local as well as those from the diaspora, came. In his remarks at the service, the Rev. Robert Chase said: "We, the Collegiate Church, recognize our part in your suffering. . . . We consumed your resources, dehumanized your people, and disregarded your culture, along with your dreams, hopes and great love for this land. We express sorrow for our part in these actions."[43] Ron Holloway, chair of the Sand Hill (Lenape) Band of Indians, offered an expression of appreciation in reply: "Today, the descendants of the original explorers who landed here have come to the descendants of those who have always been here, and openly apologized for their respon-sibility in policies that so decimated our peoples. They have extended their hands in friendship to chart a new course of race relations, to usher in a new era of healing and reconciliation that can only have beneficial results for the whole of humanity."[44] Looking back today at New Netherland from Indian country—the Massapeag and Freeman archaeological sites—leads us to consider the ways in which the lives of all these groups intersected and their sometime mutual dependence, especially in the anxious years when fears of the French, the English, and other Indian nations, loomed. Stuyve-sant, Sisiadego, and Tackapausha were each concerned with promoting the interests of their own people. But they were also astute enough to know that these interests were entangled with those of others and so they chose to become necessary, if sometimes uneasy, allies. We might even regard the actual construction of the fortifications at Massapeag and Freeman, visible and prominent on the seventeenth-century landscape, as bearing material witness to those alliances and the future they were all hoping to build. But that future was not to be.

Acknowledgments

An earlier version of this chapter was presented as a talk for the general public at the Marble Collegiate Church in New York City as part of a Dutch Days celebration in 2009. We thank Kenneth Chase for inviting us to participate. Fur-thermore, we thank Oscar Hefting of the New Holland Foundation and Lucianne Lavin of the Institute for American Indian Studies for inviting us to participate in their scholarly conferences in 2016. We are also very grateful to Lucianne for including us in this volume and for her comments on an earlier version of the chapter. We are deeply indebted to Paul Huey for his advice and generosity in supplying us with information and documents about the Freeman Site and for reading a first draft of this manuscript; to Wayne Lenig, for his advice about the Freeman Site and introducing us to the Mohawk Valley; and Arnold Pickman, for his technological support. Paul Wegner of the Institute for American Indian Studies provided the map in figure 4.1.

Notes

1. Lawrence H. Keeley, Marisa Fontana, and Russell Quick, "Baffles and Bastions: The Universal Features of Fortifications," *Journal of Archaeological Research* 15 (1) (2007): 58.

2. For disrepair of Dutch forts in New Netherland, see Paul R. Huey, "Dutch Colonial Forts in New Netherland," in *First Forts: Essays on the Archaeology of Proto-colonial Fortifications*, ed. Eric Klingelhofer (Leiden: Brill, 2010), 153–155 and 144–155; and Jaap Jacobs, *Dutch Colonial Fortifications in North America, Historical Research in the Netherlands and the United States of America: Contributions to the Atlas of Dutch North America 1.0* (Amsterdam: New Holland Foundation; Dundee: Bommelstein Historical Consultancy, 2015).

3. For discussions of the Munsee that include archaeology, see Anne-Marie Cantwell and Diana diZerega Wall, *Unearthing Gotham: The Archaeology of New York City* (New Haven: Yale University Press, 2001); Robert S. Grumet, *The Munsee Indians: A History* (Norman: University of Oklahoma, 2009); Herbert Clemens Kraft, *The Lenape-Delaware Indian Heritage* (Elizabeth, NJ: Lenape Books, 2001); and John A. Strong, *The Algonquian Peoples of Long Island from Earliest Times to the Present* (Interlaken, NY: Heart of the Lakes, 1997). For discussions of the Mohawk, see James Wesley Bradley, *Before Albany: An Archaeology of Native-Dutch Relations in the Capital Region, 1600–1664* (Albany: University of the State of New York, State Education Department, 2007); W. E. Engelbrecht, *Iroquois: The Development of a Native World* (Syracuse: Syracuse University, 2003); T. Grassman, *The Mohawk Indians and Their Valley: Being a Chronological Documentary Record to the End of 1695* (Schenectady: J. S. Lischyninsky, 1969); Dean R. Snow, *Mohawk Valley Archaeology: The Sites. Occasional Papers in Archaeology* 23 (University Park: Matson Museum of Anthropology, Pennsylvania State University, 1995). For descriptions of New Netherland, see Jaap Jacobs, *New Netherland: A Dutch Colony in Seventeenth-Century America* (Leiden: Brill, 2005); for a general discussion, see Cynthia J. van Zandt, *Brothers among Nations: The Pursuit of Intercultural Alliances in Early America, 1580–1660* (New York: Oxford University Press, 2008). See Audra Simpson, *Mohawk Interruptus: Political Life across the Borders of Settler States* (Durham: Duke University Press, 2014), 7–114, for a critique of the anthropological literature.

Here, we are using the term Munsee to refer to the Native inhabitants of coastal New York at the time of the Dutch arrivals. Although we collectively call them the Munsee, after their dialect, we emphasize that there was no single Munsee political unit at that time. There were, however, a number of autonomous groups named after a popular leader or place. The Munsee dialect is spoken by the northernmost Delaware, an Eastern Algonquian language family. They had ties with similar Munsee speakers living across a wide area from western Long Island, the lower Hudson Valley, to northern New Jersey, and across to eastern Pennsylvania. See Paul Otto, *The Dutch-Munsee Encounter in America: The Struggle for Sovereignty in the Hudson Valley* (New York: Berghahn Books, 2006), 20–22, fn. 7, for an extensive discussion about the scholarly debate on the use of the terms Munsee, Lenape, and Delaware for the seventeenth century.

4. A. J. F. Van Laer, trans., "Council Minutes," *New York Historical Manuscripts Dutch Vol. IV* (Baltimore: Baltimore Genealogical Publishing, 1974), 279–80; Berthold Fernow, ed. and trans., *Documents Relative to the Colonial History of the State of New York, XIII* (Albany: Weed, Parsons and Co., 1881), 18. During that war, according to some estimates, sixteen hundred Native men, women, and children had been killed. Native and colonial farms were destroyed. Some captured Natives were given to Dutch soldiers, others sent as gifts to the English governor of Bermuda, and many Europeans emigrated from the colony. For accounts of that war, see Mark Meuwese, *Brothers in Arms, Partners in Trade: Dutch–Indigenous Alliances in the Atlantic World, 1595–1674* (Leiden: Brill, 2012); Otto, *The Dutch-Munsee*, 113–26; Allen W. Trelease, *Indian Affairs in Colonial New York: The Seventeenth Century* (Ithaca: Cornell University Press, 1960), 60–84. Also see Andrew Lipman, *The Saltwater Frontier: Indians and the Contest for the American Coast* (New Haven: Yale University Press, 2015), who put the war in a regional perspective. For Tackapausha's lineage, see Grumet, *The Munsee*, 20–23. Tackapausha also appears in the records as Antimome, Mayauwetinnemin, Wittahom, and Wittaneyen (*Grumet, The Munsee*, 302–303 fn. 33).

5. For instances of such conflicts, see, for example, Otto, *Dutch-Munsee*, 142–143.

6. See Trelease, *Indian Affairs*, 138–148, for a detailed report of the conflict. There are differing accounts of this war and the identities of the Natives involved.

7. See Charles Gehring, trans. and ed., *Council Minutes, 1655–1656* (Syracuse: Syracuse University Press, 1995), 144–165, for the minutes of the meeting; see 145 for the quotations.

8. Benjamin Hicks, *Records of the Towns of North and South Hempstead, Long Island, New York*, 8 vols. (Jamaica, NY: Long Island Farmer Print, 1896–1904), 1:42–43. See also Ralph Solecki, "The Archaeology of Fort Neck and Vicinity, Massapequa, Long Island, New York," in *Native Forts of the Long Island Sound Area*, ed. by Gaynell Stone (Stony Brook: Suffolk County Archaeological Association, 2006), 151–152, for an extended discussion.

9. See Ralph Solecki, "Indian Forts of the Mid-17th Century in the Southern New England–New York Coastal Area." *Northeast Historical Archaeology* 22 (1) (1992–93), and Solecki, "The Archaeology," for a history of excavations at the site. Carlyle S. Smith also became a professional archaeologist and his doctoral dissertation at Columbia University, which was subsequently published, included a discussion of Fort Massapeag. The present discussion is based upon Solecki "Indian Forts" and "The Archaeology" and Carlyle S. Smith, "The Archaeology of Coastal New York," *Anthropological Papers of the American Museum of Natural History* 43 (1950), and

"A Note on Fort Massapeag," in *Native Forts of the Long Island Sound Area,* ed. Gaynell Stone (Stony Brook: Suffolk County Archaeological Association, 2006).

10. See Keeley, Fontana, and Quick, "Baffles and Bastions," for an excellent discussion of fortification features.

11. See Solecki, "The Archaeology," 158, and Smith, "The Archaeology," 3, for lack of evidence for burning.

12. Solecki, "The Archaeology," 167–174. See Smith, "The Archaeology," 162–163, and Smith, "A Note," for the suggestion that it might be a refuge, but see Daniel Denton, *A Brief History of New York, Formerly Called New Netherlands* (Cleveland: Burrows Brothers, 1902), 9, for an alternate view.

13. Solecki, "The Archaeology," 215.

14. For mouth harps, see Solecki, "The Archaeology," 216, and Jaspar Danckaerts and Peter Sluyter, *Journal of a Voyage to New York and a Tour in Several of the American Counties in 1679–80* (Ann Arbor: University Microfilms, 1966), 126. Donald A. Rumrill, "An Interpretation and Analysis of the Seventeenth-Century Mohawk Nation: Its Chronology and Movements," *Bulletin and Journal of the Archaeology for New York State* 90 (1985): 20, cites a personal communication from Jan Baart that these brass ones were all made by a single craftsman in Amsterdam from 1640 to 1680. See also Rumrill, "An Interpretation and Analysis of the Seventeenth-Century Mohawk Nation," 9.

15. Solecki, "The Archaeology," 188.

16. For De Vries, see J. Franklin Jameson, ed., *Narratives of New Netherland, 1609–1664* (New York: Charles Scribner's Sons, 1909), 229.

17. For the importance of copper in Native belief systems, see James W. Bradley, *Evolution of the Onondaga Iroquois: Accommodating Change, 1500–1635* (Syracuse: Syracuse University Press, 1987); George Hamell, "Trading in Metaphors: The Magic of Beads, Another Perspective upon Indian-European Contact in Northeastern North America," in *Proceedings of the 1982 Glass Trade Bead Conference,* ed. C. F. Hayes III, *Research Records* 16 (Rochester: Rochester Museum and Science Center, 1983); George Hamell, "Mythical Realities and European Contact in the Northeast during the Sixteenth and Seventeenth Centuries," *Man in the Northeast* 33 (1987); and Christopher Miller and George Hamell, "A New Perspective on Indian-White Contact: Cultural Symbols and Colonial Trade," *Journal of American History* 73 (1986): 311–328.

18. Forts/trading posts like this are rare in the Northeast. There were not many of them and they were around for a very short time. See Lynn Ceci, "The Effect of European Contact and Trade on the Settlement Patterns of Indians in Coastal New York, 1524–1665" (PhD diss., City University of New York, 1977), 44; Hicks, *Records,* 43–44; Solecki, "The Archaeology," 214; as well as various papers in Gaynell Stone, ed., *Native Forts of the Long Island Sound Area* (Stony Brook: Suffolk County Archaeological Association, 2006).

19. Charles T. Gehring, trans. and ed., *Fort Orange Court Minutes 1652–1660* (Syracuse: Syracuse University Press, 1990), 304. In October of the following year Sisiadego and other sachems were back in court for help in their relations with the French in Canada (*Fort Orange Court Minutes*, 411).

20. *Fort Orange Court Minutes*, 453–54; quotes on 454. As they made this particular request, they laid down a beaver and a beaver coat. Jeremias van Rensselaer and Arendt van Curler represented the court of Rensselaerswijck. Mohawk concerns about the need for powder and the cost of gun repairs underline their dependence on guns as their wars are increasing.

21. See Fernow, *Documents Relative*, 116; Gehring, *Fort Orange*, 455–456. In discussing this two days later, on September 8, 1659, the court concluded that they should tell the Mohawk that "there was no doubt of the brotherly union which many years ago was concluded between the Dutch and the Maquaas and this shall always be maintained and held securely together by a chain"; Gehring, *Fort Orange*, 455. At that time, they were waiting for Peter Stuyvesant to come and consult on this. On September 16, 1659, another session of both courts was held in Fort Orange to discuss the fact that Stuyvesant was ill and could not come. They decided to send some members of the court to Kaghnuwage. For variations in the place names of the community represented at the Freeman site and in the spelling of Kaghnuwage and Caughnawaga, see Snow, *Mohawk Valley*, 362–411.

22. Jon W. Parmenter, "Separate Vessels: Hudson, the Dutch, and the Iroquois," in *The Worlds of the Seventeenth Century Hudson Valley*, ed. Jaap Jacobs and Louis Roper (Albany: State University of New York Press, 2014), 118.

23. See Gehring, *Council Minutes*, 456–60, for an account of this meeting; the quote is from 458. See also Grassman, *The Mohawk*, 209.

24. For the Freeman site, see Kingston Larner, "Field Notes: The Freeman Site Collection," Paul Huey, Private Collection, 1971; Rumrill, "An Interpretation," 25–27; and Snow, *Mohawk Valley*, 371–376. Paul Huey, personal communication, 2016, and Wayne Lenig, personal communication, 2016. Snow, *Mohawk Valley*, 365, estimates that Freeman had a population of around 374. Seventeenth-century French Jesuit missionaries working in Iroquoia wrote that in the late 1650s a large percentage of the Iroquoian population was made up of refugees or captives adopted from other nations. Reuben Gold Thwaits, ed., *The Jesuit Relations and Allied Documents; Travels and Explorations of the Jesuit Missionaries in New France, 1610–1791*, 73 vols. (Cleveland: Burrow Brothers, 1896–1901), 45:205–209; see also Daniel Richter, *The Ordeal of the Longhouse: The Peoples of the Iroquois League in the Era of European Colonization* (Chapel Hill: University of North Carolina Press, 1992), 65–66.

25. David H. Dye, "Rotten Palisade Posts and Rickety Baffle Gates: Repairing Native Eastern North American Fortifications," 2012, 21. Accessed September 8, 2017. https://www.academia.edu/1987842/Rotten_Palisades_and_Rickety_Baffle_Gates_Fortifying_Native_Eastern_North_Ameri-ca, citing William David Himlayson and

Mel Brown, *Iroquoian Peoples of the Land of Rocks and Water, AD 1000–1650: A Study in Settlement Archaeology* (Ottawa: London Museum of Archaeology, 1998), 398, 408, and Conrad Reidenreich, *Huronia: A History and Geography of the Huron Indians, 1600–1650* (Toronto: McClelland and Stewart, 1971), 152.

26. Keeley, Fontana, and Quick, "Baffles and Bastions," 79, for a discussion of types of forts. For a discussion of the Garoga site, see Robert E. Funk and Robert D. Kuhn, *Three Sixteenth-Century Mohawk Iroquois Village Sites* (Albany: New York State Museum/New York State Education Department, 2003), 83–129. For the Caughnawaga site, also known as the Veeder site, see Rumrill, "An Interpretation," 32–33, and Snow, *Mohawk Valley*, 431–443. The site is on a property owned by Order Minor Conventuals, a Franciscan order that maintains a shine near the site. The shrine is dedicated to Kateri (Catherine) Tekakwitha, who was canonized in 2012 by the Roman Catholic Church (Grassman, *The Mohawk*, 312–314; Simpson, *Mohawk Interruptus*, 5). Some believe Tekakwitha, the first Mohawk and the second Indigenous saint in church history, lived there. For this reason, Father Thomas Grassman, O.F.M. Conv., and members of the Van Epps-Hartley Chapter of the New York State Archaeological Association tested the site and eventually completely excavated it. They, and others, saw the site as likely occupied from 1666 to 1693 and therefore associated with Tekakwitha, who would, along with her community, have moved there after the De Tracey raid in 1666 destroyed their village at Kaghnuwage, the Freeman site (see below). She was likely baptized in 1676. However, Snow's reexamination of the data leads him to date the Caughnawaga site to 1679–93. This would make it too late to be associated with Tekakwitha, since the majority of Catholic Mohawks had moved to Canada in 1679. Snow has argued that she was born probably when her community was living at Kaghnuwage, the Freeman site. After the De Tracy raid in 1666 that destroyed her village, she and her community at Kaghnuwage moved to what is now known as the Fox Farm site (1666–79). Soon after, Jesuit missionaries returned to the Mohawk Valley, having left in 1655, and many of their converts, probably including Tekakwitha, moved to Canada in 1679. For a discussion of this, see Snow, *Mohawk Valley*, 361–365, 415–419, 429–443. See also Rumrill, "An Interpretation," 32–33. For variations in the place names and spelling of Caughnawaga, see Snow, *Mohawk Valley*, 362, 411, 418. For the life of Tekakwitha, see Darren Bonaparte, *A Lily among Thorns: The Mohawk Repatriation of Káteri Tekahkwítha* (Ahkwesahsne, Mohawk Territory: Wampum Chronicles, 2009); see 120 and 122 for artifacts from the Freeman site. Unfortunately, the site attributions for some of the artifacts are incorrect. The metal scabbard part and the knife blade illustrated on page 120 are from the Freeman site and the metal utensils and miniature cup illustrated on page 121 are from the Fox Farm site (Paul Huey, personal communication).

27. For a discussion of this, see, among others, Thomas S. Abler, "European Technology and the Art of War in Iroquoia," in *Cultures in Conflict: Current Archaeological Perspectives*, ed. T. C. Tkaczuk and B. C. Vivian (Calgary: University

of Calgary, 1989), 277; W. M. Beauchamp, "Earthworks and Stockades," *American Antiquarian and Oriental Journal* 3 (1) (1891): 149; George R. Milner, "Warfare in Prehistoric and Early Historic Eastern North America," *Journal of Archaeological Research* 7 (2) (1999): 125; Solecki, "The Archaeology," 158; E. G. Squier, *Aboriginal Monuments of the State of New York* (Washington, DC: Smithsonian Contributions to Knowledge II, 1850), 82; and Snow, *Mohawk Valley*, 429. But see Susan Prezzano, "Longhouse, Village, and Palisade: Community Patterns at the Iroquois Southern Door" (PhD diss., State University of New York at Binghamton, 1992), 253, and Engelbrecht, *Iroquoia*, 98, for precontact bastions in the area. Peregrine A. Gerard-Little et al., "Understanding the Built Environment at the Seneca Iroquois White Springs Site Using Large-Scale, Multi-Instrument Archaeogeophysical Surveys," *Journal of Archaeological Science* 39 (7) (2012): 2043, wrote that although there were watchtowers there were no bastions, but straight-edged polygonal palisades have been found in Iroquoia prior to extensive contact with Europeans and that includes the sixteenth-century Adams site.

The distinction between passive and active defense is from Abler, "European Technology," 276, citing Christopher Duffy, *Siege Warfare: The Fortress in the Early Modern World, 1494–1660* (London: Routledge and Keegan Paul, 1979), 1–7. See also Keeley, Fontana, and Quick, "Baffles and Bastions," 67–79, for a comparative history of bastions.

28. Adriaen van der Donck, *A Description of New Netherland* (Lincoln: University of Nebraska Press, 2008), 83; but see 164, fn. 15.

29. Thwaites, *The Jesuit*, 53, cited in Abler, "European Technology," 277; see Abler for a detailed discussion of this as well as Snow, *Mohawk Valley*, 429, and Milner, "Warfare in Prehistoric and Early Historic Eastern North America," 125.

30. See, among others, discussions in A. M. Krus, "The Timing of Precolumbian Militarization in the US Midwest and Southeast," *American Antiquity* 81 (2) (2016); "Refortifying Cahokia, More Efficient Palisade Construction through Redesigned Bastions," *Midcontinental Journal of Archaeology* 36 (2) (2011); Dye, "Rotten Palisade"; George Milner, "Palisaded Settlements in Prehistoric Eastern North America," in *City Walls: The Urban Enceinte in Global Perspective*, ed. James D. Tracey, 46–70 (New York: University of Cambridge Press, 2000); and Milner, "Warfare in Prehistoric and Early Historic Eastern North America."

31. For bastion spacing and defenders' choice of weapons, see Keeley, Fontana, and Quick, "Baffles and Bastions," 55, and Milner, "Warfare in Prehistoric and Early Historic Eastern North America," 119–20, and "Palisaded Settlement," 55, 64, as well as C. S. Keener, "An Ethnohistorical Analysis of Iroquois Assault Tactics Used against Fortified Settlements of the Northeast in the Seventeenth Century," *Ethnohistory* 46 (4) (1999). For the bastion at the Boland site, see Susan Prezzano, "Longhouse, Village, and Palisade: Community Patterns at the Iroquois Southern Door" (PhD diss., State University of New York at Binghamton, 1992), 253.

32. See Krus, "Refortifying Cahokia," for a discussion of variability in bastion design over time in the eastern woodlands, as well as how this variability might be related to amounts of available timber. See also Krus, "The Timing," as well as Milner, "Palisaded Settlements," 58–59, for detailed discussions of palisaded settlement in eastern North America. Milner, "Palisaded Settlements," suggests that bastions might also be built to reinforce vulnerable parts of a wooden palisade. See also Finlayson, *Iroquoian Peoples*, 398, 408; Heidenreich, *Huronia*, 152; Garry Warrick, "Estimating Ontario Iroquoian Village Duration," *Man in the Northeast* 36 (1988): 49–50, and Prezzano, "Longhouse, Village," 253–256, for detailed discussions of the longevity of palisades and problems of maintenance.

33. Gehring, *Fort Orange*, 459, and Fernow, *Documents Relative*, 122–123. For accounts of the Esopus wars, see Trelease, *Indian Affairs*, as well as Otto, *The Dutch-Munsee*, 149–155. Otto refers to the two Esopus wars collectively as the Third Dutch-Munsee War. See Fernow, *Documents Relative*, 260, for the compensation Stuyvesant was offering to those colonists willing to fight in the war. For general discussions of Iroquois wars, see Richter, *The Ordeal*, and Trelease, *Indian Affairs*.

34. Gehring, *Fort Orange*, 463–464.

35. Trelease, *Indian Affairs*, 153.

36. Fernow, *Documents Relative*, 143. See also Jacobs, *New Netherland*, 368–369, for difficulties Stuyvesant had in recruiting volunteers for these wars.

37. There is a great deal of evidence pointing to the importance of Tackapausha and his people to Stuyvesant and his. In September 1659, Stuyvesant, in writing to the director in the Netherlands, referred to the Long Island Indians as "our friends" (Fernow, *Documents Relative*, 125). In an agreement with local Indian groups, signed on March 6, 1660, mention was made of Tackapausha and the Massapequa that "if it should happen, that any harm was done to him or his people, it should be considered as having been done to us [the Dutch]" (Fernow, *Documents Relative*, 148). When the peace treaty of July 15, 1660 ending the First Esopus War was signed (Fernow, *Documents Relative*, 179–181), it included those who were in friendship with Stuyvesant, "especially the chief of Long Island" (Fernow, *Documents Relative*, 180).

38. For the Second Esopus War, see Trelease, *Indian Affairs*, 160–168. For Tackapausha's bargaining, see Fernow, *Documents Relative*, 295–296, and 375–777, for signing of the second peace treaty. For role of Africans, see 296, 284, 330, 328. Jacobs, *New Netherland*, 382, writes that the Africans were deployed in "fighting functions and in supporting duties." In the literature, the Massapequa are sometimes referred to as the Marsepinghs; see, for example, Fernow, *Documents Relative*, 295–316, and Otto, *Dutch-Munsee*, 147–148.

39. For the surrender of New Netherland, see, among others, Oliver A. Rink, *Holland on the Hudson: An Economic and Social History of Dutch New York* (Ithaca: Cornell University Press, 1986), 260–263. Le Mercier's description of the raid can

be found in Thwaits, *The Jesuit 50*, 141–145. The first quote is 142; the description of the village is 143; the second quote is 144.

40. Anne-Marie Cantwell, " 'Who Knows the Power of His Bones'? Repatriation Redux," in *Ethics and Anthropology: Facing Future Issues in Human Biology, Human Rights, Globalism, and Cultural Property*, ed. Anne-Marie Cantwell, et al. (New York: New York Academy of Sciences, 2000), 93–96.

41. The National Museum of the American Indian had a traveling exhibit on the role the Mohawk played in the building of New York and the recovery work at the World Trade Center, *Booming Out: Mohawk Ironworkers Build New York* (Smithsonian, Traveling Exhibition Service, 2004), accessed August 31, 2017. http://sitesarchives.si.edu/exhibitions/exhibits/archived_exhibitions/booming/main. htm. For health problems of those rescuers, see Christopher Curtis, "Doc Tells Story of Mohawk Ironworkers Who Helped in Wreckage of 9/11," *Montreal Gazette*, September 13, 2016, accessed August 31, 2017. http://montrealgazette. com/news/doc-tells-story-of-mohawk-ironworkers-who-helped-in-wreckage-of-911; and Jed Morey, "A Mohawk Ironworker's Widow Remembers 9/11," *Jed Morey: So Far Left, We're Right*, September 12, 2011, accessed August 31, 2017. http://www. jedmorey.com/2011/a-mohawk-ironworker%E2%80%99s-widow-remembers-911/. For Mohawk rescue workers going to a tobacco burning ceremony at the National Museum of the American Indian, see Joseph Bruchac, "Indian Renaissance," in *National Geographic Magazine*, September 2004, accessed August 31, 2017. http:// ngm.nationalgeographic.com/ngm/0409/feature5/fulltext.html. For work on the Freedom Tower, see Ian Oakes, "Kahnawake Mohawk Fastens Milestone Bolt at 'Freedom Tower,' " *Indian Times*, May 3, 2012, accessed 8/31/2017. http://www. indiantime.net/story/2012/05/03/news/kahnawake-mohawk-fastens-milestone-bolt-at-freedom-tower/0504201220 28560174118.html; and Kim Mackrael, "Quebec Mohawk Turns Freedom Tower Site into New York City's Tallest Skyscraper," *Globe and Mail*, April 30, 2012, accessed August 31, 2017. https://www.theglobeandmail. com/news/world/quebec-mohawk-turns-freedom-tower-into-new-york-citys-tallest-skyscraper/article2418629/. For a discussion of contemporary Mohawk at Kahnawake, see Simpson, *Mohawk Interruptus*. For discussion of contemporary Natives of New Jersey, see John R. Norwood, *We Are Still Here: The Tribal Saga of New Jersey's Nanticoke and Lenape Indians* (Bridgeton: Native New Jersey Publications, 2007).

42. According to church records, the grist mill was located on what is now 32–34 South William Street. For the history of the Collegiate Church, see Marble Collegiate Church, accessed September 4, 2017. http://www.marblechurch.org/ welcome/history/ and Collegiate Churches of New York, accessed September 1, 2017. http://collegiatechurch.org/about-us/historical-timeline. See also Jameson, *Narratives of New Netherland*, 83–84 fn. 1, 212–213. In 1642, Kieft began raising money for a stone church to be built within the fort's walls (312, 325–326).

43. Representatives of the Collegiate Church and the Lenape signified their reconciliation by exchanging wampum, which Native Americans traditionally used

to seal a treaty (see Intersections International, "Healing Turtle Island," January 7, 2010, accessed August 31, 2017. http://www.intersections.org/healing-turtle-island-1. For a video of the event, see Healing Turtle Island Highlight Video—YouTube, https://www.youtube.com/watch?v=1oWDsuP4TdY. The Marble Collegiate Church also sponsored an opera, telling the story of the sale of Manhattan from a Native point of view; see James Barron, "The Sale of Manhattan, Retold from a Native American Viewpoint." *New York Times*, November 18, 2014, accessed August 31, 2017. https://www.nytimes.com/2014/11/19/arts/music/the-sale-of-manhattan-retold-from-a-native-american-viewpoint.html?mcubz=3.

44. Intersections International, "Healing Turtle Island," January 7, 2010, accessed August 31, 2017. http://www.intersections.org/healing-turtle-island-1.

5.

Mohawk and Dutch Relations in the Mohawk Valley

Alliance, Diplomacy, and Families from 1600 to the Two Row Treaty Renewal Campaign

PAUL GORGEN

This chapter gives a short history of relations between the Mohawk Nation and the Dutch settlers in the colony of New Netherland. Focusing on experiences in the Mohawk Valley, it looks at key aspects of the Mohawk-Dutch alliance, their trade relations, diplomatic ventures, and experiences on the personal level in Mohawk and Dutch families. This chapter also discusses the legacy of the Mohawk-Dutch alliance as it extended beyond the end of the Dutch colonial era, and its ongoing significance today.

Colonial European trade and settlement in northeastern North America had clearly negative and often devastating effects on the Native people of the region. The Mohawks and other nations in the Haudenosaunee Confederacy were no exception. But at the start of the colonial era, the relationship between the Mohawks and the Dutch was exceptional for its time—it at least aspired to be and was to some extent an equal partnership. It was certainly more equal and harmonious than subsequent Mohawk experiences with the British and American governments, which ended in almost total loss of ancestral lands in the Mohawk Valley.

The Mohawk-Dutch partnership included mutual defense against common enemies, joint diplomatic missions, legal redress of Native concerns, and acknowledgments of Native sovereignty over the land. These were key parts of an evolving, enduring alliance that the two groups forged between themselves and extended to others. The treaty that they made is still recognized today, both as an active treaty that is still in effect and as a model for agreements offering equal sovereignty to Native peoples and settler societies elsewhere in the world.

Some Background on the Mohawk Homelands, History, and Culture

The true name of the Mohawks is Kanien'kehá:ka—People of the Flint. They are the Keepers of the Eastern Door for the Haudenosaunee (Iroquois) Confederacy. Their traditional territory centers on the Mohawk Valley, with hunting lands and trade routes extending north into Canada, west along the Ohio Valley, and south through Kentucky and beyond. Not coincidently, these modern geographic place names that outline this territory are all based on original Mohawk words and phrases.

Mohawk oral tradition says that the Haudenosaunee people originally migrated north from Mesoamerica, then traveled east from the plains region and along the Ohio Valley to what is now New York State. There the Mohawks, Oneidas, Onondagas, Cayugas, and Senecas eventually formed the Haudenosaunee Confederacy, under the Great Law of Peace that ended a long period of internecine conflict. They were later joined by the Tuscarora, speakers of a related Iroquoian language from the Carolinas, who became the sixth Haudenosaunee nation.

Haudenosaunee society is matrilineal, organized into clans, with Bear, Wolf and Turtle clans for the Mohawks. Clanmothers, and the chiefs whom they appoint, work to resolve any issues and make decisions by consensus, within their own nations and within the Confederacy. Faithkeepers focus on spiritual matters, supporting traditional ceremonial ways and upholding Haudenosaunee culture. A grand council of fifty chiefs deliberates and settles issues at the Confederacy level, including questions regarding outside nations. In the early 1600s, those outside nations suddenly included a wave of incoming foreigners—traders and immigrant settlers from across Europe, arriving and building outposts on the eastern and northern borders of Mohawk land.

The Dutch, the Fur Trade, and Treaties

The Mohawks' first European contact was with fur traders—French traveling west along the Saint Lawrence, and Dutch traders sailing north up the Hudson River. The Mohawks called the traders *Rona'sharón:nih* (axe makers),[1] and the Dutch called the Mohawks *Maquas*—from the Mohican word *Machquas*, meaning "bears."[2]

The fur trade brought new tools and weapons, and intense competition among the fur buyers and suppliers for control of the trade. Competition for a limited supply of beaver pelts caused conflicts along the trade routes, which also became highways for the spread of epidemic European diseases. The pressures of conflict and disease erupted into the aptly named Beaver Wars between the Haudenosaunee, the French, and other Native peoples, causing massive population losses among all the Native peoples of the region throughout the seventeenth century. For the Haudenosaunee in general and the Mohawks in particular, one way to mitigate the losses was to accept new residents into their territory and society. Those new residents would include both other Native peoples and new Dutch settlers in the Mohawk Valley.

Around 1613, Dutch traders established an outpost and trading site, Fort Nassau on Castle Island in the Hudson River just south of modern-day Albany, New York, near the mouth of Tawasentha Creek. A Mohawk fishing village stood there by the creek mouth, an ideal spot for harvesting ocean fish such as shad and herring during spring spawning runs. The creek, and a portage route to it from the Mohawk River, soon served as a conduit for furs from the north and west, carried by Mohawks for sale to the Dutch.

According to Haudenosaunee oral tradition and written accounts dating from the late 1600s,[3] the Mohawk and Dutch made an early trade agreement at the Tawasentha site, pledging to trade and coexist without interfering in each other's internal affairs. A key tenet of the agreement was equality, which the Mohawks insisted upon in reply to an initial Dutch demand for their subservience. Their primary agreement, recorded on a wampum belt and known to the Haudenosaunee as the Two Row Wampum Treaty, guaranteed equal sovereignty for all parties and became the basis for future pacts with the Europeans.

The treaty was recorded on a wampum belt with a white background and two parallel rows of purple beads depicting the Native people in their canoes and the Dutch in their ships, traveling side by side down the river of life, respecting and not interfering with each other's traditions and sovereignty (figure 5.1). A Mohawk-Dutch alliance based on that treaty prospered and

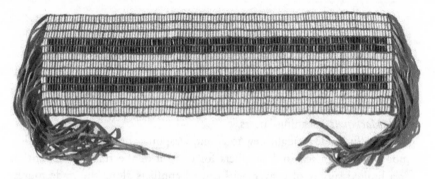

Figure 5.1. The Two Row Wampum Belt (courtesy of Darren Bonaparte).

grew into a mutual defense agreement, particularly against incursions by the French from Canada. On at least one occasion, during a rare era of peace with the French, Mohawk leaders and a Dutch representative invited the French and their Native allies to join the alliance with them.[4]

The Two Row Wampum Treaty's agreement to equal partnership was exceptional, given prevailing trade practices of the day. In that same era, Dutch traders often used brutal methods to control trade with Native peoples elsewhere in the world, particularly in the Spice Islands of the South Pacific. Individual Dutch traders sometimes used similar tactics on the Hudson River as well, including kidnapping Native leaders and holding them for ransom.[5] There are a number of documented cases of this practice, including one of a kidnapped Mohawk chief who was tortured and killed by his Dutch captors onboard their ship, *after* the ransom demand was paid.[6]

Mohawks were also sometimes beaten by Dutch traders while carrying pelts to market if they refused to sell to the traders who accosted them on the trail. Mohawks raised complaints against this treatment in the local Dutch courts, and laws were passed to ban the practice. Dutch laws were also passed to prevent settlers' cattle from straying into the Natives' corn-fields. These ordinances are good examples of the respect that the Dutch community afforded to their Native neighbors. Around that same time, the Dutch courts also passed ordinances limiting the baking of cakes, white bread, and sugar buns for sale to Native people—not for repressive reasons, but because those quintessentially Dutch products were so popular, and their sale so profitable, that Dutch bakers depleted their scarce supply of white flour and sugar trying to meet the demand.[7]

Such challenges, large and small, were generally resolved by peaceful means, and the Mohawk-Dutch alliance grew stronger as a result. The fur trade also tied the groups together, providing large profits for the Dutch and essential tools for the Mohawks and other Native peoples, including metal goods such as axes and cookware, guns, cloth, and other items that proved invaluable and eventually became essential to life in the midst of similarly armed and equipped neighbors.[8] After decades of trade and successful alliance, Mohawks allowed the Dutch to move west from the shores of the Hudson River to farm and settle in their home territory of the Mohawk Valley. This new phase of relations was exemplified by the settlement of Schenectady in 1661.

Schenectady Village: A Mohawk-Dutch Venture

The main Dutch settlement on the upper Hudson River was the town of Beverwyk (later Albany), which stood at the eastern end of a trail that led northwest through a pine forest to the Mohawk River, bypassing the Cohoes Falls. That trail, and the one from Tawasentha, met the Mohawk River at a village site called Ska-neh-tati, meaning "other side of the pines."[9] Control of that Mohawk River site was essential to controlling the flow of beaver pelts from western lands where fur was plentiful. The flat lands there along the Mohawk River were also ideal for growing corn.

Previously occupied by Mohicans, by the 1650s the Schenectady site was under Mohawk control and was being farmed by two sons of a Dutch official and his Mohawk wife: Cornelius Van Slyke and Otsistókwa (Ots-tok), a woman from the upriver Mohawk village of Canajoharie. In 1661, after the death of the eldest son, Martin Van Slyke, his brother Ackes (also called Jacques) entered into an agreement with Arent Van Curler and twelve Dutch partners from Albany to build a farming town on the Schenectady site. Built on land deeded by the Mohawks in 1663, the new town had both Dutch and Mohawk residents, and was in effect a joint venture. Documents from that era show that Mohawk leaders had intended for the farmland at Schenectady to be held in Ackes Van Slyke's name, with his Dutch partners having rights to the crops grown on it.[10] A rich and strategic site for defense, trade, and farming, the Schenectady settlement showed both the benefits and hurdles of close political and personal relations between the two cultures.

One Family's Experience

In 1680, a Dutch traveler, Jasper Dankaerts, met Ackes Van Slyke, his sister Hillitie, and their nephew Wouter in Schenectady, and wrote extensively about them in his journal. By that time, Ackes was a successful fur trader, farmer, and tavern keeper in his mid-forties, with a growing family. Hillitie was a member of the Dutch Reformed Church, married to a Dutchman, and actively encouraging her fellow Mohawks to be baptized in and join the church. Their nephew Wouter, a young man in his early twenties, struggled to fit into either Dutch or Mohawk society.

Hillitie Van Slyke described some of her Mohawk relatives as very anti-Dutch, and her family stories show some significant frictions between the two groups. In Dankaert's account, Hillitie vividly described verbal abuse she had received from Dutchmen, who mocked her religious aspirations and her ethnic background. She was called a pig, or a "sow converted," and was directed to go to the nearest tavern "for swill" when she ventured to criticize Dutchmen for their lewd behavior, probably in front of her small children.[11]

Ackes Van Slyke was a hardworking farmer who plowed his own land and supported his nephew Wouter (probably the son of his late brother Martin) along with his own large family. Dutch neighbors accused Ackes of stifling Wouter's ambitions, by having his nephew work for him as a fur trapper and by speaking only Mohawk with him—not teaching him Dutch—and for resisting Wouter's wish to depart with Dankaerts and join his Dutch religious sect. But a modern-day reader might find Ackes well justified in his actions.

He is quoted as telling Dankaerts: "Well, gentlemen, I understand Wouter is going to Holland with you. . . . What trade would you teach him?" Dankaerts replied, "Whatever God wished." "And if he should be taken by the Turks," Ackes asked, "Who would be his security, who would redeem him?" The answer—"God gives no security and makes no agreement"—was not what most guardians of a young adult would want to hear. To his credit, Ackes did not give up Wouter easily.[12] Wouter himself expressed a deep sense of frustration at being caught between his Mohawk village and Dutch culture: "I am like a man who has three knives," he said, "but has lost one he has most need of, or is the most serviceable or necessary, and without which the others are of little use."[13] Dankaerts describes Wouter as a full-blooded Mohawk unable to speak Dutch, but still hoping strongly to join Dutch society. Indeed, Wouter discussed leaving with Dankaerts and his companion to join their Labadist sect, but he never connected with them at the end of their journey. Wouter also disappears from the local records at that time. He may have gotten lost or died on a journey to rendezvous with Dankaerts in Boston for a voyage back to Holland. Speaking no English or Dutch, Wouter would have had trouble getting into Boston, which by law banned Native people from the city.[14] At the end of his journal, Dankaerts simply shrugs off Wouter's disappearance, writing "we must offer up our poor Indian to the pleasure of the Lord."[15]

Local records in Albany and Schenectady show that by the late 1680s, Hillitie Van Slyke was working as a translator for one of the Dutch ministers, assisting him in baptisms and in new church memberships for Mohawk children and adults. One early record shows a young woman named Moeset, baptized at age twenty with a group of other Mohawk young people on April 13, 1696. She was clearly joining on her own terms, as revealed in the minister's notes, which say that she kept her original name at baptism, instead of taking a new biblical name—something that had never happened in that church for any Native person.[16]

Moeset appears again in the church records just eight months later, on December 27, 1696—this time for the baptism of her newborn son. The child, named Johannes, is listed as "illegitimate" on the margin of the page, "the father a Christian" (i.e., European) whose name is not given. Sponsoring the baby was Hillitie herself, clearly acting to support the mother and child, despite the unfortunate circumstances. One suspects that Hillitie may have arranged for Moeset's April baptism before her pregnancy would be obvious to the minister, and they may have hoped there would be a wedding before the child arrived.

A few years later, that marriage did take place—Moeset Tassama and John Harris were wed in Albany on May 3, 1701, at 3:00 in the afternoon, by an alderman—not by the minister. Then they are back in the church records again just a month later, on June 29, 1701, for the baptism of their first daughter, Lisbeth. This time, the sponsors of the child include one of Albany's civic leaders from a leading Dutch family—Philip Schuyler. Moeset was clearly fighting, and finally winning, a battle for respect and equal treatment. The couple went on to have three more children—Thomas, Jacob, and Francyntje, all baptized in the Albany church, all with prominent Dutch sponsors including Schuylers and Van Rensselaers. Moeset had defied social restrictions and managed to gain acceptance in Dutch society. Her Mohawk-Dutch marriage and family was one of very few recorded in the Albany church books.[17]

Despite the Difficulties . . .

Barriers to full acceptance in the Dutch church and society, rough treatment by Dutch traders, land-use disputes, and double standards in general all caused tensions between the Mohawks and the Dutch. Nevertheless, the two groups remained allies and partners. Later in the century, French raiders attacked and burned the village of Schenectady, late on a winter night in 1690, killing scores and taking many captives. Local Mohawks immediately set out on a rescue mission and managed to save many of the captives before their retreating captors reached Montreal. The Mohawks also held several traditional Condolence Ceremonies to draw the Dutch survivors back to Schenectady and rebuild the town.[18] The Mohawks helped defend the rebuilt Schenectady stockade, placing their longhouses within its walls. In that recovery era, the Mohawks also attended and became members of the rebuilt Schenectady church in large numbers.

Five years after it was burned, Schenectady was largely rebuilt. A 1695 map, drawn by a visiting British minister, John Miller, shows the rebuilt fort, with houses, barns, pens for livestock, and two large longhouses inside the walls, housing Mohawk defenders (figure 5.2). This map appears often in local history books of the Mohawk Valley, showing the Schenectady fort on the left below. An accompanying map by Miller, held in the British Library, also shows another fort standing on the river flats—a large Native fort with five large longhouses, shown on the right below.

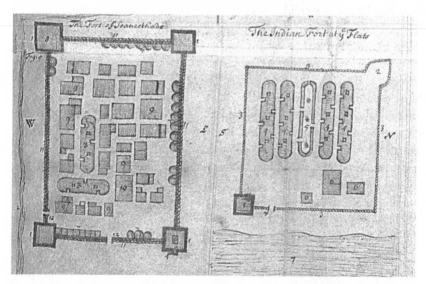

Figure 5.2. 1695 maps of (left) the Schenectady fort and (right) a Native fort containing five large longhouses that once stood on the river flats (courtesy of the British Library/GRANGER).

Just as the Schenectady fort contained longhouses for its Native defenders, the Native fort also contained a blockhouse and several guardhouses for use by their allied soldiers. After the 1690 burning of Schenectady, many Mohawk villages had been burned by the French in the winter of 1693, so their mutual defensive arrangements in 1695 were well considered.

Schenectady Reformed Church Baptisms

The Schenectady Dutch Church records show a growing congregation of Europeans and Mohawks at the end of the seventeenth century. This typical page from May 1700 lists twelve baptisms from a mix of local families (figures 5.3a and 5.3b). It also reflects the social hierarchies of the day.

Eight girls and four boys were baptized in Schenectady that day in May 1700. The order of the baptisms in the records, presumably the order in which they were performed, seems to reflect the parents' social status—a leading European family comes first (the Glens), followed by mixed-race couples (Van Slykes, Borsbooms, Stevens, and Philipsen), and ending with three Mohawk couples and their children. There are no racial or social divisions among the sponsors (the godparents), however. Hillitie Van Slyke appears as sponsor for her twin grandnieces, Helena and Feytja, born to her niece Grietje and her Dutch husband, Harmon Vedder; Mary Groot, who had French and Dutch parents, sponsors a Mohawk girl named Mary, probably named for her; and Dutchman Adam Vrooman sponsors Dina, daughter of the Mohawk woman Lea and her English husband John Stevens. Moeset (Maset) Tassama appears, too, as sole sponsor for Lowisa, daughter of Mohawk chief Onekaheriako and his wife Lowisa.

Diplomacy and Relations with Other Nations

When the Dutch ceded New Netherland to Britain in the 1670s, the Mohawks extended their alliance to the British as did most of the local Dutch population. Mohawks also allied with, took in, and protected other groups—Mohicans in Schaghticoke, New York; Palatine German immigrants in Schoharie; Lenape at Kookoose (present-day Deposit, New York); and Tuscaroras from Carolina, who became the sixth Haudenosaunee nation around 1720. Alliances also grew through marriage and adoption.

Hendrick Peters Theyanoguin was a Mohawk Bear Clan leader born to a Mohawk mother, Kanastatsie, and a Mahican father, Peter; Nicholas

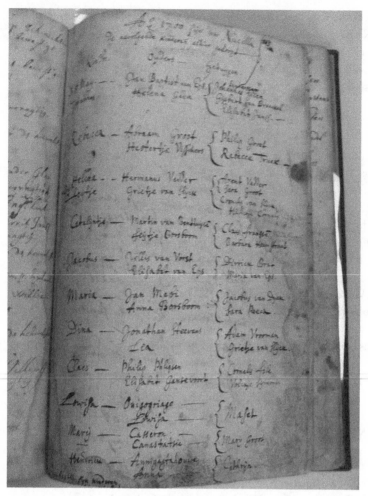

Figure 5.3a. May 5, 1700 list of baptisms at the Schenectady Dutch Reformed Church.

Etowaucum (Mohican) was married to a Mohawk Turtle Clanmother; Molly Brant was a Mohawk who became the partner of the British leader Sir William Johnson. Another British official who knew the Haudenosaunee well, and wrote about them extensively, Cadwallader Colden, described their common practice of adoption, which applied to both individuals and groups: "The Five Nations have such absolute Notions of Liberty that they allow of no Kind of Superiority of one over another, and banish all Servitude from their Territories. They never make any prisoner a slave, but it is customary among

Children	Parents	Sponsors
Johannes	Jan Baptist Van Eps Helena Glen	Johannes Sanderse Glen
		Gysbert Van Braackel
		Elisabeth Janse
Rebecca	Abraam Groot	Philip Groot
	Hestertie Visschers	Rebecca Truex
Helena & Feytie twailings (twins)	Harmanus Vedder	Arent Vedder, Sara Groot
	Grietje Van Slyck	Cornelis Van Slyck
		Hillitie Cornelis
Catalyntie	Martin Van Benthuiyse	Class Franze Vande Borgart
	Feytie Borsboom	Barbara Heemstraat
Jacobus	Jellis Van Vorst	Derrick Brat
	Elysebet Van Eps	Maria Van Eps
Maria	Jan Mebie	Jacobs Van Dyck
	Anna Borsboom	Sara Peek
Dina	Jonathan Stevens	Adam Vrooman
	Lea	Grietje Van Slyck
Claes	Philip Philipsen	Cornelis Fisk
	Elizabeth Gansevoort	Volckie Symonse
Lowisa	Onigogriage	Maset
	Lowisa	
Mary	Casseron	Mary Groot
	Canastatsie	
Hendrick	Annigagtahouwe	Cathryn
	Anna	

Figure 5.3b. Transcription of figure 3a.

them to make a Compliment of Naturalization into the Five Nations."[19] Haudenosaunee population numbers fell precipitously in the seventeenth century, due to epidemic diseases and warfare with the French and their allies. The Mohawks, as the easternmost Haudenosaunee nation, suffered perhaps the worst losses as they were exposed first and probably the most to those decimating forces. To compensate and recover from their losses, Mohawks relied on a traditional practice of absorbing and adopting outsiders into their society. Individuals, families, and larger groups were assimilated and given new identities, often replacing Mohawk people who had been lost, taking the same names and roles in their predecessors' families and clans. When a new identity was taken, the old one was not to be spoken of again.

Some Dutch captives taken from Schenectady to Canada after the French raid in 1690 were adopted into Mohawk families living in Canada. One young man, taken captive at age twelve, was Laurens Claese van der Volge. He lived with his adopted family for ten years and intended to stay with them. He made a brief visit back to Schenectady as a young man in 1700, speaking and clad as a Mohawk, with his hair braided. According to a family story, while he was sleeping one of his sisters cut off his hair with scissors; he felt disgraced and unable to return to his Mohawk family until his hair grew back. While waiting, his life took another path, and he ended up staying in the Dutch village. Van der Volge went on to serve as a leading Mohawk-Dutch interpreter in the Mohawk Valley, and he translated several books from Dutch into the Mohawk language (figure 5.4).[20]

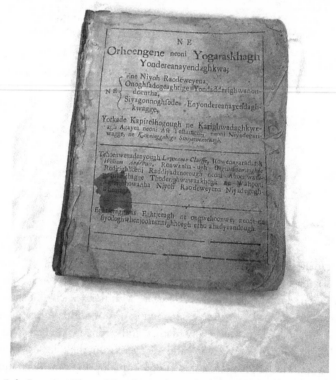

Figure 5.4. Laurens Claese Van der Volge's Mohawk translation of the Book of Prayer, 1710.

Adoptions of other Native peoples were equally common. One prominent family naturalized from another Native nation was that of Chief Shenendoah, who was among many Susquehannock people adopted by the Haudenosaunee in the early 1700s. Adopted as equals and taking on new names and identities, some rose to positions of leadership; among their descendants are members of many Haudenosaunee families today, some still bearing Shenendoah's name. They include political, spiritual, and cultural leaders, such as the late Leon Shenendoah, a leader in the Haudenosaunee Grand Council, and the world-renowned singer Joanne Shenendoah.

By contrast, Susquehannocks who remained in Pennsylvania, outside the protection of the Six Nations, suffered a tragic fate. During Pontiac's War in 1763, a band of Susquehannocks who were living peacefully alongside their white neighbors in Lancaster, Pennsylvania, far from the fighting, were set upon by a white mob, beaten and hacked to death in the county workhouse where they had been taken for protection. Their attackers were known, and even published a feeble defense of their actions, but they were never charged in a crime that was clearly a racial mass murder.[21]

Mohawk Diplomacy in War and Peace

As allies, the Dutch relied on the Mohawks to negotiate for them with other Indigenous nations. In some cases, Mohawks helped resolve conflicts that the Dutch had instigated themselves. The Dutch supported Mohawk diplomatic ventures in return.

In 1643, Dutch governor Willem Kieft led attacks on Lenape villages in southern New Netherland, touching off a war that could have wiped out the Dutch colony. Mohawk leaders were called to help negotiate a peace, which took effect later that year. The Mohawks provided similar assistance when the Esopus people attacked the Dutch town of Wiltwyck (later Kingston) in the years following.

On August 13, 1658, a group of fifteen Mohawk leaders asked the Dutch court at Fort Orange for assistance—they needed someone who spoke French to accompany them on a mission to Quebec, to exchange prisoners and extend a shaky peace with France. When the court hesitated at first, the Mohawk leaders reminded the Dutch of their help in resolving the 1643 conflict known as Kieft's War, according to the court minutes: "Whereupon the said Maquas explained that at the time of the war with the Indians they had gone down to the Manhatans and done their best to bring about peace and that it was our duty to do the same in such circumstances for them, promising in the future to do their best between us and other Indians."[22]

The Dutch court then put out a call for volunteers, and a Dutch army officer, Hendrick Martensen, who spoke French and Mohawk, agreed to be part of the Mohawk delegation. Thus began an intensive diplomatic mission that was well documented in Quebec, in an account published in the *Jesuit Relations* for the year 1658. At their Quebec meeting, the Mohawk leader Tekarihoken spoke at length with the French governor (called Onnontio in Mohawk), laying out his goals and exchanging gifts in long and precise negotiations aimed to improve their relations: "We are seven allied nations. . . . Withdraw not from our alliance. All our allies have deputed me to come and get thy opinion. . . . Otsindiakon, namely, the Captain of New Holland, is my companion in this Embassy. . . . I appoint my country of Anniege as the place of the council, at which I will gather all our nations. Onnontio and myself, during the five years in which we have had peace, have held each other by the arm."[23]

Tekarihoken made sixteen points in his speech to the French governor, each illustrated and conveyed with the presentation of a wampum belt. His seventh and eighth points were a request for the French to enter into a formal alliance with the Haudenosaunee, the Dutch, the Hurons, and Mahicans, followed by a belt affirming his own authority to make this request on behalf the Haudenosaunee and their allies. Tekarihoken seems to have made his ninth point with a presentation of the Two Row Wampum Belt itself. Describing the belt's design and offering it to the French leader, he said this: "Again, I put the river in order; we and our children will hereafter be able to navigate it in peace."[24]

In reply, the French governor gave the Mohawks gifts to support their peace mission, and he offered a long-term peace on French terms: asking the Mohawks to leave their homelands and move to Quebec, to live under French leadership. This proposal was not accepted at the meeting, but further peace negotiations were agreed to.[25]

The 1658 diplomatic mission ended with a partial exchange of prisoners and the dispatch of a French priest to accompany the Mohawks back to their villages for further negotiations. The peace that they sought with France did not endure, but the Mohawks' mission to Quebec was a well-executed, remarkable interlude in an otherwise war-torn era.

Diplomats to Europe, 1710

Perhaps the most famous diplomatic venture by Mohawks was a later journey to London in 1710, undertaken by four leaders who traveled with the

Dutch mayor of Albany, Peter Schuyler, to meet British Queen Anne. Their mission was to strengthen their alliance, and obtain forts and reinforcements against the French. Three Mohawks—Hendrick Teionihokarawa, Brant Sakwankwarakton, and Johannes Onekaheriako—traveled with Nicholas Etowaucum, the Mohican leader (figure 5.5). Their negotiations with the queen were successful, resulting in a new fortification, Fort Hunter, and a new chapel that were built by the British the following year in the Mohawk village of Tionondéroga, just west of Schenectady.

Figure 5.5. The Four Kings—Mohawk leaders and a Mohican ally. Mezzotint by Bernard Lens (courtesy of the Albany Institute of History and Art).

Schenectady Dutch Reformed Church— new Mohawk members.

In 1701, a number of Mohawk couples became members of the Schenectady Dutch Reformed Church. The following page, in the original Dutch, shows the new members, including three of the four leaders who went to London in 1710, listed together with their wives (figure 5.6).

Mohawk-British Alliance and Aftermath

After resisting the French together for 150 years, the Mohawks and their allies defeated them for the last time in 1763. The British took control of French Canada, and together with them the Mohawks enjoyed a brief era

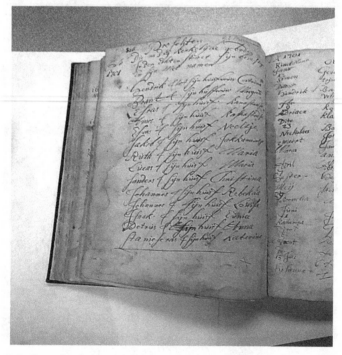

Figure 5.6. Record of new Mohawk members joining the Schenectady Dutch Reformed Church, 1701.

of peace. But increasing settlement pressures and the end of the fur trade led to large land sales, many fraudulent. The Mohawk leaders Hendrick, Joseph Brant, and Molly Brant kept a close alliance with Britain through Sir William Johnson, but the cost was a vast loss of land—most remaining Mohawk territory was opened for European settlement under Johnson's 1768 Fort Stanwix Treaty.

The American Revolution led to further displacements, and to conflicts within the Haudenosaunee Confederacy itself. Loyalists, rebels, and neutrals all suffered from civil war and dislocation. After the war, the Paris Peace Treaty of 1783 made no provision to protect Haudenosaunee lands or rights in New York. The new national and state governments aggressively sought to acquire those remaining lands, and the final Mohawk rights to their New York lands were taken in 1797. Most Mohawks moved to Canada or the border area, forming several new communities there—Six Nations and Tyendinaga in Ontario—and expanding the Akwesasne community on the border of New York, Ontario, and Quebec.[26]

The nineteenth and early twentieth centuries saw many efforts by the United States and Canada to force the surviving Mohawk communities to assimilate into European society, including the introduction of elected councils to replace the traditional leadership. Mohawk oral tradition includes many family stories of dislocation from that era, including the widespread seizure of children for reeducation in residential schools, where many lost their language and were taught to hate their culture. The first and most notorious of these schools was the Carlisle Indian Industrial School in Carlisle, Pennsylvania.

Paul Bero, one of its many Mohawk residents, later told his family stories about the brutal conditions there, which he tried to flee multiple times. He was sent back each time until he finally ran in harsh winter weather in January 1907, escaping by walking hundreds of miles over the mountains, all the way home to far northern New York. Another Mohawk at Carlisle at that time, Louis Chubb, remembered being sent out to work for local Pennsylvania farmers. While farmed-out all day for little pay, he was tormented by one boss in particular who mocked his powerlessness, boasting: "We got the money, we got the power, and sh_t on John Brown," which was essentially a way of saying: "I'm your master now, and you're my slave." The last residential schools finally closed in the 1960s, and many survivors, their families, and whole communities have struggled to recover from the trauma of them ever since.[27]

Mohawks Return to the Valley

After two hundred years, the Kanien'keha:ka people fulfilled a long-held prophecy and moved back to New York's Mohawk Valley in 1993, when the Kanatsiohareke Mohawk Community, near Fonda, New York, was founded by Bear Clan elder Sakokwenionkwas (Tom Porter) and many others. Kanatsiohareke (a modern Mohawk spelling of Canajoharie, meaning "place of the pot that washes itself") is a community dedicated to preserving the Mohawk language and culture, restored to their original homelands. Standing on the site of original Mohawk villages dating back centuries, the community serves as a center for Haudenosaunee cultural revival. Eight contemporary Mohawk reserves and communities are strong and growing today, and Kanatsiohareke is a common ground for all Mohawks and their allies to gather and reconnect with traditional ways. Kanatsiohareke recognizes and follows the Two Row Treaty as a model for relations with its European neighbors.

The Two Row Treaty Renewal Journey, 2013

In July and August 2013, hundreds of Haudenosaunee, other Native peoples, and allies took part in a canoe voyage across New York State, along the Mohawk and Hudson Rivers, in recognition of the Two Row Wampum Treaty (figure 5.7). The journey ended with official meetings of recognition at the United Nations (UN) in New York City, and later in the Netherlands (figure 5.8).

At the UN meeting, in a conference for Indigenous People's Day, UN member-state representatives described successful programs to return land to the control and protection of their Indigenous populations in Central and South America. North American Indigenous leaders discussed similar goals, based on the sovereignty promised them in the Two Row Wampum Treaty and subsequent treaties, most since broken by the United States and Canada (figure 5.9). The UN Secretary for Human Rights outlined a new UN policy to address treaty violations as human rights violations, and to help enforce treaties like the Two Row in the future. Paul Sena, chair of the UN Permanent Forum on Indigenous Issues, also discussed the UN Declaration on the Rights of Indigenous Peoples, which affirms the need to respect and promote the rights of Indigenous peoples regarding treaties, agreements, and other arrangements with UN member states.[28]

Figure 5.7. Haudenosaunee paddlers carrying a copy of the Two Row Wampum Treaty down the Mohawk River, welcomed at Kanatsiohareke by Sakokwenionkwas Tom Porter in July. 2013.

Figure 5.8. Netherlands consul general Rob DeVos smokes a pipe with Haudenosaunee leaders and allies in honor of the Two Row Wampum Treaty, New York City, 2013 (photo courtesy of Charlotte Logan).

Figure 5.9. Onondaga leader Oren Lyons describes the Two Row Wampum Treaty to the United Nations Secretary-General and member-state representatives at the UN, August 2013.

Recognition of the Two Row Treaty in the Netherlands

In September 2013, Mohawk and Onondaga elders were invited to Holland for events recognizing the Two Row Wampum Treaty. They traveled using their Haudenosaunee passports, as citizens of sovereign nations based on the treaty. In a ceremony at The Hague, Turtle Clan Faithkeeper Oren Lyons spelled out the treaty's significance:

> The Dutch were the first to come to our territories and request a trade agreement. Our leaders observed that you were not going home any time soon. They suggested that rather than just a trade agreement, we should establish a relationship. This resulted in the Guswenta (the Two Row Wampum treaty). You in your ship and we in our canoe flowing side by side down the river of life in Peace, Friendship, for as long as the sun rises in the east and sets in the west, as long as the waters flow downhill, and as long as the grass grows green. This is the grandfather of all subsequent treaties in North America.[29]

Figure 5.10. Mohawk language class, Kanatsiohareke, February 2012 (photo courtesy of Sherry Zwetsloot).

MOHAWK LANGUAGE REVIVAL AT KANATSIOHAREKE

As part of its mission to preserve the Mohawk language and culture, Kanatsiohareke holds language classes every year. The class shown in the following photo, with students at all levels, was held in February 2012 (figure 5.10). As is typical, the students included residents of Kanatsiohareke, other Mohawk communities, and local people of European descent. The instructors, seated left to right in the first row, are Bonnie Maracle, Mina Beauvais, and Nikki Auten.

Haudenosaunee Communities Today

Haudenosaunee territories today are spread throughout the US and Canada, with some as far west as Wisconsin and Oklahoma. Of the eight Mohawk communities, Kanatsiohareke is the only one located in the original homelands along the Mohawk River, where it serves as a common gathering place and cultural center for people from the other communities (figure 5.11).

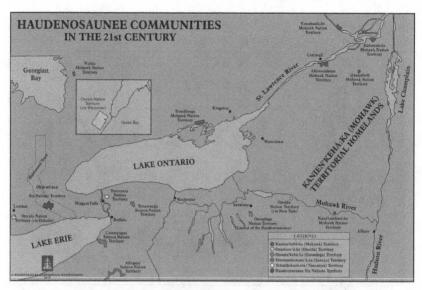

Figure 5.11. Map of current Haudenosaunee communities in the twenty-first century (photo courtesy of Kanien'kehá:ka Onkwawén:na Raotitióhkwa Language and Cultural Center).

Kanatsiohareke, and the ongoing Mohawk and Haudenosaunee cultural revival today, are fundamentally built upon the equal sovereignty agreement that was made between Native peoples and the Dutch in seventeenth-century New Netherland. Despite colonial practices that did not always live up to the Two Row Wampum Treaty's ideals, then and since, that agreement on equal sovereignty has been preserved within the Haudenosaunee communities, and is now making itself felt for the Mohawks, for other Native peoples, and for settler societies in the wider world today.

Acknowledgments

I would like to acknowledge and thank Kay Olan, Mohawk educator and storyteller, and Tom Porter, Mohawk Bear Clan spiritual leader, for their generous contributions and encouragement; Laura Lee, Schenectady historian and archivist, for access to the original records of the First Reformed Church of Schenectady; Jan Longboat, Mohawk elder and counselor; Oren Lyons,

Onondaga Turtle Clan Faithkeeper; and Doug George and John Fadden, Mohawk scholars and historians, for their invaluable insights and assistance. I would also like to acknowledge and thank my family relatives who were part of this story and helped shape Mohawk and Dutch relations—my eighth great-grandfather Hendrick Martensen (Otsindiakon), great-aunt Moeset Tassama, and cousins Ackes and Hillitie Van Slyke—niawen'ko:wa, tewatate:ken.

Notes

1. Jeremy Green, Six Nations Polytechnic Institute, electronic message to the author, May 5, 2017.

2. Carl Masthay, editor, Johan Schmick's *Mahican Dictionary, 1755* (Philadelphia: American Philosophical Society, 1991), 94. (Sample text with English translation: "Pajachquenaxo machqua—For a long time I have seen no bears.").

3. Edmund O'Callaghan, ed., *Documents Relative to the Colonial History of the State of New York* (Albany: Weed, Parsons, 1887), vol. 2, 712–713; vol. 3, 483–485, 774–775; vol. 4, 51. The 1691 text in vol. 3, 775, includes an account of the first encounter of Dutch traders by the Haudenosaunee and the alliance they made: "We have been informed by our forefathers, that in former times a ship appeared here in this country, which was a source of great Admiration to us . . . in that ship were Christians and among the rest one Jacques, with whom we made a Covenant of Friendship . . . in which covenant it was agreed that whoever should hurt or prejudice, that one should be guilty of injuring all, all of us being comprehended in one common league."

In 1967, L. G. Van Loon published a document purporting to be the text of that original covenant or treaty. For more on that document, see Charles Gehring, William Starna, and William Fenton, "The Tawagonshi Treaty of 1613: The Final Chapter," in *New York History Journal* (1987), and Robert Venables, "An Analysis of the 1613 Tawagonshi Treaty," Onondaga Nation, 2012.

4. Reuben Thwaits, ed., *Jesuit Relations Vol 44, 1656–1658* (Cleveland: Burrows, 1894), 123.

5. Hubert de Leeuw and Timothy Paulson, *Coming to Terms with Early New Netherland–New York History: 1610–1614* (Albany: New Netherland Company, 2013), 11, 50–51.

6. A. J. F. Van Laer, trans. and ed., *Van Rensselaer Bowier Manuscripts* (Albany: State University of New York Press, 1908), 302–304.

7. A. J. F. Van Laer, trans. and ed., *Minutes of the Court of Fort Orange and Beverwyk* (Albany: State University of New York Press, 1920), vol. 1, 242–243; vol. 2, 215, 219.

8. Thomas E. Burke Jr., *Mohawk Frontier—The Dutch Community of Schenectady, 1661—1710* (Albany: State University of New York Press, 1991), 26–29.

9. Konwaia'tanonhnha Eba Norton, oral Mohawk language translation of local place names, at Kanatsiohareke, NY, July 2010.

10. Jonathan Pearson, *History of the Schenectady Patent in Dutch and English Times* (Albany: Munsell, 1883), 20–21.

11. Jasper Dankaerts, *Journal of a Voyage to New York, 1679–80* (New York: Redex, 1867), 305.

12. Dankaerts, *Journal,* 309.

13. Dankaerts, *Journal,* 312.

14. *Records of the Colony of the Massachusetts Bay in New England, 1675.* Accessed January 20, 2018. http://www.mass.gov/courts/docs/lawlib/docs/1675bostonindians.pdf.

15. Dankaerts, *Journal,* 379.

16. Barbara Sivertsen, *Turtles, Wolves and Bears: A Mohawk Family History* (Bowie, MD: Heritage Books, 2006), 38.

17. David Payne-Joyce, ed., *Records of the Reformed Dutch Church of Albany, NY 1683–1809.* Accessed January 19, 2018. http://aleph0.clarku.edu/~djoyce/gen/albany/refchurch.html.

18. Cadwallader Colden, *History of the Five Nations of Canada* (London, 1747), 116–118.

19. Colden, *History,* 10.

20. Susan Staffa, *Schenectady Genesis* (Fleischmanns, NY: Purple Mountain Press, 2004), 100.

21. Henry Eshleman, *Annals of the Susquehannocks* (Lancaster, PA: Eshleman, 1909), 375–386.

22. Charles T. Gehring, trans. and ed., *Fort Orange Court Minutes, 1652–1660* (Syracuse: Syracuse University Press, 1988), 400–401.

23. Thwaits, *Jesuit Relations Vol. 44,* 122–125.

24. Thwaits, *Jesuit Relations Vol. 44,* 123.

25. Thwaits, *Jesuit Relations Vol. 44,* 129.

26. Kayeneseh Paul Williams, "The Mohawk Valley: Yesterday, Today and Tomorrow" in *Kanatsiohareke—Traditional Mohawk Indians Return to Their Ancestral Homeland,* by Tom Porter (Kanatsiohareke Mohawk Community, NY: 2006), 9.

27. Porter, *Kanatsiohareke,* 89.

28. "Indigenous Canoe Trip Celebrating 400-Year-Old Peace Treaty Culminates with UN Event," United Nations News Centre, August 9, 2013. Accessed January 20, 2018. http://www.un.org/apps/news/story.asp?NewsID=45601#.

29. Oren Lyons, in Kenneth Deer, "Haudenosaunee Renew Two Row Wampum with Dutch," *Indian Country Today,* October 6, 2013. Accessed January 20, 2018. http://indiancountrymedianetwork.com/news/opinions/haudenosaunee-renew-two-row-wampum-with-dutch/.

6.

The Dutch and the Wiechquaeskeck

Shifting Alliances in the Seventeenth Century

MARSHALL JOSEPH BECKER

Individual Dutch colonists often had extremely good relationships with nearby Native communities in the 1620s, especially with the Manhatan band of the Wiechquaeskeck tribe who continued to live on the island during parts of the year. After the massacre known as "Kieft's War," in 1642–43, the survivors of the Manhatan band, and others of the Wiechquaeskeck, relocated to the Raritan Valley and into the adjacent highlands of present-day New Jersey. Most of the other Wiechquaeskeck remained in their home territory (present-day Westchester County, New York and southwestern Connecticut) until the late 1700s. Over time, some Wiechquaeskeck, some Waping, and many Esopus of southeastern New Jersey also relocated into the Jersey "highlands," forming an amalgamated group called "Munsee." Other Wiechquaeskeck merged with colonists.

When Hendrick Hudson made his famous 1609 trip up the river that came to bear his name, the Indians living on Manhattan Island and along the next twenty miles on the eastern bank were members of the Wiech- quaeskeck tribe (figure 6.1). The earliest history of the Dutch colony on Manhattan Island is little known, but after the Dutch West India Company formed in 1621 the extent of Dutch life and trading activities, from Maine down to the Delaware Bay, became better recorded. The many Native tribes in this extensive region, and how each of them interacted with the traders and colonists from Holland and England, are only now being worked out.

The early European arrivals in this region carried important commodities valued by all of the Native populations. Woolen cloth was the most important of the high demand goods, followed by metals, and then a long list of other products that were produced in early industrial Europe. The Native product in greatest demand by European trading groups was pelts. Skins and hair were actually the by-products left over from animals that were hunted for meat by the several tribes living along the Hudson River[1] as well as those interior tribes such as the Five Nations Iroquois.

Figure 6.1. The Wiechquaeskeck territory and its rivers, being on the east side of the Hudson River and including Manhattan Island; map by Julie B. Wiest (courtesy of the Archaeological Society of Connecticut).

In 1624 Cornelius Jacobsen May, the first director of the Dutch West India Company's New Netherland expedition, arrived at the mouth of the North (later Hudson) River with a number of colonists to establish an outpost. The earliest settlers encamped on Nut Island (now Governor's Island) in the same year that an outpost was built on Burlington Island in the South (later Delaware) River. Both were focused on the pelt trade.

The following director, Willem Verhulst, also lasted only a year in this position. Verhulst identified the important elders of the different tribal groups, enabling him to develop elaborate and mutually productive interchanges. Most significantly, Verhulst understood the relatively small sizes of these Native populations and their complex tribal antagonisms. He determined that he could safely relocate his people from Nut Island to the extreme southern tip of the much larger Manhattan Island, where there were ample lands to develop an agrarian support system while expanding the regional pelt trade. Verhulst erected Fort New Amsterdam to defend against European competitors, not the local Natives. It was not until 1653 that a "wall" (wooden palisade) was set up to separate the early farmsteads from the large expanse of forested Manhattan that continued to be foraged by their Native neighbors. The wall, now the path of Wall Street in southern Manhattan, also kept free-ranging livestock within a defined area. There was never any instance of this palisade serving as a defensive construction against the neighboring Wiechquaeskeck or any other Native group.

The extensive records of early Dutch business dealings with the Natives are far from ideal ethnographic records. On the other hand, there are some impressive early documents relating to various Native people throughout the Northeast, and more emerge every year. Among the primary tasks are to use these records to identify each specific tribe and to understand their locations in aboriginal times. This often can be done by using those documents and deeds that relate to the earliest purchases of land from the Indians.[2]

The Wiechquaeskeck

The Wiechquaeskeck tribe occupied the entire eastern side of the lower Hudson River Valley, from Annsville Creek and its major feeder, Peekskill Hollow Creek (just above present-day Peekskill, New York) on the north, all the way south to the tip of Manhattan Island. Their lands also extended from the Hudson River on the west to the present New York–Connecticut border area and possibly beyond.[3] The neighbors of the Wiechquaeskeck to the north were the Waping (Wappinger). To the east, we know of the

Paugussett in present-day Connecticut, but are less certain about other tribes along the eastern margins of Wiechquaeskeck territory.[4]

My studies lead me to conclude that the Wiechquaeskeck were a hunting and gathering tribe. All of the evidence now available supports this interpretation, although other nearby tribes, with fewer fish and other resources, may have used other systems. The Wiechquaeskeck tribe was composed of a number of separate and independent bands (extended families), each with as few as a dozen members, but rarely more than fifty. Based on the signatures on land transactions, average band size is estimated to have been about twenty-five to thirty members. I propose that they were primarily hunting and gathering, perhaps as late as the late 1600s, although tribes further up the river and certainly in the interior may have been progressively more dependent on supplementary maize production. This would conform to optimal foraging theory models in which the Wiechquaeskeck had the resources of the ocean as well as the Hudson River available to them.[5] Each band used a distinct portion of the entire tribal area, and drew its name from that specific location. If a band decided to sell part or all of its land, all the adult males, and sometimes one or more adult females, signed the agreement of sale (deed).[6]

The problem with delineating the Wiechquaeskeck tribe, and identifying the Manhatan band within it, is that there is no known deed of sale for Manhattan Island. There may never have been one. All we have to indicate that any purchase was made of Manhattan Island is an indirect reference to the transaction found within a document penned by P. Schagen. Schagen's inventory of various goods brought to Amsterdam on the *Arms of Amsterdam* is mostly a count of animal pelts and reference to timber, dated November 5, 1626. This document now is in the Rijksarchief in The Hague. A translation of a portion of this brief record follows:

High and Mighty Lords,

Yesterday the ship the Arms of Amsterdam arrived here. It sailed from New Netherland out of the River Mauritius on the 23d of September. They report that our people are in good spirit and live in peace. The women also have borne some children there. They have purchased the Island Manhattes from the Indians for the value of 60 guilders. It is 11,000 morgens in size [about 22,000 acres].[7]

The "purchase" must have been made before the sailing of the *Arms of Amsterdam* from North America, on September 23, 1626, suggesting that the "purchaser" was Peter Minuit, director general of the colony from May 1626 until 1631. The brief two lines in Schagen's text name no vendors or purchaser, and no terms of sale are given. The agreement may have been a type of "handshake deal" such as are implied in many of the very earliest colonial arrangements made with Native people. The probable date of this transaction, during the fall of 1626, is similar to many well-documented sales; they usually take place in late summer or fall, before the vendors went out for winter hunting.

The format of early land transactions in the Northeast rapidly evolved into carefully worded indentures, providing the names and signatures (or marks) of all the vendors, as well as all Native and colonial witnesses plus the metes and bounds of the lands purchased. These deeds of sale, carefully preserved as legal documents, allow us to delineate the entire territory of many tribes, such as the Lenape in southeastern Pennsylvania and the Lenopi of southern New Jersey. At present we have only a small sample of Wiechquaeskeck deeds, many of which may have been lost in a fire at the archives in Albany.[8]

A Theory of Boundaries and Buffers

A century ago, several diligent historians made efforts to reconstruct the complex Native past in the area of and around Manhattan, based on their readings of some of these early records.[9] Their efforts revealed the abundant land sale records, but they made no effort to use these documents to understand cultural borders.

The modern idea that "boundaries" between properties, territories, and nations can be traced as linear dividers has a history of only a few hundred years. Our perception of modern property "lines" derives from ideas that emerged with the development of modern surveying instruments and the desire of modern states to delineate their frontiers.[10] Archaeologists and ethnohistorians now recognize that tribal areas are often surrounded by extensive buffer zones.[11] Buffer zones, also called "shared-resource-areas" or "no-man's lands," are neutral territories that lie between and separate the home territories of two or more tribes. The resources of a buffer zone can be extracted by the peoples living adjacent to it, but the land itself is not claimed nor occupied on a long-term basis. By the 1630s, Five Nations' policies of extermination, Mahican raiding of the Waping (Wappinger, and so forth) and others, and colonial expansion all combined to displace some or all members of a number of tribes.[12] Displacement led individuals or entire bands within a targeted tribe to pursue one of several possible options to maintain most aspects of traditional culture:

1. Remain scattered within their home territory, but avoid summer aggregation.

2. Maintain cultural ways, but relocate into buffer lands.

3. Join Praying Indian communities, and be subject to significant cultural change.

All of above options were used by some members of almost every tribe.

Pelt Trade and Opportunities on the Raritan

The Wiechquaeskeck, as the Native tribe operating around the center of the new Dutch colony, had minimal access to pelts from outside their own territory. Wiechquaeskeck hunters had to travel great distances to enter lands where they could compete for game and peltry with all the tribes in the area. Following a series of attacks by the Mahican in the 1630s,[13] possibly stimulated by competition for peltry, some Wiechquaeskeck relocated from their homeland into the Raritan River Valley, immediately west of lower Manhattan (figure 6.2).[14]

After 1630 one of the more prominent Native place names found in the New Netherland documents is "Raretangh," a locative referring to the place of residence of a Native group whose original identity was Wiechquaeskeck. By occupying the Raritan buffer strip, some members of this tribe took control of the game in that area and also gained influence over traders bringing peltry down the river from hunting grounds in the Jersey highlands. Whether these relocators were all the members of a single band, as was the case with one Lenopi band that moved into Pennsylvania in 1733, or a collection of families from among the many bands of the tribe, is not known.

The buffer zones that separated relatively stable traditional cultures before 1600 soon became new homelands for displaced members of various

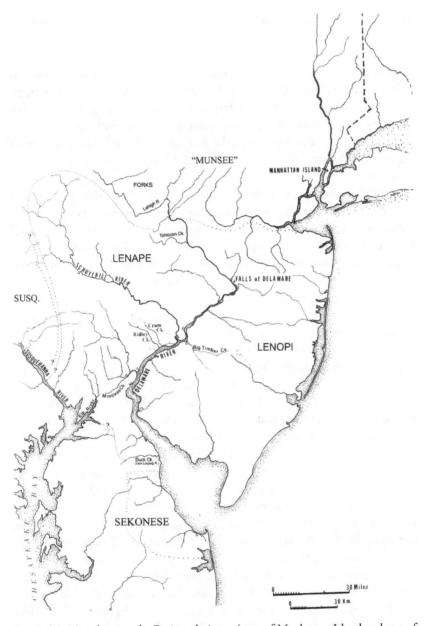

Figure 6.2. Map showing the Raritan drainage (west of Manhattan Island and east of "Munsee") and identifying the locations of the tribes south of the Wiechquaeskeck region of the lower Hudson River Valley (courtesy of the Archaeological Society of Connecticut).

tribes.[15] In the Northeast, these buffers rapidly diminished in size as fewer locations were available to groups stressed by colonial settlement.[16]

The Raritan River basin itself is an enormously rich area, with anadromous fish available for much of the year[17] and easy access to the western uplands via the tributaries forming the river. The entire valley of the Raritan River, which flows into Raritan Bay immediately south of Staten Island, long served as a buffer zone between the Lenopi of southern New Jersey and the Esopus.[18] The territory of the Esopus is difficult to determine from the colonial documents, but in 1677 a full description was provided to the governor.[19]

At the eastern end of the Raritan River, where it enters Raritan Bay and the Atlantic, is a large island that provided an extension of the Raritan Valley buffer zone. In effect, the Raritan resource area included Staten Island. Even the Dutch colonists recognized that the Raritan Valley long had served as a passageway for Native movement between the New Jersey highlands in the west to Manhattan Island and the area surrounding Staten Island.[20] My suggestion that Staten Island was part of this buffer strip is based on the many land sale documents for this island alone, each of which has some peculiar aspects suggesting that they were not valid "deeds."

These many "sales" of the island, or sometimes just parts of it, were opportunistic dealings that generated what I term "buffer deeds,"[21] a land sale document drawn up between Native "vendor/s" and colonial purchaser/s that purports to sell a tract of land lying within a buffer zone, or land that, as a shared resource area, had no legitimate claimants. These dealings were not quite Native "scams," but rather represent a generic category of sales involving lands not owned by the Native vendors nor by any other Natives.

Barbara Graymont comments on her interesting finding that Staten Island, either in its entirety or as parcels, had been sold and resold several times by various individuals over a period of several decades, not only to the Dutch and later to the English, but to a wide range of purchasers. She does not recognize that the various "vendors" of Staten Island were not all from the same tribe, an observation confirming that no one tribe actually owned it.[22] The seven distinct known "sales" of Staten Island during the 1600s and other related documents have been reviewed by the author.[23] One of these "deeds" to Staten Island, in which it is identified as "Eghquaons," provides a particularly egregious example of nearby people selling land they did not own. The text of this document lists fourteen "vendors," all Esopus from the area immediately to the north, each with their Esopus band name.[24] The famous Oratam signs as one of the seven witnesses. While sales of Native lands to several different European buyers were not uncommon, legitimate vendors were always from the owner tribe.

The Wiechquaeskeck as Described after 1632

While we know that Mohawk aggression against the Mahican was increasing during this period, and that the Mahican (or possibly the Mohawk) were regularly attacking the Waping, there do not appear to have been any significant effects on Dutch life and trade in Manhattan. While the competition among Native tribes called the "Beaver Wars" are commonly believed to have begun in the 1640s, the evidence indicates that various tribes of the Five Nations were raiding their neighbors long before that decade.[25]

In 1632 Sebastiaen Jansen Krol, who had been commander at the important Dutch outpost of Fort Orange (now Albany), was assigned to Fort New Netherland to succeed Peter Minuit as its director. Krol acted as director until a replacement was sent to take over. This was achieved within the year and Krol returned to his command at Fort Orange.[26] Unfortunately, the records of Krol and even of his successor, Wouter van Twiller, regarding their dealings with local Indians are minimally represented among the known documents.

As noted above, the Wiechquaeskeck who took up residence in the Raritan Valley, becoming known as "Raritan," arrived in the early 1630s and became part of Native realignments involved with the pelt trade. In addition to the emergence of this "Raritan" group, a group of Waping had shifted their area of operation into the Pompton Plains region of northern New Jersey and became known as the "Pompton." An important source of the deeds and other information allowing us to reconstruct buffer zones and to identify the Native groups who moved into them has been published in the form of the colonial records of the various states. The three tribal entities of New Jersey, as they were known in the 1750s, are delineated in New Jersey treaties of 1756 and 1758 in which the elders of three tribes are identified: the Lenopi, the Esopus, and the newly formed "Pompton."

By 1634 the immigrant Wiechquaeskeck were recognized by the Dutch as a population newly arrived along the Raritan River. The good relations maintained by Wouter van Twiller with the several local tribes during his term as director of New Netherland (1633–38) are evident in those few records that we have. These positive interactions were even recognized in the comic history of New York written by Washington Irving, who refers to the "golden reign" of Wouter van Twiller.[27] His skills in this office are best understood by contrasting the historical record for his tenure and leadership with that of his successor, Willem Kieft, who took over in 1638. The last part of van Twiller's tenure saw the emergence of Native hostilities among the English settlements to the east of New Amsterdam. The outbreak of the Pequot War, 1636–37, and the extensive disruptions within various English villages, had no immediate and obvious effects on the Dutch and their Native neighbors. That part of the Dutch realm that is now Connecticut had been increasingly invaded by growing numbers of English trading stations and colonial outposts. The disruptive effects of the Pequot War and tribal realignments during this period had social and political effects that are still playing out in Connecticut.[28]

Enter Willem Kieft: A Decade of Conflict

Willem Kieft's appointment as the fifth director general of New Netherland (1638–47) immediately followed the end of the Pequot-English War. His governance was a disaster for Dutch-Native relations in the area of Manhattan Island. General living conditions for the Dutch and other colonists under Kieft's command deteriorated and he was ultimately fired, concluding a decade of disastrous leadership. His problems with the citizenry and many conflicts with neighboring tribes have led the editors of the New Netherland Institute to state that "his governmental career was probably the stormiest of all" of the company's governors.[29] Kieft came to the directorship with his own set of personal problems, exacerbated by his paranoid concern for his Wiechquaeskeck neighbors taking in refugees displaced from other tribes, perhaps even some Pequot.

The effects of southern New England's Pequot War should be considered as a backdrop to Kieft's paranoia. The Pequot War led many Native families to relocate into the buffer zone at the western margins of Wiechquaeskeck territory. After 1639, increasing English settlement all along the Connecticut coast led more Natives to relocate into the buffer zones surrounding the Dutch. Displaced Pequot may have joined the Wiechquaeskeck, who themselves were adjusting to the effects of increasing numbers of Dutch farmsteads. However, there is good reason to believe that hostile activities on the part of some Natives in the years following 1639 were a direct consequence of nasty actions taken by Willem Kieft, whom Irving parodied with the name "William the Testy."[30] This epithet greatly understates the many disasters of Kieft's tenure.

The problems that the Wiechquaeskeck faced ten years earlier, when Mahican raids from the north led many Wiechquaeskeck to relocate to the Raritan Valley, were now exaggerated by the Pequot War and colonial population pressures along all of their territory.[31] The arrival in New Jersey of at least some of these Wiechquaeskeck immigrants from various parts of their home area was the result of events that also were stressful to those colonists who were trying to establish farmsteads in unprotected areas beyond Fort Amsterdam.

Dutch immigrant farmers generally had excellent relations with their Native neighbors. Peltry, wild game, and a wide array of goods and services were exchanged through informal trade between these groups.[32] However, Kieft perceived the Native population, and his fellow colonists, as hostile and problematical to his authority. His continuing mismanagement led Cornelis Melyn to seek release from his contract to purchase rights to Staten Island from the West India Company, citing the farmers that had been killed there by Natives as a result of Kieft's antagonistic policies. A release was granted to him on August 15, 1640.[33]

The earliest record specifically stating that Indians were resident in the Raritan Valley before 1634 appears in the Council minutes that were drafted on July 16, 1640. This important document, suggesting that these same Natives there had initiated trade some years before 1634, reads as follows:

> Whereas the Indians, living in the Raretangh have before now shown themselves very hostile, even to the shedding of our blood, notwithstanding a treaty of peace made with them Ao [Anno] 1634, under which we continued to trade with them by sending a sloop there every spring and whereas in the spring of this year 1640 they have tried to capture our sloop, manned by only three men . . . [who escaped] . . . with the loss of a canoe only then they came to Staten Island and killed the Company's pigs and plundered "the negro's house."[34]

Of interest here is the mention of a sloop trading somewhere along the Raritan River every spring since 1634, and reference to a treaty made in 1634, for which no record now is known.[35] Such a treaty would suggest that in 1640 or 1641, only a few years after Kieft's arrival, the company leadership had created a conflict situation with the Natives along the Raritan for which the cause is not evident. There is a discrepancy between a supposed Native invitation to trade and the Natives' supposed actions, after several peaceful years of interactions, when a possible trading party arrived, possibly during the winter of 1640–41. Part of this encounter is confirmed in a Dutch deposition of July 17, 1647 signed by Harman M. Bogardus, Harman Downer, and Cors Pitersen: "we, being in the Company's service in the year 1640, were at the request of the savages, called the Raritans, sent by the Honorable Director Kieft to trade. Arrived at the usual trading place in the yacht 'de Vreede' [The Peace] these Raritans in stead of showing the customary friendship . . . began to scoff" and otherwise treated the traders very badly, threatening them and stealing the ship's canoe.[36] (The 1640 date cited in the 1647 deposition above is clarified by David De Vries in his *Korte Historiael.*[37]) On July 4, 1641 a resolution that was presented at the Council meeting of New Amsterdam was passed, indicating the colonists' perception of the situation:

> The Indians of the Raretangh are daily exhibiting more and more hostility, notwithstanding they have solicited of us peace, which we consented to, permitting him [an emissary?] to depart unmolested on his promise to advise us within twelve days of the resolution of his chief, which has not been done; and whereas the aforesaid Indians, who experienced every friendship at our hands, have in the meantime on the plantation of Mr. de Vries and Davit Pietersen . . . partners, situated on Staten Island, murdered four tobacco planters and set fire to the dwelling and tobacco house, . . . we have therefore considered it most expedient and advisable to induce the Indians, our allies here-about, to take up arms, in order to cut off stray parties who must pass through their territory, so they can not reach our farms and plantations . . . and in order to encourage them the more, we have promised them ten fathoms of seawan for each head, and if they succeed in capturing any of the Indians who have most barbarously murdered our people on Staten Island we have promised them 20 fathoms of seawan for each head.[38]

Presumably any Natives brought in alive could be sold as slaves. These various accounts suggest that trade on the Raritan River had been going on for some years, but Natives coming to trade at Manhattan Island may have been from among any of a number of tribes in this area, including the Wiechquaeskecks who were related to the people identified as the Raritans.

The specifics of the Native-Dutch interaction on the Raritan in 1639 and just after are few but de Vries provides an important source for these data, and for other data about the various Native groups around Fort Amsterdam. De Vries was strongly opposed to the Indian policies of Governor Willem Kieft. I believe the documents speak for themselves, and here offer portions of several relevant passages in chronological order as taken from Graymont's translated versions of De Vries's *Korte Historiael.*[39]

De Vries's memoirs first mention the people called "Raritanghe" on July 16, 1639, but his recall may refer to the above-noted event that took place between 1639 and July 1641. De Vries states that after these events Cornelis van Thienhoven led one hundred armed men to seek out "the Raritanghe, a nation of savages who live where a little stream runs up about five leagues behind Staten Island" to punish them for "killing my swine and those of the Company, which a negro watched."[40] De Vries states that the troopers, acting on their own, killed several Natives and took the brother of the chief as hostage. Details of the attack followed De Vries's presentation of information regarding their location in what now is northern New Jersey. These Native peoples living in northern New Jersey who were attacked by these colonists in 1639 or 1640 probably were a group of relocated Wiechquaeskeck, but possibly they were marauding traders from another tribe. That attack on the Natives living on the Raritan led to reprisals prior to July 4, 1641, during which the Indians killed four of De Vries's men and burned his buildings.[41]

De Vries's *Korte Historiael* offers no further comment on what he believed was a 1639 expedition, but recounts Indian information from his own journey up the Hudson three months later, on October 20, 1639, "to Tapaen in order to trade for maize or Indian corn." When De Vries arrived at Tapaen he found the Company sloop there and the representatives trying to extract a "contribution" from the Indians.[42] Once again De Vries is reporting on the less charming behaviors of Kieft, acting as the representative of the Dutch West India Company.

Since the entire Raritan River Valley had once formed a traditional buffer zone,[43] unclaimed by any specific tribe, any group of Natives moving into it and establishing foraging patterns there might be seen by previous users as a potential threat to free trade along that waterway. The Raritan River formed a significant conduit to the New Jersey highlands and the vast area beyond to the west that was part of the Five Nations foraging (and pelt collecting) region. Despite the 1640 Dutch resolution to attack these Natives, nothing more now is known about the "Indians living in the *Raretangh*" until a year later. On July 4, 1641 the record indicates that the "Indians of the Raretangh are daily exhibiting more and more hostility" including burning the Staten Island house and tobacco facilities belonging to the partners "*Mr. de Vries and Davit Pietersen.*"[44] Not surprisingly an "Ordnance offering a reward for the heads of Raritan Indians passed" that same day.[45]

The Native attack was confirmed by De Vries who reported, on September 1, 1641, that "my men on Staten Island were killed by the Indians and the Raritans told an Indian . . . that we [Dutch] might now come to fight them [the unnamed Indians] on account [of the power of] our men."[46] De Vries appears to indicate that the Indians along the Raritan as well as another group, perhaps one or more bands of Lenopi, or perhaps Esopus, were involved (see below). Another report, dated September 12, 1641, confirms that a short time before "some of our people on *Staten-Island* have been murdered by the savages."[47]

The Dutch erected "a small redoubt" (fortification) on Staten Island in response, presumably near the location of that attack, which led Kieft to orchestrate the massacre of two groups of Native American peoples—Esopus and Wiechquaeskeck (and their guests?), who were long-time residents on Manhattan Island or who had recently taken refuge at Corlaer's Hook, in the immediate area to the east of the fort in New Amsterdam. These dreadful events took place during one night in the winter of 1642–43. Two documents dated February 25, 1643 describe these bizarre attacks.[48] These massacres, called by some "Kieft's War," victimized groups who usually are described in the literature either as Esopus or "Wappingers" (Waping). Now we can specifically identify one of these groups as Esopus (in New Jersey) and the other as the Wiechquaeskeck still living on Manhattan Island, among whom may have been some Waping or other refugees.[49] These needless assaults on Indian allies were generally seen by the Dutch colonists as part of Kieft's failings, yet it took another four years for the Company to get rid of him.

In general, the marauding Natives had remained respectful of De Vries and his staff; people who had maintained good relations with these tribes throughout these difficult times. The Wiechquaeskeck bands along the Hudson suffered from Mahican raiding, were stressed by the Pequot War, and then by the continuing power struggles between the Dutch and the westward expanding English colonies taking over the Connecticut River trade.[50] During the Pequot War some Wiechquaeskeck sought neutral ground on which to relocate. Their problem was where to go.

The option of joining New England Native groups living in what are identified as "praying towns" was not yet available. The Puritans began to develop these communities during the 1640s, and after that date some Wiechquaeskeck *may* have joined them. This strategy involved the Natives placing themselves under the limited protection of the colonists, but it required a significant alteration in their foraging lifestyle. These Native religious communities also tended to include members of several different tribes, thereby accelerating culture change and a drift toward European economic and linguistic systems. These praying towns also tended to be on the fringe of colonial settlement, possibly in former buffer zones where they were subject to raiding by the Iroquois Confederacy as well as from colonists seeking "open" land along the frontier.

Following the firing of Willem Kieft in 1647, Peter Stuyvesant was appointed as director general of New Netherland and served in that capacity until the English conquest in 1664.[51] Stuyvesant's seventeen-year tenure is marked by a number of positive events, but toward the end of Dutch rule the various tribes under Dutch hegemony became increasingly hostile.[52] The reasons for this dynamic are left to others to investigate. Here the primary concern is with what the records reveal about those Wiechquaeskeck then living along the Raritan River and their main bands still in their traditional range north and east of Manhattan.

A Wiechquaeskeck origin for this group along the Raritan is specifically indicated in July 1649 when one of the chiefs assembled for a meeting, named Pennekeck and identified as a chief from "achter Col," is quoted as follows: "*Pennekeck* said the tribe called *Raritanoos*, formerly living at *Wiquaeskeck* had no chief, therefore he spoke for them."[53] That is, they had no elder among them and deferred to Pennekeck, identified in this document as their neighbor, to represent them.

The Wiechquaeskeck: 1650

The earliest document that most clearly offers the name and location of the Wiechquaeskeck was issued by the Dutch in 1650. Review of this Dutch description allows us to reconsider what now can be interpreted from the earliest records of these people and their interactions with the Dutch. On March 4, 1650 the Dutch West India Company, in an effort to stimulate settlement of towns and farms throughout New Netherland, issued a listing of several areas within their jurisdiction that might be particularly attractive to prospective farmers.[54] The merits of each location were described, including mention of the presence or absence of Native inhabitants. The New Netherland colonists' recent confrontations with several of the tribes in and around the sparse settlements that constituted this Dutch colonial venture may have remained as fresh memories, but they were not mentioned in this brochure.

This 1650 brochure was issued just after the end of the Thirty Years' War (1618–48), during which period life in the Netherlands was far worse than life in New Amsterdam.[55] The West India Company brochure was intended to dispel thoughts regarding the dangers of life in America. The various "areas" listed in this 1650 document provide us with some clues to the locations inhabited by various groups of Natives, allowing us to infer the tribal units to which each belonged. The area identified as "Wiequaeskeck, on the North river, five leagues above New Amsterdam, is very good and suitable land for agriculture, very extensive maize land on which the Indians have planted—proceeding from the shore and inland 'tis flat and mostly level, well watered by small streams and running springs. It lies between the East and North Rivers and is situate between a rivulet of Sintinck and Armonck1."[56]

O'Callaghan's editorial note "1," appearing after the word "Armonck," reads as follows: "This tract extends across the county of Westchester, from Sing Sing [Ossining?] to the Byram river."[57] O'Callaghan identified the Byram River as the eastern border of Wiechquaeskeck land from a 1685 sale of land at Ossin Sing that was signed by only six vendors, all identified as "Sintsink," one of the Wiechquaeskeck bands.[58] The original of this 1685 document now is unknown, and nothing similar to it appears in Graymont.[59] Graymont does provide a transcription of a deed from the Wiechquaeskeck to what is now the eastern half of Westchester County, also giving its eastern margin at Seweyruc (Byram River).[60]

Today the Byram River forms the most southerly section of the New York–Connecticut state line. The actual presence in 1650 of Indians at the location called "*Wiequaeskeck*" is not emphasized in the Dutch brochure of March 4, 1650, suggesting a benign presence of any Natives who happened to be resident there. These few probably were there only during a portion of the year. An absence of Natives is made more explicit at the end of the second entry in this 1650 Dutch account, which also provides a description of the nearby area of the Raritan Valley, into which some Wiechquaeskeck had been relocating since around 1630:

> The district inhabited by a nation called Raritangs, is situate on a fresh water river that flows through the centre of the low

land which the Indians cultivated. This vacant territory lies between two high mountains, fair distant out one from the other. It is the handsomest and pleasantest country that man can behold, and furnished the Indians with abundance of maize, beans, pumpkins, and other fruits. This district was abandoned by the natives for two reasons; the first and principal is that finding themselves unable to resist the Southern Indians, they migrated further inland; the second, because this country was flooded every spring like Rensalaer's colonie, frequently spoiling and destroying their supplies of maize which were stored in holes underground.

Throughout this valley pass large numbers of all sorts of tribes, on their way north or east; this land is therefore not only adapted for raising grain and rearing all description of cattle, but also very convenient for trade with the Indians.[61]

In 1652, twelve years after he had abandoned his hopes for developing a plantation on Staten Island, Melyn renewed his efforts to develop his land. He returned having "strengthened himself upon Staten Island, where he resides with 117 or 118 Raritans and Southern Indians [Lenopi] each armed with a musket, to defend him against the Director" of the West India Company.[62] Following his horrid experience with Kieft, Melyn may have been wary of the recently appointed Stuyvesant. These "Raritans" in 1652 were mostly if not all Wiechquaeskeck who relocated to this area, but who maintained close contacts with the other bands of their tribe. The people here identified as "Southern Indians" were from one or more of the northern bands of Lenopi, then living in the area immediately south of the Raritan buffer zone.[63]

Unfortunately, we do not know how many of these 117 or 118 adult males represented each tribe but I infer that more than half were Raritan-Wiechquaeskeck. If at least sixty or seventy adult male "Raritans" were employed by Melyn, their population at that time would have been at least 240, if not more. A population of this size would have represented quite a substantial group.

The Esopus Wars

Although Governor Stuyvesant tried to maintain good relations with his Native neighbors, continued aggression and terrible treatment of local Indians by individual colonists led the Esopus to conduct raids on Dutch farmsteads in two brief "wars." Dutch policies managed to maintain an uneasy peace with their Long Island Native allies, with relatively few "incidences" of open conflict on that front. Only the Esopus undertook direct confrontation with the Dutch, who were receiving little actual support from home or from their Native allies.

While we cannot know the extent to which the Wiechquaeskeck and their Native neighbors were aware of the status of New Netherland on the world stage, by 1659 the Esopus recognized the fragile state of Dutch power, leading these Natives to be less tolerant of Dutch abuses.[64] A period of stress began on September 20, 1659 with a series of clashes between the Dutch and the Esopus who then were resident in present-day New Jersey. This "First Esopus War" continued until a truce was signed on July 15, 1660. On March 6, 1660, "*Achkhongh*, one of the chiefs councilors of *Wiechquaskeck*" (emphasis in original) was consulted by the Dutch along with the Wiechquaeskeck elder named Sauwenar and others.[65] On May 18, 1660, prior to signing a treaty with the Esopus, the Dutch arranged peace treaties with many of their other neighbors to limit the spread of the Esopus war. At this May 18 gathering "Sauwenaro" of the Wiechquaeskeck is listed third among the elders representing the various tribes, demonstrating that the Wiechquaeskeck elders continued to maintain tribal integrity as well as relatively peaceful interactions with the Dutch.

Relations between the Dutch and the Esopus, however, continued to be strained. In early June 1663 the "Second Esopus War" erupted. This time the Dutch called in their traditional Mohawk allies as mercenaries to do the dirty work, and all hostilities ended by September 1663. On December 28, 1663 an armistice was arranged between the Dutch and the Esopus, and afterwards various Dutch treaties or alliances were arranged, involving Oratamy of Hackingkesack and others.[66] Almost immediately, in March 1664, a delegation of Esopus and Waping traveled to Westchester to plot with the English.[67] Most likely the Wiechquaeskeck also were involved as the meeting location was within their territory.

In the spring of 1664, while the Esopus and others were conspiring with the English, the Dutch drew up Articles of Peace for the region that were signed on May 15, 1664, formally ending the conflict with the Esopus and their allies. The names of fourteen Natives appear on this treaty but, unfortunately for my effort to delineate individual tribes, many of the signatories are identified only with their band name, leaving their tribal affiliations to be worked out.[68] Six Esopus are listed by name on this 1664 peace document. The name of many of these same Natives that appear on the treaty of May 18, 1660 also appear here. The May 15, 1664 treaty reads in part as follows:

> Council Chamber at Fort Amsterdam.
> Seweckenamo, Onagkotin, Powsawagh, chiefs of the Esopus,
> T'Sees-Sagh-Gauw, chief of the Wappinghs,
> Meeght Sewakes, chief of Kightewangh,
> Ses-Segh-Hout, chief of Rewechnongh or Haverstraw,
> Sauwenarocque, chief of Wiechquaskeck,
> Oratamy, chief of Hackingkesacky and Tappaen, [is he an Esopus?]
> Matteno, chief of the Staten-Island and Nyack savages,"
>   [originally from Long Island?]
> Siejpekenouw, brother of Tapusagh, chief of the Marsepingh
>   etcetera [Long Island] with about twenty other savages of
>   that tribe.

The Dutch asked why other "chiefs of the Esopus had not come, to wit: *Keercep, Pamyrawech,* and *Niskahewan.*"[69] One was said to be too old to attend, and the others were excused. Seweckenamo acted as speaker for the assembled Indians. He was particularly pleased that this treaty included groups that extended as far north as Maquas (Mohawk) territory, and that the Marsepingh of Long Island also were included. This document was signed only by Seweckenamo and Powsawagh, both Esopus, on behalf of all the Natives, as well as by a Dutch contingent along with their translator. The last signature is that of Maerhinnie Tuwee, whose role is not identified. In what appears to be a separate signing, "Otatam" (Oratamy) and Matteno sign, along with "Hans alias Pieweserenves" who is not among the Natives listed in the document. Probably unknown to the Dutch at the time of the signing of this treaty (May 16, 1664) was that three months earlier, in March 1664, Charles II had presented this entire region to his brother, the Duke of York, in advance of an English invasion.

The significant English fleet arrived in the fall, and on September 8, 1664 the Dutch surrendered the actual colony. Richard Nicolls, as the military governor under the Duke of York, then took command of Fort Amsterdam and renamed it Fort James of the colony of New York. Nicholls immediately began negotiation with the local Indians and by 1665 he had reached an agreement concerning this new group of Christians: the English (figure 6.3).

Figure 6.3. "An Agreement made between Richard Nicolls Esq.ʳ Governoʳ under his Royall Highnesse the Duke of Yorke and the [Indians] and Poeple [sic] called the Sopes Indyans" (Wikipedia, public domain).

Nicolls served admirably until Francis Lovelace took charge in 1668. Lovelace served until 1673 when the Third Anglo-Dutch War in this area resulted in the reconquest of New York. The peace treaty of 1674 returned New Amsterdam to the English, but allowed the Dutch to retain Dutch Guiana, now known as Surinam. That colonial outpost was deemed to be more profitable at that time.[70]

Tribes of New Jersey

Only two aboriginal tribes are consistently identified as resident in New Jersey prior to 1630, the Esopus along the Hudson in the north and the Lenopi, commonly identified as "Jerseys" in contemporary documents, south of the Raritan Valley.[71] Both are extensively documented in the New Jersey archives as well as in New York's colonial records.[72] The buffer lands between these two tribes have been roughly delineated.[73] Many early documents suggest that the Hackensack and other groups were separate tribal entities, but further study is needed to identify tribal and band territories. For now, "*Sauwenarocque*, chief of *Wiechquaskeck*" is of primary interest. Several New Jersey scholars had culled the early documents for specific and direct evidence relating to the many named aboriginal individuals and the names of the specific bands to which they belonged.[74] These efforts began with the investigations of William Nelson[75] and were later continued with studies made by Frank H. Stewart[76] and others.

Stewart largely focused his work on the southern part of the state, among the people now identified as Lenopi. Until the 1980s many historians and linguists had conjoined both of the now identified Native tribes of New Jersey into an undefined group of "Indians," commonly using the name "Delaware" to identify them. By the 1980s the term "Lenape" became substituted for "Delaware" for questionable reasons.

The relocation of some Wiechquaeskeck into the Raritan Valley reflected a shift in their residence in hope of making a more successful adaptation to prevailing political and economic conditions. These immigrants to the Raritan buffer zone, then known as "Raritans," and their immigrant neighbors from among the Waping, who became identified as Pomptons, were relocated peoples from not far away. After many decades of residence along the lower Raritan River, both groups moved farther up the Raritan Valley, reflecting continuing changes in the world around them. At some point various families relocated even farther to the west, being invited into the southeast section of Five Nations' buffer territory. This removed the stresses suffered by Iroquoian raiding. The upland region called the Minnisincks extended west to the Delaware River. It attracted the "Raritan" as well as members of the Esopus tribe; all became "Munsee." These extensive buffer lands, surrounding the several tributaries of the Raritan, were sold at later dates by various Natives claiming to be "owners."[77] The boundaries of these tracts have rectilinear borders, very different from the boundaries of traditional Native land holdings, usually waterways (figure 6.4). These rectilinear boundaries reveal that the lands being "sold" were not traditional hunting

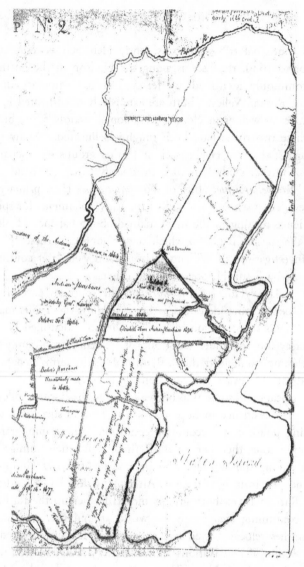

Figure 6.4. Copy of the eastern portion of "Indian Land Sales North of Raritan" from the Philhower Collection, Rutgers University Library Archives (from Becker 2016a, 70, fig. 3). Bolton (1922: map XI, following page 202) published this map (on which is written "Map No. 2") and indicates that it is "Courtesy of the New York Historical Society." Bolton suggests that it was "Drawn probably about 1750 as an exhibit in the Elizabeth boundary dispute." Note that none of the many "sales" of land on Staten Island are indicated, suggesting that the compiler may have recognized the questionable nature of those transactions (cf. Becker 1998).

territories. Graymont provides excellent transcriptions of a number of these sales of land in the Raritan Valley, often for tracts on both sides of the river, with straight line boundaries similar to those used by colonials. For example, Cornelius Longfield bought a tract on the south side of the Raritan on November 29, 1683, for which the metes and bounds in no way resemble traditional Native land holdings as revealed by countless Native deeds.[78]

The "vendors" in these many land sales of the Raritan Valley and uplands were opportunistic individuals taking advantage of the colonists' desire, or possibly need, for Native land sales documents bearing Native signatures. Since the lands of the Raritan Valley had been a shared buffer zone, the vendors "claimed" them simply by stating that they owned that area. At least they were willing to "sell" the land in question, without making reference to possible owners.[79] Lands previously used as shared resource areas had no "owners" to dispute these sales. A few of the same Natives selling tracts of buffer lands in New Jersey were later involved in specious land sales in Pennsylvania, in effect becoming specialists in the process of selling buffer lands.[80]

At a council held at Fort James on Manhattan Island, April 9, 1684, with "The Indians of Minisinck being present" there was a discussion of the purchase from the Natives of all the lands between the Hudson and the Delaware River.[81] These lands included the Raritan Valley and Raritan River headwaters plus a narrow zone along the upper Delaware River. The most interesting feature of this document is the absence of all Native names, confirming that the Indians present at this Council in 1684 had moved west from their earlier areas of activity along the Hudson, suggesting Esopus, Wiechquaeskeck, and others. Not until June 6, 1695 does a deed support the idea that the Wiechquaeskeck who had immigrated to the Raritan had "assumed" a legal claim to the valley.[82]

Edward Manning Ruttenber recognized that several groups among "the *Minsis* or Esopus living upon the east branch of the Delaware River" had relocated from their Hudson Valley homeland.[83] All Natives resident at the Minisinck, the New Jersey highlands, regardless of their cultural origins or affiliation (e.g., the Wiechquaeskeck), were identified as "Munsee."[84] Graymont's efforts to decode the cultural origins of the peoples in the Minisink area, all of them identified as "Munsee," were unsuccessful.[85]

However, a complaint by a sachem called Ankerap in 1722 identifies him as an Esopus.[86] Some people identified as "Esopus" continue to appear in the Pennsylvania colony literature into the 1770s, but gradually that aboriginal identification disappears. The large numbers of Native land sales and other documents enable us to reconstruct life histories for some individuals and extended families, and to suggest some cultural boundaries.[87]

The Waping Known as the Pompton
in New Jersey: 1695 and After

The homeland of the Waping lay along the eastern side of the Hudson River, north of Wiechquaeskeck territory, extending up to the middle of present Columbia County: an area to the south of the Mahican range as it existed after 1630.[88] In addition to describing a June 6, 1695 sale of land to Arent Schuyler, Philhower documents Waping participation in two other land agreements in New Jersey that took place fifty years apart.[89]

The earlier of these texts, dated August 13, 1708, is a deed for the Morristown area, twenty-five miles (forty km) due west of Manhattan Island and thirty-five miles (forty-eight km) southwest of the Pompton-Poquaneck area, of which Philhower presents a transcription of only a part of the text.[90] In 1758 the Esopus were represented at an important treaty at Easton in Pennsylvania, at which the Lenopi named Teedyuscung presented himself as "King of the Delaware."[91]

Teedyuscung (1709–63) was a young man of the Toms River band of Lenopi when they relocated into the Forks of Delaware buffer zone in 1733–34.[92] Teedyuscung's rise to "power" led to his false claim that he led ten Native tribes. This created some interesting problems for the New Jersey and Pennsylvania colonial governments.[93] Prior to the treaty of October 1758, Governor Francis Bernard had delegated Teedyuscung to go to the "Indians of Minisink and Pompton" (as the two northern groups in New Jersey were then identified) to invite them to the conference.[94] Bernard's effort to settle any and all land claims in the New Jersey colony caused the Five Nations to assert their hegemony over these various Indian groups, who at that time were all resident in regions under Five Nations aegis, including the Minnisincks and the vast buffer lands along the present New York–Pennsylvania border.

At meetings held on August 7–8, 1758, "John Hudson, the Cayuga" asserted Five Nations' suzerainty over these displaced peoples, stating that "I, who am the Mingoian, am by this belt to inform you, that the Munseys are women, and cannot hold treaties for themselves."[95] His declaration reveals that the people then called "Munsee" were immigrants living on former buffer lands, not their own "property," and thereby under the control of the Five Nations. To affirm this statement, John Hudson presented a belt of white wampum on which there were woven seven "figures of men in black wampum," four of whom he said represented the Five Nations, collectively, and the other three represented the subordinate peoples—the "Munseys" and any others resident in the area in question.[96] In August 1758 "the chief man of the Munseys, is Egohohoun." Land rights for "the *Delaware Indians* [Lenopi], now inhabiting near *Cranbury*, and to the Southward of *Raritan River*"[97] had been already clarified, with the upcoming treaty at Easton aimed at resolving land rights north of the Raritan.

An important document regarding early Waping activities in Morris County, New Jersey,[98] records their presence there some fifty years after the 1695 land sale noted above; as reported in the minutes of the crucial October 1758 Treaty at Easton.[99] This treaty finalized the release of all remaining Native claims to lands in New Jersey while also delineating the Native cultures of New Jersey as they were *at that time*. The people in New Jersey who in 1758 were identified in the documents as the "Wapings or Pumptons" were then considered to be a Native population. They were, however, a group that had relocated into New Jersey and were allied to, or had joined with, the Indigenous people called Esopus—the tribe that had fought two brief wars against the Dutch only a century earlier.

Treaty at Easton in Pennsylvania, October 1758: "All" the Tribes of New Jersey

The Treaty at Easton in October 1758 was a major gathering at which the government of Pennsylvania met with all of their regional Native allies as well as with Sir Francis Bernard, the new governor of New Jersey. Several Native American populations continued to live there in traditional fashion.[100] This marathon "treaty" (meeting), in the midst of the Seven Years' War, began on October 7, as the first participants arrived at Easton.[101] The meeting continued as a public discourse, ending nearly three weeks later, on October 26, 1758. The manuscript proceedings of this important event are preserved in Newark, New Jersey[102] and have been published in *The Minutes of the Provincial Council of Pennsylvania*.[103] The nearly fifty pages of published text from the minutes of this treaty provide a wealth of information concerning the Native American peoples of the region who were allied with the English in 1758.

At Easton, the Pennsylvania government and their colonial neighbors sought a guarantee from the Five Nations Iroquois regarding their amicable intent during this period of conflict. Much of what was discussed related to the attacks of certain "Delaware" on the English settlers, many of whom were illegally intruding into areas reserved by treaty for the Five

Nations and their allies. The marauders were a small group of Lenopi and others, led by Teedyuscung, living along the frontier. The English wished to consolidate their alliance with the Native American peoples with whom they had long interacted, and assure their support in the war against the French and their allies.

The roster of attending Five Nations in 1758, using the standard protocol, lists the most powerful nations at the beginning: Mohawk, Oneida, Onondaga, and so forth, but no Cayuga had yet arrived (see above for John Hudson's presentation on August 7–8, 1758). The list descends to the least powerful of the thirteen tribes attending. Near the bottom are the "landless" groups, or peoples who had sold all of their *traditional* territory and in 1758 were mostly scattered over buffer lands under the suzerainty of the Six Nations. The group third from last are identified as the "Munsies or Minnisinks—[represented by] Egohohowen," then the "Mohickons" and very last listed are the "Wapings or Pumptons," represented by "Nimhaon, Aquaywochta, with Sundry Men, Women and Children."[104] The Waping are noted in the 1758 treaty as having sold their lands in New Jersey along the Hudson, and the "Mohickons" are obviously immigrants.

At this treaty Teedyuscung spoke of the "Waping Tribes, or Goshen Indians,"[105] also as "Wapings or Pumptons" from New Jersey, as being descended from earlier Waping immigrants. The Waping who relocated to northern New Jersey after the 1630s, however, left numerous members of their tribe in their homeland. This "stay at home" population may not have included Daniel Nimham (Young Nimhan), the son of "One Shake" Nimhan. In 1758 most of these Waping were still resident in southeastern New York. "Nimhaon," the first representative of the "Wapings or Pumptons," must be "One Shake" Nimhan (also identified as Nimhan II, who died in 1762), of the famous Nimhan line of Waping from east of the Hudson.[106] Daniel Nimhan (1726–78) was the third in his line identified as a leader of the Waping.[107] The published version of this readily available 1758 treaty has been documented as a reliable transcription.[108]

Discussion

The impressive series *Early American Indian Documents: Treaties and Laws, 1607–1789* (general editor, Alden T. Vaughan) offers an excellent means by which scholars can examine the interactions among tribes and colonial immigrants from Europe. The vast numbers of documents relating to the many Native tribes presented a significant challenge to the many editors who contributed to this effort. The resulting collection is nearly complete for early Pennsylvania[109] but less inclusive in the several volumes for New York, combined with New Jersey, reflecting their political history during and after the Dutch period.[110] Delineating the home range of any Native population using land sale documents remains the best route now available to determining the boundaries of aboriginal land holdings.

The present study began with an effort to confirm Philhower's hypothesis that the aboriginal people called "Pompton" had originated among the Waping, from southeastern New York and western Connecticut. This is evident in the New Jersey Treaty of 1758. Efforts to decode the borders of the Wiechquaeskeck, and their relationship with the Waping, have clarified the process by which these Hudson River Indians became the "Raritan," as well as the "Pompton," in New Jersey. Various political factors after 1630 resulted in the migration of small groups of Wiechquaeskeck and also of Waping into the Raritan Valley.

Graymont's volumes on *Treaties and Laws, 1607–1789* had to confront the extreme complexity of Native politics involving New York's Five Nations Iroquois, plus the estimated fifteen hundred land transfer documents for New Jersey alone.[111] This plethora of information placed an enormous burden on Graymont, who made a heroic selection for publication.[112] Other New York and New Jersey documents are included in B. Fernow's works,[113] including a transcription of the deed (patent) of July 12, 1630 for the area that includes present-day Hoboken, sold by members of the Hackensack band of Esopus.

The complexity of political and military interactions among the Native tribes, amplified by the Dutch opening the pelt trade, was increased by the development of a Native-produced commodity known as "wampum."[114] This important trade product, first produced by Natives living at the margins of the pelt trade, increasingly influenced every aspect of economics throughout the region and into the world trade system.[115]

The tracing of individual biographies and tribal histories requires that we return to the many basic documents to reconstruct this period in history. For many Natives, European trade and colonization provided opportunity and abundance. Many individuals and entire tribes benefited from the new opportunities offered through trade with Europeans.[116] A major question addressed in this study concerns the matter of *where* a group of Natives *could* move if they wished to leave their traditional territorial area. One possible choice for displaced Native communities involved movement into buffer zones.[117]

Frederic Shonnard and W. W. Spooner, in examining the documents for Westchester County where the Wiechquaeskeck lived, made a simple but extremely important observation regarding Native activities following the sale of their lands: "They always remained on the lands after the sale continuing their former habits of life until forced by the steady extension of white settlement to fall back farther into the wilderness."[118]

For all the Native peoples of the Northeast, remaining in place was an option for some parts of the community. Thus, Wiechquaeskeck land sales to Adolphus Philipse and other Dutch had minimal influence on the first generation of vendors. Gradually, the inexorable population increase among the colonists exerted land pressures on the aboriginal Wiechquaeskeck, who were partly dependent on anadromous fish.[119] Their use of fish resources had facilitated the relocation of some to the Raritan Valley, a nearby coastal zone that shared many of the same fish populations seasonally available in their homeland.[120] Individuals and families made their own decisions on how to respond to changing factors. While a substantial number of the Wiechquaeskeck may have relocated to the Raritan Valley ca. 1630, most of the tribe remained in their traditional range. How many Wiechquaeskeck remained behind or shifted into the Connecticut (eastern) portion of their territory, or went elsewhere, we do not know. Unlike Mahican, Waping, and Esopus, I have yet to find any Wiechquaeskeck or Raritan operating within the Pennsylvania colony in the 1700s.

By the 1750s the Wiechquaeskeck in the area that became Westchester County, New York and southwestern Connecticut were no longer an identifiable people.[121] At least some traditionalist Wiechquaeskeck merged into the colonial population, with most of those families settling into marginal situations. Others may have been attracted to the Native praying communities then being established in several New England locations. Still others may have relocated to the upper Housatonic River Valley. Mandell indicates that by 1723 the Housatonic Valley had become an important center for Indian refugees from the Connecticut River Valley to the east,[122] and presumably also from among the several tribes from the west, including at least some of the Wiechquaeskeck. By 1739 Mahican can be documented among the peoples relocated to, or concentrated along, the Housatonic,[123] although Lavin suggests that the Housatonic Valley of western Massachusetts had always been part of the Mahican homeland, with their eastern border located within the Berkshire Mountain range.[124]

Relocations among this Native population may have shifted to the individual level soon after 1750. In the 1790s at least one individual from a New England tribe is known to have married a Lenopi woman and became resident with her in central New Jersey, where their common language was English.[125] Despite these occasional marriages and considerable population movement after 1600, the cultural integrity of the core groups of these tribes remained remarkably intact for quite some time, well into the 1800s in some cases. By the middle 1800s, descendants of the Wiechquaeskeck who were still living in the area that became southwestern Connecticut were no longer identified by that tribal name. By the later 1800s all recall or recognition of their tribal origins had vanished, as did most traces of Native traditions, as some of these people developed into an Indian "ethnic group."

Similarly, those Wiechquaeskeck who had moved into the Raritan Valley, and some Waping then in the Pompton Plains area, may have remained there even after most members of these relocated groups moved farther west into the New Jersey highlands. Groups such as the "Ramapo Mountain" people and others claiming Native ancestry may be admixed, biological descendants of early Native immigrants into northern New Jersey, but among these groups, direct descent from any known tribe has never been documented.[126]

We now need to generate standardized methods of recording and referencing data from land sales and other Native-related documents in order to enable scholars to share their databases more effectively. This might allow us to reconstruct the histories of individual Native Americans and the cultures of which they were members. Native American name searches in the many documents may help us to resolve questions concerning the origins and later movements of tribal groups such as the Wiechquaeskeck, and to learn what became of them within or beyond the lower Hudson River Valley after the 1600s.

Conclusion

The evidence indicates that the Manhattan Indians were but one band of the Wiechquaeskeck tribe. A small number of the Wiechquaeskeck people living at the northern edge of their territory moved to the Raritan region during the decades between 1630 and 1650, responding to attacks by the Mohican. Others took refuge among their kin in the Manhattan band who were still resident on Manhattan Island. The members of that band lived close to the palisade or "wall" near the lower end of Manhattan Island, in the area of Corlaer's Hook and quite close to Fort Amsterdam. Other displaced Wiechquaeskeck had taken refuge in present-day New Jersey among the Esopus, at a location just across the Hudson River from lower Manhattan. They were later joined by other kin from their aboriginal homeland.[127]

Those Wiechquaeskeck resident in the Raritan Valley became identified as "Raritan."

As Raritan they continued to move west along that river valley, foraging along with the Esopus and those Waping who had relocated to the Pompton Plains area and became known as Pompton. Whether the Esopus had joined with the Wiechquaeskeck-Raritan or with the Waping, or both, and if all were in the process of becoming the "Munsee" after the 1650s remains unclear. Ultimately, they all became conflated, by colonists and scholars, with other Delawarean language speaking groups collectively identified as the "Delaware." As generic "Delaware" (Delawarean language speakers), the people identified as Munsee lived within the vast buffer territory utilized as the southern foraging range of the Five Nations Iroquois. Some of these "Munsee" Delawarean speakers later moved to Canada while others traced an irregular journey toward the west, dispersing across North America.[128] How many Wiechquaeskeck were among them remains to be determined.

Acknowledgments

My sincere thanks are due to a number of people who have helped bring this paper into print, including Prof. Tom Arne Midtrød, Ari Samsky, John A. Strong, P. Hite, and Raymond Whritenour. Their insights and generous sharing of information are deeply appreciated. The kind encouragement and considerable aid of Lucianne Lavin in all aspects of this study and her many important insights regarding Native peoples are deeply appreciated. The extremely constructive comments of a very important anonymous reviewer also are very much appreciated.

Academic support for this research at West Chester University has been provided by Prof. Heather Wholey (Chair, Department of Anthropology) and by Prof. Mary Page (Director, University Library). The kind efforts of Stephen Marvin, Walter Cressler, Jennifer O'Leary, and many others at West Chester University in support of this research also are very much appreciated. The ideas presented here, as well as any errors of fact or interpretation, are solely my own responsibility.

Notes

1. In recent decades, finds of maize and other features at precolonial Mahican sites have led scholars to apply the term "horticulturalists" to these people whom

I had long believed were hunters and gatherers. Many scholars now interpret this evidence differently, especially Lucianne Lavin, *Connecticut's Indigenous Peoples: What Archaeology, History, and Oral Traditions Teach Us about Their Communities and Cultures* (New Haven: Yale University Press, 2013); see also Lucianne Lavin et al., "The Goldkrest Site: An Undisturbed, Multi-Component Woodland Site in the Heart of Mahican Territory," *Journal of Middle Atlantic Archaeology* 12 (1996): 113–129; Tonya Largy et al., "Corncobs and Buttercups: Plant Remains from the Goldkrest Site," in *Current Northeast Paleoethnobotany*, ed. John P. Hart, Bulletin 494 (Albany: New York State Museum, 1999), 69–84; esp. James W. Bradley, *Before Albany: An Archaeology of Native-Dutch Relations in the Capital Region, 1600–1664* (Albany: State University of New York, State Education Department, 2007). Recently J. P. Hart et al., using the same reasoning, suggest that the Esopus also had been "horticulturalists": "Maize and Pits: Late Prehistoric Occupations of the Hurley Site in the Esopus Creek Valley, Ulster County, New York," *Archaeology of Eastern North America* 45 (2017): 133–160.

In extensive reviews of the ethnohistoric literature for the Lenape, M. J. Becker demonstrates that traditional limited maize gardening in the lower Delaware Valley was amplified during the period 1640–60 to generate a cash crop that provided access to desired European goods: M. J. Becker, "Lenape Maize Sales to the Swedish Colonists: Cultural Stability during the Early Colonial Period," in *New Sweden in America*, ed. Carol E. Hoffecker et al., 121–136 (Newark: University of Delaware Press, 1995), and M. J. Becker, "Cash Cropping by Lenape Foragers: Preliminary Notes on Native Maize Sales to Swedish Colonists and Cultural Stability during the Early Colonial Period," *Bulletin of the Archaeological Society of New Jersey* 54 (1999): 45–68; see also M. J. Becker, "Lenape ('Delaware') in the Early Colonial Economy: Cultural Interactions and the Slow Processes of Culture Change before 1740," *Northeast Anthropology* 81–82 (2014): 109–129. Descriptions of economics within each Native culture merit greater scrutiny.

2. Each colonizing venture in North America had a different system for securing Native lands; see the important series *Early American Indian Documents: Treaties and Laws, 1607–1789*, 20 vols., general ed., Alden T. Vaughan (Frederick, MD: University Publications of America, 1981–2004). For example, both the earliest Dutch and Swedes along the Delaware River varied considerably in their patterns of negotiating land purchases, usually buying just the amount needed for a fort or plantation; but by the later 1600s land speculation led to huge purchases made from various Native bands. William Penn's policy was to secure title to all the Indian land in his colony, and to clear title from previous purchases made by Swedes and Dutch. The Dutch along the Hudson at first also varied in making purchases of land from the Wiechquaeskeck and others, but later the formats of deeds became more systematic.

3. See Bert Salwen, "Indians of Southern New England and Long Island," in *Connecticut Archaeology: Past, Present, and Future*, ed. Robert E. Dewar, Kenneth L. Feder, and David A. Poirier, Occasional Papers in Anthropology no. 1 (Storrs:

Department of Anthropology, University of Connecticut, 1983). The article includes important material cut from Bert Salwen, "Indians of Southern New England and Long Island," in *Handbook of North American Indians*, vol. 15: Northeast, general ed. B. Trigger (Washington, DC: Smithsonian Institution Press, 1978), 160, as noted by Dena Dincauze in "Bert Salwen's Prehistory: 1962–1983," *Northeast Historical Archaeology* 21–22 (1992–93): 9. For the Waping, the northern neighbors of the Wiechquaeskeck, see Tom Arne Midtrød, *The Memory of All Ancient Customs: Native American Diplomacy in the Colonial Hudson Valley* (Ithaca: Cornell University Press, 2013).

4. Cf. Barbara Graymont, ed., *Early American Indian Documents: Treaties and Laws, 1607–1789*, general ed. Alden T. Vaughan, vol. 7, New York and New Jersey Treaties, 1609–1682 (Frederick, MD: University Publications of America, 1985), 7:438, n40.

5. Since John P. Hart and Bernard Means published on "Maize and Villages" in the Northeast (2002), a great deal of evidence has accrued regarding maize production in this region (see also Lavin, *Connecticut's Indigenous*, 316). However, the evidence from among the Lenape (Becker, "Cash Cropping"; Becker, "Lenape Maize Sales"), plus suggestions regarding optimum foraging theory. Arthur S. Keene, "Biology, Behavior, and Borrowing: A Critical Examination of Optimal Foraging Theory in Archaeology," in *Archaeological Hammer and Theories*, edited by James A. Moore and Arthur S. Keene, 137–155 (New York: Academic Press, 1983), suggests that the Wiechquaeskeck sustained their predominantly hunting and gathering economy into the late 1600s, if not beyond. These data conform with evidence now available for population size. During the 1950s and 1960s ethnographic studies among the Dobe Ju/'Hoansi, then identified as the "Dobe !Kung" (Richard Lee, *The Dobe Ju/'Hoansi*, 3rd ed. [Toronto: Harcourt Brace, 2002]), and other hunting-gathering societies found that individual band size usually ranged between twelve and fifty members, with an average of about twenty-five. The total population for a tribe usually numbered about five hundred. These data are reviewed for the Lenape and found to be supported by the evidence from land sale documents: Marshall Joseph Becker, "Lenape Population at the Time of European Contact: Estimating Native Numbers in the Lower Delaware Valley," in "Symposium on the Demographic History of the Philadelphia Region, 1600–1860," ed. Susan E. Klepp, *Proceedings of the American Philosophical Society* 133, no. 2 (1989). Application of these population data to other hunting-gathering tribes in the region of the Delaware River drainage yield similar results: Marshall Joseph Becker, "The Lenape and Other 'Delawarean' Peoples at the Time of European Contact: Population Estimates Derived from Archaeological and Historical Sources," *Bulletin: Journal of the New York State Archaeological Association* 105 (1993): 16–25. For matters relating to "demographic pressures bearing on hunting and gathering societies, or marginally food producing ones," see Philip E. L. Smith, "Land-use, Settlement Patterns, and Subsistence Agriculture: A Demographic Perspective," in *Man, Settlement, and Urbanism*, ed.

Peter J. Ucko, Ruth Tringham, and G. W. Dimbleby (Cambridge, MA: Schenkman Publishing, 1972), 424.

6. See Timothy H. Ives, "Wangunk Ethnohistory: A Case Study of a Connecticut River Indian Community," unpublished MA thesis in anthropology, College of William and Mary, Williamsburg, Virginia, 2001. Ives's studies of documents relating to the Wangunk suggest a higher rate of female participation in land sales then is known in the Delaware Valley.

7. The P. Schagen document now is widely available, with a picture, transcription, and translation, all of which are available from the impressive website of the New Netherland Institute, https://www.newnetherlandinstitute.org/history-and-heritage/ additional-resources/dutch-treats/peter-schagen-letter/.

8. For Lenape territory, see Donald H. Kent, ed., *Early American Indian Documents, Treaties and Laws, 1607–1789, Volume I: Pennsylvania and Delaware Treaties, 1629–1737*, general ed. Alden T. Vaughan (Washington, DC: University Publications of America, 1979); M. J. Becker, "Anadromous Fish and the Lenape," *Pennsylvania Archaeologist* 76 (2) (2006): 28–40; Becker, "Late Woodland (CA. 1000–1740 CE) Foraging Patterns of the Lenape and Their Neighbors in the Delaware Valley," *Pennsylvania Archaeologist* 80 (1) (2010): 17–31; Becker, "Lenape Culture History: The Transition of 1660 and Its Implications for the Archaeology of the Final Phase of the Late Woodland Period," *Journal of Middle Atlantic Archaeology* 27 (2011): 53–72. For the Lenopi, see Becker, "Mehoxy of the Cohansey Band of South Jersey Indians: His Life as a Reflection of Symbiotic Relations with Colonists in Southern New Jersey and the Lower Counties of Pennsylvania," *Bulletin of the Archaeological Society of New Jersey* 53 (1998): 40–68; Becker, "Mehoxy of the Cohansey Band of Lenopi: A 1684 Document That Offers Clues to the Missing Part of His Biography," *Bulletin of the Archaeological Society of Delaware* 44, n.s. (2012): 1–29. The territory of the Wiechquaeskeck is worked out in Becker, "The Wiechquaeskeck and Waping of Southeastern New York and Southwestern Connecticut: History and Migrations," unpublished manuscript dated 2017, on file at the Becker Archives, West Chester University of Pennsylvania. Legal land "sales" also can be used to identify fraudulent claims made by Natives who sold lands in buffer zones, to which no one had traditional rights of ownership. Situations such as seen on Staten Island, where seven completely different groups step forward to sell the island, reveal that there was no true owner. Other buffer zone lands are sold by individuals or by only two or three men, suggesting that they are not representing the members of a band that owned the land. As more of the Wiechquaeskeck deeds come to light, we will better understand the full extent of their territory and be able to define the buffer lands surrounding their territory.

9. For example, William Nelson, *The Indians of New Jersey: Their Origin and Development (etc.)* (Paterson: Press Printing and Publishing Company, 1894); Reginald Pelham Bolton, "New York City in Indian Possession," *Indian Notes and Monographs* 2 (7) (1920): 223–397; Frank H. Stewart, *Indians of Southern New Jersey*

(Woodbury, NJ: Gloucester County Historical Society, 1932; repr. 1977); Charles A. Philhower, "Indians of the Morris County [NJ] Area," *New Jersey Historical Society, Proceedings* 54 (4) (1936): 249–267. For the use of these records in archaeology, see Foster H. Saville, "A Montauk Cemetery at Easthampton, Long Island," *Indian Notes and Monographs* 2 (3) (1920): 65–102.

10. Hugh Elton, *Frontiers of the Roman Empire* (London: B. T. Batsford, 1996).

11. William Engelbrecht and J. Brice Jamieson. "St. Lawrence Iroquoian Projectile Points: A Regional Perspective," *Archaeology of Eastern North America* 44 (2016): 81–98. See also Jennifer Birch and John P. Hart. "Social Networks and Northern Iroquoian Confederacy Dynamics," *American Antiquity* 83 (1) (2018): 14, fig. 1.

12. Five Nations' collective policies regarding their neighbors are evident in devastating raids against the Mahican, St. Lawrence Iroquoians, Huron, Erie, Susquehannock, and others. See William N. Fenton, *The Great Law and the Longhouse* (Norman: University of Oklahoma Press, 1998), 355, 453. Mahican aggression against the Waping and Wiechquaeskeck is noted in Graymont, *Early American,* 7:212–213; Becker, "The Raritan Valley Buffer Zone: A Refuge Area for Some Wiechquaeskeck and Other Native Americans during the 17th Century," *Bulletin of the Archaeological Society of Connecticut* 78 (2016): 55–93; and Becker, "The Manhatan Band of Wiechquaeskeck Relocate into the Raritan Valley Buffer Zone: A Refuge Area and the Beginning of 'Munsee' Ethnogenesis," paper presented at the 11th Annual Roundtable, Institute of American Indian Studies: "Early Encounters: Dutch-Indigenous Relations in 17th Century Northeastern North America," Washington, Connecticut, November 2016.

13. Summarized in Becker, "The Raritan Valley," and Becker, "The Manhatan Band" (see note 12).

14. I discussed this possibility twenty years ago, suggesting that some Wiechquaeskeck maintained cultural integrity through a move to northern New Jersey and now we have more evidence to confirm this idea. Becker, "Connecticut Origins for Some Native Americans in New Jersey during the Early Historic Period: Strategies for the Use of Native American Names in Research," *Bulletin of the Archaeological Society of New Jersey* 48 (1993): 62–64; Becker, "The Raritan Valley"; Becker, "The Manhatan Band of Wiechquaeskeck."

15. Becker, "Lenape Culture History"; M. J. Becker, "Ethnohistory of the Lower Delaware Valley: Addressing Myths in the Archaeological Interpretations of the Late Woodland and Contact Period," *Journal of Middle Atlantic Archaeology* 30 (2014): 41–54.

16. Heather A. Wholey and Carole L. Nash, eds., *Middle Atlantic Prehistory: Foundations and Practice* (Lanham, MD: Rowman and Littlefield, 2017).

17. Cf. Becker, "Anadromous Fish."

18. M. J. Becker, "Lenopi, or, What's in a Name? Interpreting the Evidence for Cultures and Cultural Boundaries in the Lower Delaware Valley," *Bulletin of the Archaeological Society of New Jersey* 63 (2008): 11–32.

19. See Graymont, *Early American*, 7:381, from B. Fernow, trans., comp., and ed., "Documents Relating to the History and Settlement of the Towns along the Hudson and Mohawk Rivers (with the exception of Albany) from 1630 to 1684," *Documents Relating to the Colonial History of the State of New-York*, n.s. 2 (Albany: Weed, Parsons and Company, 1881), 8:504–506.

20. Edmund B. O'Callaghan, *Documents Relative to the Colonial History of the State of New York; Procured in Holland, England and France* (Albany: Weed, Parsons, 1856), 1:366–367.

21. Becker, "Mehoxy."

22. Graymont, *Early American*, 7:428, n. 21.

23. Graymont, *Early American*, 7:158–159, 183, 330.

24. Located in the New York State Archives, Albany (Series A1810-78_V12_61).

25. José António Brandão and William A. Starna, "From the Mohawk-Mahican War to the Beaver Wars: Questioning the Pattern," *Ethnohistory* 51 (4) (2004): 725–750.

26. A. Bastiaen Jansz Eekhof, *Krol: Krankenbezoeker, kommies en kommandeur van Nieuw-Nederland (1595–1645)* (The Hague: Martinus Nijhoff, 1910), 3–5; cf. O'Callaghan, *Documents Relative to the Colonial History*, 1:45–50.

27. Washington Irving, *A History of New York, from the Beginning of the World to the End of the Dutch Dynasty*, rev. ed. (New York: Inskeep and Bradford, 1812). First revised edition 1812, from the 1809 first edition.

28. See Laurence M. Hauptman and James D. Wherry, eds., *The Pequots in Southern New England: The Fall and Rise of an Indian Nation* (Norman: University of Oklahoma Press, 1990); also Lavin, *Connecticut's Indigenous Peoples* (2013).

29. https://www.newnetherlandinstitute.org/history-and-heritage/dutch_americans/willem-kieft/

30. Irving, *A History of New York*, 41.

31. The archaeological evidence for any of this information, largely concentrated within the seventeenth century, is close to zero. All these documented killings, burnings, and other events in the historical record remain unknown from any archaeological evidence. Simply put, there is no archaeological data from the Wiechquaeskeck homeland from the Late Woodland through the early Colonial Period, or into the 1700s. A collation of the limited historical record, and its relevance to this study, will be left to scholars working in that region. Our interest here is to determine what kind of archaeological record might support the belief that the Raritan region, or part of it, served as a buffer zone between the Lenopi and Esopus tribes during the early historic period. We would expect to find very few "residential" archaeological sites of those eras in an area that was, at best, intermittently host to small groups gathering resources. An "absence" of sites, however, might be attributed to survey or other methodological problems. Therefore, we might consider the relative abundance of sites as a better indicator, with activities from earlier time periods being better represented than from the more populous Late Woodland period. In fact, that is what is indicated from the sparse archaeological record.

32. See Stephen T. Staggs, "Declarations of Interdependence: The Nature of Dutch–Native Relations in New Netherland, 1624–1664," chapter 3 in this volume, also for a discussion of this interdependence, and note 24.

33. Fernow, "Documents Relating," 8:8.

34. Fernow, "Documents Relating," 8:7, cf. 22.

35. The annual trade after 1633 or 1634 with a group living along the Raritan River appears to parallel the annual expedition sent from Fort Amsterdam to Burlington Island in the South River beginning around 1623 or 1624. Those expeditions also remain known only from inferences, and not from specific accounts in the documents.

36. Graymont, *Early American*, 7:65–66, from Fernow, "Documents Relating," 8:22–23.

37. David Pietersz. De Vries, from the "Korte Historiael ende Journaels Aenteyckeninge," 1633–1643 (1655), 181–234, in *Narratives of New Netherland 1609–1664* (New York: Charles Scribner's Sons, 1909 [1655]). David P. De Vries, taken from the section "*near America ende Nieuw-Nederlandt . . . ,*" in *Korte Historiael Ende Journaels Aenteyckeninge*, ed. H. T. Colenbrander, 227–280 ('s-Gravenhage: Martinus Nijhoff, [1655] 1911).

38. Graymont, *Early American*, 7:70, from NYCMD, 4:115–116.

39. Graymont, *Early American*, vol. 7.

40. De Vries, "Korte Historiael," 208; Graymont, *Early American*, 7:82.

41. Graymont, *Early American*, 7:65–75.

42. Graymont, *Early American*, 7:83. See also endnote 1, above.

43. Becker, "Lenopi"; Becker, "Lenopi Land Use Patterns in Central New Jersey during the Late Woodland Period as Inferred from a Deed of 1710," *Newsletter of the Archaeological Society of New Jersey*, no. 247 (March 2015): 3–5.

44. Graymont, *Early American*, 7:70.

45. Fernow, "Documents Relating," 8:7.

46. Graymont, *Early American*, 7:83.

47. Fernow, "Documents Relating," 8:9.

48. Graymont, *Early American*, 7:72–75.

49. Becker, "The Wiechquaeskeck and Waping."

50. William A. Starna, *From Homeland to New Land: A History of the Mahican Indians, 1600–1830* (Lincoln: University of Nebraska Press, 2013), 21–33.

51. Edwin G. Burrows and Mike Wallace, *Gotham: A History of New York City to 1898* (New York City: Oxford University Press, 1999), 41.

52. Discussion of growing conflicts with the Dutch on the South River are reviewed in Becker, "Lenape Culture History."

53. Graymont, *Early American*, 7:119. Italics in original. Achter Col is the area at the mouth of the Hackensack River where it enters Newark Bay, and site of a number of early Dutch farmsteads. The nearest Esopus band resident in that area are generally identified as "Hackensack" Indians in the documents.

54. O'Callaghan, *Documents Relative to the Colonial History*, 1:365–367.

55. Peter H. Wilson, *Europe's Tragedy: A New History of the Thirty Years' War* (London: Penguin, 2010), 787. Geoffrey Parker, *The Thirty Years' War* (London: Routledge, 1997), 17–18.

56. O'Callaghan, *Documents Relative to the Colonial History*, 1:366.

57. Robert, Bolton Jr., *The History of the County of Westchester from Its First Settlement to the Present Time*, vols. I and II (New York: Alexander S. Gould, 1848), I:2.

58. Bolton, "New York City in Indian Possession," 339–340.

59. Barbara Graymont, *Early American* 7:7.

60. Graymont, *Early American*, 7:116.

61. O'Callaghan, *Documents Relative to the Colonial History*, 1:366–367; Becker, "The Raritan Valley."

62. Charles T. Gehring, trans. and ed., "Correspondence, 1647–1653," *New Netherland Documents Series* (Syracuse: Syracuse University Press, 2000), 128; Becker, "Lenape ('Delaware')," 120.

63. M. J. Becker, "The Moravian Mission in the Forks of the Delaware: Reconstructing the Migration and Settlement Patterns of the Jersey Lenape during the 18th Century through Documents in the Moravian Archives," *Unitas Fratrum* 21–22 (1987): 83–172; Becker, "Teedyuscung's Youth and Hereditary Land Rights in New Jersey: The Identification of the Unalachtigo," *Bulletin of the Archaeological Society of New Jersey* 47 (1992): 37–60.

64. cf. Becker, "Lenape Culture History."

65. Attending the peace treaty between the Dutch and the Waping on May 18, 1660 were Oratam of the "Hackinkesachy" band representing the Waping, followed by "*Mattano*, late chief of *Najack*" and "*Sauweraro*, chief of *Wiechquaeskeck*" and two others, plus an interpreter (Graymont, *Early American*, 7:210–211, from Fernow, "Documents Relating," 8:166–167).

66. Graymont, *Early American*, 7:270–272.

67. Graymont, *Early American*, 7:275, 277–278.

68. Graymont, *Early American*, 7:282–285.

69. Graymont, *Early American*, 7:284.

70. J. J. Hartsinck, *Beschryving van Guiana, op de wilde Kust in Zuid-America* (Amsterdam: Gerrit Tielenburg, 1770), 27–35.

71. Becker, "Lenopi"; Becker, "Late Woodland."

72. Graymont, *Early American*, 7:8, 9: *New York and New Jersey Treaties, 1714–1753* (Bethesda, MD: University Publications of America, 1996).

73. Becker, "The Raritan Valley."

74. cf. Becker, "The Armewamus Band of New Jersey: Other Clues to Differences between the Lenopi and the Lenape," *Pennsylvania Archaeologist* 80 (2) (2010): 61–72.

75. William Nelson, *Indians of New Jersey*; Nelson, "Anthropologic Miscellanea. Indian Words, Personal Names, and Place-names in New Jersey," *American Anthro-*

pologist 4 (1902): 183–192; Nelson, *Personal Names of Indians of New Jersey: Being a List of Six Hundred and Fifty* . . . (Paterson, NJ: Paterson History Club, 1904).

76. Stewart, *Indians of Southern New Jersey.*

77. Becker, Ms. A, "Four Specious Indian Deeds from New Jersey, All Dated 18 August 1713: Transcribed in 1990 by Marshall Joseph Becker from West Jersey Deeds [Book] Liber BBB (pages 140–147) in the New Jersey Archives," Trenton, New Jersey (6 pages, April 29, 2015).

78. Graymont, *Early American*, 8:26–27. See also Becker, "Transcriptions of Indian Deeds. Manuscript copy in the Charles A. Philhower Collection, New Jersey Historical Society, Newark, New Jersey," Ms. A, unpublished manuscript of file, Becker Archives, West Chester University of Pennsylvania.

79. cf. Becker "Lenopi Land Use Patterns in Central New Jersey."

80. cf. Becker, "Mehoxy."

81. Graymont, *Early American*, 7:27.

82. Becker, "The Raritan Valley."

83. Edward Manning Ruttenber, *History of the Indian Tribes of Hudson's River* (Albany: J. Munsell, 1872), 201.

84. cf. Becker "The Boundary between the Lenape and the Munsee," 1983.

85. Graymont, *Early American*, 9:664, n18.

86. Ruttenber, *History of the Indian Tribes*, 201.

87. For example, Becker, "Teedyuscung's Youth."

88. Starna, *From Homeland*; Ted J. Brasser, "Mahican," in *Handbook of North American Indians*, vol. 15: *Northeast*, ed. B. G. Trigger, 198–212 (Washington, DC: Government Printing Office, 1978). See also Tom Arne Midtrød, *The Memory of All Ancient Customs: Native American Diplomacy in the Colonial Hudson Valley* (Ithaca: Cornell University Press, 2013).

89. Philhower, *Indians*, 255.

90. Charles A. Philhower, "Transcriptions of Indian Deeds," Ms. A, manuscript copy in the Charles A. Philhower Collection, New Jersey Historical Society, Newark, New Jersey.

91. Anthony F. C. Wallace, *King of the Delawares: Teedyuskung, 1700–1763* (Philadelphia: University of Pennsylvania Press, 1949).

92. Becker, "The Moravian Mission"; Becker, "Teedyuscung's Youth."

93. Becker, "Lenopi, or, What's in a Name?," 11–32.

94. Barbara Graymont, *Early American Indian Documents: Treaties and Laws, 1607–1789*, general ed. Alden T. Vaughan, vol. 10: *New York and New Jersey Treaties, 1754–1775* (Bethesda, MD: University Publications of America, 2001), 299–301.

95. Graymont, *Early American*, 10:302.

96. Graymont, *Early American*, 10:303.

97. Graymont, *Early American*, 10:305.

98. Philhower *Indians*, 251–254.

99. Graymont, *Early American*, 10:309–353. See also Nelson, *The Indians of New Jersey*, 117–119; also claimed by Robert S. Grumet, "Taphow: The Forgotten

'Sakemau' and Commander in Chief of All Those Indians Inhabiting Northern New Jersey,'" *Bulletin of the Archaeological Society of New Jersey* 43 (1988): 27, as from the record in the New Jersey Archives as *Liber I–2*: 89–94.

100. Becker, "Jacob Skickett, Lenopi Elder: Preliminary Notes from before 1750 to after 1802," *Pennsylvania Archaeologist* 81 (2) (2011): 65–76; Becker, "John Skickett (1823?—after 1870): A Lenopi Descent Basketmaker Working in Connecticut," *Bulletin of the Archaeological Society of Connecticut* 76 (2014): 99–118.

101. Colonial Records of Pennsylvania, *Minutes of the Provincial Council of Pennsylvania*, vol. 8, 13 January 1757—4 October 1762 (Harrisburg: Theo. Fenn & Company, 1852), 174.

102. Located at the New Jersey Historical Society, Newark, New Jersey, where they are catalogued under "L.C. 1 Vault."

103. Colonial Records of Pennsylvania, 8:174–223.

104. Colonial Records of Pennsylvania, 8:175–176; see also Philip Smith, *A General History of Dutchess County from 1609 to 1876, Inclusive* (Pawling, NY: Published by the author, 1877), 479.

105. Graymont, *Early American*, 10:333.

106. For earlier evidence, see Becker, "Cultural History in the Native Northeast" (review essay), *American Anthropologist* 99 (1997): 178–180; also Becker, "The Lenape and other 'Delawarean' Peoples."

107. Colonial Records of Pennsylvania, 8:176.

108. James H. Merrell, "'I Desire That All I Have Said . . . May Be Taken Down Aright': Revisiting Teedyuscung's 1756 Treaty Council Speeches," *William and Mary Quarterly*, 3rd ser., 63 (4) (2006): 777–826.

109. Donald H. Kent, ed., *Early American Indian Documents, Treaties and Laws, 1607–1789. Volume I: Pennsylvania and Delaware Treaties, 1629–1737*, general ed. Alden T. Vaughan (Washington, DC: University Publications of America, 1979); Donald H. Kent, ed., *Early American Indian Documents, Treaties and Laws, 1607–1789, Volume II: Pennsylvania Treaties, 1737–1756*, general ed. Alden T. Vaughan (Washington, DC: University Publications of America, 1981).

110. Graymont, *Early American*, 7:8, 9, 10.

111. Graymont, *Early American*, 7:8, 9, 10.

112. For example, see Becker, "Mehoxy of the Cohansey Band of Lenopi: A 1684 Document That Offers Clues to the Missing Part of His Biography," *Bulletin of the Archaeological Society of Delaware*, n.s., 44 (2012): 1–29.

113. Fernow, "Documents Relating," 8.

114. Jonathan Lainey, *La "Monnaie des Sauvages": Les colliers de wampum d'hier à aujourd'hui* (Quebec: Septentrion, 2004).

115. Lynn Ceci, "The Effect of European Contact and Trade on the Settlement Patterns of Indians," in *Coastal New York, 1524–1665* (New York: Garland Press, 1990); Becker, "Wampum on the Fringe: Explaining the Absence of a Post-1600 CE Native-Produced Commodity in Delaware," *Bulletin of the Archaeological Society of Delaware*, n.s., 45 (2012): 23–36; Becker, "Lenape ('Delaware')."

116. Becker, "Lenape ('Delaware')"; Becker, "Lenape ('Delaware') Mail Carriers and the Origins of the US Postal Service," *American Indian Culture & Research Journal* 39 (3) (2015): 99–121.

117. By the 1700s these buffer zones were no longer sufficient to absorb displaced Natives, leading, in the 1730s, to the formation of refuges such as the Indian town of Stockbridge in western Massachusetts (see Salwen, "Indians," 1978 and 1983).

118. Frederic Shonnard and W. W. Spooner, *History of Westchester County, New York from Its Earliest Settlement to the Year 1900* (New York: New York History Company, 1900), 33.

119. Cf. Becker, "Anadromous Fish."

120. Jan A. Moore, "Quinnipiac Fishes and Fisheries: History and Modern Perspectives on the Fishes and Fisheries in the Quinnipiac Watershed," *Transactions of the Connecticut Academy of Arts and Sciences* 57 (2001): 1–28.

121. Cf. Jason Mancini, " 'In Contempt and Oblivion': Censuses, Ethnogeography, and Hidden Indian Histories in Eighteenth-Century Southern New England," *Ethnohistory* 62 (1) (2015): 61–94.

122. Daniel R. Mandell, ed., *Early American Indian Documents: Treaties and Laws, 1607–1789*, general ed. Alden T. Vaughan, vol. 20, *New England Treaties, North and West, 1650–1776* (Bethesda, MD: University Publications of America, 2003), 10:464–465.

123. Mandell, *Early American Indian Documents*, 10:516.

124. Lucianne Lavin, Institute for American Indian Studies, personal communication to the author, September 2016. See also Lavin, "Dutch-Native American Relationships in Eastern New Netherland (That's Connecticut, Folks!)," chapter 10, this volume.

125. Cf. Becker, "Jacob Skickett."

126. A wide range of popular works review, with varying degrees of scholarly diligence, an assortment of information relating to the peoples variously identifying themselves as the Ramapo (or Ramapough) Indians, or as the Jackson Whites. See David Steven Cohen, *The Ramapo Mountain People* (New Brunswick, NJ: Rutgers University Press, 1974). The information relating to Native ancestry for the Ramapo claimants is so flimsy that none of the claimant groups using that name have even been granted Indigenous recognition by the state of New York. Koenig and Stein specifically state that the "group known as the Ramapough Mountain Indians" were denied recognition in their pursuit of a gaming license: Alexa Koenig and Jonathan Stein, "Federalism and the State Recognition of Native American Tribes: A Survey of State-Recognized Tribes and State Recognition Processes across the United States," *Santa Clara Law Review* 48, no. 1 (2007): 1–153. For related information on the "Pompton Indians," see Kate S. Ahmadi, "Pompotowwut-Muhheakanneau, Part 1: The Pomptons (Pumptons)," paper presented at the 23rd annual Highlands Archaeological and Historical Conference, Tuxedo, New York, October 24, 2009,

copy on file in the Becker Archives, West Chester University of Pennsylvania, and "Chief Towaco," paper presented at the 25rd annual Highlands Archaeological and Historical Conference, Tuxedo, New York, October 15, 2011, copy on file in the Becker Archives, West Chester University of Pennsylvania.

127. Electra F. Jones, *Stockbridge, Past and Present; or, Records of an Old Mission Station* (Springfield, MA: Samuel Bowles & Company, 1854), 13–29. This process was parallel to that of the Lenopi who relocated from New Jersey to New Stockbridge in New York. See Becker, "Jacob Skickett"; also Becker, "John Skickett." The process of a "point person" leaving a tribal area to explore a buffer zone, and then being followed by some kin, is documented in only one known example: Marshall Joseph Becker, "Keposh: First Lenopi Migrant into the Forks of Delaware in Pennsylvania," *Newsletter of the Archaeological Society of New Jersey*, no. 230 (January 2011): 1, 3–7.

128. C. A. Weslager, "Enrollment List of Chippewa and Delaware-Munsies Living in Franklin County, Kansas, May 31, 1900," *Kansas Historical Quarterly* 40 (2) (1974): 234–240; Earl P. Olmstead, *Blackcoats among the Delaware—David Zeisberger on the Ohio Frontier* (Kent, OH: Kent State University Press, 1991); Becker, "The Ganawese: Tracing the Piscataway from Their Entry into Pennsylvania ca. 1700 until They Relocated into Five Nations Territory around 1750 and Became Known as Conoy." Unpublished manuscript on file, Becker Archives, West Chester University of Pennsylvania.

Land sales from within buffer areas, all dating from a later period, reveal how the members of several immigrant Native groups morphed into "groups" with names that today are better known (e.g., Abenaki, Munsee, Delaware) than the names of their actual ancestral, aboriginal groups. Land sales by relocated populations also provide a window through which to view these people. Each document adds important information to their histories.

7.

Early Seventeenth-Century Trade in Southern New England

Kevin A. McBride

This chapter examines the nature, mechanics, and material culture of the trade between the Pequot, Dutch, and English between ca. 1611 and June 1637. The beginning date correlates with the arrival of Dutch explorers and traders in Long Island Sound, and the later date corresponds to the defeat of the Pequot in the Pequot War of 1636–37, when they fled their homeland shortly after the Battles of Mistick Fort and the English Withdrawal on May 26, 1637. The data used in this analysis is drawn from Dutch and English historical sources dating between 1611 and 1637 and archaeological data consisting of over 450 iron, brass, ceramic, and lead trade items that are believed to date to the same time period. The items are Dutch or English in origin and were recovered from five Pequot domestic sites identified during metal detector surveys of the Battle of the English Withdrawal.[1]

The Pequot War began in September 1636, when a Massachusetts Bay force of twenty men under the command of Colonel John Endicott landed in Pequot territory along the Thames River to demand the murderers of Captain John Stone and his crew who were killed by the Pequot in January 1634. The Pequot employed a number of delaying tactics and in frustration the English burned two villages and killed several Pequot. In retaliation, the Pequot laid siege to Saybrook Fort at the mouth of the Connecticut River for the next seven months, killing dozens of English soldiers, traders, and settlers. On April 23 the Pequot attacked the English settlement at Wethersfield, killing nine settlers, including women and children, and took two girls captive. In response, the English declared an Offensive War against the Pequot on May 1, 1637 and made plans to attack the Pequot fortified village at Mystic with a force of seventy-seven English soldiers and 250 Mohegan, Narragansett, Eastern Niantic, and Wangunk allies. The surprise dawn attack took place on May 26, 1637 and resulted in the deaths of four hundred Pequot men, women, and children, half of whom burned to death. The Battle of the English Withdrawal began a few hours later and consisted of a 4.5-mile, ten-hour fighting retreat against hundreds of Pequot fighting men who had mobilized after the Mistick Fort Battle in one of the longest and most intense battles of the Pequot War.[2]

Pequot Expansion, 1620–1631

Within a decade after the arrival of Dutch traders in 1611, the Pequot positioned themselves to control the fur and wampum trade over much of Long Island Sound and the Connecticut River Valley. Pequot hegemony was achieved through warfare, coercion, subjugation, and alliance building to dominate key territory and resources. Wampum (purple and white shell beads made from hard shell clam and northern whelk) from eastern Long Island Sound quickly became the most important component of the fur trade, as it was in great demand by tribes in the fur-rich interior areas of the Hudson and upper Connecticut River drainages. By the mid-1620s the Dutch acquired at least 150,000–200,000 wampum beads a year from tribes living along Long Island Sound for the northern fur trade.[3] The wampum-producing regions of eastern Long Island Sound between the Connecticut River and Narragansett Bay were the first areas to fall under Pequot control in the 1620s, followed by the middle Connecticut River Valley in the early 1630s. In 1626, the Dutch stated that the tribes on eastern Long Island "are held in subjection by, and are tributary to the Pyquans [Pequot]," and in 1628 the Dutch reported that the "whole north coast [of Long Island Sound] is tributary" to the Pequot.[4] In 1631, the Pequot defeated the Wangunk sachem Wahginnacut/Attawanhut of the middle Connecticut Valley in battle three times and claimed his territory by right of conquest.[5]

By the early 1630s the Pequot controlled a territory of over 2,500 square miles stretching one hundred miles along the Connecticut and Long Island coastlines and fifty miles up the Connecticut River. Subjugated tribes were placed in a subordinate relationship to the Pequot, who claimed their territory by right of conquest and could effectively dictate the manner and amount of furs and wampum that would reach the Dutch and English, as well as the redistribution of European trade goods to their tributary and allied tribes.

Dutch Trade, 1611–1637

While the acquisition of furs in New Netherland was the primary focus of Dutch trade, furs were largely depleted in the coastal regions of New Netherland by the second decade of the seventeenth century. The Dutch defined New Netherland as the area from Massachusetts Bay to the Delaware River. Eastern New Netherland was the area between the Connecticut River and Buzzards Bay (figure 7.1). With the arrival of the English in 1620, however, the east side of Narragansett Bay (Sloops Bay) became the eastern boundary of New Netherland. By the mid-1620s, the focus of Dutch trade in coastal areas of eastern New Netherland shifted from furs to acquiring wampum for use in the fur trade. As a result, a specialized wampum trade developed in eastern New Netherland as the Dutch sought to maintain a competitive edge in the fur trade against the French and English.[6]

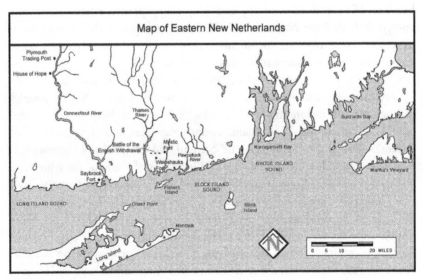

Figure 7.1. Eastern Long Island Sound and eastern New Netherland.

The Dutch were the first Europeans to systematically explore the region known as New Netherland and develop trade relationships with many of the Native groups inhabiting Long Island Sound and the Connecticut River. Soon after Henry Hudson's discovery of the Hudson River in 1609/10, individual Dutch traders began to trade with Natives throughout the region. A number of trading voyages were funded by individual Dutch merchants between 1611 and 1614, and in 1611 a consortium of merchants led by Lambert van Tweenhuysen funded several voyages of exploration and trade to survey and map what was to become New Netherland. Van Tweenhuysen's intent was to secure exclusive trading rights to the region from the States General, which first required the consortium to submit a map and description of the region; the endeavor took three years.[7]

Four captains were engaged in this effort: Jan de With, Adriaen Block, Hendrick Christiaensz Thijs, and Cornelis Jacobsz May.[8] Adriaen Block's responsibility was to map Long Island Sound from the Hudson River to Buzzards Bay. The "Report of the Discovery of New Netherland" was submitted to the States General on October 11, 1614. The original report has been lost but parts of Block's narrative and possibly those of May and Christiaensz are contained in Johannes De Laet's *The New World* and Nicolas van Wassenaer's *Historisch Verhael*.[9] A Figurative Map accompanied the report and a copy survives in the State Archives in The Hague (figure 7.2).[10] Block and Thijs may have made four voyages each to New Netherland between 1611 and 1614. With and May only appear to have made one voyage each to New Netherland.[11] While the voyages of the Tweenhuysen cartel are reasonably well documented, there were undoubtedly many other voyages by private traders that went undocumented.

Block's 1614 Figurative Map and report could only have been made by extensive exploration and information obtained from Native peoples throughout the region (figure 7.2). Block's map is striking for the cartographic detail of the Long Island Sound coastlines and the Connecticut River, as well as the highly accurate cultural and geographic information.[12] Block correctly identified the names and locations of many of the tribes and sachems inhabiting Long Island Sound and the Connecticut River Valley.

Notarial records and other sources indicate that at least sixteen ships sailed from Holland to New Netherland between 1611 and 1614.[13] Most Dutch captains left Holland for New Netherland between October and December, sailing through Long Island Sound and arriving in the Hudson River between January and March before returning to Holland by late July or early August. One voyage a year for a captain appears to be the norm.

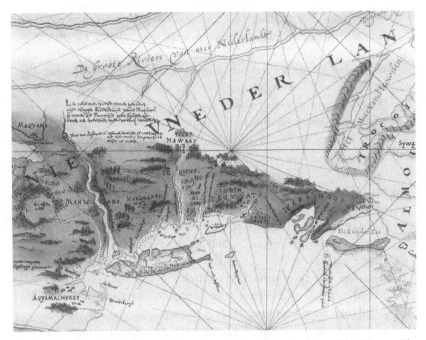

Figure 7.2. Adriaen Block's 1614 Figurative Map (State Archives, The Hague, The Netherlands).

The average stay in New Netherland appears to have been between four and five months.

If all sixteen ships stayed in New Netherland for four months, Dutch traders spent a total of sixty-four months in New Netherland between 1611 and 1614. On Block's first voyage he did not leave Holland until late May, but in subsequent voyages he appears to have followed the general pattern outlined above. If so, Block may have spent between ten and fifteen months in New Netherland over a three-year period, a sufficient amount of time to acquire extensive knowledge of the region and its people. Block's narrative, as cited by De Laet, also indicates that the Dutch had already developed trade relations with some, but not all, of the tribes in the area by 1614:

> [On the] bay of Nassau [Buzzard's Bay] the inhabitants seem sturdy and fairly tall. They are somewhat shy, however, since they are not accustomed to trade with strangers. . . . In the lower part of the bay [east side of Narragansett Bay] dwell the

Wapenocks [Wampanoags] . . . a nation of savages like the rest. Captain Adriaen Block calls the people who inhabit the west side of this bay Nahicans [Narragansetts] and their sagamore Nathattou another chief was named Cachaquant . . . another small river, which our countrymen call the river of Siccanamos [Mystic River] after the name of the Sagimos or Sacmos. . . . The people who dwell on this river, according to the statements of our people, are called Pequatoos [Pequots], and are the enemies of the Wapanoos . . . the Frisian [Thames] River, where some trade is carried on with the natives, who are called Morhicans . . . a river named by our countrymen Fresh River [Connecticut]. . . . There are few inhabitants near the mouth of the river, but at the distance of fifteen leagues above they become numerous; their nation is called Sequins . . . and in the year 1614 they had a village resembling a fort. . . . They are called Nawaas, and their sagamore was then named Morahieck. Within the land dwells another nation of savages, who are called Horikans another called the river of Royenberch [Quinnipiac]. . . . The natives who dwell here are called Quiripeys [Quinnipiac]. They take many beavers, but it is necessary for them to get into the habit of trade, otherwise they are too indolent to hunt the beaver.[14]

In 1614 the States General granted a three-year trading monopoly to the van Tweenhuysen consortium that established the New Netherland Company. The States General restricted trading ventures by any other individuals or groups while the New Netherland Company was operating, although the company didn't begin regular voyages to New Netherland until 1615. James Bradley identified four periods of Dutch trade with correlations in the nature of goods traded to Natives: independent traders (1611–14/15), New Netherland Company (1614/15–18), independent traders (1618–23), and the West India Company (1623–50s).[15] Under the New Netherland Company, trade with the Natives became more organized and regular.

The New Netherland Company's monopoly expired in 1618 and the trade once again became chaotic and unpredictable until the West India Company was formed in 1621, although it did not become operational until 1623. The West India Company began to construct fortifications and trading houses along the Hudson and Delaware Rivers, but for reasons that remain unclear the Dutch did not construct a fort and trading post on the Connecticut River until the Huys de Hoop (House of Hope) was built in the summer of 1633 at the present site of Hartford. The fort and trading post was constructed in part to establish Dutch territorial claims to the Connecticut Valley and to intercept the furs coming from the north down the Farmington and Connecticut Rivers. In October 1633 the Plymouth Colony constructed a trading post a few miles upriver from the Dutch in present-day Windsor, effectively circumventing the Dutch position.

Permanent trading posts such as the House of Hope were an effective means to facilitate the collection of furs from trading partners in interior areas that Dutch traders could not easily reach. The wampum trade required a different strategy. Rather than fixed or permanent European trading posts and mobile Native hunters as in the fur trade, the wampum trade required the reverse: a mobile European collection strategy and fixed Native places of production. This strategy is illustrated by the number of small, shallow draft coastal sloops and yachts that visited fixed Native places (often fortified) along the coast, bays, and estuaries to trade for wampum.

The Dutch referred to wampum as the "source and mother of the fur trade" and to eastern New Netherland as the "mint" of wampum production.[16] Within a decade of initiating trade with Natives in New Netherland, wampum became the most important item in the fur trade. Dutch trader Jaques Elckes kidnapped the chief Pequot sachem (perhaps Tatopan) "in the year 1622 in his yacht and obliged him to pay a heavy ransom, or else he would cut off his head. He paid one hundred and forty fathoms of Zeewan" (approximately fifty thousand wampum beads).[17] This is the first mention of wampum by the Dutch, but indicates that wampum had already become a very important commodity in the fur trade. This incident most likely occurred on the Thames or Mystic Rivers in Pequot territory.

The need for wampum became so great by 1626 that Isaac de Rasieres, secretary of New Netherland, requested funds from the directors of the West India Company to construct two or three sloops to pursue the wampum trade. He estimated that a thousand yards of wampum (approximately 350,000 beads) would be necessary for Dutch traders to have any success in acquiring furs from their northern trading partners during the winter of 1626.[18] Wampum production was greatly facilitated by the use of iron drills (*muxes*), which became a common item traded to Natives along the coast. Dutch traders in shallow draft vessels acquired wampum from tribes along coastal areas of eastern New Netherland and transported it to Albany or the House of Hope, where it was traded to interior tribes.

After the West India Company became operational in 1623, they began to construct extensive trade networks throughout New Netherland and defined rules of conduct for their traders regarding the quality of trade goods and how to maintain good relations with their Native trading partners. The rules and regulations established by the West India Company was in direct response to a number of incidences that occurred in the "chaotic" period between 1618 and 1623 and threatened to disrupt the trade, such as the Jaques Elckes kidnapping of the Pequot sachem. In 1625 the directors of the West India Company sent detailed instructions to Willem Verhulst, secretary of New Netherland, regarding the conduct of traders, the quality of trade goods, developing exclusive relations with their Native trading partners, and a strategy to keep the French and English from impinging on the Dutch trade:

> And for the better security of the trade and the exclusion of foreign nations he is to consider whether it would be practicable to contract with the natives of the country in various districts as would make them promise us to trade with no one but those of the company, provided that we on our part should bind ourselves to take all the skins, which they would us upon such terms as would be considered reasonable, or at such price as we have hitherto bought them.
>
> And whereas those tribes are very quarrelsome among themselves, suspicious and vindictive, he shall be very careful not lightly to embroil himself in their quarrels or wars, or to take sides, but to remain neutral and to pacify and reconcile the respective parties by the most suitable means.
>
> He shall by small presents seek to draw the Indians to our service, in order to learn from them the secrets of that region and the condition of the interior, but not feed them in idleness or give in too much to their wanton demands.
>
> He shall also as far as feasible avoid getting into any dispute with the French or English, and especially avoid all acts of violence, unless he is obliged to defend himself and those who are committed to his charge against open aggression.
>
> He shall endeavor to increase the trade in skins and other articles that are obtained in the country, and at the place of trading. With the Indians have a cabin erected so that the goods may be stored therein, and at a suitable time he shall send one or more sloops thither to carry on trade, taking for that purpose such persons as are most competent as are able to write, in order that they keep a record thereof.

> He is to take good care that the stock of hatchets, mattocks, knives, and other hardware does not rust, but is kept clean, and that other goods do not spoil through neglect.[19]

The strategy worked and competent and fair Dutch traders began to forge exclusive trading relations with groups throughout the region. Following the incident with Jaques Elckes "the chief of this nation [Pequot] has lately made an agreement with Pieter Barentsz not to trade with any other than him . . . on this account he has no confidence in any one but this one [Barentsz] now."[20] Barentsz and many other Dutch traders also learned the language of their trading partners to better facilitate trade: "This Pieter Barentz, already spoken of, can understand all the tribes thereabout; he trades with the Sickenames, to whom the whole north coast is tributary; with the Zinnekox, Wappenox, Maquaes and Maikans, so that he visits all the tribes with sloops and trades in a friendly manner with them, only for peltrie."[21]

English Arrival and Conflict, 1633–1637

Between 1611 and 1633 the Dutch and Pequot maintained a monopoly over their respective areas of the trade, exercising control over their economic and political spheres. This period could be described as relatively calm, but potentially volatile. The careful balance was disrupted in 1633 with the arrival of English traders and settlers in Long Island Sound and the Connecticut River Valley, and by a smallpox epidemic that swept across the Northeast in 1633 and 1634, killing thousands of Native people.

Tensions increased and regional stability waned as the English and other Native tribes attempted to break Pequot and Dutch dominance over the region. Anticipating that the English planned to construct a trading post on the Connecticut River, in 1633 the Dutch purchased a tract of land called Sickajoock from the Pequot, "a flat extending about one league down along the river and one-third of a league in width" to establish a trading post "on condition that all tribes might freely, and without any fear or danger, resort to the purchased land for the purposes of trade."[22]

Unlike the Dutch, who purchased the land for their trading post from the Pequot and recognized Pequot rights to the territory by right of conquest (which was also acknowledged by the Narragansett enemies of the Pequot), when Plymouth established their trading post in present-day Windsor in the fall of 1633 they ignored Pequot claims to the area and purchased the land from the Wangunk sachem Wahginnacut/Attawanhut, who was subjugated by the Pequot in 1631. Tatopan, the chief Pequot sachem, was angered by the purchase, and Lieutenant Holmes, commander of the post, related the following:

> I brought in Attawanhut, and there left him, where he lived and dies upon the ground, whom Tatopan [chief Pequot sachem], the tyrant had before expelled by war; that this Attawanhut, by the relation of Lieutenant Holmes, if he would have given way to it, would have cut off the Dutch, because they came in by Tatopan . . . but one thing more of great consequence I call to mind, that Tatopan, for so we termed him, after he had chide me for bringing in his mortal enemy [Attawanhut] and countenancing him, as he did, would have had me (when indeed he durst not attempt it againe upon him) to have given him but a knife, or but an awl blade, for his consent, to what I had done, which I utterly refused.[23]

English settlers from Massachusetts Bay also disregarded Pequot claims to the Connecticut River Valley, and they too purchased land from local sachems that had been subjugated by the Pequot; Wethersfield was settled in 1634, Windsor in 1635, and Hartford in 1635. Saybrook Fort at the mouth of the Connecticut River was also established in 1635, but the land was purchased from the Western Niantic Indians, allies of the Pequot. As English settlers and traders flooded into the Connecticut Valley, they provided new trade opportunities for the Pequot, although the English ignored Pequot hegemony and developed independent trade relations and sought alliances with other tribes in the region. These actions undoubtedly angered the Pequot, but they continued to trade with the English nonetheless, in part because trade with the Dutch had been interrupted by the Pequot-Dutch War in 1634.

Pequot-Dutch War, 1634

Little is known about the Pequot-Dutch War of 1634, the first major conflict between Native Americans and Europeans in New England. It was also the first time that a Native tribe (the Narragansett) formed an alliance with a European power against a Native enemy. The war probably began in the winter or early spring of 1634 and continued through the fall of 1634. In

January 1634, John Winthrop reported that the Pequot had killed Captain John Stone and his crew of eight at the mouth of the Connecticut River. The Pequot justified their actions by claiming Stone had kidnapped several of their Western Niantic allies, and either during a rescue attempt or retribution (or both) the Pequot killed the English. This incident was a major cause of the Pequot War that began two and a half years later.

Winthrop reported in his journal entry for November 6, 1634 that "a messenger from the Pekod sachem [arrived], to desire our friendship" and make amends over the deaths of Captain Stone and his crew. Winthrop reported that "the reason why they desired so much our friendship was, because they were now in war with the Narragansets, whom, till this year, they had kept under, and likewise with the Dutch."[24]

Winthrop's statement suggests that the Pequot may not have been trading with Massachusetts Bay on a regular basis at that time, if at all, but the Pequot were likely trading with independent English traders from the Connecticut Valley settlements and with Plymouth. Nonetheless, the statement suggests that the loss of their Dutch trading partners was a significant blow to the Pequot.

An account likely provided to Plymouth governor William Bradford by either Lieutenant Holmes or Jonathan Brewster stationed at the Plymouth trading post states that after the Pequot killed Stone and his crew in early 1634, "They made a pray of what they had, and chafered away some of the things to the Dutch that lived there [House of Hope]. But it was not long before a quarrel fell between the Dutch and them, and they would have cut off their bark, but they slew the chief sachem with the shot of a murderer."[25] Winthrop also stated that the Dutch "had killed their sachem [Pequot sachem Tatopan] and some other of their men, for that the Pekods had killed some Indians, who came to trade with the Dutch at Connecticut; and, by these occasions, they could not trade safely anywhere. Therefore they desired us to send a pinnace with cloth, and we should have all their trade."[26] Winthrop's information also likely originated from Holmes or Brewster via Bradford as the Plymouth men were the only English "on the ground" in the Connecticut Valley in 1634 and would have witnessed the events that unfolded.

Stone was well known to the Dutch in the Hudson River, and presumably the Dutch at the House of Hope, and he was friends with the Dutch governor. It may be that when the Pequot tried to trade Stone's goods, the Dutch discovered the Pequot had killed Stone, which caused the "quarrel." The quarrel escalated into a major conflict when the Dutch killed Tatopan and several Pequot men. The reference to the bark and murderer suggests that the Pequot attempted to attack the bark from canoes. In retaliation the Pequot may have sought to disrupt trade between the Dutch and other Natives by killing some Indians who had come to trade at the House of Hope. The Narragansett likely declared war on the Pequot either because the Natives who were killed were Narragansett or the Narragansett had a responsibility to seek retribution on behalf of their allies in the Connecticut River Valley.

The Pequot may have faced seventy Dutch marines who were stationed at the House of Hope at the time, sent to the Connecticut Valley in the fall of 1633 to drive the English from the newly established Plymouth trading post at Windsor. Winthrop made an interesting observation when the Endicott expedition tried to engage the Pequot in battle in September 1636. During the encounter the Pequot kept retreating beyond the range of English gunfire "but when they were gone out of musket shot, he [Endicott] marched after them, supposing they would have stood to it awhile, as they did the Dutch."[27] This statement clearly indicates the Pequot had engaged in a major battle with the Dutch.

English Traders, 1633–1637

Saybrook Fort's location at the mouth of the Connecticut River became an important trading center, as more than a dozen traders constructed warehouses at Saybrook Point to house their trade goods and ply their trade upriver and along the coast. The men stationed at Saybrook Fort under the command of Lieutenant Lion Gardiner often traded with the Pequot and knew many of the Pequot men. Saybrook men accompanied the Endicott expedition to the Thames River in September 1636, and during the drawn-out negotiations to obtain Stone's murderers Gardiner mentioned that the Pequot "talked with my men who they knew."[28] The English did not begin to trade in Long Island Sound or the Connecticut River Valley until mid-1633. In 1631 the Wangunk sachem Wahginnacut/Attawanhut from the Wethersfield area, and recently conquered by the Pequot, went to Boston to meet with Governor Winthrop to convince him to trade and settle in the Connecticut Valley:

> The said Wahginnacut was very desirous to have some Englishmen
> to come plant in his country, and offered to find them com, and

give them yearly eighty skins of beaver, and that the country was very fruitful, etc., and wished that there might be two men sent with him to see the country. The governor entertained them at dinner, but would send none with him. He discovered after, that the said sagamore is a very treacherous man, and at war with the Pekoath [Pequot] (a far greater sagamore). His country is not above five days' journey from us by land.[29]

Plymouth traders were the first English to establish regular trade relations with Native people in the Connecticut Valley and Long Island Sound. Governor Edward Winslow went to the Connecticut River in 1632, at which time he purchased the land in Windsor that was to become the site of the Plymouth trading post. Bradford suggests there were a number of trading ventures prior to the establishment of the Plymouth trading post in 1633:

And having now good store of commodities, and also need to look out where they could advantage themselves to help them out of their great engagements, they now began to send that way to discover the same, and trade with the natives. They found it to be a fine place, but had no great store of trade; but the Indians excused the same in regard of the season, and the fear the Indians were in of their enemies. So they tried diverse times, not without profit, but saw the most certainty would be by keeping a house there, to receive the trade when it came down out of the inland.[30]

The first mention of traders from Massachusetts Bay in the Connecticut Valley and Long Island Sound wasn't until late August 1633. Winthrop mentioned that "about ten days before this time [September 4], a bark was set forth to Connecticut and those parts, to trade."[31] In his September 4 entry Winthrop also reported that John Oldham "went over land to Connecticut to trade. The sachem used them kindly, and gave them some beaver."[32] The overland route from Massachusetts Bay to Connecticut was not the most efficient way to carry on trade with the Natives in the Connecticut Valley, and all subsequent trading ventures to the Connecticut Valley and Long Island Sound were by ship. Because of the shallowness of the mouth of the Connecticut River as well as the bays and estuaries of Long Island Sound, the types of ships most often referenced in the trade were smaller vessels of less than sixty tons such as pinnaces, pinks, shallops, and barks. At least two dozen different English ships are mentioned as trading in Long Island Sound or the Connecticut River Valley on a regular basis between 1633 and 1637.[33]

There is no specific mention of the Pequot trading at either the Dutch or Plymouth trading posts, and it appears that most of the trade was conducted in Pequot territory as per the necessities of acquiring wampum. When Jaques Elckes kidnapped the Pequot sachem and took him aboard his ship in 1622 and held him for ransom it was likely on the Thames or Mystic Rivers. Dutch sources mention that Pieter Barentz "trades with the Sickenames [Pequot] . . . he visits all the tribes with sloops and trades in a friendly manner."[34] In the fall of 1634 when a Pequot delegation went to Boston to make retribution for the murder of Captain John Stone and his crew eighteen months before, Winthrop reported "they desired us to send a pinnace with cloth, and we should have all their trade."[35]

The most likely anchorage for trading vessels was Pequot Harbor in the Pequot (Thames) River, as it is sufficiently deep with a wide estuary and harbor where ships could easily maneuver. The Mystic River is located seven miles to the east but is very shallow, with a narrow channel, making it difficult for even small ships to maneuver, and, therefore, they would be at risk of being attacked from canoes.

Relations between the Pequot and English continued to deteriorate over the murder of Captain Stone and his crew, and the increasing tensions began to affect the trade. In February 1635 Winthrop reported to Governor Winslow of Plymouth that "we are now preparing to send a pinass unto them [i.e., Pequot]," but a short time later Winthrop reported that "Our pinass is lately returned from the Pequents; they put off but little comoditie, and found them a very false people, so as they mean to have no more to doe with them."[36] The pinass Winthrop referred to may have been that of Oldham, who often traded with the Pequot. Oldham was killed in his ship off Block Island in July 1636 by the Manisses of Block Island, who were apparently paid to do so by several petty Narragansett sachems because "he went to make peace, and trade with the Pekods last year."[37]

Plymouth trading vessels appear to have visited Pequot territory on a fairly regular basis between 1633 and 1636 until they too stopped all trade out of fear of Pequot attacks. Jonathan Brewster reported in June of 1636 that he

had occasion to send my man who hath the Indian language to a place called Munhicke [Mohegan on the Thames River], distant from the Pequents 12 myles, partly upon business of my own, and partly to discover the proceedings of the Pequents . . . the sachem thereof called Woncase [Uncas], sent me word that upon the 23rd of May last, Sasocuse [Sassacus], chief sachem of the Pequents, with his brother Sacowauein, and the old men held consultation one day, and most part of one night, about cutting off of our Plymouth Barke, being then in their harbor weakly manned, who resolving thereupon appointed 80 men in armes before day to surprise her: but it pleased the over ruling power of God to hinder them, for as soon as those bloody executioners arose out of the ambush with their canoes, they discerned her under sail; with a fayre wind returned home: which act of theirs (circumstances considered) is intolerable for us to put up.[38]

Brewster also reported an incident that occurred two years earlier (possibly in the spring of 1634): "The Pequents confessed that if our barke had but stayed 6 hours longer in their harbor, they had cut her off, or at least attempted it."[39] The first report from Uncas should be taken with a grain of salt given that Uncas had cause to increase tensions between the English and the Pequot, but the second report is credible as it was probably obtained by Brewster directly from a Pequot. If these reports are true it is hard to understand why the Pequot would take any action that would cut off trade with the English. It is interesting that almost all of the references to English ships trading with the Pequot describe a failed trading venture or potential hostility from the Pequot. By the early spring of 1635, Massachusetts Bay was no longer trading with the Pequot and by June 1636, if not before, Plymouth was not either. Individual traders from Connecticut (such as Oldham) and men with warehouses at Saybrook Point may have continued to do so even on the eve of the Pequot War. The Dutch continued to trade with the Pequot even after the English declared war and were preparing to attack the Pequot fortified village at Mistick:

A little before wee set forth, came a certaine shippe from the Dutch Plantation; casting an ankor under the command of our Ordnance, we desired the Master to come ashore, the Master and Marchant willing to answer our expectation, came forth, and sitting with us awhile unexpectedly revealed their intent, that they were bound for Pequeat river to trade; our selves knowing the accustome of warre, that it was not the practise in a case of this nature, to suffer others to goe and trade with them our enemies, with such commodities as might be prejudiciall unto us, and advantageous to them, as kettles, or the like, which make them Arrowheads; wee gave command to them not to stirre, alledging that our forces were intended daily to fall upon them.[40]

In July 1636 John Winthrop Jr. received orders from Governor Henry Vane of Massachusetts to meet with the Pequots at Saybrook Fort and demand that the murderers of Stone be turned over for justice and that the remaining wampum the Pequot promised in recompense for Stone's murder be turned over as well. Winthrop's instructions were that if any Pequot was "found guilty of any of the sayd Murthers and will not deliver the Actors in them into our hands, that then, (as before you are directed) you return them the Present [a gift of wampum and furs given by the Pequot in November 1634] and declare to them that we hold ourselves free from any league or peace with them and shall revenge the blood of our Countrymen as occasion shall serve."[41] There is no record of what happened at the meeting, but the presents of wampum and furs were returned, and as a result the Pequot and Massachusetts Bay were in an undeclared state of war. Nonetheless, Lieutenant Gardener reported:

2 or 3 dayes after [the meeting] came an Indean from pequit, whose name was cocommithus who had lived at Plimmoth and could speake good English, he desired yt Mr Steven winthrop would goe to pequit with an 100"s worth of trucking cloath and all other trading ware for they knew yt we had a great cargoe of goods of Mr Pinchons & Mr Steven winthrop had ye disposing of it And he said yt if he would come he might put off all his goods.[42]

Gardiner sent Steven Winthrop and five men in his shallop to the Thames River to trade with the Pequot. Anticipating trouble, he gave specific instructions to anchor in the middle of the river and not go ashore. He also instructed the men to be well armed with muskets and swords and only allow one canoe with no more than four Pequots at a time to come aboard the ship "as I durst not trust them." Gardiner reported they "found but little trade."[43] Against Gardener's orders the men went ashore, and when one of the men entered a sachem's wigwam his wife "made signs to him yt he should be gone for they would cut off his head."[44] This was apparently the last English attempt to trade with the Pequot.

With the exception of a six- or eight-month period during the Pequot-Dutch War, the Dutch were the primary trading partner with the Pequot for twenty-five years. In comparison, the English did not begin to establish trade relations with the Pequot until mid-1633 and by 1635–36 both Massachusetts Bay and Plymouth ceased trading with the Pequot. Even when the English did send out trading vessels to the Pequot they often reported little success in the trade. Based on this subjective analysis, it is likely that most of the trade goods found in Pequot domestic sites from the period 1611–37 are of Dutch origin.

Pequot Domestic Sites

Although only 2.5 miles of the Battle of the English Withdrawal has been investigated through metal detector surveys and limited excavations, over 1,250 seventeenth-century artifacts were recovered. Approximately eight hundred of the objects were English battle-related objects such as musket balls, gun parts from flintlock, matchlock, and wheelock firearms, as well as a variety of other weapons (pikes, knives), equipment (e.g., buckles, musket rests, touch hole cleaners, gun worms), and personal items (jaw harps, buttons, dice, scissors). Battle-related and personal objects associated with the Native combatants included brass arrow points, breastplate, beads, brass and lead amulets, scissors, knives, and jaw harps (figures 7.14–7.17).

The most significant and surprising outcome of the metal detector survey of the Battle of the English Withdrawal was the identification of five, possibly six early (ca. 1611–37) seventeenth-century Pequot domestic sites (figure 7.3). One of the sites (59-73) is located approximately half a mile from the Mistick Fort and was likely occupied and abandoned just before the English–Native Allied column passed by it on their withdrawal after the Mistick Fort battle.[45]

Two radiocarbon samples dates from sites 59-73 and 59-111 were submitted to PaleoResearch Institute, Inc. A date of 235±15 RCYB (PRI-6004) was obtained from hickory shell from Site 59-73, which calibrates to 310–280 BP or AD 1640–70, and a date of 235±15 RCYBP (PRI-6006) was obtained from maize from Site 59-111, which calibrates to 310–280

BP or AD 1640–70. Site 59-111, possibly a large village, is not believed to have been occupied at the time of the battle but may have been abandoned shortly before.

It cannot be determined if any of the other domestic sites were occupied at the time of the battle, as the English narratives are silent on the matter, but they likely were not. However, based on the beginning date of Dutch trade and the end date of Pequot occupation in the area it is safe to infer that the remaining four or five domestic sites date between ca. 1611 and mid-1637. It is not possible to seriate the sites into a more refined chronology at this time, but based on the known terminal date of the briefly occupied Site 59-73 (May 26, 1637), and comparative analyses with assemblages of Dutch trade goods recovered from reasonably well-dated early seventeenth-century Mahican, Mohawk, and Dutch sites, the remaining Pequot domestic sites should be able to be placed in more precise temporal contexts in the near future.[46]

The only potentially diagnostic artifacts recovered from the Pequot domestic sites were clay pipes, English North Devon Gravel Tempered Ware, a single fragment of delft (presumably Dutch), a blue glass seed bead that Bradley dates between 1625 and 1635, blue tubular glass beads, and Pequot ceramics of the Hackney Pond Variety.[47] The English North Devon Gravel Tempered Ware recovered from Site 59-73 is consistent with the later date of the site, as the Pequot did not begin to trade with the English until 1633. The Hackney Pond ceramics recovered from all of the Pequot domestic sites have been consistently dated to the late pre-Contact and early Contact Periods, and were replaced by Shantok Ware ceramics immediately after the Pequot War (figure 7.5).[48]

The Pequot hamlet (Site 59-73) burned by the English was identified based on a brief reference in Captain John Mason's narrative of the Pequot War. Mason stated that the English–Native Allied force stopped to rest at a stream at the bottom of Pequot Hill following the attack on the Mistick Fort: "There was at the Foot of the Hill a small Brook, where we rested and refreshed ourselves, having by that time taught them a little more Manners than to disturb us. We then marched on towards Pequot Harbor; and falling upon several Wigwams, burnt them."[49]

Mason's account indicates the hamlet was not far from the brook, as it was the next action he described after the column resumed their march. He also indicated the potential size (several wigwams) and possible archaeological signature (domestic artifacts, possible features, and evidence of burning). A metal detector survey located the village based on the initial recovery of

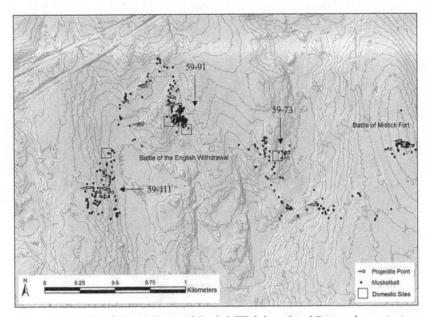

Figure 7.3. Battles of Mistick Fort and English Withdrawal and Pequot domestic sites.

several fragments of brass scrap from reprocessed trade kettles. Subsequent metal detector surveys and excavations recovered over 125 brass and iron objects, most of them reprocessed to make other objects such as brass and iron arrow points, brass beads, awls, wedges, and chisels (figures 7.9, 7.13, 7.30–33). European clay pipes and early seventeenth-century Pequot (Hackney Pond Ware) and English ceramics (North Devon Gravel Tempered Ware), lead cloth seal, and blue glass seed beads were also recovered, indicating an early seventeenth-century occupation (figures 7.5, 7.18, 7.26). Phosphate testing to identify burned areas suggests the presence of several structures (figure 7.4). Two shell middens with faunal and botanical remains and dozens of reprocessed iron and brass objects along with a group of post molds were found adjacent to the high phosphate areas. The thinness of the middens and the recovered botanical and faunal remains suggest the site was occupied for only a few weeks in the spring.

It is believed that the village represented by Site 59-73 had been recently relocated from the coast to its present location just a few weeks prior to the battle. The site was strategically located between the two Pequot fortified villages at Mistick and Weinshauks (Fort Hill), suggesting the village was

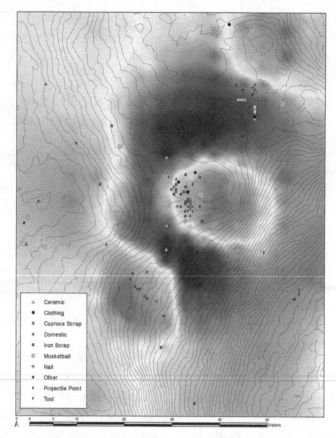

Figure 7.4. Site 59-73, phosphate analysis. Dark indicates burned areas.

relocated in anticipation of an English attack. With the discovery of Site 59-73, it was apparent that metal detected concentrations of brass scrap were a signature for Pequot domestic sites. As a result, four and possibly five additional domestic sites were identified along the route of withdrawal based on the recovery of concentrations of brass from reprocessed trade kettles and other objects as well as reprocessed iron trade goods and scrap.

These objects were originally thought to be part of the battlefield assemblage of Native and English dropped and broken personal items, weapons, and equipment. But when the more obvious battle-related objects such as musket balls and dropped and discarded English weapons and equipment and brass points were removed from the battlefield assemblage, it became clear that hundreds of trade objects and reprocessing debris were concentrated in several areas along the route of withdrawal, indicting areas of domestic activity (figure 7.3). Excavation units placed within the highest concentrations of brass scrap and reprocessed trade items in three of the domestic areas (in addition to Site 59-73) yielded Hackney Pond ceramics, Native clay and steatite pipes, European clay pipes, European ceramics (North Devon Gravel Tempered Ware and Delft), and a number of features including hearths, post molds, and small refuse areas (figures 7.5, 7.6, 7.17, 7.26, 7.27).

Several caches of two or three sets of iron trade goods were also recovered from the battlefield. When Mason described the attack on the Mistick Fort he stated that the original intent was "to destroy them by the Sword and save the Plunder."[50] As English casualties mounted after the English entered the fort, Mason decided to burn the fort and form a perimeter around the fort to prevent any Pequot from escaping.

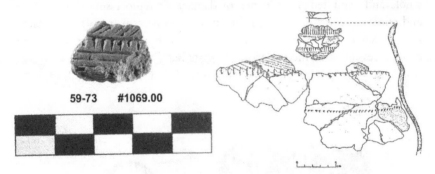

59-73   #1069.00

Figure 7.5. Site 59-73, Hackney Pond ceramics.

59-91   #787.00

Figure 7.6. Site 59-91, Pequot incised pipe bowl.

Although the fort was burned, iron trade items would survive the flames and it appears that the English and their Native allies "plundered" many valuable iron trade items that were easily transportable such as mattocks, axes, hoes, trenchers, and a hammer. Most of these objects were likely taken from the Mistick Fort (Site 59-19) but a few may have been taken from Site 59-73 if it was quickly abandoned as the English–Allied Native column approached the village. In the heat of battle these objects were either cached with the intent of returning to retrieve them or they were simply dropped or discarded along the route of withdrawal.

The axe, hoe/mattock, and hammer depicted in figure 7.7 (#s 338, 340, 341) were found within inches of one another in the same pit feature. The mattocks depicted in figure 7.8 were recovered in a similar context in another location on the battlefield. All of the objects recovered from battlefield contexts (i.e., those that were not associated with domestic sites) were whole and exhibited no evidence of damage or reprocessing (i.e., cutting and removing constituent parts). In contrast, 63 percent (n=10) of the large iron objects recovered from domestic contexts exhibited evidence of damage or reprocessing with their constituent parts removed or modified, and they could no longer function as originally intended (figures 7.9–7.13).

Figure 7.7. Site 72-40, cached iron trade goods; #341 ax, #340 mattock, #338 masonry hammer, # 137 trencher.

Figure 7.8. Site 59-111, cached iron mattocks.

Figure 7.9. Reprocessed iron hoe and iron arrow point, Site 59-73.

59-91 #311.00   59-91 #313.00

Figure 7.10. Site 59-91, reprocessed iron axe with scoring.

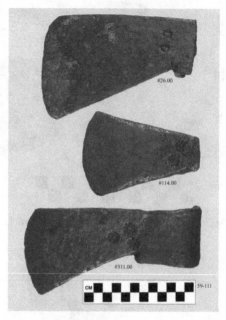

Figure 7.11. Site 59-111, reprocessed iron axes with poll (eyelet) removed (poll removed on reverse side of #311).

Figure 7.12. Site 59-111, reprocessed iron axe with blade and poll.

The reprocessed hoe in figure 7.9 was cut at an angle at the end of the blade where the cross section was thinnest. An iron arrow point was recovered from the battlefield with exactly the same cross section, suggesting it may have been made from the section of the hoe blade that was removed. The axe depicted in figure 7.10 was reprocessed to remove the thinner iron that formed the poll (eyelet) and exhibits an uneven cut, indicating the cutting method was sawing and cutting by abrasion using a heavy cord and sand rather than a file. Of the six reprocessed axes recovered, all had their polls removed (figures 7.10–13). The blade of the ax may have been cut longitudinally to make celts, as depicted in figure 7.13.

Figure 7.14 depicts all brass arrow points recovered from the Battles of Mistick Fort and the English Withdrawal. Several distinct styles can be identified, some of which can be attributed to the Pequot, Mohegan, Narragansett, Eastern Niantic, and Wangunk tribes based on their context within the battlefield. The conical points in the top row are associated with the Wangunk of the Middle Connecticut River Valley.[51] Points numbered 716–718 are Pequot, as they were recovered from within the Mistick Fort. Points numbered 114 and 648 are believed to be associated with the Eastern Niantic based on similarities with points recovered from the Fort Ninigret

59-73 #378.00

59-73 #357.00

CM

Figure 7.13. Site 59-73, reprocessed iron mortise/felling ax (top) and reprocessed iron axe to form celts.

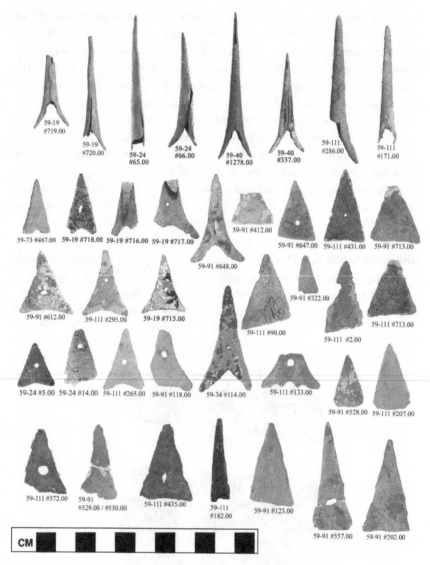

Figure 7.14. Brass and iron (59-11 #182) arrow points.

site, and points numbered 295, 612, and 715 are believed to be associated with the Narragansett. The iron point (#182) may be Pequot.

The number and variety of trade goods provide an opportunity to examine the nature, mechanics, and evolution of trade between the Pequot and the English and Dutch. It is believed that most of the trade goods recovered from the Pequot domestic sites are of Dutch origin, based on the simple calculation that the Pequot were trading with the Dutch for twenty-five years and with the English for only three to four years. In addition, in 1635 and in the first half of 1636, most of the English trading ventures to the Pequot seemed to have ended in failure either because of Pequot belligerence or the Pequot did not have anything to trade.

There are many questions regarding the nature of European-Native trade that have rarely been addressed, in part because European sources do not provide much information on Native perspectives on trade or how the process of trade and redistribution of trade objects functioned in Native communities. To what extent did Natives dictate the terms of trade, and the trade inventory carried by traders? Who conducted trade in Native communities: sachems and social and political elites, specially designated traders, or any individual within the community? How were trade goods redistributed within the community and to leaders and individuals in other communities or tribes? Did Native leaders form exclusive trading relationships with certain Dutch or English traders? Did the Pequot control access to

Figure 7.15. Site 59-40, modified iron knife.

Figure 7.16. Site 59-40, brass pipe refashioned from trade kettle.

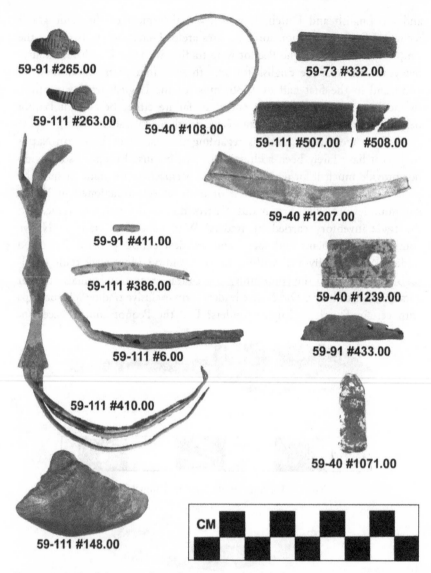

59-91 #265.00

59-111 #263.00

59-40 #108.00

59-73 #332.00

59-111 #507.00 / #508.00

59-40 #1207.00

59-91 #411.00

59-111 #386.00

59-40 #1239.00

59-111 #6.00

59-91 #433.00

59-111 #410.00

59-40 #1071.00

CM

59-111 #148.00

Figure 7.17. Lead, brass, and graphite native personal objects. #s 263 and 265 brass Jesuit rings, #108 Dutch brass bracelet, #s 332, 433, 1239, 1071 reprocessed brass and lead amulets, # 507/508 steatite pipe, #1207 reprocessed brass pipe, #s 6, 386, 411 reprocessed brass beads, #410 reprocessed brass comb/hairpiece, #148 graphite.

Dutch and English traders in return for tribute in trade goods, wampum, furs, and other goods from subjugated and allied tribes? Did the Pequot have differential access to Dutch and English trade goods because of their power and influence and control of the wampum trade?

Native Traders

It is not at all clear how Native trade with the Europeans was conducted. Did the sachems or other high-status individuals such as councilors oversee trade and identify preferences and priorities of trade goods? How were trade goods disseminated within the community and throughout the tribe? Could any individual conduct trade with Europeans? How was wampum production organized? Was each community responsible for producing its own wampum for trade or was it a tribal-wide effort?

The historical sources do not provide a lot of information to address these questions, but some inferences can be made with the little information available. The Pequot sachems may have been personally involved in some trade transactions or at least established protocols that were followed throughout the tribe. When Jaques Elckes kidnapped the chief Pequot sachem in 1622 and "imprisoned him on his yacht," the sachem was probably already onboard the Dutch ship perhaps to trade or negotiate.[52] In 1626 the Pequot chief sachem made an agreement with Pieter Barentsz "not to trade with any other than him," suggesting the sachem was making a policy for the entire tribe.[53]

Tatopam met with Lieutenant Holmes of the Plymouth trading post and chided him for not seeking permission or not giving him a gift for purchasing the land for the post from the Wangunk sachem Attawanhut. While we do not know if there was any other purpose to the meeting, the account certainly indicates the sachem was directly involved in some of the negotiations and discussions with the English. In 1636, a Narragansett man was reported to have "carried three beaver skins and beads for Caunounicus's [chief Narragansett sachem] son, and came home with five fathom [of wampum] and three coats," suggesting trade was carried out on behalf of a sachem or person of status.[54]

Most of the references to Natives trading with Europeans involve individuals or groups with no apparent direction or oversight from Native sachems or leaders. Gardiner's instructions to his men when they went to trade at Pequot

Harbor was "yt they should let but one canoe cum aboard at once with no more but 4 Indeans in her, & when they had traded then another."[55] While these instructions were in anticipation of a potential attack, it does suggest that at other times several canoe loads of Native traders would get onboard a ship to trade. Roger Williams's *A Key into the Language of America* makes several references to trade, and the context suggests individuals were trading on their own behalf: "I have bought, I will buy of you, I come to buy this, Have you any cloth?, You ask too much, How much shall I give you, You have deceived me, Let us trade, Have you this or that?, I want this, I like this, I do not like, I want many things, I come to buy."[56]

Material Culture

Dutch and English sources identify a variety of items typically traded to Natives. By far the highest volume was cloth. Duffel, a coarse woolen or Kersey cloth, is the most frequently mentioned trade item, although a wide variety of different types of cloth were traded. Cloth was always the most important item in Dutch and English trade inventories: "They all generally prize a mantle of English or Dutch cloth before their own wearing of skins and furs, because they are warme enough and lighter, Cloth inclining to white they like not, but desire to have a sad color without any whitish hairs."[57] The importance of duffel in the trade with Natives is indicated in a letter from Isaack de Rasieres, secretary of New Netherland, to the West India Company in 1626:

> They [Northern or French Indians] come to us for no other reason than to get wampum, which the French cannot procure unless they come to barter for it with our natives in the north, just as the brownists of Plymouth come near our places to get wampum in exchange. I beg to submit to your honors whether, if we could overtake French and English sloops here, it would not be well by some means or other to take the trade away from them, either by force or by spoiling their trade by outbidding them with duffels or hatchets, in order that they themselves would have to come to us to get wampum, or that we in going to them could exchange the wampum for skins in their possession. And instead of giving the Indians 2 ½ hand-lengths, we could give them three or four hands. To do this, there would have to be

two or three large sloops more. If it will please the honorable gentlemen to supply me continually with duffels, I shall know how to get wampum and to stock Fort Orange in such a way that the French Indians will never come here again in vain, as they have done heretofore. . . . I hope this winter before the frost sets in to stock Fort Orange with a thousand yards of wampum [350,000 beads], nearly all of which I have in my possession, in order that Crool may have success. Only I am very much afraid that I shall be short of duffels when the time comes, so that I am again obliged to beg the honorable gentlemen to assist me towards the end of March or the beginning of next April with 200 pieces, in order that I may be enabled to keep the sloops continually going, and thereby prevent the Indians in the north from going to the English [with] their skins, as they did last spring.[58]

I have only about 30 pieces of cloth in colors that are in demand, that is blue and standard grey; the rest which I have are all red, whereof I can hardly sell a yard, because the Indians say that it hinders them in hunting, being too far off. They all call for black, the darker the color the better, but red and green they will not take. If by that time your Honors will be pleased to provide me with duffels as hereinbefore mentioned, I hope to send back about 10,000 skins in return, and that in time for the Amsterdam fair. Why should we go hunting? Half the time you have no cloth.[59]

The link between wampum and duffel cloth is underscored by the fact that the Pequot largely controlled the wampum trade and were constantly requesting that the English (and presumably the Dutch) bring cloth to trade for their furs and wampum. The importance of cloth in relation to other trade goods is indicated in a bill from John Pynchon to John Winthrop Jr. for trade goods Winthrop purchased from Pynchon in March 1635. The total worth of the cloth purchased was 197 pounds, and all other goods were worth only 3 ½ pounds.[60] Cloth does not survive in archaeological contexts, but lead bale seals that are attached to bolts of cloth used to identify the maker, quantity, and quality of the cloth are commonly found within archaeological sites. While only one bale seal was recovered from the five domestic sites (Site 59-73; figure 7.18) it certainly does not reflect the amount of cloth traded to the Pequot.

Figure 7.18. Lead bale/cloth seal. Note the P in right/middle of the seal (left).

The other most frequently traded items mentioned by English and Dutch sources were hatchets/axes, knives (the Dutch distinguish between French knives [folding/clasp?] and straight knives), kettles (brass and to a lesser degree iron), glass beads, and mattocks. Mattocks are agricultural tools that are a combination of an ax blade and an adze shaped like a pickax and used for breaking up new or hard ground (figure 7.8). Mattocks have a rectangular eyelet with a wider and thicker blade while hoes have an ovate eyelet and the blade is wider and thinner. Hoes are used primarily for weeding (figures 7.19 and 7.20).

De Rasieres testified to the importance of mattocks in the trade when he requested of the directors of the West India Company, "Your honors will also be pleased to send me by the next ship 3000 or 4000 mattocks, for I fear that by the time the Indians will wish to plant I shall be short of mattocks."[61] There's no information on what the Dutch meant by mattocks and the term could have included mattocks and hoes, although de Rasieres's reference to planting suggests they were used to break new ground. Mattocks (n=5) and hoes (n=4) were the most common iron trade objects recovered from the battlefield and domestic sites, followed by axes (n=5). There could be other examples of mattocks, hoes, and axes represented in the overall assemblage, but they may have been so modified they no longer retain any evidence of their original form. Several of the iron objects identified as chisels, planes, or celts are likely reworked axes or mattock/hoes (figure 7.13).

The maker's marks on the axes, combined with the distinct ovate shape of the eye, identify them as Biscayne axes (figures 7.10–7.12, 7.22). The axes were hand-wrought and made from a single strap of iron and folded over to form the poll (eyelet). They were manufactured by blacksmiths along the Bay of Biscayne in southwestern France and northern Spain from the sixteenth through the late seventeenth centuries and traded throughout North America by the Spanish, French, Dutch, and English, and were considered the best quality axes in the world.

59-123 #502.00   59-73 #9.00   59-123 #20.00   59-111 #262.00

Figure 7.19. Narrow iron hoes.

59-122 #39.00

Figure 7.20. Repurposed broad iron hoe.

Figure 7.21. Iron punch.

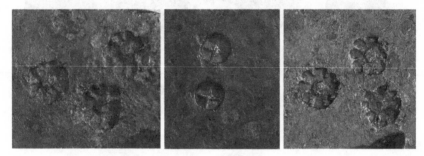

Figure 7.22. Biscayne axe makers' marks; (L) 59-111 #114, (M) 59-123 #26, (R) 59-111 # 311.

William Pynchon's trade inventory from 1636 identifies a number of trade items he sold to John Winthrop Jr., intended for use in the fur and wampum trade: 2 doz. looking glasses; 3 quart potts; 4 doz. Jewes harpes; 4 doz. of Steele aule blades; 1 doz. of porengers large; 1 doz. occomy spones; 15 howes large (figures 7.19, 7.20, 7.23, 7.24).[62]

Quart pots (presumably brass), jew/jaw harps, awl blades, porringers, spoons, pot hooks, scissors, and hoes were all recovered from Pequot domestic sites (figures 7.23–7.24, 7.29–7.30, 7.32–7.34). Other trade items recovered from the battlefield and domestic sites that are not specifically mentioned in Dutch or English trade inventories include clasp or folding knives, iron and brass punches and awls, trenchers, masonry hammers, pot hooks, nails, boxes, Jesuit rings, brass beads, cuprous kettle fragments (bales, lugs, scrap), iron kettle fragments and scrap, brass escutcheons, brass box hinges and latches, bottle glass (case bottle), iron fishhooks, brass spoon fragments (bowl, handle), iron scissors, and many other as yet unidentified objects (figures 7.17, 7.28–7.34).

Ten fragments of white clay (kaolin) pipes and one complete bowl of either English or Dutch manufacture were recovered from the Pequot domestic sites (figures 7.26, 7.27). The bore diameters of the pipes measured 6/64ths (3), 7/64ths (2), and 8/64ths (1). According to J. C. Harrington's study of pipe stem diameters, pipe stem bore diameters and associated dates are as follows:[63]

9/64 inches:	1590–1620
8/64 inches:	1620–1650
7/64 inches:	1650–1680
6/64 inches:	1680–1720
5/64 inches:	1720–1750
4/64 inches:	1750–1800

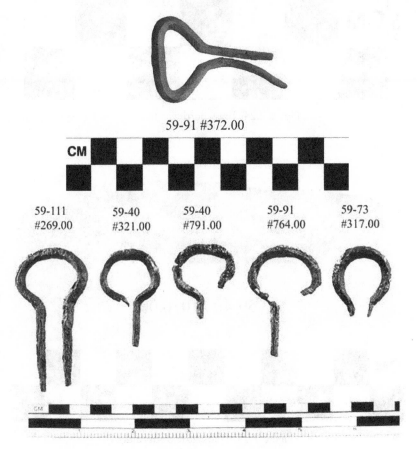

59-91 #372.00

| 59-111 | 59-40 | 59-40 | 59-91 | 59-73 |
| #269.00 | #321.00 | #791.00 | #764.00 | #317.00 |

Figure 7.23. Brass (top) and iron (bottom) jaw harps.

59-111 #64.00

Figure 7.24. Brass porringer fragment.

59-40 #1076.00

Figure 7.25. Folding or clasp knife.

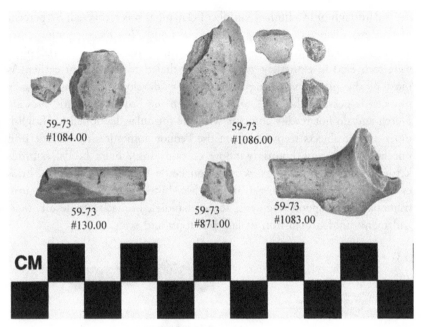

59-73
#1084.00

59-73
#1086.00

59-73
#130.00

59-73
#871.00

59-73
#1083.00

CM

Figure 7.26. European clay pipes.

59-91 #922.00

CM

Figure 7.27. European clay pipe bowl.

Although only a limited sample of clay pipes was recovered, 84 percent of the bore diameters were between 6/64ths and 7/64ths, suggesting dates in the second half of the seventeenth century. However, all of the pipes were recovered in extremely good contexts that date to 1637 or earlier. As most of the pipe-stem-dating formulas were developed for English-made pipes, it is possible the pipes recovered from the Pequot domestic sites are Dutch and do not readily compare with the formulas developed for English pipes. Other objects recovered from the Pequot domestic sites include iron pot hooks, cuprous hoops (window curtain ring), brass beads, cuprous kettle fragments (bales, lugs, scrap), iron kettle fragments and scrap, brass escutcheons, brass box hinges and latches, bottle glass (case bottle), iron fishhooks, brass spoon fragments (bowl, handle), iron scissors, Jesuit rings, and many unidentified iron or cuprous tools and scrap.

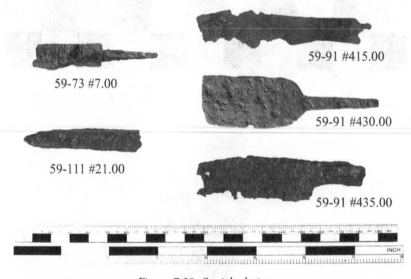

59-73 #7.00

59-91 #415.00

59-91 #430.00

59-111 #21.00

59-91 #435.00

Figure 7.28. Straight knives.

59-91 #646.00

CM

Figure 7.29. Brass awl.

Figure 7.30. Site 59-73. Reprocessed brass objects. #345 unknown; #348 knife bolster; #350 unknown; #363 folding knife scale; #367 kettle scrap; #328 bead; #332 incised caste amulet, #333; 338 kettle scrap; #31 box hinge; #37 key hole; #s 260, 159 kettle scrap.

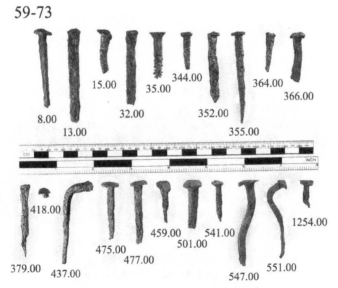

Figure 7.31. Site 59-73, rose head nails.

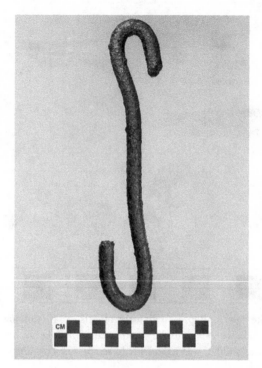

Figure 7.32. Site 59-73, pot hook.

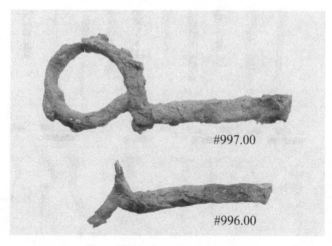

#997.00

#996.00

Figure 7.33. Site 59-73, scissors.

Figure 7.34. reprocessed brass objects; #s 200 and 27 kettle scrap; #40 escutcheon; #s 178 and 130 wire; #s 767, 150, 224 unknown; #279 spoon handle; #s 175, 191, 454, 270 kettle lugs.

Conclusion

The five Pequot domestic sites constitute the largest assemblage of early seventeenth-century sites associated with a single Native group yet identified in southern New England. Individually and collectively, these sites have the potential to yield important information on the nature of Pequot settlement patterns, trade with the Dutch and English, evolving Pequot technology, trade patterns, and the production of war-related materials. The number and diversity of English and Dutch trade items recovered from the five domestic sites is unprecedented in the archaeology of nonburial Contact Period sites. The hundreds of iron, brass, lead, pewter, and ceramic objects that were recovered from the Pequot domestic sites not only attest to the

212 / Kevin A. McBride

extent of Pequot trade with the Dutch and English but also to the method by which these objects were reprocessed and incorporated into Pequot social, ideological, military, and economic contexts.

The key to understanding the nature and evolution of the trade between the Pequot, the Dutch, and the English is the correct identification of whole objects, reprocessed objects before they were modified, the form and purpose of reprocessed objects, and whether the objects were of Dutch or English origin. An equally important aspect of future analysis will be to seriate the sites into more specific temporal divisions to examine the changing availability and preferences for certain trade goods by the Pequot.

Notes

1. Kevin McBride, David Naumec, Ashley Bissonnette, and Noah Fellman, "Battle of Mistick Fort: English Withdrawal and Pequot Counterattacks" (report on file with the National Park Service American Battlefield Protection Program, 2017).

2. McBride et al., "Battle of Mistick Fort."

3. Kevin McBride, "War and Trade in Eastern New Netherland," in *A Beautiful and Fruitful Place*, ed. Margriet Lacy (Albany: New Netherlands Institute, 2013), 271–285.

4. J. Franklin Jameson, ed., *The Narratives of New Netherland, 1609–1664* (New York: Charles Scribner's Sons, 1909), 87, 103.

5. Door De Heeren, H. Van Beverningk, W. Nieupoort, J. van de Perre, and A. P. Jongestal, *Verbael Gehouden*, 1725, 607. Translated by Charles Gehring. New York: New Netherland Project.

6. McBride, "War and Trade in Eastern New Netherland."

7. E. B. O'Callaghan, *Documents Relative to the Colonial History of the State of New York, Vol. I* (New York: Weed Parsons and Company, 1856), 10–11; Simon Hart, *The Prehistory of the New Netherland Company: Amsterdam Notarial Records of the First Dutch Voyages to the Hudson* (Amsterdam: City of Amsterdam Press, 1959).

8. O'Callaghan, *Documents Relative to the Colonial History of the State of New York, Vol. I*, 11; McBride, *War and Trade*; I. N. Phelps Stokes, *The Iconography of Manhattan Island, Volume 2* (New York: Robert H. Dodd, 1928), 68.

9. Johan de Laet, "New World," in *The Narratives of New Netherland, 1609–1664*, ed. J. Franklin Jameson (New York: Charles Scribner's Sons, 1909), 29–58; Nicolas van Wassenaer, "Historisch Verhael 1624–1630," in *The Narratives of New Netherland, 1609–1664*, ed. J. Franklin Jameson (New York: Charles Scribner's Sons, 1909), 61–90.

10. Stokes, *The Iconography of Manhattan Island, Volume 2*, 68.

11. Hart, *Prehistory of New Netherland Company*; Wassenaer, *Historisch Verhael*, 78.

12. Howard M. Chapin, *Cartography of Rhode Island, Contributions to Rhode Island Bibliography*, No. 3 (Providence: Preston and Rounds Co., 1915); Stokes, *The Iconography of Manhattan Island, Volume 2*, 5–29, 66–78.

13. Hart, *Prehistory of New Netherland Company*; Stokes, *The Iconography of Manhattan Island, Volume I*, 52–58; de Laet, *New World*; Wassenaer, *Historisch Verhael*.

14. De Laet, *New World*, 41–44.

15. James Bradley, *Before Albany: An Archaeology of Native-Dutch Relations in the Capitol Region 1600–1664*, Bulletin 509 (Albany: New York State Museum, 2008).

16. O' Callaghan, *Documents Relative to the Colonial History of the State of New York, Vol. II*, 543.

17. Wassenaer, *Historisch Verhael*, 78.

18. Letter of Isaack de Rasieres to the Directors of *the Amsterdam Chamber of* the West India Company, *Fort Amsterdam on Manhattan Island, September 23, 1626*, in A. J. F. van Laer, ed., *Documents Relating to New Netherland, 1624–1626* (San Marino, CA: Henry E. Huntington Library, 1924), 224–227.

19. Instructions for Willem Verhulst, Director of New Netherland, January 1625, in van Laer, *Documents Relating to New Netherland, 1624–1626*, 52–68.

20. Wassenaer, *Historisch Verhael*, 78.

21. Wassenaer, *Historisch Verhael*, 87.

22. O' Callaghan, *Documents Relative to the Colonial History of the State of New York, Vol. II*, 543.

23. William Bradford, *History of Plymouth Plantation 1620–1647, Volume II* (Boston: Massachusetts Historical Society, 1912), 168.

24. James Kendall Hosmer, ed., *Winthrop's Journal, Vol. I* (New York: Charles Scribner's Sons, 1908), 139.

25. Bradford, *History of Plymouth Plantation, Vol. II*, 192.

26. Hosmer, *Winthrop's Journal, Vol. I*, 139.

27. Hosmer, *Winthrop's Journal, Vol. I*, 189.

28. Lion Gardener, *Relation of the Pequot Warres* (Hartford, CT: Hartford Press, 1901), 10.

29. Hosmer, *Winthrop's Journal, Vol. I*, 189.

30. Bradford, *History of Plymouth Plantation, Vol. II*, 192.

31. Hosmer, *Winthrop's Journal, Vol. I*, 189.

32. Hosmer, *Winthrop's Journal, Vol. I*, 108.

33. Hosmer, *Winthrop's Journal, Vol. I*; *Winthrop Papers, Vol. III, 1631–1637* (Boston: Massachusetts Historical Society, 1943).

34. Wassenaer, *Historisch Verhael*, 87.

35. Hosmer, *Winthrop's Journal, Vol. I*, 139.

36. Bradford, *History of Plymouth Plantation, Vol. II*, 192.

37. Hosmer, *Winthrop's Journal, Vol. I*, 184.

38. Bradford, *History of Plymouth Plantation, Vol. II*, 270.

39. *Winthrop Papers, Vol. III, 1631–1637*, 271.

40. John Underhill, *Newes from America* (Lincoln: University of Nebraska Digital Texts, [1638] 2007), 23.

41. *Winthrop Papers, Vol. III, 1631–1637*, 285.

42. Gardener, *Relation of the Pequot Warres*, 7–8.

43. Gardener, *Relation of the Pequot Warres*, 8.

44. Gardener, *Relation of the Pequot Warres*, 8.

45. Thomas Prince, ed., *A Brief History of the Pequot War Written by John Mason* (Boston: S. Kneeland and T. Green, 1736), 11.

46. Bradley, *Before Albany*; Paul Huey, "Aspects of Continuity and Change in Colonial Dutch Material Culture at Fort Orange, 1624–1664," PhD diss., University of Pennsylvania, 1988.

47. Bradley, *Before Albany*; Kevin McBride, "Prehistory of the Lower Connecticut River Valley," PhD diss., University of Connecticut, 1984.

48. McBride, "Prehistory of the Lower Connecticut River Valley."

49. Prince, A *Brief History of the Pequot War*, 11.

50. Prince, *A Brief History*, 8.

51. McBride, *War and Trade in Eastern New Netherland*, 279–280.

52. Wassenaer, *Historisch Verhael*, 86.

53. Wassenaer, *Historisch Verhael*, 86.

54. Glenn W, LaFantasie, ed., *The Correspondence of Roger Williams, Volume I, 1629–1653* (Providence: Brown University Press, 1988), 171.

55. Gardener, *Relation of the Indian Warres*, 8.

56. Roger Williams, *A Key into the Language of America* (Bedford: Applewood Books, [1643] 1936), 159–162.

57. Williams, *A Key into the Language*, 160.

58. De Rasieres, *Letter to the Directors of the Amsterdam Chamber of the West India Company, Fort Amsterdam on Manhattan Island, September 23, 1626*, 223–231.

59. De Rasieres, *Letter to the Directors of the Amsterdam Chamber of the West India Company, Fort Amsterdam on Manhattan Island, September 23, 1626*, 231.

60. *Winthrop Papers, Vol. III, 1631–1637*, 271.

61. De Rasieres, *Letter to the Directors of the Amsterdam Chamber of the West India Company, Fort Amsterdam on Manhattan Island, September 23, 1626*, 232.

62. *Winthrop Papers, Vol. III, 1631–1637*, 238.

63. J. C. Harrington, "Dating Stem Fragments of Seventeenth and Eighteenth Century Clay Tobacco Pipes," *Quarterly Bulletin of the Archeological Society of Virginia* 9 (1) (1954).

8.

Roduins

A Dutch Fort in Branford, Connecticut

JOHN PFEIFFER

The discovery of the Dutch fort in Branford raises several issues that make it imperative to rethink how we envision early colonial southern New England history. In many regards, this chapter offers several hypotheses about the earliest presence of the Dutch in southern New England that vary from the traditional view. I offer a more complex model than the contemporary view of Dutch interest in the New World as a function of the fur trade. I pose that there were far more intricate schemes put together by Dutch companies to gain an exponential return on investments. In this model of Dutch involvement in the New World, the Dutch fort at Branford takes on a new complexion.

I also investigate the relationship between the Dutch and English in southern New England and challenge how traditional history has recorded it. The Dutch fort in Branford and a careful review of early colonial documents support a greater Dutch presence in southern New England, and in this chapter I explore how this might have been incorporated into the Dutch mercantile revolution.

Finally, I review the beginnings of Dutch tolerance, its effect upon cultural diversity, the resultant stimulus to the mercantile revolution, and how this was represented in seventeenth-century Dutch material culture. From this view, the artifacts that were excavated at the Dutch fort in Branford as well as other sites in New Netherland take on special meaning.

Introduction

History teaches us lessons—the Dutch were fast learners. Dutch, or Frisian, coastal trading cities had developed during the early Middle Ages in the agriculturally rich delta lowland region north of what is now France and west of contemporary Denmark. A bustling economy based upon agriculture, local industry, and maritime shipping provided the ingredients for the development of maritime cities. By the time of the First Crusade there were two hundred Frisian ships participating, carrying knights along the routes to the Holy Land.

The Crusades were called for by Pope Urban II in 1095 with the explicit goal of freeing the Holy Land from the Moslems. His call had at its heart an extremely intolerant basis and resulted in one of the West's lowest points in history. The First Crusade succeeded in taking Jerusalem in 1099. All living things, including non-Christian men, women, and children, were brutally murdered and their bodies desecrated.[1] Blood was said to have been waist deep in the streets.[2]

Jerusalem was held by the Crusaders for the next eighty-eight years. Muslim armies under the command of Saladin retook Jerusalem in 1187. The fighting was well removed from the city at the Battle of Hattin, where a siege and smoke tactic rendered the Crusaders totally ineffective. As a result, most of the Crusader cities were reunited under Muslim control. Jerusalem was peacefully turned over to Saladin.

Saladin's policy was one of tolerance. Even though the city had been taken in a bloodbath by the Christian forces, Saladin's conquest was one without revenge. He chose to permit Crusaders to move freely about until their ransom was paid and to pledge their honor to not rise up. In doing this, Saladin's policy established the opportunity for knights to savor Islamic culture, copy its technological advancements, and acquire a taste for spices and silk from China, as well as discover the Arabic sources of gold, ivory, and slaves. In many ways, Saladin's military policy created trading partners of the descendants of the Crusaders that had eighty-eight years earlier shown nothing but brutal inhumanity.[3]

Surely, Saladin's actions were practical social adjustments that made the best out of an injurious past. He looked beyond the aspect of his own hate and need for revenge, and instead looked at how the situation could serve as an opportunity for the long term. He embraced a mercantile perspective.

By the end of the Crusades, Frisia, or Holland, was in a key position to take up the Arab trade. It had the fleets, the knowledge of the world outside of Europe, and had experienced the benefits of a tolerant perspective. It is often noted by historians that Holland has been characterized by extremely tolerant people. Clearly, they accepted others who were being persecuted throughout Europe. Whether it was during the Inquisition in Spain, the Cromwellian regicide in England, or the torture and murder of the Huguenots in France, such groups were permitted to live in Holland. They looked beyond religious differences and hostilities and organized instead toward capitalizing on opportunity—mercantile opportunity. While I cannot say that their action was based upon what they had experienced in Jerusalem, their policy demonstrated the same practical bottom-line approach.[4] As historian Allan Bikk noted: "As the Dutch economy prospered, it demanded new modes of interaction. Quite simply, identifying people through their religious denomination alone and then dismissing or in some way injuring them was not only impractical but also stupid. Dutch tolerance therefore presumed a new set of values about how people should relate to one another."[5]

Discovery of a Dutch Fort in Branford

In the early 1990s, I went through all of the journals and miscellaneous papers of Ezra Stiles (1727–95) that were housed on microfilm at Olin Library at Wesleyan University; originals are at the Beinecke Library of Yale. I had read the article by William Sturtevant of the wigwams at Niantic in *American Antiquity*, and I was interested to find out if there were further references to Native Americans along Stiles's path of commuting between Newport, Rhode Island and New Haven, where he was the president of Yale College.[6]

What I discovered were hundreds of documents, letters, maps, and journal entries from the colonial period. Stiles had many personal observations, but he was also one of those individuals who was contacted by learned individuals of the time (or those that wished to be thought of as learned). Within the hundreds of papers were letters from Benjamin Franklin, German historians seeking information on colonial New England, and colonial census records identifying all occupants, including Indians and slaves, who are rarely enumerated elsewhere. There was discussion of the day about religion, the problem of the dilution of the races, mathematical calculations, discourses in Hebrew and classical Greek, and his own sketches along the route of his travels. To my absolute amazement, there were many pages of Indian information, based both upon his own observation as well as data sent to him by those that knew he would be interested.

In the *Itineraries and Miscellanies of Ezra Stiles 1755–1794* was a map of Branford, Connecticut (figure 8.1).[7] Within it was a reference to the Totokett Tribe and a *Dutch Fort*. Clearly, it was one of his own observations as he notes, "this is the largest body of shells that I have seen." He placed an "X" where the fort was located. As often happens in historic document research, I did not immediately follow up on the tantalizing lead but rather continued to conduct research of the Nehantic group of Native Americans who were situated in Lyme. I made a copy of the Branford map and filed it in a folder labeled "future potential research."

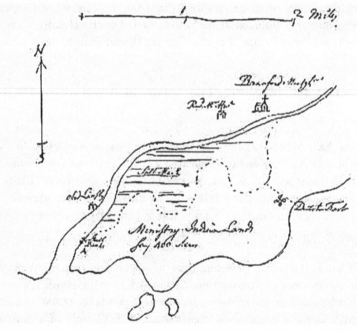

Figure 8.1. Stiles 1790 map of Totokett (from Franklin B. Dexter, *Extracts from the Itineraries and other Miscellanies of Ezra Stiles 1755–1794* [New Haven: Yale University Press, 1916], 413).

Dutch in Connecticut: The Traditional View

History is an interpretation of the past based upon various selected data as well as the paradigm under which such data are organized. Depending upon the sources used and the organizing elements employed by the historian, various interpretations can be made. There are, therefore, multiple histories for any said people, event, or time. Our history textbooks paint a view of the Dutch in Connecticut as traders. They set up trading posts positioned in such a way as to facilitate their acquiring furs from the Native populations in exchange for materials the Dutch had brought along as trade goods.

The traditional account of the timing of Dutch arrival as traders in Connecticut has been indicated as slightly prior to the English and then immediately being overshadowed. In some interpretations, it is suggested that the Dutch attempts in Connecticut were the direct result of their trying to compete with the English and beat them to the new resources, thus gaining an economic advantage.

Regarding exploration by the Dutch, the traditional view begins with Hudson's reconnoitering of the river that is identified by his name. It occurred toward the end of the first decade of the 1600s. In this view, the Hudson River became the center of Dutch settlement in North America. The Dutch exploration in Connecticut was undertaken in 1614 by Adrian Block sailing on the ship *Onrust*. However, such exploration was not significantly followed up until the early 1630s.

Dutch in Connecticut: A More Comprehensive View

While the traditional view persists, its accuracy is questionable. It is said that history is written by the victors, and in this case we have been subject to a clear dose of English bias. Our history of the colonial period is an English history, produced from English documents, and interpreted through an English viewpoint. Compounding this phenomenon is the fact that the English, at the time of documentation, intentionally underreported or left out direct references to other national or commercial interests. They probably did this because they did not want to put in place documents that could support competing colonial interests. This pattern of behavior is also apparent in their continual approach with Native American land transactions. They would purchase the same parcel multiple times from different native sellers in the quest for one of those sellers to be the rightful seller and thus avoid potential claims later on.

In the Connecticut colonies, there are only cursory references to the Dutch. In Hartford, for instance, as late as 1654, there is clear evidence of a Dutch land ownership around the Fort of Good Hope.[8] Another record is a complaint about Dutch cattle in Englishmen's corn.[9] In New Haven, there is a protracted discussion about shipping and trading in the other's territory. Peter Stuyvesant and Theophilus Eaton write back and forth, pointing out that the issues are capable of upsetting the agreement between the Dutch and English regarding their presence in the other's colony.[10] Yet when it comes to the writing of histories, the Dutch presence is understated or omitted. There is an interesting account by the Dutch commissary of the House of Good Hope where Gysbert Opdyck narrates an exchange over dinner with the English colony of Hartford's governor, John Haynes:

> The commander gave me orders to make a protest against them, as they were using our own land, which we had bought of the Indians. Some of our soldiers had forbidden them to put the plough into it; but they had disregarded them, and had cudgelled some of the Company's soldiers. Going there, I was invited by the English governor to dine; when sitting at the table, I told him that it was wrong to take by force the Company's land, which it had bought and paid for. He answered that the lands were lying idle; that though we had been there many years, we had done scarcely anything; that it was a sin to let such rich land, which produced such fine corn, lie uncultivated; and that they had already built three towns upon this river in a fine country.[11]

By English standards, ownership rights were invalidated if nothing had been done to improve the land. Clearing the ground, turning the soil, fencing, weeding, and manuring (an English term for managing) were necessary to literally maintain a claim. This argument was central to English having a right to the land of the Indians as well as the Dutch.

In New Haven, the colonial records show that Thomas Mullinar/ Molinar/Mouleno, of the eastern part of the colony—Totokett, or Branford—was harassed unmercifully by the ecclesiastical society. He was brought before the court on multiple occasions accused of not paying his men at the mill according to the set wage, drinking in public, failing to keep his animals enclosed within a fence, and not maintaining his property in a proper fashion. In November 1640, Mr. Mullinar "is commanded by the courte to stay his proceedings at Totokett inasmuch as what he hath done is disorderly."[12]

Mullinar is not on the list of English landowners or freemen to come to New Haven in 1639.[13] He is already there. He is noted as the first settler of Totokett and "gained ownership from the Indians."[14] He came from Ipswich, England, which had been heavily populated by the Dutch since the early Medieval period. The name Mullinar means miller in Dutch. Throughout the colonial records of New Haven, Mullinar was being harassed by the English in the same way that other Dutchmen were being treated in Hartford.

Finally, between 1639 and 1641 there are several long discussions regarding Dutch settlement in Hartford.[15] The Dutch and English go back and forth, each complaining to the court about hay being taken off of the fields by nonowners, men beaten as they attempt to protect their property, English planting the land that the Dutch plowed, cows and calves taken and subsequently sold because they had wandered into English fields, a Dutch mare feasting on an Englishman's green grass, and so on. The evidence is pretty conclusive that there is more going on, regarding Dutch presence, than just trading.

> There is also a good amount of information suggesting that there was an earlier exploration and occupancy of the east coast of North America by the Dutch. Based upon these data, both Hudson and Block knew where they were going because earlier Dutch companies had already investigated and profited from being there. The Greenland Company formed by a group of investors claimed from the Virginia capes to Cape Cod:
>
> New Netherlands, situate in America between English Virginia and New England, extending from the South River lying in 341/2 degrees to Cape Malabar of 411/2 degrees, was first frequented by the inhabitants of this country in the year 1598, and especially by those of the Greenland Company, but without making any fixed settlements, only as a shelter in the winter for which purposes they erected on the North and South rivers there, two little forts against the incursions of the Indians.[16]

Another document indicates that a privateering venture of the Dutch East Indies Company in 1606 was sailing the southeast coast of Newfoundland

and taking whale oil from Basque ships as well as their ordinance, and selling it at auction in Amsterdam:

> De Witte Leeuw was a heavily-armed trading ship of 320 tons, sailing out of Amsterdam. While looking for a profitable cargo in the fishing grounds off Newfoundland It captured two vessels in St. Mary's Bay. One was a Spanish ship from which the Dutch crew took 107 barrels of train oil and seven guns, the other was a Portuguese ship carrying 24,000 pieces of cod. Although a complaint to the King of France forced the owners to return the naval ordinance from the two ships, the merchants back in Amsterdam must have been satisfied with the return on their investment from the sale of the cod and train oil.[17]

This type of mercantile venture was commonplace and sanctioned by various governmental and royal agencies. Privateering was a form of investment activity that funded many treasuries across Europe during the sixteenth century and later. As an example, Queen Elizabeth I commissioned Sir Francis Drake and others, known as the "Seadogs," for such undertakings. Armed with a letter of marque (a permit), such ships and crews went out onto the high seas to intercept shipping and steal the cargo, take it back to a home port, auction it off, and disperse the revenue among the investors and, to a lesser degree, the ship's crew. All involved profited. Dutch investors formed companies to do similar things to generate profit.[18]

Initially the *mercantile revolution* began as trade with the Arabs following the Crusades, but evolved into accessing sources of profitable cargo from around the world. Coupled with the Age of Discovery, sending out explorers to find new trade goods—whether it was spices, gold, slaves, or potatoes—could lead to considerable profits. Complex partnerships were arranged. Funds from investors were pooled and ships, crews, and trade goods amassed to be used as barter items throughout the far reaches of the world. Return voyages with valuable goods from the exotic ports produced great interest in home ports and immense return on investments.

Multifaceted business endeavors (schemes) were put together to generate further profits. As an example, in 1585 the Roanoke Settlement was started by Sir Walter Raleigh under a 1584 charter issued by Queen Elizabeth I. The venture started off with five ships and privateering in Majorca and Puerto Rico, focusing upon Spanish galleons. After that phase, the ships were to proceed to Mexico and further loot Spanish shipping, but it was clear that it was too risky. The English vessels then set sail for eastern North America and the Virginia capes to establish a settlement where a tobacco plantation would be started. They dropped off over one hundred settlers and promised to return the following year. Each step of the plan was envisioned to generate a financial benefit for the investors (who numbered approximately 118), including Raleigh and the queen.[19]

While the queen hoped for a profitable investment, she was also initiating the first English settlement in the New World. This was a settlement that could send profitable raw materials back to England, as well as a place that afforded a prime location from which to prey upon Spanish shipping. Privateering was sensationally profitable.

The purpose of settlement in the New World was far more than what traditional history reflects. Our history books indicate that Plimoth Plantation, for instance, was established for religious reasons. It is undeniable that the investors who backed the settlement had profits as their motivation. It is not insignificant that board and plank were the first raw materials shipped back to England in 1623.

Wood was a commodity that Europe desperately needed, and local sources were significantly disappearing. By 1600, European supplies were greatly reduced and predominantly situated in the northern Baltic regions. Relations with that region were not overly cordial and other sources were necessary. Eastern North American wood supplies as reported by early explorers surely did not go unnoticed, and timbering operations had to be considered. The Dutch ship *White Lion*, which laid in wait for the Basque ships off of Newfoundland, carried a large complement of *coopers*, or barrel makers.

While hypothetical, it would not be too outlandish to put together a scheme where the crew cut oak in southern New England, made barrels, and then transported these to southern Labrador to sell to the Basques. Once the Basques filled them with whale oil, the Dutch ship intercepted the Basque cargo ships, and stole the cargo. Not only would they profit from the sale of the whale oil but they also would get paid for the wood, staves, and barrels. That scheme would have clearly made the investors back in Amsterdam extremely pleased. This was the way companies were doing business at the time.

What we can postulate is that the Dutch may have had a timber operation in Branford run by Thomas Mullinar prior to English establishment of New Haven in 1638. It is also pretty reasonable to suggest that Branford was not the only Connecticut location for Dutch timbering operations. Balthazar DeWolf established timber operations in the eastern part of the

Saybrook Colony, which later on became Lyme, after residing in Branford during the first half of the seventeenth century. The DeWolf family in the ensuing centuries opened many lumber mills throughout coastal southern New England. They took their profits from the sale of board and plank and invested in the lucrative slave trade, becoming one of the wealthiest families in America prior to the Civil War.[20]

We know that both English colonies of New Haven and Connecticut, as soon as they were established, immediately placed restrictions on wood cutting and the transporting of board, plank, and staves to foreign ports. It can be assumed that prior to the English presence there had already been wood milling operations in many parts of Connecticut. I would suggest that these were Dutch. In 1639, the newly established New Haven Colony ordered that "after this day no man shall cut any tymber downe butt where he shall be assigned by the Magistrate or on his own ground—It is ordered that Seely and Gordon shall walk the woods and if they finde any wood cut, squared, and uncrosst, they must acquaint the Magistrate therewith. They have the liberty to seize half for themselves and half for the towne."[21] This was an operation significant enough to force immediate regulation by English authorities. While rarely citing the Dutch as being present in the colony undertaking "illegal" activity, there are references to magistrates being appointed to straighten out the differences between the "Dutch and us." One reference follows immediately the wood restrictions in the Colonial Records of Connecticut: "And for the bettering of preserving of tymber that the country may have provisions of pypestaves. It is ordered that no tymber shall be felled fro the bounds of these plantations without lycence . . . nor sold or transported into foreign ports."[22] Note that immediately following these regulations is the following sentence: "Mr. Hopkins is desired by the courte if he see an opportunity to arbitrate the difference betwixt the Dutch and us." Wood was an important resource that could reap considerable profit for investors, and the control of the timber market was central to English colonial policy.

Toward the end of the sixteenth and beginning of the seventeenth century, competition between companies and countries was considerable. Heightening this competition was the commercial practice of privateering on the high seas. What you stole was sold at auction. As a result, the investors and companies they formed found it necessary to arm merchant ships and convince the monarchies to strengthen navies for protection. Sea dominance passed from the Spanish, after the loss of the Armada in 1588, to the Dutch when they maintained most of the world's ships. Finally, in the late seventeenth century, England claimed control of the seas.

Branford: Archaeology of the Dutch Fort

In 1998 it was time to open the folder marked "future potential research data." In the spring I went to Branford, crossed over to Indian Neck, and from the high point on Linden Avenue I gazed to the west overlooking Totokett (the location as Stiles had indicated). I wondered what was it that Ezra Stiles saw some one hundred or more years after the Dutch had built the fort. I guessed that it had to be earthworks.

To the south of Linden Avenue at the crest and narrows of Indian Neck was the region where Stiles indicated the fort's location. As I looked in that direction I saw an expansive area in lawn, undeveloped and abutting Long Island Sound. A hedgerow of shrubs dissected the high point into two parcels. East of the hedge was property of the Owenego Inn and to the west was the property of Chet and Angelica Bentley. From the crest of the hill to the beach was a drop of approximately thirty feet, and the exposed bank was red sand.

In the 1880s postcard in figure 8.2, the bank of Red Dunes can be seen in the far left of the image. To the south of the beach lay innumerable

Figure 8.2. Postcard circa 1880 of Red Dunes, courtesy of John Kirby.

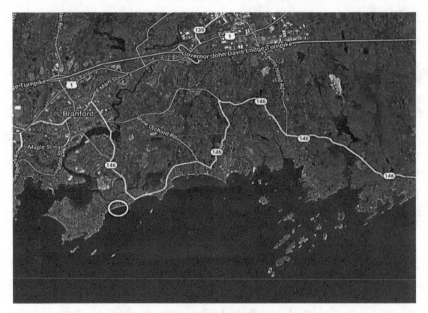

Figure 8.3. Aerial view of Totokett; red circle identifies Dutch fort.

rock piles and treacherous rock shoals as well as the Thimble Islands (figure 8.3; white circle indicates Dutch fort location). A navigational nightmare awaited the unacquainted sailor.

I made contact with the landowners as well as local historians and societies to gain permission to excavate as well as seek any of their information regarding Dutch presence in their town. There was clearly local tradition of the Dutch being in Branford. There was also much enthusiasm for my plans to investigate. The landowners gave permission, and in the summer of 1998 I offered a field school in archaeology through Wesleyan University's Graduate Liberal Studies Program.

Our first field approach was to place a test trench parallel to the hedge running south in the direction of Long Island Sound (figure 8.4). It was a very dry and hot summer; the lawn was parched brown and the underlying soil was powder dry. Even so, features were discernable. Toward the bottom of the image of the trench, a daub discoloration was initially seen. Figure 8.5 focuses upon the daub feature, and figure 8.6 identifies the two-by-three-foot rectangular daub outline within the feature.

The first season's test excavation yielded tantalizing material. As seen in the one-foot gridded photo of figure 8.6, a light colored and pasty soil outline appeared below the surface. The matrix of the light-colored feature

Figure 8.4. Test trench.

Figure 8.5. Daub feature.

Figure 8.6. Rectangular daub outline, indicated by trowel placement.

was identified as daub. The daub was a mixture of ground shell, fiber that may have been from local reeds, and a mixture of dung and clay.[23]

Colonial material was found within the daub outline. Two whelk columella, four black, dark green glass beads of approximately ¼ inch in size, a small sheet copper rolled bead, and flat fragments of a ceramic plate were excavated (figures 8.7, 8.8, 8.9). At the end of the field school we covered the daub feature with polyethylene and carefully backfilled. We planned to come back the next summer to extend the excavation and define the daub feature.

The ensuing fall, we excavated on the Owenego property on the east side of the hedge. Toward the southern end of the hedge, two post molds appeared in the topsoil and extended down nearly two feet into the sand. The post molds were each within a roughly squared hole. The post molds themselves were approximately 6–8 inches in diameter. No associated artifacts were recovered. There was evidence of a trench, however; it appeared that the trench terminated before the most southerly post mold. A large nineteenth-century stone and plaster cistern was directly to the east of the hedge by ten feet. It extended down to eight feet below the surface and was twenty feet in diameter. Inside was trash relating to the early twentieth century.

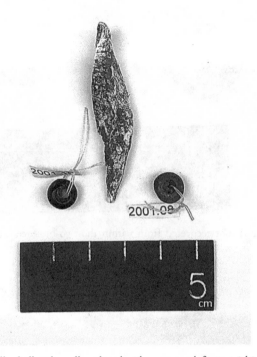

Figure 8.7. Whelk shell columella, glass beads recovered from within the two-by-three-foot daub outline.

In the summer of 1999, we returned to the Bentley Locus on the western side of the hedge, reopened the previous year's excavation, and studied the daub outline. Within the excavation of the daub outline were more colonial artifacts including lead shot (figure 8.8), a wrought iron pierced tubular fragment that may have been part of a pike, a copper alloy button (figures 8.9 and 8.10), and more fragments of the ceramic plate (figures 8.11 and 8.12).

The daub outline was sectioned and it appeared that the daub rested upon wooden logs or timbers. Apparently, there had been a wattle wall plastered and seated upon a subterranean wood foundation. The general outline of the walls and daub was probably octagonal. However, the western end of the structure was disturbed by the recent drilling of a well that was immediately to the west of the outline and associated with the Bentleys' house. Colonial artifacts characterized the interior of the octagonal feature, but no historical materials were discovered outside the wall perimeters.

Figure 8.8. Lead shot recovered from within the two-by-three-foot daub outline.

Figure 8.9. Copper alloy button found within the two-by-three-foot daub outline, top (L) and bottom (R) surface views.

Figure 8.10. Profile view of copper alloy button shown in figure 8.9.

Figure 8.11. In situ discovery of ceramic fragments within the two-by-three-foot daub outline.

Figure 8.12. Ceramic fragments shown in figure 8.11; probable jug fragments with Arabic design and paste and slip of Spanish origin.

As excavation extended to the south from the structure, there was a little prehistoric debitage and as we extended the 1998 excavation some seventy feet toward the bank overlooking the beach. At this point there was evidence of several post molds. To the west of the post molds was a thirty-inch deep trench and related berm. This feature was also picked up in several lateral eighteen-inch-by-five-foot sampling trenches that ran back toward the west. The excavation the previous fall identified a similar post mold pattern and trench system on the east side of the hedge.

At the end of the season the site was backfilled. The daub structure outline was left sampled but predominantly unexcavated. The lawn was raked, rolled, and reseeded. The Bentleys' property was no longer an active archaeological excavation. Over 50 percent of the site and its features were still intact and could potentially be studied for further analysis at some future date. At this point the focus of the investigation went back to the search for documentary evidence. Jaap Jacobs, a Dutch scholar and graduate student, was contracted to undertake research for supporting written records in Amsterdam and Leiden. His research suggested that "Dutch activity in the area between 1611 and 1626 makes it a distinct possibility that there was a Dutch presence, most likely of a seasonal nature, on the north shore of the Long Island Sound."[24]

Maybe the most convincing documentary evidence is a sea chart first produced by Sir Robert Dudley for publication in 1645 (figure 8.13). On the Dudley sea chart, there is a symbol for a fort in Branford. The same symbol is employed on the chart for a known fort at Manhattan (note black arrows in figure 8.14).

Dudley was a naval explorer and privateer in the late 1500s and early 1600s. He focused like many of the Seadogs on Spanish ships returning from Central and South America. Such ships were forced (due to prevailing winds) to sail along the East Coast of America, including Long Island, New England, and the Canadian Maritimes. It is unclear whether Dudley successfully privateered off the New England coast. However, his maps and charts are based upon his personal knowledge while navigating throughout the New World. It is known that his ship *Beare* sailed off New England in 1595 and returned to port in St. Ives in Cornwall. It did carry material taken off of Spanish shipping.[25]

Based upon maritime experience and sea charts, Dudley worked on the compilation of his sea *Atlas Dell'Arcano del Mare*. His works first appeared in 1645 written in Italian. The engraving was done by Antonio Francesco Lucini of Florence and had taken twelve years and five thousand pounds of copper to produce the plates for the publication of the charts and maps.[26]

The importance, from our perspective, is that Dudley handed over the drafts in 1633 to Lucini. His knowledge of what was to become coastal Connecticut clearly predates English settlement of the region. The expanded

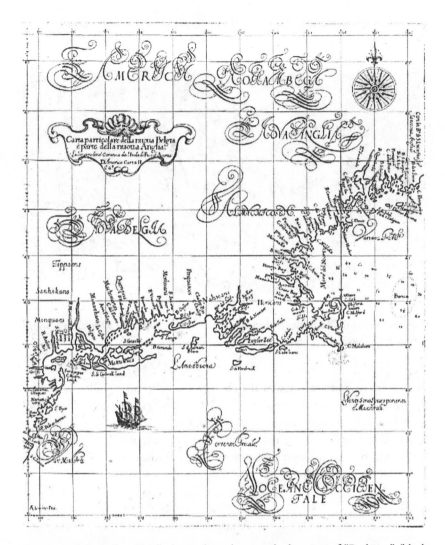

Figure 8.13. Sir Robert Dudley's sea chart showing the location of "Rodwins" (black arrow) just north of present Long Island ("Matouwacs" on map). See figure 8.14 for detail of that section (from the New York Public Library, http://digitalcollections. nypl.org/items/510d47d9-7c00-a3d9-e040-e00a18064a99).

view of the sea chart (figure 8.14) supports an early seventeenth-century, pre-English, Dutch fort in Branford. The site in Branford is identified on the chart as Roduins (Rodwins). The word is Dutch for "Red Dunes."

234 / John Pfeiffer

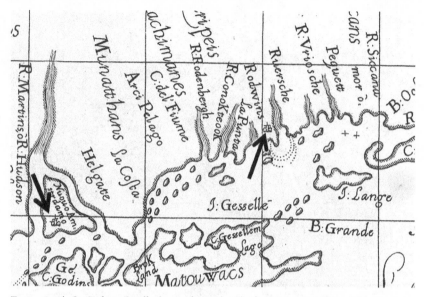

Figure 8.14. Sir Robert Dudley's sea chart, detail of section identifying New Amsterdam and Roduins (Rodwins) by fort symbols (black arrows); the white arrow points to Dudley's symbols signifying islands and underwater rock obstructions.

It is also noteworthy that the chart of the coast off Roduins identifies, in two sweeping dotted lines, the islands and underwater obstructions that encircle the shore (white arrow, figure 8.14). Certainly, this was an important feature that a navigator needed to consider while sailing in the vicinity. This is the kind of notation that probably indicated Dudley's personal experience of the surrounding waters.

Analysis

FEATURES

Several features were discovered during the three seasons of excavation. The daub outline may well have been a structure. It measured a little over sixteen feet across. Its general shape suggested a polygonal rather than a square or rectangular structure; it well may have been octagonal. The depth of the daub from the beginning of its first appearance was ten to twelve inches.

The feature continued below the daub for another foot where sterile sand deposits were observed. The matrix of the below daub layer was an organic dark soil. No wood was encountered in the test sections that were made across the daub and below. Carved into the reddish sand were rounded channels that were likely the imprint of logs, which may have held up the wattle and daub walls of a building.

I suspect that the building was utilized on a temporary basis, as there were only a few associated artifacts. Also, there was no apparent packed floor or sheet midden within or, for that matter, outside the outline. Occupants had not trodden the dirt floor into a compact layer nor had much refuse been deposited.

Both the 1999 and 1998 fall excavation revealed a post mold, trench, and berm pattern approximately seventy feet to the south of the daub outline and closest to the bank overlooking Long Island Sound. The trench and berm system may have been a moat that ran parallel to the posts but terminated before the line of posts turned at right angles to form a squared abutment. This arrangement of posts, trench, and berm was apparent on both sides of the hedge that separated the Owenego and Bentley loci. A small fragment of ceramic plate similar to that found in the daub feature was found in the bottom of the moat. Together these data probably indicate a southern end to a fortification and possibly a bastion. Further work would be necessary to confirm this possibility.

ARTIFACTS

There were several categories of artifacts that were recovered during the 1998 and 1999 season that came directly from the structure. All were excavated from the two-foot-by-three-foot rectangular daub stain seen in figure 8.6.

The two whelk columella were related to wampum production and the four glass trade beads were early black, dark green examples (figure 8.7). These were approximately a quarter inch in diameter and while spherical were not symmetrical but globular. One specimen was broken in half and showed that the dark color was continuous in cross-section. Upon showing these beads to archaeologist Kevin McBride, it was indicated that the beads were early representatives of such trade items.

The half inch in diameter flat button was of copper alloy and had a partially damaged circular loop adhered to the back (figures 8.9 and 8.10). Its condition was poor and was likely undecorated. A three-inch-long iron tubular fragment with a one-inch diameter was also found that clearly had a punched hole in its midsection. The hole may have been a rivet attachment to a wooden shaft or handle.

The most significant artifact was a fragmented ceramic vessel, possibly a jug (figure 8.11 and 8.12). I took the ceramic specimen to several historical archaeologists who were involved in early colonial sites. One of these experts, the prominent James Tuck of Memorial University who had discovered the earliest colonial site in North America known as Ferryland in eastern Newfoundland, reaffirmed what others had said in that they had seen nothing like it.[27] The sherds were glazed on one surface and smoothed on the alternate surface. The thickness was a consistent 3/16 of an inch, no sign of temper, and the body of the sherds was very homogenous.

I showed the ceramics to Charlotte Wilcoxen, the ceramic specialist who analyzed the material from Fort Orange, New York for archaeologist Paul Huey. Her analysis of the Branford shards was quite interesting. She suspected that the clay may have originated in southern Spain where small amounts of fine mica are naturally found within the deposits. She also indicated that the painted slip technique witnessed on the fragments could also have a Spanish origin. The design on the other hand was reminiscent of an Arabic style. The date of the ceramic material was probably before the seventeenth century. She was not at all surprised to hear that the fragments were found at a potential Dutch site. She remarked how at many Dutch sites the number of artifacts that originated in other countries was very significant. She noted that it is characteristic of seventeenth-century Dutch sites to have a preponderance of exotics. After all, they were traveling around the world trading and undoubtedly picking up material culture from all corners of the globe.

Beyond that, Holland was a tolerant melting pot, accepting refugee individuals and groups who were being forced out of their home countries for religious and political reasons. During the sixteenth and seventeenth centuries, Holland had accepted both Jews and Moslems from Spain during the Inquisition. Likewise, they welcomed Huguenots from France. In the late sixteenth and early seventeenth centuries, English Puritans took refuge in Holland, and later during the Civil War and regicide many loyalist Cavaliers and Catholics retreated there. During that time Sir Isaac Newton moved to Holland, and his scientific ideas were embraced and encouraged in a free-thinking academic environment.[28]

It is obvious that a wide spectrum of material culture existed in this tolerant environment. Clearly, the archaeological record reflects this cultural diversity. It is, therefore, highly likely that Roduins was within this sphere of tolerance that reflected a broad range of divergent material culture.

Discussion

The 1998 and 1999 archaeological excavations found evidence of a colonial Dutch fort in Branford, as Stiles had indicated on his 1790 map of Totokett. The excavations revealed a ditch-berm and post-mold system that potentially indicated some sort of earthen and post fortification. There was very clearly a daub and timber structure, probably octagonal in shape, and artifacts consistent with such occupation.

The subsequent analyses and documentary research seems to bolster the Stiles notation. The Dudley sea chart, or map, dates prior to English settlement in Connecticut and the name that he uses on the chart is Dutch. Roduins or Red Dunes is likely based upon the color of the sand and bluff bank seen in the 1880s postcard of the Owenego Inn (figure 8.2). Similarly, the Dutch name for New Haven was Rodenbergh (Red Hill), probably because of the reddish basaltic East Rock and West Rock prominent on the northern horizon to the sailor entering the mouth of the Quinnipiac River.

The purpose of the Dutch fort is unclear. It appears that it was used for a short duration. Potentially, it may have been the very first structure that the Dutch built in the area and placed in the region as a position to which they could retreat if threatened. Such strategies were employed from at least Roman times on.[29]

It is accurate to consider the Dutch entrance into the New World to be motivated by profit. They were the center of the mercantile revolution during the sixteenth and early seventeenth centuries. While trade with the Indigenous population was crucial, it was by no means the only approach to making a return on investments. Resource acquisition was also very important. Lumbering activity and marketing of timber resources was certainly part of the Dutch investment plan. Coupled with a fair amount of privateering, significant profits were netted.

While speculative at this juncture, it is possible that the Dutch had a tidal sawmill operation that was the focal point of their presence in Branford. In 2000, I spent several weeks testing a mill site on the west bank of the Branford River at the confluence of Mill Creek. The excavation did reveal a well-stratified site with early colonial materials overlying wood chips, sawdust, and some yellow ballast bricks. The deposits were unfortunately seven feet below the surface. The depth of the site's earliest colonial strata, and continual groundwater flooding, precluded further testing. The sawdust, wood chips, and the yellow brick probably indicate a Dutch or Dutch-affiliated sawmill operation. Land records indicated that an English colonial mill had been there in the later part of the seventeenth century. The stratigraphy demonstrated that both an English component and an older, probably Dutch, component existed at the site.

Had there been an earlier Dutch mill that failed to be noted in the land records? Was this Thomas Mullinar's mill? If this were the case, the Dutch interest in Branford was relatively easy access to timber resources, a power source where lumber could be sawn, as well as proximity to a deep water river from where the materials could be loaded and shipped. This may well have been the real focus of Dutch interest in the Branford region.

The purpose of Roduins could have been multifaceted. It afforded an opportunity to monitor activity within the adjacent Native village.[30] It placed the Dutch in a position to readily trade with the Natives for furs and other resources. The location also situated the Dutch where they would be able to enlist the services of their neighbors to cut wood in the forests. Governor William Leete of Guilford described this practice later in 1659. He asked that "they (his Indian men) are not to be molested" as they were cutting wood for him.[31]

Roduins's position on top of the hill and at a narrows on the peninsula also made it easier to defend if any hostilities occurred. The high ground location overlooking the Native American Totokett village certainly had logistical benefit. Likewise, the location permitted a good view of potential threats. Such threats were not necessarily posed by the Native population. More likely, the Spanish and other countries' forces were seeking to stop the Dutch from privateering.

The selection for the location of Roduins comes into more clarity here. Approaching the fort and the Branford River by sea was a very dangerous proposition. Rocks, reefs, and small islands greeted the sailor. Nature provided a significant first line of defense. Dudley's double dotted lines on his chart clearly indicates the threat. Without knowledge of the obstructions, picking a way through would be slow and arduous at best. In the meantime, such an oncoming hostile force would be a sitting duck for the Dutch cannon mounted within the fort. Evidence of this ordinance was found adjacent to Roduins—a cannonball found three hundred feet west of the fort, depicted in figure 8.15.

Figure 8.15. Cannonball found three hundred feet west of Roduins.

Acknowledgments

This study evolved over the years and prospered from the input and support of various scholars, organizations, and individuals. In many ways it was an additive and combined process that was nurtured in a vibrant and stimulating academic environment. Feedback flowed into the study from many quadrants and backgrounds, making this far more than just a site report.

I wish to thank Charles Gehring of the New Netherlands Research Center at the New York State Library for his interest and suggestions regarding this research. His knowledge of the early Dutch in the Northeast and his directing me toward the supporting documents opened the door to many of my ideas. I wish to thank Paul Huey for his support and suggestions. Paul was kind enough to bring to my attention a map within Stokes titled "Carta particolare della Nuoua Belgia e parte della Nuoua Anglia," made by Lucini, that indicated the presence of a Dutch fort at Roduins.[32] He also directed me toward Charlotte Wilcoxen to inspect the ceramics found during the 1998 and 1999 excavations. I gratefully appreciate Charlotte's hospitality at her home in Boston and the valuable feedback regarding the ceramics from Roduins. The Robert Powers Company of Philadelphia conducted the daub analysis. I also want to recognize my friend and partner over the years, the late Robert Funk, who dug with me at Roduins in 1998 and 1999, encouraged my research, and arranged contacts with New York State New Netherland experts Gehring and Huey. I wish to acknowledge the Graduate Liberal Studies Program at Wesleyan University for sponsoring the field schools in Historic Archaeology in both 1998 and 1999. Finally, I need to recognize the community of Branford: Branford historian John B. Kirby Jr.; the Bentley family, who not only permitted excavation on their property but also flew the Dutch flag while we were excavating; the Owenego Inn permitted access to the east side of the site; the Branford Historical Society; as well as the First Selectman "Unk" DaRos and his daughter Maureen. They were all tremendously helpful and supportive. Without them, this study would not have been complete.

Notes

1. August C. Krey, *The First Crusade: The Accounts of Eyewitnesses and Participants* (Princeton: Princeton University Press, 1921).

2. Roger B. Beck, et al., *World History: Patterns of Interaction* (Evanston, IL: McDougal and Littell, 2005).

3. Beck, *World History*.

4. Allan Bikk, *Tolerance as Value-Neutrality in the Seventeenth Century Dutch Republic* (New York: Nightingale-Bamford School, 2007), accessed February 18, 2018. http://www1.umassd.edu/euro/2007papers/bikk.pdf.

5. Bikk, *Tolerance as Value-Neutrality*, 7.

6. William C. Sturtevant, "Two 1761 Wigwams at Niantic, Connecticut," *American Antiquity Society for American Archaeology* 40 (1975): 437–444.

7. Franklin B. Dexter, *Extracts from the Itineraries and Other Miscellanies of Ezra Stiles 1755–1794* (New Haven: Yale University Press, 1916), 413.

8. William D. Love, *The Colonial History of Hartford Gathered from the Original Records* (Hartford, CT: Rev. William DeLoss Love, 1914), 113–114.

9. *Public Records of the Colony of Connecticut, 1636–1776*, vol. 1 (Hartford: Brown & Parsons, 1850), 51.

10. Charles J. Hoadley, *Records of the Colony and Plantation of New-Haven, from 1638 to 1649* (Hartford, CT: Case, Tiffany and Company, 1857), 507–536.

11. Love, *Colonial History*, 107–108.

12. Hoadley, *Records of New Haven*, 47.

13. Hoadley, *Records of New Haven*, 18.

14. Edward E. Atwater, et al., *History of the Colony of New Haven to Its Absorption into Connecticut* (Meriden, CT: Journal Publishing Company, 1902), 606.

15. Love, *Colonial History*, 109–110.

16. Edmund B. O'Callaghan, *Documents Relating to the Colonial History of the State of New York* (Albany: Weed, Parsons and Company Printers, 1856), 149.

17. Charles T. Gehring, "The Dutch among the People of the Long River," *Annals of New Netherland*, New Netherland Project (New York: Consulate General of the Netherlands, 1993), 4.

18. John Pfeiffer, "Privateers on the Shoreline," *Newsletter of the Old Lyme Historical Society* 4 (2008): 2.

19. Ivor N. Hume, *The Virginia Adventure: Roanoke to Jamestown* (Charlottesville: University of Virginia Press, 1997).

20. John Pfeiffer, "Wood the First Resource," *Lyme Public Hall Newsletter* 15 (2016): 4–6.

21. Hoadley, *Records of New Haven*, 25.

22. *Public Records of the Colony of Connecticut*, 60.

23. Personal communications with James Powers regarding his brother Robert's company, the Robert Powers Company in Philadelphia, Pennsylvania, which performed analysis of the daub, 1999.

24. Jaap Jacobs, *Dutch Colonial Fortifications in North America 1614–1676* (Amsterdam: New Holland Foundation and Bommelstein Historical Consultancy, 2015), 66.

25. John T. Leader, *Life of Sir Robert Dudley Earl of Warwick and Duke of Northumberland* (Florence, UK: G. Barbara, 1895).

26. Leader, *Life of Sir Robert Dudley*.

27. Personal communications with Dr. James Tuck, Ferryland, Newfoundland, 2000.

28. Beck, *World History*.

29. Hume, *Virginia Adventure*. Note: even if the Roman legion was to stay in a location for one night the first thing that they did was to secure the location with stockade and moat. The 1584–85 English expedition that eventually settled Roanoke was initiated as a multifaceted investment scheme that initially sought wealth through privateering of the Spanish fleets in Puerto Rico and Mexico. The first thing they did in Puerto Rico was establish a fort with stockade and moat.

30. Dexter, *Itineraries of Ezra Stiles*, 413.

31. Bernard C. Steiner, *A History of the Plantation of Menunkatuck* (Baltimore: Steiner, 1897), 72.

32. Isaac N. P. Stokes, "Carta particolare della Nuoua Belgia e parte della Nuoua Anglia," Miriam and Ira D. Wallach Division of Art, Prints and Photographs: Print Collection (New York: New York Public Library, 1930). New York Public Library Digital Collections, accessed January 1, 2018. http://digitalcollections.nypl.org/items/510d47d9-7c00-a3d9-e040-e00a18064a99.

9.

The Fresh River and the
New Netherland Settlement

"House of Good Hope"

Richard Manack

Adriaen Block, a Dutch navigator who sailed along the northern coast of North America, "discovered" the Fresh River in 1611.[1] It was known as the Connecticut, or "long tidal river," to the local Algonquian-speaking Native Americans whose ancestors were its original discoverers. Not long after, the Dutch began settlements in the Hudson River Valley of present-day New York, and in the Connecticut River Valley of present-day Connecticut (figure 9.1). They built a fort in present-day Hartford that they named the House of Good Hope (Huys der Goede Hoop).[2] Trade flourished with the Indian tribes occupying the valley. The Dutch continued to dominate this trade until the English arrived and began settlements in the greater Hartford region. By the middle of the seventeenth century, the Dutch had lost control of the valley due to constant English encroachment on both their real estate and their trading partners.

In American historical writing, the story of the Dutch in Hartford during the seventeenth century is seldom told. Historians tend to emphasize the success story of the victorious English and mention only in passing the Dutch presence in the area. Due to the nature of the Dutch settlers—they were mainly traders rather than colonists seeking a permanent home—the

Dutch left Hartford with few traces. The original site of the Dutch fort was eventually washed away by the Connecticut River.

These facts help to explain the lack of attention given to the Dutch in most of the published Connecticut histories. As the first white settlers in the area, any history that fails to mention their presence is incomplete. This is the story of the Dutch at the House of Good Hope, and why the Dutch left the area in the middle of the seventeenth century despite the promising foothold they had established.

The Settlement of Hartford

In 1614, with the maps produced by explorers Adriaen Block and Hendrick Christiansen for the purpose of trade with the Natives of the New World, the New Netherland Company was formed from several smaller Dutch companies. This company was given a seven-year patent for trade and became the prelude to the Dutch West India Company.[3] The Dutch were to have established other trading houses along Long Island Sound. The North Atlantic was very dangerous to cross in the winter. To make this trade viable, trading houses were constructed to warehouse furs so that seagoing ships could pick up this cargo. Often Indians and traders were to live together and collect furs to be loaded onto arriving ships in the spring.[4]

Along the Connecticut coastal area, the three main rivers for trade were the Thames or "Pequoots," the Connecticut or "Versche" (Fresh), and the Housatonic or "Rodenburg." At present-day Saybrook Point, at the mouth of the Connecticut River, an early trading house was erected (figure 9.1).[5] The exact date of this construction is not known; however, researchers estimate it was somewhere around 1614–16. Charmed by the song of the bird known as the *kievit*, or lapwing, the Dutch called it Kievits Hoek. The trading post at Saybrook Point was important for controlling the trade on the Connecticut River.[6]

To secure the trade of the upper river valley, in 1633 Wouter van Twiller, newly appointed director of New Netherland, who was originally from Nijkerk, sent Jacob van Corlaer (or van Curler) with a party of men up the Connecticut River. They were to purchase a tract of land, then erect and fortify a trading post. Van Corlaer and his company sailed upstream searching for a suitable place. Some miles upriver, they came upon a natural clearing that offered easy access to the river and a natural defensive perimeter

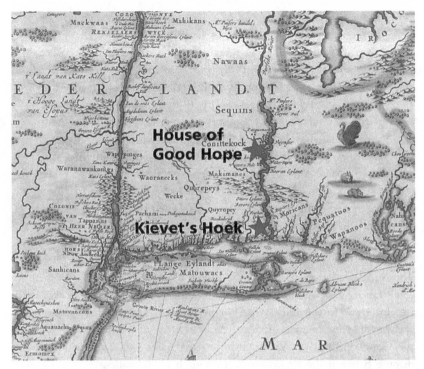

Figure 9.1. The locations of two early seventeenth-century Dutch settlements in the Connecticut River Valley, overlain on the seventeenth-century map "Novi Belgii Novaeque Angliae nec non partis Virginiae tabula multis in locis emendate" by Nicolaes Visscher, ?1655 (from the New York Public Library, Image ID 54910).

of rocks on a small hill. On this very spot, in the region called Suckiaug, on the west bank of the river, the city of Hartford is located today.

Van Corlaer could apply to two parties for the purchase: the Pequot, who claimed the country by right of conquest over the resident Wangunk tribe, or the Sequeen, or Sequassen, the former Wangunk sachem who was in exile.[7] Van Corlaer decided to turn to Tatobem, the grand sachem of the Pequot. Tatobem sold lands that he held by an uncertain tenure, and on June 18, 1633, a treaty of sale resulted between the two parties. This new purchase included lands that encompassed parts of the waterfront of present-day Hartford.[8]

The record of a treaty made with the Indians, embodying the rights of both parties and witnessed by the Dutchmen who were present, reads as follows:

The aforesaid Curler, and the sachem named Wapyquart or Tattoepan, chief of Sickenames river, and owner of the Fresh river of New Netherland, called, in their tongue, Conettecuck, have amicably agreed for the purchase and sale of the tract named Sickajoock on condition that all tribes might freely, and without any fear of danger, resort to the purchased land for the purposes of trade, and whatever wars might arise between them and others, may be waged or carried on without any of them entering on our said territory. The chief of Sickenames is paid for the said land by Jacob Curler one piece of duffel 27 ells long, six axes, six kettles, 18 knives and one sword-blade, one shears and some toys. All, which was signed by Jacob van Curler, Frederick Lubbersen, Giffis Pieters, Claes Jans Ruyter, Domingo Dios, Barent Jacobs Cool (Pieter Louweresen).[9]

The Suckiaug land was thus purchased by van Corlaer and his men for some fabric, axes, kettles, knives, shears, and toys. The territory was made free for trade to the Dutch and to the Indians. Due to this agreement, it was possible for Sequassen, the former sachem of Suckiaug, to return to the Connecticut River Valley, an event that later would contribute to the dispute between the English and the Dutch in the valley.

With tools they had brought with them, van Corlaer and his men cut timber and constructed a small fort, which, in expectation of profit, they christened Huys der Goede Hoop, or House of Good Hope. Bricks brought from Holland by ship were used in the fort's construction. It has been suggested that the fort was an earthwork with brick or stone corners. It is also possible that the bricks were used in the construction of chimneys for the buildings within the enclosure. The House of Hope was twenty-six feet, nine inches long, two stories high, and boasted a pavilion-like shingled roof. Beneath the fort was a cellar equal in length and width to the upper floor. The first floor rested upon eight beams and was divided into two compartments. In the north end was a room 16–17 feet wide, while the south portion had an entry ten feet wide. On the second floor was the courtroom, accessed by a ladder through a trapdoor in the floor.[10] David de Vries, a Dutch navigator who visited the House of Hope in 1639, described the fort in these words: "This redoubt stands upon a plain on the margin of the rivers, and alongside it runs a creek to a high woodland. It was a one acre tract, beside the Little River and adjoining the landing place, from which a lane 24 feet wide led to the 'highway from ye meadow gate to the

Indian land.' "[11] The House of Good Hope was surrounded by a *bouwerie*, or cultivated farm, of about twenty-five acres. In 1633 the fort sheltered approximately thirty settlers, including women and children.

An inventory of the estate of Caspar Varlett, a Dutch merchant in the Connecticut region, dated September 22, 1662, gives an indication of what one home inside the fort may have contained.[12] The Varlett house was divided into one large room and a hall or entry on the ground floor, two upper chambers and a garret, a kitchen and a buttery. Both of the upper rooms contained bedsteads, bedding, and yellow curtains. The stock of linen and bedding was typical of a Dutch household: six feather beds, three bolsters, six pillows, ten blankets, seven other sheets, sixteen towels and napkins, and seven tablecloths. There were prints, books, and a looking glass (or mirror) valued at six pounds, five shillings. Looking glasses were also situated in the bedrooms and living rooms. In the garret were five additional looking glasses, which may have been intended for use in trade with the Indians. The garret also held six pairs of combs for wool and the tack for a horse.

In the buttery and kitchen were brass, iron, and earthen pots, six brass kettles, frying pans, a "scummer," and a ladle with a spit. Brass, iron, and pewter candlesticks, a pestle and mortar, a chopping knife, and a broad platter were also mentioned. The chests also contained tape, silk, maps, fine thread, and writing paper. Two cattle, two steers, two cows, and a pig were among the livestock. The barn held eight loads of hay. Two mares and their colts were in a pasture. The value of these household goods, including the clothing, was 205 pounds, fourteen shillings.

Van Twiller appointed Jacobus van Corlaer, who was also from Nijkerk, as commander of the House of Hope. Hans Janse Eencluys was placed in charge of the two cannons that defended the fort. Upon this military foundation, the Dutch threatened to stop the progress of the English.[13]

Trade in the Connecticut River Valley

The Connecticut River Valley was a region of remarkable fertility and other natural advantages. The Connecticut River was ideal for travel by canoes. The valley's woods were filled with game, its streams with fish, and its soil was good for growing corn. Here the Native river communities lived on friendly terms with one another. There were three major Indian villages in this part of the valley: Matianuck, Saukiog, and Pyquag.[14] They are now the towns of Windsor, Hartford, and Wethersfield, respectively. Through this rich valley the Pequots had forced their way and conquered the river tribes.

With the establishment of the New Netherland Company in 1614 and the West India Company in 1621, the Dutch established a prosperous trade with the Natives. The annual trade amounted to at least a thousand beaver skins along with other commodities. Year after year, Dutch traders sailed the coast entering the Thames, Connecticut, and Housatonic Rivers for the purpose of trading with the Indians. The fur trade was the primary activity throughout the first quarter of the seventeenth century. Items commonly traded in exchange for furs included glass beads, knives, adzes, axes, hoes, copper and iron kettles, and duffel cloth.[15]

The Dutch in the Connecticut River Valley were heavily involved in the wampum trade. They referred to the shell wampum beads as "the source and mother of the fur trade."[16] Jacques Elckings/Elckes, who kidnapped the Pequot grand sachem Tatobem in 1622, demanded 140 fathoms of wampum, rather than furs, as ransom. This appears to confirm the importance of the commodity.[17] The Dutch, however, were not the only traders in the area. The English were also becoming increasingly interested in trade with the Indians.

By the mid-1620s, the nature of Dutch trading activities in eastern New Netherland changed dramatically, the focus shifting from furs to the acquisition of wampum for use in interior areas of New Netherland. Subsequently, a specialized wampum trade developed in eastern New Netherland, creating a triangle of trade. In exchange for wampum, European investors to the wampum-producing zone first sent manufactured goods. Next, the wampum was transported upriver and exchanged for furs. Finally, the furs were shipped back to investors and sold at a great profit.

As early as 1623, the Dutch and English were engaged in direct competition for furs throughout Narragansett Bay and Cape Cod.[18] At the beginning of the seventeenth century, the Dutch were able to gain the advantage in the fur trade due to the high quality of trade goods they offered and their ability to attain vast amounts of wampum. The Dutch offered to sell the English any goods they might need while purchasing their furs at a fair price. By doing this they hoped the English would employ the wampum elsewhere and not pursue trade in eastern New Netherland. The strategy worked for a while, but in the end, by investing some profits from the fur trade to purchase better quality trade goods, the English became more competitive in the region and began to trade furs and wampum. Competition came from Native entrepreneurs like the Pequots, whose geographic location between the coastal wampum trade and the local fur trade placed them in an advantageous position.

The shell Indian beads were identified by a variety of names: wampum, wampum peage, *wampeage, peage, peak, sewan,* or *zewand.* Commercial transactions in wampum frequently employed the word "fathom," a unit of length (equaling six feet) normally used to measure the depth of water. The Dutch most commonly used the term "sewan," while the English generally preferred wampum. The Indians divided their beads into two general classes, the "wompam," derived from "*wompi*" or "white," and "*sukauhock,*" a compound word combining "sucki" or "dark colored" and "hock" or "shell." The white wampum was created from the central column (or columella) of the whelk shell, and the black was composed of the eye of hard shell clams. Three black beads were equal to one English penny. The white beads were only worth half as much, perhaps because the material from which they were made was more abundant or more easily worked. Wampum gradually became common currency among Europeans. In addition to being used as currency, wampum was also woven into garters, belts, bracelets, collars, earrings, neck ornaments, bags, wallets, and other articles of dress.[19]

The invasion of English traders into eastern New Netherland precipitated the establishment of the only major permanent Dutch trading post in the area. As noted previously, the House of Good Hope was built in 1633 on the Connecticut River at Hartford, mainly to seize furs coming downriver from the north. The ability to carry out successful trade in the area depended on the Natives' goodwill. In the agreement between the Dutch and Pequots quoted above, the territory had been made free to all Indians for trading purposes. Unfortunately, this liberal agreement could not withstand the long-standing hostility.

Tension and conflict developed in the region as Native communities began to compete for control of the fur and wampum trade. The Pequots first broke the contract by killing some of their enemies who had come to trade at the House of Good Hope. The Dutch, infuriated by this violence, punished the offenders. In doing so, Tatobem, the leader of the Pequots, was killed, which resulted in the trade being interrupted.

In the early 1630s, the Pequots found themselves in an awkward position. Their Indian enemies had become more hostile and trade with the Dutch had come to a halt. Needing support, they sought the friendship of the English of Massachusetts Bay, inviting them to settle in Connecticut.[20] Simultaneously, other tribes disputing the right of the Pequots to the territory sold to the Dutch also encouraged the English to settle in the Connecticut River Valley.[21]

The Relationship with the English

The Dutch were not the only Europeans present in Northeastern North America. As early as 1620, the first English Separatists had arrived in Plymouth to establish a community where they could live according to their religious beliefs.[22] Originally supporting themselves by agriculture and fishing, the pioneers soon found trading with the Indians a profitable activity. From 1622 onward scattered colonies were established at other points along the coast. Plymouth continued to be the largest single English settlement in New England, remaining so until the migration of Puritan refugees into Massachusetts Bay in 1630 challenged its position. However, there was growing discontent in the Massachusetts Bay settlements with the existing administration of the affairs of the colony.[23] The consensus was that the government had failed to fulfill the Separatist hope of spiritual freedom. This discontent, bolstered by reports of the beauty and fertility of its valley, induced English migration toward the Connecticut River.

There were several reasons the English colonists were enticed to settle in the Connecticut River Valley. First, the rich farmland with its access to trade on the river was very attractive. In 1633 John Winthrop, the governor of Massachusetts Bay, announced that from the northern Connecticut River Valley and Lake Champlain "come most of the beaver which is traded between Virginia and Canada. . . . There comes yearly to the Dutch about ten thousand skins, which might easily be diverted if a course of trade were settled above that river."[24] John Oldham of Massachusetts Bay had explored the Connecticut River, trading and establishing friendships with the residents of Pyquag and other Algonquian-speaking Indians in the vicinity of present-day Wethersfield. Oldham noted that good quality Indian hemp grew naturally in the river meadows and that Connecticut contained many promising sites for settlements.[25]

Additionally, the English were invited by Native American tribes to settle in the Connecticut River Valley. The Pequot especially needed the support and protection of the English, since they had lost their trade with the Dutch. Other tribes, the Podunk, for instance, whose homelands were located on the east side of the Connecticut River across from present-day

Hartford, urged the Puritan Separatists to settle in Connecticut in hopes that the English could become their military allies against the invading Pequot.[26]

Prior to the arrival of the English in the Connecticut River Valley, the relations between the English and the Dutch had been peaceful. The Dutch had congratulated the colonists of Plymouth by both letters and messengers on their "prosperous and praise-worthy undertakings," and had offered to trade with them as honored good friends and neighbors.[27] In 1627, Secretary Isaac de Rasieres of New Amsterdam sailed up to Plymouth with friendly proposals for a joint commercial venture.[28] The Plymouth leaders, however, were suspicious and no agreement was reached at this time. Following his visit, Governor Bradford addressed a letter to Peter Minuit, the Dutch governor, cautioning him not to allow his people to settle where they had no title or to extend their trade too near the English plantation.[29]

When news of Dutch activities in the summer of 1633 reached New Plymouth and Boston, Governor Winthrop wrote a letter to van Twiller clearly stating English territorial claims to the area.[30] Winthrop's letter warned van Twiller not to erect fortifications in the valley lest such a move be "misinterpreted." The English believed they had rights in the territory based on the voyages of John and Sebastian Cabot who, in 1497 and 1498, had sailed along the eastern coast of North America.[31] Furthermore, the king of England had granted the river and lands of Connecticut to his own subjects.[32] Van Twiller received the letter some weeks later and dashed off a reply that attempted to avoid a confrontation. The director general's letter feigned surprise at the hostile tone of the English governor's warning and expressed dismay that two longtime allies should initiate a correspondence with such hostile language. Van Twiller described the House of Good Hope as simply a trading post. He also pointed out that Dutch claims to the Connecticut River Valley preceded those of the English by some years.[33]

The English did not recognize the claims of the Dutch. In 1633 Plymouth colony sent out William Holmes, guided by friendly Podunks.[34] When his vessel arrived opposite the Dutch fort at Hartford, he heard drums and saw cannoneers beside the guns with lighted torches standing beneath the banner of the Netherlands. The commander, Jacob van Corlaer, ordered Holmes to halt while an inquiry as to his intentions was conducted. Holmes replied that he held a Plymouth commission with orders to proceed upriver to trade. The Dutch threatened to open fire, but Holmes disregarded the threat. No shot was fired. On September 26, upon reaching the point just below the mouth of the Farmington River, they landed and hastily constructed a house. They then erected a palisade around it to protect them from the Dutch. It was thus that the present village of Windsor was founded.

The Dutch quickly retaliated by sending an expedition of seventy men against the settlement. Since an evacuation could only be achieved by fighting and not by parliamentary negotiations, the Dutch returned to New Amsterdam accomplishing little. The instructions from the Dutch command were to avoid warfare at all cost because Holland could not afford another war. The directors of the West India Company served a grievance upon Holmes.[35] It stated that he depart with all his people, and break up his settlement on the Fresh River. In case of refusal, the company would protest against all loss and damage that they may sustain. Although the complaint was forcefully written, it was to no avail.

In the spring of 1634 additional settlers came from Massachusetts Bay to found present-day Wethersfield. The English also founded "about a small gunshot from Fort Hope, the town called Hertfoort, and other settlements on the company's purchased lands, contrary to previous complaints; so that the English of Hertfoort left to Fort Hope scarcely ground enough to grow corn and vegetables necessary for the people living there."[36] In 1635 Governor Winthrop pulled down the arms of Holland at Saybrook. When van Twiller learned of this he sent a sloop from New Amsterdam with soldiers to regain possession. The commander of this sloop found the fort armed with two cannons, necessitating a battle. Not willing to risk a clash of arms, the sloop returned to New Amsterdam.

In June 1636, Thomas Hooker of Newtown (present-day Cambridge, Massachusetts) and his Puritan Separatist followers traveled overland to Connecticut and settled in the Connecticut River Valley.[37] They acquired an Indian title from Sequassen, sachem of the "River Indians" of that area, for the territory bounded by the river from Windsor to Wethersfield. Right in the middle of this region was the Dutch fort and the "Bouwerie." In making this purchase of the "Sequins," a Wangunk tribal community and the ancient owners of the Connecticut River Valley, the English declared that the subjugation of this tribe by the Pequot did not give the conquerors the right of ownership. This increased the animosity between the English and the Dutch. The commissary of the fort opposed the intrusion by the English as long as he could, but eventually had to submit under protest.

Thus the English and the Dutch were living in close proximity to one another. The Dutch were surrounded by an active, vigorous group of Englishmen and trouble between them was bound to occur. It could hardly be expected otherwise, for both people sought to dominate the fur and wampum trade. In this the Dutch would prove to be at a disadvantage, simply because they did not have a large enough population to compete.

The Dutch looked upon the flourishing English settlements with envious eyes. They regarded this territory as their own for three reasons: (1) original discovery; (2) constant visitation; and (3) purchase from the Native owners. The English denied Dutch claims to any land around the fort. In 1636 the English secured deeds from Sequassen, who testified in the Hartford court that he never sold any land to the Dutch nor was he at any time conquered by the Pequot, nor did he pay any tribute to them. He also claimed that he had sold the same territory to the English.[38]

English and Dutch relations were now very hostile as a result of the territorial disputes. In addition, the goals of the two countries were quite different. The primary goal of the English was colonization, while the main objective of the West India Company, whose directors oversaw New Netherland, was trading for profits only. The Dutch settlers themselves were more involved with permanent settlement. William Kieft, the newly appointed Dutch governor, went so far as to forbid English trade with the Dutch at Hartford.[39]

Trouble erupted in 1639 when the English damaged Dutch crops under cultivation. David de Vries arrived at the House of Hope on June 9, 1639. He described the incident as follows:

> The commander gave me orders to make a protest against them, as they were using our own land, which we had bought from the Indians. Some of our soldiers had forbidden them to plow, but they had disregarded them and had beaten some of the Company's soldiers. Going there, I was invited by the English governor (John Haynes) to dine. When sitting at the table, I told him that it was wrong to take by force the Company's land, which they had bought and paid for. He answered that the lands were lying idle and although we had been there for many years, we had done scarcely anything and that it was a sin to let such rich land lie uncultivated.[40]

These complaints from both sides were typical of the differences between the English and the Dutch. The Dutch dwelled upon their rights to the land while the English colonists were irritated by the fact that the disputed land remained uncultivated. This situation characterized the different objectives between the two peoples.

The following spring brought even more problems. On April 23, 1640, the Dutch informed the English governor, Edward Hopkins, of their intention to plow a piece of land lying behind Fort Hope and forbade the English to interfere. The usual dispute concerning Indian titles followed. Hopkins said, "Show your right, we shall show ours."[41]

He continued on to say he sought to deal in friendship with the Dutch. Gysbert Opdyck, the Dutch commissary at the fort, replied that this was also their intention, but that meanwhile he wished to have use of the land, being Dutch ground. Hopkins did not agree. The next day the Dutch began plowing the land. The English constable came with a dozen men armed with sticks. With blows and shouting they frightened the horses, who broke their harnesses and ran. An hour later the Dutch resumed plowing with no interference. However, that night the English planted corn in the furrows prepared by the Dutch the day before. Opdyck wrote a grievance to the governor, who refused to make any reply, as it was written in "Low Dutch."[42]

When the Dutch attempted to plant barley on the same ground, the English drove them off. Evert Duyckink ran past the English with a hatful of barley. When he began to plant the seed, an Englishman struck him on the arm with a club, immobilizing him. Another struck him with an axe and the blood streamed down his face and clothes. Opdyck protested, saying, "You do us wrong and with violence." Both parties resorted to an uneasy truce, the dispute temporarily settled.[43]

Problems resumed, however, as early as May 1640, when a Dutch mare grazed upon an Englishman's land. Governor Hopkins's servant confiscated the mare for trespassing. Afterwards, Opdyck was told that if he paid for the damage, they would return the animal. His answer to this was that the ground and grass belonged to the Dutch and that the English had nothing to do with the horse. Therefore, they should bring it back. Three weeks later trouble erupted once again when Dutch cattle wandered into the English cornfield, prompting the English to confiscate the cattle. The General Court promptly prosecuted the matter as a case of trespass. The outcome was that the Dutch were to pay for the damages; if not, their cattle were to be sold. Opdyck's reply was that he did not intend to pay for any damages since the cattle grazed on land purchased by the Dutch and no damage had been done.[44]

On June 28, 1640, as told by the Dutch, an English minister took a load of hay that had been grown and cut on land owned by a Dutchman. The minister took it for his own use without any compensation to the owner of the land. Opdyck at once filed a grievance, which was overlooked.[45] There was even further friction at harvest when Peter Colet, who was cutting grain, was driven off his land. Another complaint was again filed in vain. Governor Haynes answered that he had nothing to do with any grievances.[46]

In 1640, Opdyck returned to Holland and Jan Hendricksen Rosen was appointed commissary of the House of Hope in his place. A garrison of about fifteen soldiers supported him. By this time the Dutch were confined to the territory upon which the fort stood and the "Bouwerie" around it, where the Dutch Point on the north bank of the river is located today.

The most serious clash occurred on April 17, 1641. Three Dutchmen were plowing a disputed field near the fort and were attacked by the English. The English cut the ropes, freeing the horses, and threw the plow into the river. Two days later, the Dutch again proceeded to work their land only to be driven off once again by the Hartford men. This time the English not only threw the plows into the river but placed a sturdy barricade across the road leading from the fort to the woods, thus preventing the Dutch from using this access road to their woods and hayfields. The Dutch quickly dismantled it.[47]

Hope Elsie Goossens, the widow of the recently deceased commissary, reported to Fort Amsterdam on the English outrages.[48] The English reported their troubles with the Dutch to the Council of Massachusetts, which, without deciding the case for either side, recommended the Hartford people allow the Dutch more than thirty acres of land, the limits to which the English restricted Fort Hope.[49]

In 1642, the English magistrates of the river towns protested the Dutch sale of firearms to the Indians. They also complained that the Dutch were putting their cattle into the English town fields, entertaining English fugitives, and helping them to file their irons. They accused the Dutch of buying stolen goods and also persuading servants to run from their masters.[50]

In July 1643, Winthrop received a letter from William Kieft, the Dutch governor of New Amsterdam, complaining of injuries received from the Connecticut and New Haven colonists and requesting a definite answer as to whether Governor Winthrop would aid or desert them. Kieft wanted to know who were his friends and who were his enemies. Winthrop replied that the controversy at Hartford was over a small piece of land, and in so vast a continent was of too little value to make a breach between the Dutch and the English.[51]

The Dutch began to prepare a military expedition but the outbreak of an Indian war interceded, taxing their resources. The onset of this Indian war, known as Kieft's War, even impelled the Dutch to request the assistance of the United Colonies. A volunteer force led by the English captain John Underhill of Stamford fought on behalf of the Dutch in western Connecticut and Long Island, the force slaying around five hundred Natives in about two years' time.[52]

In 1646, the Dutch were refusing to cooperate with English efforts to keep law and order. They protected Indians who were guilty of crimes, and when the Dutch made purchases from the English they refused to make payment.[53] A meeting of the Congress of United Colonies held at New Haven in that same year was enlivened by the submission of the correspondence between Governor Theophilus Eaton of the New Haven Colony and Governor Kieft. Connecticut pressed a complaint against the Dutch commissary at Good Hope for having willfully detained an Indian woman, a fugitive from justice and servant of one of the English colonists, from her rightful owners. In his reply to this correspondence, Kieft flatly denied the charges, reiterating that the English had no right to any part of the coast of Connecticut. He also threatened that if he did not receive better treatment he would avenge himself by an appeal to arms. He refused to submit the differences to any arbitrators, either in Europe or America, and demanded to know what right the Congress of the United Colonies had to hold their meeting within the limits of New Netherland. No agreement was reached between the two parties.[54]

By 1647, Opdyck reported that the House of Good Hope was in a ruinous condition and demanded immediate repairs. It was estimated that six thousand guilders would be required to restore it to its original sound state. The money was never authorized.[55] The situation at the House of Good Hope continued to decline, indicating the post was no longer economically viable. The arguments for repairing the fort were political and not economic; the Dutch wished to maintain the post as a tenuous claim on the Connecticut River.

In May 1647 Peter Stuyvesant, the new director of New Netherland, took office. The English commissioners wrote him a congratulatory message while at the same time renewing their complaints of ill treatment. The message was ignored but the argument continued. Eventually both parties petitioned to have the boundaries of their jurisdiction settled.[56]

The commissioners of the four colonies—Massachusetts, Plymouth, Connecticut, and New Haven—met Peter Stuyvesant at Hartford in 1650. The conference was held at the House of Good Hope, where an agreement was made to settle the jurisdiction and boundaries of the colonies. However, the treaty remained operative for only a short time because it threatened to ruin the Dutch fur trade, and the supply of wampum from the region was effectively reduced.[57] This Navigation Act by the English would ultimately lead to a war between the two groups.

The End of the House of Good Hope

In 1652, rumors had spread that Stuyvesant was inviting the Indians to exterminate the English in the colonies.[58] Stuyvesant was enraged that a charge like this was credited on the testimony of Indians. The commissioners of New England took the rumors seriously, however, and in April 1653 called a special meeting of the confederation at Boston to investigate the Dutch threat. After several futile attempts to uncover evidence of a conspiracy, the commissioners satisfied themselves by drawing up a long document. This document accused the New Netherlanders of being in "bloody colors" with the Indians of New England.[59]

Meanwhile, Holland and England were at war and the English colonies were authorized by Parliament to open hostilities against the Dutch. Rumors circulated that a Dutch attack was imminent on the coast of Long Island. Turning to Captain John Underhill, who had participated in the Connecticut campaign against the Pequot, the citizens of the colony authorized the equipping of a force of men under his command for an attack against the Dutch House of Good Hope. Underhill took possession of the fort on June 27 and 28 without opposition. By the time Stuyvesant heard about the capture of the House of Good Hope, it was too late. John Underhill was already in the process of selling the Dutch land to William Gibbons and Richard Lord from Hartford.[60]

But on April 6, 1654, the General Court in Hartford confiscated the House of Good Hope; therefore, Underhill's attempts to sell Dutch property around the fort were illegal.[61] Any sale or rental of the land was forbidden without the permission of the court. Underhill naturally objected to having the spoils of war taken from him, and he sent a petition to the court to allow him to proceed with the sale of the property. He expressed his willingness at all times to act in the interest of the colony. His request was denied. Despite this fact, Underhill proceeded to sell the property.[62] On July 18, 1655, he sold the House of Good Hope and about thirty acres of Dutch land to Richard Lord and William Gibbons. By March 5, 1659, Gibbons's share was 12.5 acres at the west end of the "Bouwerie," and Lord's share included Dutch Point and 9.5 acres east of Gibbons's lot.

The colony received a one-acre parcel while the remaining 1.5 acres were sold to John Gilbert on March 11, 1662.

Thus the Dutch colonial effort in Connecticut was brought to a close. Most of the Dutch residents moved to New York.[63] Only the name "Dutch Point" remained to testify to the occupation of land in the city of Hartford by the citizens of Holland. That particular area of Hartford is still, today, known as Dutch Point.

Conclusion

The story of the Dutch in Hartford ends like an extinguished fire, despite the flourishing start they had made in the Connecticut River Valley. The Dutch discovered the Connecticut River almost a quarter of a century before the English arrived, and they had peacefully acquired land along this river. Yet the English gradually drove them out. Their surrender to the English was accomplished with little more than a noisy protest on their part. In this period, the West India Company had few resources to spare due to their ongoing conflict with the Portuguese over control of the sugar trade in Brazil. In 1654, the Dutch silently left their outpost in the Connecticut River Valley. The weight of numbers, and the tenacity of the English colonists, decided the issue once and for all.

Numerical weakness was a basic drawback of the Dutch colony. The flourishing trade and industry of the Netherlands made it difficult to convince large numbers of Dutch people to seek a new life for themselves in a wilderness three thousand miles across the ocean. Periodic problems with the Indians also hindered the development of the colony. News of bloody encounters with Native tribes made the settlement less appealing.

The real cause of the confined growth of the settlements in New Netherlands, however, was the policy of the West India Company. The company was organized for commerce; colonization was secondary. As New Netherland continued to fail in its efforts to attract more settlers, the position became increasingly unstable. By contrast, the English immigrated to America in much greater numbers and were more inclined to remain there.

As we have seen, friction between the Dutch and the English developed, increasing day by day as the English intruded on the company's land. Disputes occurred regarding the legitimacy of land purchase agreements. The Dutch bought the land from the Pequot, who had conquered the "Sequin" (i.e., Wangunk), the original masters of the Connecticut River Valley. Therefore, the Pequot's ownership of the land was uncertain, especially when Sequassen, the sachem of the Sequins in the Hartford area, returned to the valley and proceeded to sell the same territory to the English. The English and the Dutch both believed that they were the rightful owners of the land.

Tension also arose due to the different objectives of the Dutch and English colonists. The most fundamental and compelling cause for the early English migration was the desire for religious freedom. Before the English came to the Hartford area, the two nationalities lived on friendly terms in the American colonies. The Dutch had even proposed a joint commercial venture in the Connecticut River Valley. Problems began only when the English intruded on the Hartford land. The characteristics distinguishing the English and Dutch became evident in their quarrels. The fact that the Dutch cultivated so little of their land was unbelievable to the English, who coveted this rich terrain. As a result, confrontations arose. Another problem that caused disputes was trespassing cattle. The Dutch became defensive because their economic interests were at stake.

These two groups found it increasingly difficult to live together as good neighbors. The Dutch occupied Fort Hope on the Connecticut River until the middle of the seventeenth century but were becoming increasingly isolated by the presence of English colonists in that area. As we have seen, the English had deep roots in the disputed soil and were eventually able to dominate the fur and wampum trade. As a result, the Dutch foothold in the area deteriorated.

The first white settlers/explorers had undeniably been the Dutch. Even though they were servants of a commercial company, by international law the Dutch were the earlier claimants. If the territory could have been held by force, the legal title of the original settlers may have held. The general character of the Dutch colonies and the country's priorities may explain why the Dutch did not resort to violence. Holland, still engaged in a struggle with the Spanish Empire, could not afford another war. In addition, the sensible business spirit of the Dutch made them hesitant to begin an armed conflict.

Stuyvesant, aware of the prosperity and strength of the English townships in the Connecticut River Valley, realized that the tenure of the Dutch was uncertain, not only because of the disputed Indian tribes but also due to the fact that the English outnumbered the Dutch. Therefore, Stuyvesant agreed to retreat from an indefensible position in the Hartford area. Thus, the Dutch experiment at the House of Good Hope came to an end. With all the pioneer hardiness and commercial aggressiveness of the Dutch settlers who journeyed to the American colony, and with all the advantages this had given them, the Dutch seemed to have lost their opportunity to succeed.

260 / RICHARD MANACK

Acknowledgments

The author wishes to thank the following for their help in the preparation of this article: Bill Mead, founder of Adriaen's Landing, Hartford; exchange student Eveline S. van Rossum; and staff of the Connecticut Historical Society and the University of Connecticut History Department. Kelly Lund provided the map for figure 9.1.

Notes

1. J. H. Trumbull, *The Memorial History of Hartford County Connecticut, 1633–1884* (Boston, E.L. Osgood, 1886), 16.

2. Adam S. Eterovich, ed., *The Dutch in New Netherland and the United States 1609–1909* (New York: New Netherland Chamber of Commerce in America, 1909), 22.

3. Eterovich, *The Dutch*, 25.

4. Eterovich, *The Dutch*, 25.

5. J. W. DeForest, *History of the Indians of Connecticut from the Earliest Known Period to 1850* (Hartford: W. J. Hamersley, 1851), 71–72.

6. DeForest, *History of the Indians*, 1–72.

7. DeForest, *History of the Indians*, 71–72.

8. DeForest, *History of the Indians*, 71–72.

9. DeForest, *History of the Indians*, 71–72.

10. "Dutch Land in Early Hartford," *Hartford Times* (February 24, 1905), 10.

11. J. F. Jameson, ed., *Narratives of New Netherland 1609–1664* (New York: Charles Scribner's Sons, 1909), 203.

12. Charles F. Johnson, "The Dutch in Hartford," in *Hartford in History*, a series of papers by resident authors, ed. Willis I. Twitchell (Hartford: Plimpton, 1899), 43.

13. Ellen Terry Johnson, "The House of Hope of the First Connecticut Settlers," a paper read before the Connecticut Society of the Colonial Dames of America, in Hartford, November 19, 1895 (New Haven: Tuttle, Morehouse & Taylor Press, 1897), 20–21.

14. William Bradford, *History of Plymouth Plantation* (Boston: Wright & Potter, 1898), 4.

15. DeForest, *History of the Indians*, 70–71.

16. Kevin McBride, "The Source and Mother of the Fur Trade: Native-Dutch Relations in Eastern New Netherland," in *Enduring Traditions. The Native Peoples of New England*, ed. Laurie Weinstein (London: Bergin and Garvey, 1994), 42.

17. McBride, "The Source," 42.

18. McBride, "The Source," 38.

19. Ashbel Woodward, *Wampum* (Albany, NY: J. Munsell, Printer, 1878), 9.

20. Woodward, *Wampum*, 6.

21. Forrest Morgan, *Connecticut as a Colony and a State, or One of the Original Thirteen* (Hartford: Publishing Society of Connecticut, 1904), 84.

22. Karen Ordahl Kupperman, "The Connecticut River: A Magnet for Settlement," *Connecticut History Review* 35 (1) (1994): 55.

23. Kupperman, "The Connecticut River," 55.

24. James Kendall Hosmer, ed., *Winthrop's Journal*, 1630–1649, vol. 1, "History of New England" (New York: C. Scribner's Sons, 1908), 110.

25. E. B. O'Callaghan, *Documents Relative to the Colonial History of New York*, vol. 3 (Albany: Weed Parsons, 1850), 181.

26. Albert E. Van Dusen, *Connecticut* (New York: Random House, 1961), 55.

27. Bradford, *Of Plymouth Plantation*, 268.

28. Hosmer, *Winthrop's Journal*, 109.

29. Hosmer, *Winthrop's Journal*, 109.

30. Oliver A. Rink, *Holland on the Hudson: An Economic and Social History of Dutch New York* (Ithaca: Cornell University Press, 1986), 22.

31. Hosmer, *Winthrop's Journal*, 109.

32. Hosmer, Winthrop's Journal, 109.

33. C. W. Burpee, *The Story of Connecticut* (New York: Belknap Press of Harvard University Press, 1939), 22.

34. Burpee, *The Story*, 22.

35. O'Callaghan, *Documents Relative to the Colonial History of New York*, 9:140.

36. O'Callaghan, *Documents Relative to the Colonial History of New York*, 7:543.

37. O'Callaghan, *Documents Relative to the Colonial History of New York*, 9:152.

38. J. H. Trumbull, ed., *The Public Records of the Colony of Connecticut Prior to the Union with New Haven Colony* (Hartford: Brown & Parsons, 1850), 1:56.

39. Trumbull, *The Public Records*, 1:56.

40. Jameson, *Narratives of New Netherland*, 203.

41. O'Callaghan, *Documents Relative to the Colonial History of New York*, 9:141.

42. O'Callaghan, *Documents Relative to the Colonial History of New York*, 9:141.

43. O'Callaghan, *Documents Relative to the Colonial History of New York*, 9:141.

44. O'Callaghan, *Documents Relative to the Colonial History of New York*, 9:142.

45. O'Callaghan, *Documents Relative to the Colonial History of New York*, 9:142.

46. O'Callaghan, *Documents Relative to the Colonial History of New York*, 9:142.

47. O'Callaghan, *Documents Relative to the Colonial History of New York*, 9:143.

48. O'Callaghan, *Documents Relative to the Colonial History of New York*, 3:35.

49. "Governor John Winthrop Letter," *Connecticut Historical Society Bulletin* 17 (3) (July 1952).

50. "Governor John Winthrop Letter."

51. Lewis S. Mills Jr., "Long Ago in Connecticut: Of the Seizure of the House of Hope," *The Lure of the Litchfield Hills* 12 (June 1953).

52. Mills, "Long Ago in Connecticut."

53. Mills, "Long Ago in Connecticut."

54. Mills, "Long Ago in Connecticut."

55. E. B. O'Callaghan, *History of New Netherland or, New York under the Dutch* (New York: D. Appleton & Co., 1848), 22–23.

56. O'Callaghan, *History of New Netherland*, 22–23.

57. Ebenezer Hazard, *Historical Collections: consisting of State Papers and other authentic documents; intended as materials for a history of the United States of America* (Philadelphia: T. Dobson, 1794), 2:172.

58. O'Callaghan, *History of New Netherland*, 22–23.

59. Sylvester Judd, "The Dutch House of Good Hope at Hartford," in *New England Historical and Genealogical Register* (Boston: New England Historic, Genealogical Society, 1852), 6:368.

60. Judd, "The Dutch House," 368.

61. Howard Bradstreet, *Citations from Authorities Regarding the Dutch in the Connecticut Valley* (Cambridge, MA: Riverside Press, 1933), 29.

62. Bradstreet, *Citations*, 29.

63. Bradstreet, *Citations*, 29.

10.

Dutch–Native American Relationships in Eastern New Netherland

(That's Connecticut, Folks!)

LUCIANNE LAVIN

The goals of this chapter are to discuss (1) the strong Dutch presence in seventeenth-century western Connecticut, (2) the relationships the Dutch developed with the local Indigenous communities, and (3) the significant, often long-term effects of those relationships on our state and federal histories. As nineteenth-century scholar and New York historian John Romeyn Brodhead once wrote, "It seems to me that it is due to historical truth that the influence and the character of the Dutch who first explored and settled the coasts of New York and New Jersey should be fairly set forth."[1]

As the title of this chapter notes, what is now the state of Connecticut was once part of the early Dutch Empire. New Netherland extended from Cape Cod west to Delaware Bay from 1614 to 1650.[2] In 1650, the Dutch gave up most of their claim to Connecticut to the English at the Treaty of Hartford, retaining control only in the southwestern part of the state.[3] Peter Stuyvesant, the Dutch director general of New Netherland at the time, likely agreed to this arrangement because the English colonists far outnumbered the Dutch and armed resistance would have been futile.[4] Even more importantly, Stuyvesant knew that the fur trade in the Connecticut Valley had just about died out,[5] and that the Dutch no longer controlled the wampum trade along the New England coast.[6] Because New Netherland was originally founded to promote commerce, its director general most likely thought it best to relinquish that portion of the colony that was fast becoming economically ineffectual.

Dutch Traders

According to a 1644 Dutch document on the "Condition of New Netherland," Dutch explorers had been sailing the coasts and rivers of what eventually became New Netherland as early as 1598, especially agents of the Greenland Company, a Dutch trading company.[7] In 1609 Henry Hudson, an Englishman employed by the Dutch East India Company, sailed into what is now New York harbor and up the river that now bears his name in search of the northwest passage to the Spice Islands of Southeast Asia. Hudson did not find that route, but what he did discover were friendly Native Americans and potential trading partners.[8] At that time, beaver fur felt hats and other kinds of fur clothing were the fashion rage in Europe.[9] The main source for pelts was Russia and Poland, which were being rapidly depleted through overhunting. Happily for the Dutch, Native Americans were more than willing to barter their fur pelts for European metal tools, bolts of cloth, and other items.[10]

Soon after Hudson's return to Holland, a brisk trade network quickly emerged between tribal communities and Dutch sea captains/traders Adriaen Block (for whom Block Island is named), Hendrick Christiaenszen, Cornelius May, Jacob Eelkens/Elckes, and others.[11] Based on his voyages, Block produced a map of New Netherland in 1614 (figure 10.1).[12] It detailed coves and peninsulas along coastlines, navigable rivers, islands, and the locations of several Native American communities with a considerable degree of accuracy. The map confirms that the Dutch were quite knowledgeable about the region and its inhabitants very early on.

By 1615, Block and the other traders represented a newly formed trading company, the United Company of Merchants to New Netherlands. The company had been granted a three-year charter by the States-General.[13] The States-General was the national assembly and governing body of the Dutch Republic. After the expiration of the charter in 1621, the States-General chartered the West India Company, a Dutch trading company whose charter gave it a monopoly on all trade within the Americas, Africa, and the general Atlantic region "with power to colonize and govern" any place it might occupy.

Figure 10.1. Adriaen Block's 1614 "Figurative Map" of New Netherland (Wikipedia, public domain).

The company quickly built three forts: Fort Orange on the Hudson River near present-day Albany in 1624, Fort Amsterdam at the Hudson's mouth in 1626, and, a little later, Fort Nassau on the Delaware River. In

1633 the company built a fort and trading-house called the Huys der Goede Hoop (House of Good Hope) on the Verse River, Dutch for "Fresh River" (aka Connecticut River), at present-day Hartford (figure 10.2). Erected on twenty acres of land purchased from the Pequot tribe, its location is called Dutch Point to this day.[14] Its name symbolized the Dutch hope for peaceful trading relationships with and among all of their Indigenous trading partners, who represented diverse tribal communities. The transaction for its land clearly noted this requirement for its purchase:

> The aforesaid Curler, and the sachem named Wapyquart or Tattoepan, chief of Sickenames river, and owner of the Fresh river of New Netherland, called, in their tongue, Conettecuck, have amicably agreed for the purchase and sale of the tract named Sickajoock on condition that all tribes might freely, and without any fear of danger, resort to the purchased land for the purposes of trade, and whatever wars might arise between them and others, may be waged or carried on without any of them entering on our said territory.[15]

Having spent many years among them, the Dutch were quite cognizant of local Indigenous histories and Indigenous-Indigenous political relationships. They did not want intertribal hostilities interfering with their trade. As historian John Menta aptly noted, "Knowing that intertribal warfare was destructive to the fur trade, the Dutch designated the House of Good Hope as a neutral trading zone open to all Algonquians."[16]

The West India Company also early established several trading houses on Long Island Sound and its navigable rivers. They included settlements in present-day Connecticut at Totoket (present-day Branford)[17] and Zeebrugge/Seabroek (present-day Old Saybrook; a Dutch trading house and farming settlement, were established at Saybrook Point, called by the Dutch Kievet's Hoek—see below), and possibly at Mattabesek (present-day Middletown) on the Connecticut River.[18] The Dutch were also trading in the Quinnipiac and Housatonic drainages as well. The importance of the Dutch-Indian trade on those rivers was emphasized in Dutch documents.

Adriaen Block's 1614 map depicts the mouth and lower reaches of a river entitled "verse rodenbergh," or River of the Red Hills (the Quinnipiac River), likely because it was located near the conspicuous red-colored cliffs of East Rock and West Rock, twin hills in the present-day New Haven area.[19] In 1642, Dutch political leader and historian Adriaen van der Donck

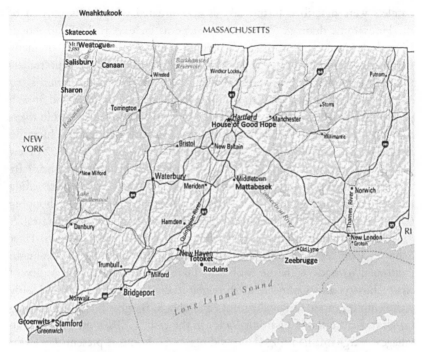

Figure 10.2. Map of a portion of eastern New Netherland showing localities mentioned in the text (from OnTheWorldMap web site, Connecticut Highway Map. http://ontheworldmap.com/usa/state/connecticut/connecticut-highway-map.jpg).

remarked: "Red Hills . . . the Querepees inhabit its banks; many beavers are taken here, since a demand for our goods has stimulated the naturally slothful savages."[20]

Four years later Willem Kieft, the director general of New Netherland, complained in a letter to the governor of New Haven Colony that a recently established English trading post on the Housatonic River would "not only disturb our trade . . . but utterly destroy it."[21] An overland route from the Hudson Valley also connected Dutch traders with Algonquian-speaking communities in the Housatonic and Connecticut River drainages. The trail began in the Dutch town of Kinderhook, New York Province, and led eastward through the Berkshires of southwestern Massachusetts into the Housatonic River Valley, where major Mohican villages were located at Wnahktukook and Skatecook (present-day Stockbridge and Sheffield, Massachusetts), and at Weatogue in present-day Salisbury, Connecticut. Smaller Mohican villages/

hamlets were described historically as also situated within this portion of the Housatonic drainage. The trail extended as far east as the Connecticut River Valley, which comprised the highly populated homelands of many Indigenous communities. The path was used so frequently by fur traders that it was known as the "Indian Fur Trail" in old Berkshire diaries.[22]

Dutch traders traveled the Indian Fur Trail and other inland Indian paths,[23] and plied the waters of coastal Connecticut and its navigable rivers throughout *and after* the existence of New Netherland,[24] reaping lucrative rewards in furs and shell beads called wampum.[25] For example, in 1624 New Netherland traders shipped 4,700 beaver and otter pelts to Holland.[26] By 1635 the number of skins had almost quadrupled, with 16,304 pelts selling for about 135,000 guilders, or 13,500 English pounds,[27] or a whopping 63,450 American dollars (based on eighteenth-century conversion rates).[28]

Dutch traders from the Hudson Valley such as Dirck Wessels, Peter Schuyler, Conraet Burghardt, Elias Van Schaak, and Joachim Van Valkenburgh continued to trade with the Mohicans in the upper Housatonic Valley of Massachusetts and Connecticut throughout the late seventeenth and early eighteenth centuries. Originally from Kinderhook, Burghardt and Van Valkenburgh moved to the Housatonic Valley in the early 1700s, close by Mohican villages. Burghardt had huge landholdings and a home at present-day Great Barrington. Van Valkenburgh set up house at Wnahktukook (present-day Stockbridge), where he became the resident trader, interpreter, and farmer of a 290-acre homestead. He bought the property from the Mohican sachem John Konkapot, who was a close friend. The historic house presently standing on the property is known as the Merwin House.[29]

Fur-bearing animals were overhunted to such an extent that southern New England and southern New York were soon depleted of these resources.[30] When fur pelts disappeared from the Connecticut coasts, trade in white and purple shell beads called wampum and *sewan* took their place. The white beads were manufactured from whelk shells, while the purple beads were made from the interior of quahog clam shells.[31] Collected along both sides of Long Island Sound, the shells held significant spiritual and political meanings for Indigenous peoples.[32] Strings and belts were used to convey social and political messages, confirm alliances, and finalize treaties. The Dutch were the first Europeans to discover the sociopolitical significance of wampum and how its incorporation as a trade good could enhance their commercial efforts.[33] Interior tribes such as the Mohawk in upstate New York and the Susquehannock in central Pennsylvania, where beaver and otter were plentiful, willingly exchanged many pelts for wampum beads.

Discoveries at archaeological sites confirm a strong Dutch presence in Connecticut. In 1998 and 1999, archaeologist John Pfeiffer discovered the remains of an early historic site on Indian Neck Peninsula in Branford that he has identified as an early seventeenth-century Dutch fort. Pfeiffer uncovered the remains of a wooden and daub structure within a moated enclosure, trade items, and exotic, fine-earthenware ceramic fragments. The trade goods included wampum, glass and copper beads, a copper alloy button, musket balls, and other historic items.[34] The site is located in the midst of Quinnipiac Indian homelands. Recent excavations under the direction of archaeologist Kevin McBride at several early seventeenth-century Pequot village sites in southeastern Connecticut uncovered numerous Dutch trade goods.[35]

Altercations between traders and Native Americans did occur,[36] but they appear to have been relatively uncommon. As McBride noted, "The ability of these traders to carry on the trade depended on good relationships with the natives."[37] The trade continued because of its substantial economic, social, and political value to all concerned parties.

Dutch Settlers

The Dutch West India Company was never interested in settling North America. Their interests lay strictly in commercial enterprise. Much of their financial and military efforts from the second through the fourth decades of the seventeenth century were focused on South America and wars with Spain and Portugal over control of sugar-rich Brazil.[38] They never encouraged settlers and did little to renovate or maintain the facilities and structures in their forts to accommodate them.[39] This was not the case with other Dutchmen, however, such as Adriaen van der Donck, who actively promoted colonizing efforts.[40] The company did, however, ship over settlers to establish permanent colonies to provide sustenance for West India Company traders and staff, and whenever anxieties intensified over English competition for Dutch lands.[41]

Consequently, the Dutch traders were closely followed by Dutch colonists. Besides the trading posts mentioned previously, Dutch farming communities sprang up in New Netherland, including Connecticut.[42] In 1623, the Dutch trading house at present-day Old Saybrook was enhanced by the arrival of men and women settlers from Holland.[43] Dutch colonists settled near the Dutch fort in present-day Branford as well. By 1639 New Netherland contained thirty *bouweries* (farming settlements).[44]

Thomas Mullinar/Molinar was the first settler of Totoket (the original, Algonquian name for Branford), having purchased land directly from its Indigenous inhabitants prior to English settlement in 1638.[45] John Pfeiffer speculates that Mullinar—who owned a mill and whose surname means "miller" in Dutch—ran a timber operation in the area.[46] Europe was experiencing a wood shortage, and lumber would have been an important and lucrative export for the Dutch.

Some of the first settlers of present-day Greenwich ("Groenwits") and Stamford in coastal southwestern Connecticut were the Dutch by at least 1640 and 1641, respectively.[47] In present-day Salisbury and Canaan in northwestern Connecticut, *all* of the earliest documented European residents were Dutch families. The Dutchers, Knickerbockers, Hollenbecks, Hoogebooms, and Van Deusens are all mentioned in the earliest town records—overland migrants from a patroonship in eastern New York.[48]

The Dutch were purchasing land from the Mohicans in Salisbury and Canaan, Connecticut as early as 1685.[49] Some were living in Salisbury by 1714, but the earliest documented European resident landowners were the Van Deusens and Whites in 1719–20 (White was an Englishman living among the Dutch who married a Dutch woman, Goodeth Deeker; their previous home was the Livingston patroonship).[50] The Dutch were active town members. They regularly attended town meetings, some of which were held in their homes. Some owned businesses that fostered town development. William White owned half interest in a Salisbury saw mill; Abraham Van Deusen ran a grist mill in the Lime Rock section of the town.[51] Local features were named after them; for example, Knickerbocker Pond, Dutcher's Bridge, and Hollenbeck River.

In 1749, Cornelius Knickerbocker moved his family south to Sharon, Connecticut; they were some of the earliest residents of that town.[52] A number of Dutch families dwelled across the state border in western Massachusetts as well.[53] Dutch descendants continued to reside in northwestern Connecticut and adjacent Massachusetts in the subsequent centuries.[54]

Dutch Effects on Indigenous Communities

In effect, Native American communities in western Connecticut were virtually surrounded by Dutch settlements consisting of traders, settlers, and businessmen. The physical closeness only intensified Dutch-Indigenous working relationships.[55]

PROMOTION OF INCREASED TECHNOLOGICAL EFFICIENCY AND SOCIAL RANKING

Native American communities improved their economic efficiency through their growing use of Dutch metal tools, guns, textiles, and other items that made life easier for them.[56] Ownership and control of European trade goods also enhanced the social status of those Indigenous individuals and communities most closely involved in trading activities.[57] Professor Kathleen Bragdon of William and Mary College, a specialist in New England Native American history and culture, has suggested that this unequal access to European trade items may eventually have led to an incipient social stratification, particularly along the southern New England coast, where "limited access to restricted resources and increasing localized populations may well have created the necessary conditions for emerging centralization, hierarchy, and managerial control known cross-culturally to be most commonly associated with . . . chiefdoms,"[58] and where sachems appeared to wield more authority than their inland counterparts.[59]

Tribes acting as middlemen in the European trade network achieved greater political power as a result of their accumulating wealth and their heightened social status as direct trading partners and allies of the Dutch. One example is the powerful Pequot tribe of southeastern Connecticut, who early enjoyed the fruits of political alliance with the Dutch. Prior to the Pequot War of 1637, the Pequots controlled trade throughout much of Connecticut and Long Island; Indigenous communities regularly paid tribute to the Pequot leadership.[60]

The Mohawks from northern New York are another example of tribal power enhanced by European trade. Their receipt of Dutch guns and ammunition for furs increased their reputation as fierce, cannibalistic conquerors. They, too, regularly collected tribute from many apprehensive tribes, including those resident in Connecticut.[61]

CHANGES IN INDIGENOUS-INDIGENOUS SOCIOPOLITICAL RELATIONS

The fear that these two tribes aroused among their contemporaries is high-lighted by John Menta's description of a 1638 meeting between Quinnipiac leadership and English colonists. At this meeting the Quinnipiac sachems admitted that they so feared Pequot and Mohawk attacks that they had temporarily removed from their villages along Long Island Sound and New Haven Harbor inland to central Connecticut, seeking protection from the

English residing in the Wethersfield-Middletown areas. As Menta reported: "The Quinnipiac sachems then addressed what was for them the main issue: their desire for English military protection from their Indian enemies. The sachems acknowledged that the threat they felt from the Pequot, Mohawk, and others had forced the Quinnipiac to seek refuge close to the English towns on the Connecticut River."[62] Many of the Indigenous palisaded "forts" mentioned by early seventeenth-century European explorers/settlers were likely built for protection against these Native American adversaries. One example in which the historical record specifically noted such a function is the "strong fortress, with flankers at the corners," built by the Paugussetts under the sachemship of Ansantaway north of Washington Bridge in present-day Milford "as a defense against the Mohawks," to whom they were tributaries.[63]

Indigenous-Indigenous political dynamics were even more complex. In his latest book on the history of the Mohican tribe from 1600 to 1830, William Starna clearly shows that the European presence and the new trade economy it created among Indigenous communities disrupted the latter's old alliances, created new ones, and in general fueled competition and jealousies to such magnitudes that the end result was pervasive and persistent distrust and contention, even warfare.[64] A good example is the early seventeenth-century conflict between the Pequots and the Wangunks over control of the fur trade in the lower Connecticut Valley. Three battles were fought. The Pequots won the final battle and with it political and economic control of the valley.[65]

The animosity engendered by this outcome, fueled by intertribal competition for material wealth and political power, continued to create cultural and social discord that involved Native American and European communities. The Pequot-Wangunk conflict and its aftermath, for example, was one of the contributing factors to the Pequot War.[66] In that war, several tribes remained neutral, and some—such as the Mohegan, Niantic, and Narragansett—openly allied themselves with the English against the Pequot.[67]

DISRUPTION OF NATURAL ENVIRONMENTS AND SUBVERSION OF
INDIGENOUS SPIRITUAL DOCTRINE

Not only did the fur trade promote imbalances in Indigenous sociopolitical environments, but in their natural environments as well. As noted previously, fur-bearing animals were overhunted to virtual extinction. Tribal peoples traveled long distances in search of new trapping grounds, encroaching on the homelands of other Indigenous peoples as far away as Michigan, Virginia, and the Carolinas.[68] These forays surely must have created animosity and opposition among the involved parties, further intensifying intertribal conflicts.

Most importantly, as Timothy Paulson and Hubert de Leeuw have noted, the "indiscriminate slaughter" of wildlife and the use of sacred shell beads for mundane economic purposes violated Indigenous sacred teachings. Key concepts in Native American belief systems include spiritual reverence for Nature and all living things, the interconnectedness of natural and social environments—humans as part of Nature, and their "duty to always harmonize with and maintain the natural world order."[69] Paulson and de Leeuw are correct that "the issues at stake were the environment and belief systems, subject[s] about which natives would have a deep, intuitive understanding. We think they saw it coming. With the Two Row Wampum Belt, they made at least a bid to stave off what must have looked like an ecological and spiritual apocalypse."[70]

Early Dutch sources suggest that Indigenous communities originally did resist the temptation to sacrifice the traditional teachings of their spiritual leaders for material gain. As noted previously, in 1642 van der Donck referred to the Quinnipiacs as "slothful" because they refused Dutch demands that they increase their normal kill of beavers (prior to European traders, beavers and other fur-bearing animals were killed solely to provide food and other staples for tribal members). He was probably citing a 1625 publication by the popular Dutch writer Johannes de Laet, *Extracts from the New World*, which was based on the log books/journals of the early Dutch traders, including Adriaen Block. De Laet reported that "the Natives who dwell here are called Quirepeys. They take many beavers, but it is necessary for them to get into the habit of trade, otherwise they are too indolent to hunt the beaver."[71]

Archaeology shows that the Quinnipiac had been trading with other Indigenous communities for thousands of years prior to European visitation.[72] They had no need to "get into the habit of trade." Taking into consideration their traditional spiritual beliefs, it is far more reasonable that the Quinnipiacs's aversion to overharvesting the local beaver population at the beginning of the fur trade had little to do with commercial naïveté or laziness and everything to do with upholding the teachings of their elders. That a more secular and materialistic faction in the tribe won out is demonstrated by the fact that overharvesting of fur-bearing animals in the next few years caused such a decline in peltries that "by 1630 the coastal fur trade was dead" in Connecticut.[73]

Death and Social Upheavals due to European Diseases
and Alcoholism

The most frightening consequence of European trade was the introduction
of virulent diseases for which Native Americans had no immunity. Traders,
sailors, and settlers transmitted plague, smallpox, tuberculosis, cholera, syphilis,
dysentery, and other ailments and Indigenous peoples died in great numbers.
Several "plagues" and smallpox epidemics were reported by seventeenth-
century historians. The earliest known epidemic, which decimated New
England coastal communities from Massachusetts northward in 1616–19,
appears to have spread along traditional Indigenous communication and
trade routes.[74] William Bradford, the governor of Plimoth Colony in eastern
Massachusetts, had this to say about a 1634 smallpox epidemic in the Connecticut River Valley, which occurred soon after European settlement of the
Hartford-Windsor-Wethersfield region: "They dye like rotten sheep. . . . they
were (in the end) not able to help one another; no, not to make a fire, nor
to fetch a little water to drinke, nor any to burie the dead. . . . The cheef
Sachem himself now dyed, & almost all his friend & kindred."[75]

Many Indigenous peoples also died from the effects of alcoholism,
another European introduction. Rum and brandy were staple trade items,
and Dutch traders often offered alcoholic drinks to Indigenous trading
partners prior to trade, in order to give them an advantage in the business
transaction.[76] The Rev. John Sergeant, the first minister to the Mohicans at
early eighteenth-century Stockbridge, wrote in his journal that "the Dutch
traders . . . make vast Profit by selling them [the Mohicans] Rum, and
making Bargains with them when they are drunk."[77]

Researchers have estimated that from 77 to 90 percent of the Native
American population in New England had died off by 1650.[78] Their low
populations not only signified low manpower and military strength. Many
of the dead were political, religious, and medical leaders, elders who carried special information important to the tribe, and children who were the
tribe's future members. They were crippled societies—economically, socially,
and politically.

Dutch Application of the Principles of Equality and
Tolerance in Indigenous Relations

The most impressive contribution to Indigenous histories was the Dutch
recognition of tribal sovereignty and equality. In general, Dutch officials

and settlers alike treated tribal communities as independent, self-governing nations—equal partners in both governmental and personal relationships.[79] The Dutch agreed that the tribal communities with whom they came into contact were the earliest settlers and owners of the land. In contrast, the English "believed that all titles to colonial land resided in the King, and that natives living on the land had no rights to any part that was not actually under cultivation and then only if they had a grant from the King of England."[80] Unlike their English counterparts, the Dutch exhibited social and religious tolerance of Native American cultural traditions, and often lived in close association with Indigenous neighbors.[81] These observations are echoed in several of the chapters comprising this volume.[82] Tolerance was a fundamental principle in seventeenth-century Dutch society. As Russell Shorto noted in his award-winning book on New Amsterdam:

> Tolerance was more than just an attitude in the Dutch Republic. Following the bloody religious persecution of thousands in the previous century at the hands of the Spanish, the Dutch provinces had broken new ground in writing into their 1579 de facto constitution the guarantee that "each person shall remain free, especially in his religion, and that no one shall be persecuted or investigated because of their religion" . . . diversity was good for business.[83]

Dutch beliefs in Indigenous sovereignty, universal tolerance, and neighborliness extended into eastern New Netherland as well. The Dutch were always careful to purchase land directly from the local Indigenous leadership, unlike their English contemporaries, as the Dutch farmers in Salisbury were quick to point out in their 1736 and 1738 memorials (petitions) to the English Connecticut General Assembly.[84] Citing the October 1736 memorial, historian Shirley Dunn wrote: "The Mohican Indians had complained angrily [to the Dutchmen] that the government of Connecticut had never given them any consideration for their lands."[85]

Mohican leadership continued to accuse the English of fraudulent land dealings in northwestern Connecticut, particular in present-day Sharon, where they claimed the English took lands that the tribe never sold.[86] Mohican settlements were located within the Salisbury Dutch land purchases, the Dutch allowing Mohican villagers to continue living on the land unmolested.[87] For their part, the Mohicans provided military support against incursions by the Mohawks, other hostile Indians, and the French, to which the Dutch farmers testified in their 1738 petition to the English Connecticut General Assembly.[88] Not insignificantly, the tolerance, diversity, and individual freedom practiced by the Dutch in Europe and in New Netherland eventually became the cornerstones of the later United States of America.

Conclusions

In summary, Dutch explorers and traders were the first documented Europeans to visit Connecticut. New Netherland settlers were the first to plant colonies in Connecticut. They were the first documented Europeans to not only interact with Connecticut's First Nations, its Indigenous tribes, but the first to make Connecticut history as well. Dutch relationships with the local tribal communities well outlasted the New Netherland political entity, and stimulated many changes in tribal societies that had long-term consequences for future Indigenous-Indigenous and Indigenous-European liaisons in our American history. These facts all demonstrate that the Dutch deserve a more prominent position in future Connecticut history books and museum exhibits than they have previously enjoyed. Moreover, Dutch-American history and Dutch contributions to American culture should be mandated topics in Connecticut's school curriculum.

Acknowledgments

I wish to thank Stephen McErleane and the New Netherland Institute for inviting me to present an earlier version of this chapter on June 10, 2017 at a conference hosted by the New Netherland Institute in Hartford, Connecticut entitled "The Dutch in Connecticut: Exploring New Netherland's Fresh River." Craig Nelson and Laurie Weinstein kindly reviewed earlier drafts of this paper. Paul Wegner supplied the map for figure 10.1.

Notes

1. This quote by John Romeyn Brodhead was published by Russell Shorto in his comprehensive masterwork on the Dutch in early America, which focuses on the establishment of New Amsterdam in what is now New York City: *The Island at the Center of the World* (New York: Vintage Books, 2005), 312. Shorto explains

that the quote was part of Brodhead's response to some ugly newspaper reviews of his public lectures in the 1840s and 1850s "for the unheralded legacy of the Dutch colony" (Shorto, *The Island*, 311).

2. John Romeyn Brodhead, "Oration on the Conquest of New Netherland, Delivered before the New York Historical Society, on Wednesday, the 12th of October," in *Coming to Terms with Early New Netherland—New York History: Commemoration of the Two Hundredth Anniversary by the New York Historical Society* (New York: New York Historical Society, 1864; repr. 2015, Albany: New Netherland Company), appendix: note A, The First New Netherland Charter, granted by the States-General on October 11, 1614, 61–62. See also Kevin A. McBride's publications for geographical descriptions of New Netherland and "Eastern New Netherland," such as "The Source and Mother of the Fur Trade: Native-Dutch Relations in Eastern New Netherland," in *Enduring Traditions*, ed. Laurie Weinstein (Westport, CT: Bergin and Garvey, 1994), 31–32; and "Fort Island: Conflict and Trade in Long Island Sound," in *The Native Forts of Long Island Sound Area*, ed. Gaynell Stone (Stony Brook, NY: Suffolk County Archaeological Society, 2006), 255. The Englishman John Smith, of Pocahontas's fame, sailed to New England and drew a map of it in 1616. It showed English New England well to the north of Cape Cod. Brodhead's "Oration," 14–15 (including unnumbered footnotes), showed that the wording of King James I's patent of 1620 disallowed settlement in areas already inhabited by other Christians (i.e., New France and New Netherland); Brodhead also noted that the Mayflower Pilgrim settlement at Plymouth received its charter from the Virginia Company, to whom James I in 1606 had granted a patent for colonization between the 34th and 38th parallels—which is Virginia and the Middle Atlantic, not Massachusetts. In sum, the Dutch had every right to purchase land from the Indigenous owners and to found New Netherland.

3. Ronald D. Cohen, "The Hartford Treaty of 1650: Anglo-Dutch Cooperation in the Seventeenth Century," *New-York Historical Society Quarterly* 52 (1969): 311–332. But see Richard Manack, "The Fresh River and the New Netherland Settlement, House of Good Hope," chapter 9, this volume, for another take on the permanence of that treaty. See also Missy Wolfe, *Insubordinate Spirit: A True Story of Life and Loss in Earliest America 1610–1665* (Guilford, CT: Globe Pequot Press, 2012), 158–169.

4. Manack, "The Fresh River," chapter 9, this volume.

5. Thomas E. Burke, "The New Netherland Fur Trade, 1657–1661: Response to Crisis," in *A Beautiful and Fruitful Place: Selected Rensselaerswijck Seminar Papers*, ed. Nancy Anne McClure Zeller, 283–289 (Albany: New Netherland Publishing, 1991), 287.

6. McBride, "The Source and Mother of the Fur Trade," 41. McBride believes that the Dutch monopoly on the wampum trade was destroyed in 1637, when the English gained control of much of the wampum manufacturing regions after their defeat of the Pequot in the 1636–37 Pequot War.

7. "Report of the Board of Accounts on New Netherland," dated December 15, 1644, in an ms. in the Royal Archives in The Hague, in the *Loketkas* of the States-General, Rubric, West Indische Compagnie, no. 30; 1st Division, in E. B. O'Callaghan, *Documents Relative to the Colonial History of the State of New York*, vol. 1, ed. E. B. O'Callaghan (Albany: Weed, Parsons, and Company, 1856), 149.The quote is cited by John Pfeiffer, "Roduins: A Dutch Fort in Branford, Connecticut," chapter 8, this volume. Charlotte Wilcoxen, "Dutch Trade with New England," in *A Beautiful and Fruitful Place: Selected Rensselaerswijck Seminar Papers*, ed. Nancy Anne McClure Zeller (Albany: New Netherland Publishing, 1991), 235. Citing seventeenth-century secretary of New Netherland Isaack de Rasieres and nineteenth-century American historian Justin Winsor, Charlotte Wilcoxen noted that Dutch traders may have frequented New England shores as early as 1598–1601.

8. Charles T. Gehring, "Sources Relating to Dutch-Indian Relations," chapter 2, this volume; Shirley W. Dunn, "Henry Hudson Goes Ashore on Castle Hill," chapter 1, this volume. For detailed descriptions of all four of Hudson's voyages to the New World, see Timothy Paulson and Hubert de Leeuw, *Coming to Terms with Early New Netherland–New York History: 1609, Henry Hudson Revisited* (Albany: New Netherland Company, 2014).

9. At the time, Europeans were enduring a "Little Ice Age," a climatic period of cool, wet weather that lasted from ca. A.D. 1500 to 1850: see Lucinda McWeeney, "A Review of Late Pleistocene and Holocene Climatic Changes in Southern New England," *Bulletin of the Archaeological Society of Connecticut* 62 (1999):10–11. To reduce the chill, fur clothing would have been a most efficient item as well as an aristocratic social marker.

10. For a summary of the importance of the beaver and the early Dutch fur trade, see Stephen T. Staggs, "Declarations of Interdependence: The Nature of Dutch–Native Relations in New Netherland, 1624–1664," chapter 3, this volume.

11. Gehring, "Sources"; Timothy Paulson and Hubert de Leeuw, *Coming to Terms with Early New Netherland–New York History: 1610–1614* (Albany: New Netherland Company, 2013).

12. Lynn Ceci, "Native Wampum as a Peripheral Resource in the Seventeenth-Century World-System," in *The Pequots in Southern New England: The Fall and Rise of an American Indian Nation*, ed. Laurence M. Hauptman and James D. Wherry (Norman: University of Oklahoma Press, 1990), 53–57, figs. 4 and 5.

13. "Report of the Board of Accounts on New Netherland," 149; Brodhead, "Oration," 61–62.

14. "Report of the Board of Accounts on New Netherland," 149–150; William A. Fletcher, *A History of New England, Volume 1, Massachusetts, Connecticut and Rhode Island* (Boston: Crocker and Company, Publishers, 1880), 311; Lauric Henneton, "The House of Hope in the Valley of Discord: Connecticut Geopolitics and 'Anglo-Dutch' Relations (1613–1654)," in *The Worlds of the Seventeenth-Century*

Hudson Valley, ed. Jaap Jacobs and L. H. Roper (Albany: State University of New York Press, 2014), 180–186; Manack, *Nijkerk*, 5–6, 8–16, 38; Paulson and de Leeuw, *Coming to Terms . . . 1610–1614*, 24–26. For a detailed description and history of the Dutch trading house at present Hartford, see Richard Manack, "The Fresh River," chapter 9, this volume.

15. John W. DeForest, *History of the Indians of Connecticut from the Earliest Known Period to 1850* (Hartford: W. J. Hamersley, 1851), 71–72, as cited in Richard Manack, "The Fresh River and the New Netherland Settlement, 'House of Good Hope,'" chapter 9, this volume.

16. John Menta, *The Quinnipiac: Cultural Conflict in Southern New England*, Yale University Publications in Anthropology 86 (New Haven: Peabody Museum of Natural History, 2003), 68, citing Neal Salisbury, *Manitou and Providence: Indians, Europeans, and the Making of New England 1500–1643* (New York: Oxford University Press, 1982), 207.

17. John Pfeiffer, "Roduins," chapter 8, this volume. Pfeiffer's archaeological excavations in the late 1990s uncovered what appears to have been a Dutch fort and trading center in present Branford, Connecticut, with European trade goods. Pfeiffer also cites historical documentation for a Dutch fort in Branford—an early seventeenth-century sea chart by explorer and privateer Robert Dudley that depicts a fort symbol in the Branford area, and the 1761 writings of minister, educator, and seventh president of Yale College Ezra Stiles that also included a map of the ruins of a Dutch fort in Branford.

18. Old Saybrook Historical Society, "Old Saybrook Historical Society," accessed August 8, 2015, http://www.saybrookhistory.org/web_page.php?id=13.

19. New Netherland Institute, "A Tour of New Netherland: Connecticut, Rodenburgh," on the website *Exploring America's Dutch Heritage*, https://www.new netherlandinstitute.org/history-and-heritage/digital-exhibitions/a-tour-of-new-netherland/connecticut/rodenburg/, accessed January 14, 2018. Robert Novak, "The Dutch in the Housatonic Valley," *Huntington Herald*, July 1998, accessed on the Derby Historical Society website, January 19, 2018, http://derbyhistorical.org/dutch.htm. Novak was the town historian for Derby, Connecticut, which is located on the Housatonic River where it is joined by its largest tributary, the Naugatuck River; the river was once navigable to large vessels up to this point (Derby Neck).

20. Quoted in Menta, *The Quinnipiac*, 65. Menta also believed that the Rodenburg River was originally the Dutch name for the Quinnipiac River, not the Housatonic as some researchers have suggested. Likely he based that assumption on Adriaen Block's 1614 map, where the name was written in the area of three coves on the central Connecticut coast; on the river's name—Red Hills; and the fact that van der Donck noted that Quinnipiac peoples resided "along its banks." Block's location of the name could also be construed as the Housatonic Valley. Later seventeenth-century Dutch and English maps show the "Quiripeys" extending into

the Housatonic Valley as well as the Quinnipiac, and identify the Housatonic as the Rodenburg River. See Visscher's seventeenth-century maps of Nova Belgii for examples. See also Pfeiffer, "Roduins," and Novak, "The Dutch."

21. Novak, "The Dutch."

22. Gary Leveille, *Eye of Shawenon: A Berkshire History of North Egremont, Prospect Lake, and the Green River Valley* (Great Barrington, MA: Berkshire Archive. com, 2011), 18, 20, 21, 42. The Indian Fur Trail was also known as the Great New England Path. Leveille emphasizes the fact that it was not the only major Indian trail in the region, that there were numerous other trails. This statement is also true for the Indigenous pathways in Connecticut, many of which are now part of the state's highway system. See Mathias Spiess and Hayden L. Griswold, *Map of Connecticut, circa 1625, Indian Trails, Villages, Sachemdoms*, compiled by Mathias Spiess and drawn by Hayden L. Griswold (published by the Colonial Dames of America, 1930. Map and Geographic Information Center, University of Connecticut Libraries, Storrs). A version of the map, illustrated in Lucianne Lavin, *Connecticut's Indigenous Peoples: What Archaeology, History, and Oral Traditions Teach Us about Their Communities and Cultures* (New Haven: Yale Peabody Museum and Yale University Press, 2013), 306–307, shows the location of tribal homelands and their respective villages in the Housatonic and Connecticut drainages circa 1625.

For the location of Wnahktukook, Skatehook, Weatogue, and other Mohican settlements in southwestern Massachusetts and northwestern Connecticut, see Shirley W. Dunn, *The Mohicans and Their Land, 1609–1730* (Fleischmanns, NY: Purple Mountain Press, 1994), 33, 62; Shirley W. Dunn, *The Mohican World 1680–1750* (Fleischmanns, NY: Purple Mountain Press, 2000), especially 56–59. For the location of Mohican settlements in northwestern Connecticut, see Timothy L. Binzen, "Mohican Lands and Colonial Corners: Weataug, Wechquadnach, and the Connecticut Colony, 1675–1750," master's thesis, University of Connecticut Department of Anthropology, 1997; see also *The History of Litchfield County* (Philadelphia: J.W. Lewis & Co., 1881), 519, for the locations of Mohican villages in Salisbury, Connecticut (the book lists no authors, just a mention of anonymous "compilers").

23. See Spiess and Griswold, *Map of Connecticut*, for the location of other major Indian paths in Connecticut.

24. Wilcoxen, "Dutch," 235. Citing James Bradley, Wilcoxen related that the Dutch continued to trade in southern New England after New Netherland had fallen to the English in 1664. James W. Bradley, "Blue Crystals and Other Trinkets: Glass Beads from 16th and 17th Century New England," in *Proceedings of the 1982 Glass Bead Conferences*, ed. Charles F. Hayes, Research Records no. 16 (Rochester, NY: Rochester Museum and Sciences Center, 1983), 35.

25. Ceci, "Native Wampum," 55, 58–59; McBride, "The Source and Mother of the Fur Trade," 35–49.

26. Allen W. Trelease, *Affairs in Colonial New York: The Seventeenth Century* (Ithaca: Cornell University Press, 1960), 43.

27. In 1630, ten guilders were worth one English pound. See Francis Turner, "Money and Exchange Rates in 1632," Official 1632 Fan site, 1632, accessed August 29, 2015, org/1632Slush/1632money.rtf.

28. Trelease, *Affairs*, 43. In the eighteenth century one pound was worth $4.70. See Travelex web site, "US Dollar to British Pounds Exchange Rates," accessed June 6, 2017, https://www.travelex.com/currency/currency-pairs/usd-to-gbp.

29. Dunn, *The Mohican World*, 111–112; Leveille, *Eye of Shawenon*, 71–72; local Stockbridge historians Rick Wilcox and Barbara Allen, personal communication, 2016.

30. McBride, "The Source and Mother of the Fur Trade," 31; McBride, "Early Seventeenth-Century Trade in Southern New England," chapter 7, this volume.

31. Lavin, *Connecticut's Indigenous Peoples*, 300.

32. Lavin, *Connecticut's Indigenous Peoples*, 300. Connecticut coastal peoples supplied such great quantities of wampum beads that those living in southwestern Connecticut were called Siwanogs/Siwanoys by Europeans (see Spiess and Griswold, *Map of the State of Connecticut*), even though the villagers appear to have been members of the Wiechquaeskeck tribe. For a description of the Wiechquaeskeck, see Marshall Joseph Becker, "The Dutch and the Wiechquaeskeck: Shifting Alliances in the Seventeenth Century," chapter 6, this volume.

33. McBride, "The Source and Mother of the Fur Trade," 39–40.

34. Pfeiffer, "Roduins," chapter 8, this volume; John Pfeiffer, "Preliminary Results: Historical and Archaeological Evidence Demonstrating an Early 17th Century Dutch Presence in Branford, Connecticut," *De Nieu Nederlanse Marcurius* 14 (4) (1998) (cited by Paul Huey, "Archaeology of 17th Century New Netherland since 1985: An Update," *Northeast Historical Archaeology* 34 [2005], 106). For the presence of Dutch trade goods at other Branford archaeological sites, see also F. Lawrence and H. Gordon Rowe, "Indian Sites in and Near Pine Orchard," *Bulletin of the Archaeological Society of Connecticut* 27 (1953): 30–34.

35. Kevin A. McBride, director of research at the Mashantucket Pequot Museum, personal communication to the author, 2017 and 2018; McBride, "Early Seventeenth-Century Trade," chapter 7, this volume.

36. Lavin, *Connecticut's Indigenous Peoples*, 300; Gehring, "Sources," chapter 2, this volume.

37. McBride, "The Source and Mother of the Fur Trade," 38.

38. Joep M. J. de Koning, "From Van der Donck to Visscher: A 1648 View of New Amsterdam," *Mercator's World* (July/August 2000): 2–3.

39. See Shorto, *The Island*, and Manack, *Nijkerk*, for the Dutch West India Company's history governing New Amsterdam and other parts of New Netherland, particularly Connecticut.

40. Adriaen van der Donck, *A Description of the New Netherlands* [1655], ed. Thomas F. O'Donnell, trans. Jeremiah Johnson (Syracuse: Syracuse University Press, 1968), xxx–xxxviii, 133–139. See also Gehring, "Sources," chapter 2, this volume;

Staggs, "Declaration of Interdependence," chapter 3, this volume; and Shorto, *The Island*, especially chapter 11, for detailed descriptions of van der Donck's life and his commitment to Dutch colonization of New Netherland.

41. Such as at Old Saybrook in 1623 and later at Hartford; see "Brief History of Old Saybrook"; McBride, "The Source and Mother of the Fur Trade," 41; and Manack, "The Fresh River," chapter 9, this volume.

42. Shorto, *The Island*, 40–49; Manack, *Nijkerk.*

43. "Old Saybrook Historical Society." In 1623, a small Dutch colony of settlers was planted in what is now Old Saybrook, Connecticut. In 1632 the Dutch West India Company formally purchased land at Saybrook Point from the Nehantics and built a trading post. In 1631 the English claimed this area as part of the Warwick Patent, a deed of conveyance awarded to eleven patentees (four others joined a year later) by the Council of New England as represented by its president, the Earl of Warwick, to lands stretching from the Narragansett River in present-day Rhode Island westward along the coastal region to the Pacific Ocean. By 1636 the English had built a fort at the Point and eventually forced out the Dutch militia. But see Manack, chapter 9, this volume, who notes that a trading post was constructed at "Kievits Hoek"—present-day Saybrook Point in Old Saybrook—in ca. 1614–16, prior to the arrival of the Dutch settlers in 1623. That makes sense, since the original reason for settlers was to supply food for the Dutch traders.

44. Report of the Board of Accounts on New Netherland, 150.

45. E. E. Atwater, L. M. Hewitt, B. E. Beach, and R. A. Smith, *History of the Colony of New Haven to Its Absorption into Connecticut* (Meriden, CT: Journal Publishing Company, 1902), 606, as cited in Pfeiffer, "Roduins," this volume

46. Pfeiffer, "Roduins," chapter 8, this volume. Citing records of the New Haven Colony, he reports that Molinar owned a "mill."

47. Spencer P. Mead, *Ye Historie of Ye Town of Greenwich, County of Fairfield and State of Connecticut* (New York: Knickerbocker Press, 1911); Elijah Baldwin Huntington, *History of Stamford, Connecticut: From Its Settlement in 1641, to the Present Time, Including Darien, Which Was One of Its Parishes until 1820* (Stamford, CT: Published by the author, 1868), 81–82.

48. J. Goddard, "An Historical Discourse of Occasion of the 150th Anniversary of the Congregational Church in Salisbury, Connecticut, November 23, 1894," in *The Congregational Church of Salisbury, Connecticut 1744 to 1994* (undated pamphlet with no publication information on file at the Scoville Library, Salisbury, CT), 1–2; Julia Pettee, *The Rev. Jonathan Lee and His 18th Century Salisbury Parish: The Early History of the Town of Salisbury, Connecticut* (Salisbury, CT: Salisbury Association, 1957), 21–22, 52–57; Salisbury Association, *Salisbury Town Meeting Minutes 1741–1784* (Salisbury, CT: Salisbury Association, 1988); Dutcher Family Association, *Bulletin* 1 (1) (February 1935); *Bulletin* 1 (3) (April 1935); *Bulletin* 3 (2) (December 1938), accessed January 15, 2018, http://www.witsend.org/gen/

dutcher/dfa12.htm; Town of North Canaan website, "Canaan History," accessed January 19, 2018, http://www.northcanaan.org/nc/history.html.

49. Binzen, "Mohican Lands and Colonial Corners," 23–24.

50. Arthur H. Hughes and Morse S. Allen, *Connecticut Place Names* (Hartford: Connecticut Printers, 1976), 505; *The History of Litchfield County* (Philadelphia: J. W. Lewis & Co., 1881), 520–521. Dutch settlers encroached on Mohican homelands in Salisbury just south of the tribe's village of Weataug as early as 1714, mistakenly believing that the land was part of Livingston manor; see Binzen, "Mohican Lands," 27, citing Pettee, *The Rev. Jonathan Lee and His 18th Century Salisbury Parish*, 22.

51. Salisbury Association, "Salisbury Town Meeting," esp. 161–162.

52. Hughes and Allen, *Connecticut Place*, 500.

53. For example, see Dunn, *The Mohican World*, 65, 68–76, 111–112, and Leveille, *Eye of Shawenon*, 14, 25, 70, 71, 74–84.

54. Dutcher Family Association, *Bulletin* 1 (2): 3; Dutcher Family Association, *Bulletin* 1 (3): 2; Dutcher Family Association, *Bulletin* 3 (1): 1–2; Roelof Dutcher and his descendants owned a 135-acre farm near Dutcher's Bridge in Salisbury from 1720 until they sold it in 1933. Witsend, "Connecticut Dutchers," 1–7.

55. For examples of intensive, continued, even intimate Dutch-Indigenous relationships, see Gorgen, "Mohawk and Dutch," chapter 5, this volume, and Staggs, "Declarations of Interdependence," chapter 3, this volume.

56. Lavin, *Connecticut's Indigenous Peoples*, 270–271, 300, 308–309.

57. For example, see the discussion on Dutch-Indigenous trade in Staggs, "Declarations of Interdependence," chapter 3, this volume, which describes the Dutch practice of giving gifts to Indian traders prior to trading, and concludes with the statement that "exorbitant gifts were yearly given to Indian brokers."

58. Kathleen J. Bragdon, *Native People of Southern New England 1500–1650* (Norman: University of Oklahoma Press, 1996), 77–78.

59. Bragdon, *Native People*, 143–150; Paulette Crone-Morange and Lucianne Lavin, "The Schaghticoke Tribe and English Law: A Study of Community Survival," *Connecticut History* 43 (2) (2004): 143–145.

60. Edward R. Lambert, *History of the Colony of New Haven before and after the Union with Connecticut* (New Haven: Hitchcock & Stafford, 1838); reprinted in 1976 by the Rotary Club of Milford, CT, 40; McBride, "The Source and Mother of the Fur Trade," 43–49; McBride, "Early Seventeenth-Century Trade," chapter 7, this volume; Menta, *The Quinnipiac*, 67; Manack, *Nijkerk*, 20, 23.

61. Menta, *The Quinnipiac*, 60–61, 80,124; Orcutt and Beardsley, *History of the Old Town of Derby*, lxxv–lxxvi; Margaret Bruchac and Peter Thomas, "Locating Wissatinnewag," *Historical Journal of Massachusetts* 34 (1) (2006): 56–82; Lavin, *Connecticut's Indigenous Peoples*, 299. The name "Mohawk" is an Algonquian term that was applied to them by their enemies. It means "eaters of men," according to Chandler Whipple, *First Encounter: The Indian and the White Man in Massachusetts*

and Rhode Island (Stockbridge, MA: Berkshire Traveler, 1974), 27. The Mohawks' name for themselves was the Iroquoian term "Kanienkehaka" or "Kanien'Kahake," which means "people of the flint," referring to the extensive toolstone resources in their homelands.

62. Menta, *The Quinnipiac*, 86.

63. Lambert, *History of the Colony of New Haven*, 126, 129.

64. William A. Starna, *From Homeland to New Land: A History of the Mahican Indians, 1600–1830* (Lincoln: University of Nebraska Press, 2013). See also Kevin McBride's description of Pequot conflicts with other southern New England tribes as a consequence of the Dutch trade (McBride, "The Source and Mother of the Fur Trade," 44–49).

65. Menta, *The Quinnipiac*, 67, and McBride, "The Source and Mother of the Fur Trade," 36, 48—both citing early Dutch sources.

66. Edward E. Atwater, *History of the Colony of New Haven to Its Absorption into Connecticut* (New Haven: Published by the author, 1881), 325–326; *Battlefields of the Pequot War* website, accessed January 22, 2018, http://pequotwar.org/about/. When the Wangunk sachem Sowheage was driven out of Wethersfield by the English, contra to his land transaction with them, Sowheage appealed to the Pequot for help. Because the Wangunks were tributaries to the Pequot, the latter retaliated on April 23, 1637 with an attack on Wethersfield, killing six Englishmen and three women and abducting two girls. The raid on Wethersfield was the spark that formally ignited the Pequot War. On May 1, 1637, Connecticut Colony declared war on the Pequot tribe.

67. Kevin A. McBride, "The Historical Archaeology of the Mashantucket Pequots, 1637–1900," in *The Pequots in Southern New England: The Fall and Rise of an American Indian Nation* (Norman: University of Oklahoma Press, 1990), 104–105; *Battlefields of the Pequot War* website, accessed January 22, 2018, http://pequotwar.org/about/.

68. See Robert Grumet, *First Manhattans: A History of the Indians of Greater New York* (Norman: University of Oklahoma Press, 2011), 125–128, citing English and French sources, of Mahikans and other southern New England Indians traveling long distances (Michigan, Virginia, Carolinas) for new trapping and trading grounds for furs.

69. Lavin, *Connecticut's Indigenous Peoples*, 277.

70. Paulson and de Leeuw, *Coming to Terms . . . 1610–1614*, 33.

71. Johannes de Laet, quoted in J. Franklin Jameson, ed., *Narratives of New Netherland, 1609–1664* (New York: Charles Scribner's Sons, 1909), 44.

72. Lavin, *Connecticut's Indigenous Peoples*.

73. Menta, *The Quinnipiac*, 67; Francis X. Moloney, *The Fur Trade in New England, 1620–1676* (Hamden, CT: Archon Books, [1931] 1967), 42. Cited by Menta, *The Quinnipiac*, 66, that although "by 1640 the era of the coastal fur trade was passing," Dutch traders were still visiting the Indigenous coastal communities up to 1647.

74. Dunn, *The Mohican World*, 51, 54, 197. Lavin, *Connecticut's Indigenous Peoples*, 315–316; Lion Miles, *A Life of John Konkapot: The Mohican Chief Who Sold His Berkshire (Massachusetts) Hunting Grounds to Puritan Settlers Hoping That Their Faith and Example Would Benefit His People* (Troy, NY: Troy Bookmakers, 2009), 8.

75. William Bradford, *Of Plimoth Plantation* [1650], ed. Harvey Wish (New York: Capricorn, 1962), 176.

76. Dunn, *The Mohican World*, 103–105.

77. Rev. Samuel Hopkins, *Historical Memoirs Relating to the Housatunnuk Indians* (Boston: S. Kneeland, 1753), 15. Cited in Dunn, *The Mohican World*, 177.

78. Lavin, *Connecticut's Indigenous Peoples*, 316.

79. See Paul Gorgen, "Mohawk and Dutch," chapter 5, this volume, for a discussion of equality between the Dutch and the Mohawk that began with the early seventeenth-century Two Row Wampum Treaty and continues to this day. It is true that the Dutch and local Indigenous communities became embroiled in the bloody Kieft's War of 1643–45 (see Anne-Marie Cantwell and Diana diZerega Wall, "Building Forts and Alliances: Archaeology at Freeman and Massapeag, Two Native American Sites," chapter 4, this volume). But that war was instigated by the unpopular Director-General Willem Kieft and his cronies; the Dutch colonists and their leaders were totally against the war. For a thorough and detailed discussion of the causes and effects of Kieft's War, see Shorto, *The Island*, 118–128, 161–164, and Wolfe, *Insubordinate Spirit*, 94–131. See also Walter Giersbach, "Governor Kieft's Personal War," accessed September 1, 2016, http://www.militaryhistoryonline.com/indianwars/articles/kieftswar.aspx.

80. Dunn, *The Mohicans and Their Land*, 129.

81. Dunn, *The Mohicans and Their Land*, 124–131; Shorto, *The Island*, 95–98.

82. Gorgen, "Mohawk and Dutch Relations in the Mohawk Valley," chapter 5, this volume; Pfeiffer, "Roduins," chapter 8, this volume; Staggs, "Declaration of Interdependence," chapter 3, this volume.

83. Shorto, *The Island*, 96. See Gehring, "Sources," chapter 2, this volume, for a summary of fourteenth- to sixteenth-century Dutch history and the forces that led to their deep concern for tolerance and individual freedom. In particular, Catholic Spain's religious persecution of the Protestant Dutch under King Philip II sparked a Dutch revolt against the Habsburg Empire in 1568 that exploded into the Eighty Years' War with Spain. Pfeiffer, "Roduins," chapter 8, this volume, goes back even farther in history to show how Dutch experiences during the Crusades may have instilled the high regard for tolerance.

84. Dunn, *The Mohican World*, 132–133.

85. Dunn, *The Mohican World*, 132.

86. Binzen, "Mohican Lands," 44–50.

87. Dunn, *The Mohican World*, 134.

88. Dunn, *The Mohican World*, 135.

Bibliography

Abler, Thomas S. "European Technology and the Art of War in Iroquoia." In *Cultures in Conflict: Current Archaeological Perspectives*, edited by T. C. Tkaczuk and B. C. Vivian, 273–82. Proceedings of the Twentieth Annual Conference of the Archaeological Association of the University of Calgary, 1989.

Abler, Thomas S. "Longhouse and Palisade." *Ontario History* 63 (1970): 17–40.

Ahmadi, Kate S. "Chief Towaco." Paper presented at the 25th annual Highlands Archaeological and Historical Conference, Tuxedo, New York, October 15, 2011. Copy on file in the Becker Archives, West Chester University of Pennsylvania.

Ahmadi, Kate S. "Pompotowwut-Muhheakanneau, Part 1: The Pomptons (Pumptons)." Paper presented at the 23rd annual Highlands Archaeological and Historical Conference, Tuxedo, New York, October 24, 2009. Copy on file in the Becker Archives, West Chester University of Pennsylvania.

Armbruster, Eugene L. *The Ferry Road on Long Island*. New York: G. Quattlander, 1919.

Atwater, Edward E. *History of the Colony of New Haven to Its Absorption into Connecticut*. New Haven: Published by the author, 1881.

Atwater, E. E., L. M. Hewitt, B. E. Beach, and R. A. Smith. History of the Colony of New Haven to Its Absorption into Connecticut. Meriden, CT: Journal Publishing Company, 1902.

Axtell, James, ed. *The Invasion Within: The Contest of Cultures in Colonial North America*. New York: Oxford University Press, 1985.

Baart, Jan. "Combs." In *One Man's Trash Is Another Man's Treasure: The Metamorphosis of the European Utensil in the New World*, edited by Alexandra van Dongen, 175–187. Rotterdam: Museum Boymans-van Beuningen, 1996.

Bachman, Van Cleaf. *Peltries or Plantations: The Economic Policies of the Dutch West India Company in New Netherland, 1623–1639*. Baltimore: Johns Hopkins University Press, 1969.

Barron, James. 2014. "The Sale of Manhattan, Retold from a Native American Viewpoint." *New York Times*, November 18, 2014. Accessed August 31, 2017. https://

www.nytimes.com/2014/11/19/arts/music/the-sale-of-manhattan-retold-from-a-native-american-viewpoint.html? mcubz=3.

Battlefields of the Pequot War website. Accessed January 22, 2018, http://pequotwar.org/about/.

Beauchamp, W. M. "Earthworks and Stockades." *American Antiquarian and Oriental Journal* 3 (1) (1891): 42–51.

Beck, Roger B., L. Black, L. S. Krieger, P. C. Naylor, and D. I. Shabaka. *World History: Patterns of Interaction.* Evanston, IL: McDougal and Littell, 2005.

Becker, Marshall Joseph. "Anadromous Fish and the Lenape." *Pennsylvania Archaeologist* 76 (2) (2006): 28–40.

Becker, Marshall Joseph. "The Armewamus Band of New Jersey: Other Clues to Differences between the Lenopi and the Lenape." *Pennsylvania Archaeologist* 80 (2) (2010): 61–72.

Becker, Marshall Joseph. "The Boundary between the Lenape and the Munsee: The Forks of Delaware as a Buffer Zone." *Man in the Northeast* 26 (Fall 1983): 1–20.

Becker, Marshall Joseph. "Cash Cropping by Lenape Foragers: Preliminary Notes on Native Maize Sales to Swedish Colonists and Cultural Stability during the Early Colonial Period." *Bulletin of the Archaeological Society of New Jersey* 54 (1999): 45–68.

Becker, Marshall Joseph. "Connecticut Origins for Some Native Americans in New Jersey during the Early Historic Period: Strategies for the Use of Native American Names in Research." *Bulletin of the Archaeological Society of New Jersey* 48 (1993): 62–64.

Becker, Marshall Joseph. "Cultural History in the Native Northeast" (review essay). *American Anthropologist* 99 (1997): 178–180.

Becker, Marshall Joseph. "Ethnohistory of the Lower Delaware Valley: Addressing Myths in the Archaeological Interpretations of the Late Woodland and Contact Period." *Journal of Middle Atlantic Archaeology* 30 (2014): 41–54.

Becker, Marshall Joseph. "John Skickett (1823?—after 1870): A Lenopi Descent Basketmaker Working in Connecticut." *Bulletin of the Archaeological Society of Connecticut* 76 (2014): 99–118.

Becker, Marshall Joseph. "Jacob Skickett, Lenopi Elder: Preliminary Notes from before 1750 to after 1802." *Pennsylvania Archaeologist* 81 (2) (2011): 65–76.

Becker, Marshall Joseph. "Keposh: First Lenopi Migrant into the Forks of Delaware in Pennsylvania." *Newsletter of the Archaeological Society of New Jersey,* no. 230 (January 2011): 1, 3–7.

Becker, Marshall Joseph. "Late Woodland (CA. 1000–1740 CE) Foraging Patterns of the Lenape and Their Neighbors in the Delaware Valley." *Pennsylvania Archaeologist* 80 (1) (2010): 17–31.

Becker, Marshall Joseph. "The Lenape and Other 'Delawarean' Peoples at the Time of European Contact: Population Estimates Derived from Archaeological and

Historical Sources." *The Bulletin: Journal of the New York State Archaeological Association* 105 (1993): 16–25.

Becker, Marshall Joseph. "Lenape Culture History: The Transition of 1660 and Its Implications for the Archaeology of the Final Phase of the Late Woodland Period." *Journal of Middle Atlantic Archaeology* 27 (2011): 53–72.

Becker, Marshall Joseph. "Lenape ('Delaware') in the Early Colonial Economy: Cultural Interactions and the Slow Processes of Culture Change before 1740." *Northeast Anthropology* 81–82 (2014): 109–129.

Becker, Marshall Joseph. "Lenape ('Delaware') Mail Carriers and the Origins of the US Postal Service." *American Indian Culture & Research Journal* 39 (3) (2015): 99–121.

Becker, Marshall Joseph. "Lenape Maize Sales to the Swedish Colonists: Cultural Stability during the Early Colonial Period." In *New Sweden in America*, edited by Carol E. Hoffecker, Richard Waldron, Lorraine E. Williams, and Barbara E. Benson, 121–136. Newark: University of Delaware Press, 1995.

Becker, Marshall Joseph. "Lenape Population at the Time of European Contact: Estimating Native Numbers in the Lower Delaware Valley." In "Symposium on the Demographic History of the Philadelphia Region, 1600–1860," edited by Susan E. Klepp. *Proceedings of the American Philosophical Society* 133 (2) (1989): 112–122.

Becker, Marshall Joseph. "Lenopi Land Use Patterns in Central New Jersey during the Late Woodland Period as Inferred from a Deed of 1710." *Newsletter of the Archaeological Society of New Jersey*, no. 247 (March) (2015): 3–5.

Becker, Marshall Joseph. "Lenopi, or, What's in a Name? Interpreting the Evidence for Cultures and Cultural Boundaries in the Lower Delaware Valley." *Bulletin of the Archaeological Society of New Jersey* 63 (2008): 11–32.

Becker, Marshall Joseph. "The Manhatan Band of Wiechquaeskeck Relocate into the Raritan Valley Buffer Zone: A Refuge Area and the Beginning of 'Munsee' Ethnogenesis." Paper presented at the 11th Annual Roundtable, Institute of American Indian Studies, "Early Encounters: Dutch-Indigenous Relations in 17th Century Northeastern North America," Washington, Connecticut, November 2016.

Becker, Marshall Joseph. "Matchcoats: Cultural Conservatism and Change." *Ethnohistory* 52 (4) (2005): 727–787.

Becker, Marshall Joseph. "Mehoxy of the Cohansey Band of Lenopi: An 1684 Document That Offers Clues to the Missing Part of His Biography." *Bulletin of the Archaeological Society of Delaware*, n.s., 44 (2012): 1–29.

Becker, Marshall Joseph. "Mehoxy of the Cohansey Band of South Jersey Indians: His Life as a Reflection of Symbiotic Relations with Colonists in Southern New Jersey and the Lower Counties of Pennsylvania." *Bulletin of the Archaeological Society of New Jersey* 53 (1998): 40–68.

Becker, Marshall Joseph. "The Moravian Mission in the Forks of the Delaware: Reconstructing the Migration and Settlement Patterns of the Jersey Lenape during the 18th Century through Documents in the Moravian Archives." *Unitas Fratrum* 21–22 (1987): 83–172.

Becker, Marshall Joseph. Ms. A, "Four Specious Indian Deeds from New Jersey, All Dated 18 August 1713: Transcribed in 1990 by Marshall Joseph Becker from West Jersey Deeds [Book] Liber BBB (pages 140–147) in the New Jersey Archives." 6 pages. Trenton, NJ, April 29, 2015.

Becker, Marshall Joseph. Ms. B, "The Ganawese: Tracing the Piscataway from Their Entry into Pennsylvania ca. 1700 until They Relocated into Five Nations Territory around 1750 and Became Known as Conoy." Unpublished manuscript on file, Becker Archives, West Chester University of Pennsylvania.

Becker, Marshall Joseph. "The Raritan Valley Buffer Zone: A Refuge Area for Some Wiechquaeskeck and Other Native Americans during the 17th Century." *Bulletin of the Archaeological Society of Connecticut* 78 (2016): 55–93.

Becker, Marshall Joseph. "Teedyuscung's Youth and Hereditary Land Rights in New Jersey: The Identification of the Unalachtigo." *Bulletin of the Archaeological Society of New Jersey* 47 (1992): 37–60.

Becker, Marshall Joseph. "Wampum on the Fringe: Explaining the Absence of a Post-1600 CE Native-Produced Commodity in Delaware." *Bulletin of the Archaeological Society of Delaware*, n.s., 45 (2012): 23–36.

Becker, Marshall Joseph. "The Wiechquaeskeck of Southeastern New York and Southwestern Connecticut: History and Migrations." 2017. Unpublished manuscript on file, Becker Archives, West Chester University of Pennsylvania.

Bikk, Allan. "Tolerance as Value-Neutrality in the Seventeenth Century Dutch Republic." In *The Dutch Republic and Britain: The Making of Modern Society and a European World Economy.* New York: Nightingale-Bamford School, 2007. Accessed February 18, 2018. http://www1.umassd.edu/euro/2007papers/bikk.pdf.

Binzen, Timothy L. "Mohican Lands and Colonial Corners: Weataug, Wechquadnach, and the Connecticut Colony, 1675–1750." Master's thesis, University of Connecticut Department of Anthropology, 1997.

Birch, Jennifer, and John P. Hart. "Social Networks and Northern Iroquoian Confederacy Dynamics." *American Antiquity* 83 (1) (2018): 13–33.

Blackburn, Roderic H., and Ruth Piwonka. *Remembrance of Patria: Dutch Arts and Culture in Colonial America, 1609–1776.* Albany: Albany Institute of History and Art, 1988.

Block, Adriaen. "The Adriaen Block Map of 1614. First map of 'New Netherland' and the Hudson River area." Photo print in the possession of the author, 24 x 18 inches, "with the courtesy of the Algemeen Rijksarchief, The Hague, The Netherlands."

Bogaert, Harmen Meyndertsz van den. *A Journey into Mohawk and Oneida Country, 1634–35: The Journal of Harmen Meyndertsz van den Bogaert.* Translated and edited by Charles T. Gehring and William A. Starna. Syracuse: Syracuse University Press, 1988.

Bolton, Reginald Pelham. "New York City in Indian Possession." *Indian Notes and Monographs* 2 (7) (1920): 223–397.

Bolton, Robert, Jr. *The History of the County of Westchester from Its First Settlement to the Present Time.* 2 vols. New York: Alexander S. Gould, 1848.

Bonaparte, Darren. *A Lily among Thorns: The Mohawk Repatriation of Káteri Tekahkwitha.* Ahkwesahsne, Mohawk Territory: Wampum Chronicles, 2009.

Boxer, Charles R. *The Dutch Seaborne Empire, 1600–1800.* London: Hutchinson & Co., 1965.

Bradford, William. History of Plymouth Plantation. Boston: Wright & Potter, 1898.

Bradford, William. *History of Plymouth Plantation 1620–1647, Volume II.* Boston: Massachusetts Historical Society, 1912.

Bradford, William. *Of Plimoth Plantation* [1650]. Edited by Harvey Wish. New York: Capricorn, 1962.

Bradley, James W. "Blue Crystals and Other Trinkets: Glass Beads from 16th and 17th Century New England." In *Proceedings of the 1982 Glass Bead Conferences,* edited by Charles F. Hayes, 29–39. Research Records No. 16. Rochester, NY: Rochester Museum and Sciences Center, 1983.

Bradley, James W. *Evolution of the Onondaga Iroquois: Accommodating Change 1500–1635.* Syracuse: Syracuse University Press, 1987.

Bradley, James W. *Before Albany: An Archaeology of Native-Dutch Relations in the Capital Region, 1600–1664.* Albany: State University of New York, State Education Department, 2007.

Bradley, James W. *Before Albany: An Archaeology of Native-Dutch Relations in the Capitol Region 1600–1664.* Bulletin 509. Albany: New York State Museum, 2008.

Bradstreet, Howard. *Citations from Authorities Regarding the Dutch in the Connecticut Valley.* Cambridge, MA: Riverside Press, 1933.

Bragdon, Kathleen J. *Native People of Southern New England 1500–1650.* Norman: University of Oklahoma Press, 1996.

Brandão, José António. "'*Your Fyre Shall Burn No More': Iroquois Policy toward New France and Its Native Allies to 1701.* Lincoln: University of Nebraska Press, 1997.

Brandão, José António, and William A. Starna. "From the Mohawk–Mahican War to the Beaver Wars: Questioning the Pattern." *Ethnohistory* 51 (4) (2004): 725–750.

Brasser, Ted. J. "Mahican." In *Handbook of North American Indians,* vol. 15: Northeast, edited by B. G. Trigger, 198–212. Washington, DC: Government Printing Office, 1978.

Breeden-Raedt aende Vereenichde Nederlandsche Provintien . . . gemaeckt ende gestalt uyt diverse ware en waerachtige memorien. Antwerp: I. A. G. W. C., 1649.

Brink, Andrew. Invading Paradise: *Esopus Settlers at War with Natives, 1659, 1663.* Philadelphia: Xlibris Corporation, 2003.

Brodhead, John Romeyn. "Oration on the Conquest of New Netherland, Delivered before the New York Historical Society, on Wednesday, the 12th of October, 1864." In *Coming to Terms with Early New Netherland–New York History: Commemoration of the Two Hundredth Anniversary by the New York Historical Society.* New York City: New York Historical Society, 1864. Reprinted in 2015: Albany: New Netherland Company.

Bruchac, Joseph. "Indian Renaissance." *National Geographic Magazine,* September 2004. Accessed August 31, 2017. http://ngm.nationalgeographic.com/ngm/0409/feature5/fulltext.html.

Bruchac, Margaret, and Peter Thomas. "Locating Wissatinnewag." *Historical Journal of Massachusetts* 34 (1) (2006): 56–82.

Buccini, Anthony F. "Swannekens Ende Wilden: Linguistic Attitudes and Communication Strategies among the Dutch and Indians in New Netherland." In *The Low Countries and the New World(s): Travel, Discovery, Early Relations,* edited by Johanna C. Prins, Bettina Brandt, Timothy Stevens, and Thomas F. Shannon, 11–28. Lanham, MD: University Press of America, 2000.

Burke, Thomas E., Jr. *Mohawk Frontier: The Dutch Community of Schenectady, New York 1661–1710.* Ithaca: Cornell University Press, 1991.

Burke, Thomas E., Jr. "The New Netherland Fur Trade, 1657–1661: Response to Crisis." In *A Beautiful and Fruitful Place, Selected Rensselaerswijck Seminar Papers,* edited by Nancy Anne McClure Zeller, 283–289. Albany: New Netherland Publishing, 1991.

Burpee, C. W. *The Story of Connecticut.* New York: Belknap Press of Harvard University Press, 1939.

Burrows, Edwin G., and Mike Wallace. *Gotham: A History of New York City to 1898.* New York: Oxford University Press, 1999.

Cantwell, Anne-Marie. " 'Who Knows the Power of His Bones'? Repatriation Redux." In *Ethics and Anthropology: Facing Future Issues in Human Biology, Human Rights, Globalism, and Cultural Property,* edited by Anne-Marie Cantwell, Eva Friedlander, and Madeleine Tramm, 79–119. New York: New York Academy of Sciences, 2000.

Cantwell, Anne-Marie E., and Diana diZerega Wall. *Unearthing Gotham: The Archaeology of New York City.* New Haven: Yale University Press, 2001.

Cave, Alfred A. *The Pequot War.* Amherst: University of Massachusetts Press, 1996.

Ceci, Lynn. *The Effect of European Contact and Trade on the Settlement Patterns of Indians in Coastal New York, 1524–1665.* New York: Garland Press, 1990.

Ceci, Lynn. "Native Wampum as a Peripheral Resource in the Seventeenth-Century World-System." In *The Pequots in Southern New England: The Fall and Rise of an American Indian Nation,* edited by Laurence M. Hauptman and James D. Wherry, 48–63. Norman: University of Oklahoma Press, 1990.

Chapin, Howard M. *Cartography of Rhode Island, Contributions to Rhode Island Bibliography, No. 3.* Providence: Preston and Rounds Co., 1915.

Cohen, David Steven. *The Ramapo Mountain People*. New Brunswick, NJ: Rutgers University Press, 1974.

Cohen, Ronald D. "The Hartford Treaty of 1650: Anglo-Dutch Cooperation in the Seventeenth Century." *New-York Historical Society Quarterly* 52 (1969): 311–332.

Colden, Cadwallader. *History of the Five Nations of Canada*. London: Osbourne, 1747.

Collections of the Massachusetts Historical Society. Vol. 9. Boston: Hall and Hiller, 1804.

Collegiate Churches of New York. Accessed September 31, 2017. http://collegiate-church.org/about-us/historical-timeline.

Colonial Records of Pennsylvania. *Minutes of the Provincial Council of Pennsylvania*. Vol. 8 (January 13, 1757–October 4, 1762). Harrisburg: Theo. Fenn & Company, 1852.

Crone-Morange, Paulette, and Lucianne Lavin. "The Schaghticoke Tribe and English Law: A Study of Community Survival." *Connecticut History* 43 (2) (2004): 132–162.

Curtis, Christopher. "Doc Tells Story of Mohawk Ironworkers Who Helped in Wreckage of 9/11." *Montreal Gazette*, September 13, 2016. Accessed August 31, 2017. http://montrealgazette.com/news/doc-tells-story-of-mohawk-ironworkers-who-helped-in-wreckage-of-911.

Dahlgren, Stellan, and Hans Norman. *The Rise and Fall of New Sweden: Governor Johan Risingh's Journal, 1654–1655, in Its Historical Context*. Uppsala: Almquist and Wiksell International, 1988.

Danckaerts, Jasper, and Peter Sluyter. *Journal of a Voyage to New York and a Tour in Several of the American Colonies in 1679–80*. Ann Arbor: University Microfilms, 1966.

Davies, D. W. *Primer of Dutch Seventeenth Century Overseas Trade*. The Hague: Martinus Nijhoff, 1961.

Deer, Kenneth. "Haudenosaunee Renew Two Row Wampum with Dutch." *Indian Country Today*, October 6, 2013.

De Forest, John William. *History of the Indians of Connecticut from the Earliest Known Period to 1850*. Hartford: William James Hammersley, 1851.

De Heeren, Door, H. Van Beverningk, W. Nieupoort, J. van de Perre, and A. P. Jongestal. *Verbael Gehouden*. 1725. Translated by Charles Gehring. New Netherland Project. New York: Consulate General of the Netherlands, n.d.

De Koning, Joep M. J. "From Van der Donck to Visscher: A 1648 View of New Amsterdam." *Mercator's World* (July/August 2000): 2–10.

De Laet, Johannes. *Beschrijvinghe van West-Indien*. Leiden: Elzevir, 1630.

De Laet, Johannes. "New World." In *The Narratives of New Netherland, 1609–1664*, edited by J. Franklin Jameson. New York: Charles Scribner's Sons, 1909.

De Leeuw, Hubert, and Timothy Paulson. *Coming to Terms with Early New Netherland–New York History: 1610–1614*. Albany: New Netherland Company, 2013.

Deming, Dorothy. *Settlement of Litchfield County.* New Haven: Yale University Press, 1933.

Den Heijer, H. J. *De Geschiedenis van de WIC.* Zutphen: Walburg Pers, 1994; rev. ed. 2002.

Dennis, Matthew. *Cultivating a Landscape of Peace: Iroquois–European Encounters in Seventeenth-Century Iroquoia.* Ithaca: Cornell University Press, 1993.

Denton, Daniel. *A Brief History of New York Formerly Called New Netherlands.* Cleveland: Burrows Brothers, 1902.

De Vries, David Pietersz. From the "Korte Historiael ende Journaels Aenteyckeninge" by David Pietersz De Vries, 1633–1643 (1655). In *Narratives of New Netherland 1609–1664*, 181–234. New York: Charles Scribner's Sons, 1909.

De Vries, David Pietersz. Taken from the section "*near America ende Nieuw-Nederlandt . . .*" In *Korte Historiael Ende Journaels Aenteyckeninge*, edited by H. T. Colenbrander, 227–280. 's-Gravenhage: Martinus Nijhoff, [1655] 1911.

Dexter, Franklin B. *Extracts from the Itineraries and Other Miscellanies of Ezra Stiles 1755–1794.* New Haven: Yale University Press, 1916.

Dincauze, Dena F. "Bert Salwen's Prehistory: 1962–1983." *Northeast Historical Archaeology* 21–22 (1992–93): 7–10.

Donck, Adriaen van der. *Beschryvinge van Nieuw-Nederlandt (gelijck het tegenwoordigh in staet is).* Evert Nieuwenhof, 1st ed. Amsterdam, 1655; 2nd ed., Amsterdam, 1656.

Donck, Adriaen van der. *A Description of the New Netherlands.* Edited by Thomas F. O'Donnell, translated by Jeremiah Johnson. Syracuse: Syracuse University Press, 1968.

Dongen, Alexandra van, ed. *One Man's Trash Is Another Man's Treasure: The Metamorphosis of the European Utensil in the New World.* Rotterdam: Museum Boymans-van Beuningen, 1996.

Duffy, Christopher. *Siege Warfare: The Fortress in the Early Modern World, 1494–1660.* London: Routledge and Keegan Paul, 1979.

Dunn, Shirley W. *The Mohicans and Their Land, 1609–1730.* Fleischmanns, NY: Purple Mountain Press, 1994.

Dunn, Shirley W. *The Mohican World 1680–1750.* Fleischmanns, NY: Purple Mountain Press, 2000.

Dutcher Family Association. *Bulletin* 1 (1), February 1935. Accessed January 15, 2018. http://www.witsend.org/gen/dutcher/dfa12.htm.

Dutcher Family Association. *Bulletin* 1 (3), April 1935. Accessed January 15, 2018. http://www.witsend.org/gen/dutcher/dfa13.htm.

Dutcher Family Association. *Bulletin* 3 (2), December 1938. Accessed January 15, 2018. http://www.witsend.org/gen/dutcher/famassn5.htm.

Dye, David H. 2012. "Rotten Palisade Posts and Rickety Baffle Gates: Repairing Native Eastern North American Fortifications." Accessed September 8, 2017. https://www.academia.edu/1987842/Rotten_Palisades_and_Rickety_Baffle_Gates_Fortifying_Native_Eastern_North_ America.

Eekhof, A. *Bastiaen Jansz. Krol: Krankenbezoeker, kommies en kommandeur van Nieuw-Nederland (1595–1645).* The Hague: Martinus Nijhoff, 1910.

Eekhof, A. *Jonas Michaëlius, Founder of the Church in New* Netherland. Leiden: A. W. Sijthoff, 1926.

Elton, Hugh. *Frontiers of the Roman Empire.* London: B. T. Batsford, 1996.

Engelbrecht, William E. *Iroquoia: The Development of a Native World.* Syracuse: Syracuse University Press, 2003.

Engelbrecht, William, and J. Brice Jamieson. "St. Lawrence Iroquoian Projectile Points: A Regional Perspective." Archaeology of Eastern North America 44 (2016): 81–98.

Eshleman, Henry. *Annals of the Susquehannocks.* Lancaster, PA: Eshleman, 1909.

Eterovich, Adam E., ed. *The Dutch in New Netherland and the United States 1609–1909.* New York: New Netherland Chamber of Commerce in America, 1909.

Feister, Lois M. "Indian–Dutch Relations in the Upper Hudson Valley: A Study of Baptism Records in the Dutch Reformed Church, Albany, New York." *Man in the Northeast* 24 (1982): 89–113.

Feister, Lois M. "Linguistic Communication between the Dutch and Indians in New Netherland." In *Neighbors and Intruders: An Ethnohistorical Exploration of the Indians of Hudson's River,* edited by Laurence M. Hauptman and Jack Campisi, 185–190. National Museum of Man Mercury Series, Canadian Ethnology Service No. 39. Ottawa: National Museums of Canada, 1978.

Fenton, William N. *The Great Law and the Longhouse.* Norman: University of Oklahoma Press, 1998.

Fernow, B., trans., comp., and ed. "Documents Relating to the History and Settlement of the Towns along the Hudson and Mohawk Rivers (with the exception of Albany) from 1630 to 1684." In *Documents Relating to the Colonial History of the State of New-York,* vol. 8. Albany: Weed, Parsons and Company, 1881.

Fernow, B., trans., comp., and ed. "Documents Relating to the History of the Early Colonial Settlements Principally on Long Island." In *Documents Relating to the Colonial History of the State of New-York,* vol. 8. Albany: Weed, Parsons and Company, 1883.

Fernow, B., trans., comp., and ed. *Documents Relative to the Colonial History of the State of New York.* Vol. 8. Albany: Weed, Parsons & Co., 1891.

Finlayson, William David, and Mel Brown. Iroquoian Peoples of the Land of Rocks and Water, AD 1000–1650: A Study in Settlement Archaeology. Ottawa: London Museum of Archaeology, 1998.

First Reformed Church of Schenectady, Records, 1688–1750. Archives of First Reformed Church of Schenectady, Schenectady, New York.

Fletcher, William. *A History of New England. Volume 1: Massachusetts, Connecticut and Rhode Island.* Boston: Crocker and Company, Publishers, 1880.

French, J. H. *Gazetteer of New York.* Syracuse, NY: R. Pearsall Smith, 1860.

Frijhoff, Willem. Wegen van Evert Willemsz: Een Hollands weeskind op zoek naar zichzelf, 1607–1647. Nijmegen: Sun, 1995.

Funk, Robert E., and Robert D. Kuhn. *Three Sixteenth-Century Mohawk Iroquois Village Sites*. Albany: New York State Museum/New York State Education Department, 2003.

Gaastra, Femme S. *De geschiedenis van de VOC*. Zutphen: Walburg Pers, 1991.

Gardener, Lion. *Relation of the Pequot Warres*. Hartford, CT: Hartford Press, 1901.

Gastel, Ada van. "Ethnic Pluralism in Early American Literature: Incorporating Dutch-American Texts into the Canon." In *Early American Literature and Culture: Essays Honoring Harrison T. Mesorole*, edited by Kathryn Zabelle Derounian-Stodola, 109–121. Newark: University of Delaware Press, 1992.

Gastel, Ada van. "Van der Donck's Description of the Indians: Additions and Corrections." *William and Mary Quarterly*, 3rd ser., 47 (1990): 411–421.

Gehring, Charles T., trans. and ed. *Council Minutes 1655–1656*. Syracuse: Syracuse University Press, 1995.

Gehring, Charles T., trans. and ed. "Correspondence, 1647–1653." *New Netherland Documents Series*. Syracuse: Syracuse University Press, 2000.

Gehring, Charles T. "The Dutch among the People of the Long River." *Annals of New Netherland*. New Netherland Project. New York: Consulate General of the Netherlands, 1993.

Gehring, Charles T., trans. and ed. *Fort Orange Court Minutes, 1652–1660*. Syracuse: Syracuse University Press, 1988.

Gehring, Charles T., ed. and trans. *Fort Orange Court Minutes, 1652–1660*. New Netherland Document Series, vol. 16, part 2. Syracuse: Syracuse University Press, 1990.

Gehring, Charles T., trans. and ed. *New York Historical Manuscripts: Dutch. Delaware Papers 1648–1664*. Baltimore: Genealogical Publishing, 1981.

Gehring, Charles T., trans. and ed. *New York Historical Manuscripts: Dutch. Council Minutes, 1652–1654*. Baltimore: Genealogical Publishing, 1983.

Gehring, Charles T. "Privatizing Colonization: The Patroonship of Rensselaerswijck." https://www.newnetherlandinstitute.org/research/essays-and-articles/#annals.

Gehring, Charles T., and J. A Schiltkamp, trans. and eds. *Curacao Papers, 1640–1665*. Interlaken, NY: Heart of Lake, 1987.

Gehring, Charles T., and William A. Starna. "Dutch and Indians in the Hudson Valley: The Early Period." *Hudson Valley Regional Review* (September 1992).

Gehring, Charles T., and William A. Starna, trans. and eds. *Journey into Mohawk and Oneida Country 1634–1635: The Journal of Harmen Meyndertsz van den Bogaert*. Syracuse: Syracuse University Press, rev. ed., 2013.

Gerard-Little, Peregrine A., Michael B. Rogers, and Kurt A. Jordan. "Understanding the Built Environment at the Seneca Iroquois White Springs Site Using Large-Scale, Multi-Instrument Archaeogeophysical Surveys." *Journal of Archaeological Science* 39 (7) (2012): 2042–2048.

Geyl, Pieter. *The Revolt of the Netherlands, 1555–1609*. London: Williams & Northgate, 1932; paperback by Cassell History, 1988.

Goddard, Ives. "Delaware." In *Northeast*, vol. 15 of *Handbook of North American Indians,* edited by Bruce Trigger, 213–239. Washington, DC: Smithsonian Institution, 1978.

Goddard, Ives. "The Use of Pidgins and Jargons on the East Coast of North America." In *The Language Encounter in the Americas, 1492–1800,* European Expansion and Global Interaction, vol. 1, edited by Edward G. Gray and Norman Fiering, 61–78. New York: Berghahn Books, 2000.

Goddard, J. "An Historical Discourse of Occasion of the 150th Anniversary of the Congregational Church in Salisbury, Connecticut, November 23, 1894." In *The Congregational Church of Salisbury, Connecticut 1744 to 1994,* undated Pamphlet with no publication information on file at the Scoville Library, Salisbury, Connecticut.

Gosselink, Martine. *New York Nieuw-Amsterdam: De Nederlandse oorsprong van Manhattan.* Amsterdam: Nieuw Amsterdam, 2009.

"Governor John Winthrop Letter." *Connecticut Historical Society Bulletin* 17 (3) (July 1952).

Grassmann, Thomas. *The Mohawk Indians and Their Valley: Being a Chronological Documentary Record to the End of 1693.* Schenectady: JS Lischynsky, 1969.

Graymont, Barbara, ed. *Early American Indian Documents: Treaties and Laws, 1607–1789.* General editor Alden T. Vaughan, vol. 7, New York and New Jersey Treaties, 1609–1682. Frederick, MD: University Publications of America, 1985.

Graymont, Barbara, ed. *Early American Indian Documents: Treaties and Laws, 1607–1789.* General editor Alden T. Vaughan, vol. 7, New York and New Jersey Treaties, 1683–1713. Bethesda, MD: University Publications of America, 1995.

Graymont, Barbara, ed. *Early American Indian Documents: Treaties and Laws, 1607–1789.* General editor Alden T. Vaughan, vol. 9, New York and New Jersey Treaties, 1714–1753. Bethesda, MD: University Publications of America, 1996.

Graymont, Barbara, ed. *Early American Indian Documents: Treaties and Laws, 1607–1789.* General editor Alden T. Vaughan, vol. 10, New York and New Jersey Treaties, 1754–1775. Bethesda, MD: University Publications of America, 2001.

Greer, William. "Arent van Curler and the Flatts: History, Archaeology, and Art Illuminate a Life on the Hudson." https://www.newnetherlandinstitute.org/history-and-heritage/digital-exhibitions/arent-van-curler-and-the-flatts/.

Grumet, Robert S. *The Munsee Indians: A History.* Norman: University of Oklahoma Press, 2009.

Grumet, Robert S. "Taphow: The Forgotten 'Sakemau and Commander in Chief of All Those Indians Inhabiting Northern New Jersey.'" *Bulletin of the Archaeological Society of New Jersey* 43 (1988): 23–28.

Hagedorn, Nancy Lee. "A Friend to Go between Them: The Interpreter as Cultural Broker during Anglo–Iroquois Councils, 1740–1770." *Ethnohistory* 35 (1) (1988): 60–80.

Hamell, George. "Mythical Realities and European Contact in the Northeast during the Sixteenth and Seventeenth Centuries." *Man in the Northeast* 33 (1987): 62–87.

Hamell, George. "Trading in Metaphors: The Magic of Beads, Another Perspective upon Indian-European Contact in Northeastern North America." In *Proceedings of the 1982 Glass Trade Bead Conference*, edited by C. F. Hayes III, 5–28. Research Records 16. Rochester: Rochester Museum and Science Center, 1983.

Harrington, J. C. "Dating Stem Fragments of Seventeenth and Eighteenth Century Clay Tobacco Pipes." *Quarterly Bulletin of the Archeological Society of Virginia* 9 (1) (1954).

Hart, John P., Hetty Jo Brumbach, Lisa M. Anderson, and Susan Winchell-Sweeney. "Maize and Pits: Late Prehistoric Occupations of the Hurley Site in the Esopus Creek Valley, Ulster County, New York." *Archaeology of Eastern North America* 45 (2017): 133–160.

Hart, John P., and Bernard Means. "Maize and Villages: A Summary and Critical Assessment of Current Northeast Early Late Prehistoric Evidence." In *Northeast Subsistence-Settlement Change: A.D. 700–1300*, 342–358. New York State Museum Bulletin no. 496. Albany: State University of New York, 2002.

Hart, Simon. *The Prehistory of the New Netherland Company: Amsterdam Notarial Records of the First Dutch Voyages to the Hudson*. Amsterdam: City of Amsterdam Press, 1959.

Hartford Times. "Dutch Land in Early Hartford." February 24, 1905.

Hartgers, Joost. "'t Fort nieuw Amsterdam op de Manhatans." In Beschryvinghe van Virginia, Nieu Nederlandt, Nieu Englandt en d'eylanden Bermudes, Berbados, en S. Christoffel. Amsterdam, 1651. Accessed July 20, 2013, http://luna.wustl.edu:8180/luna/servlet/detail/JCB~1~1~492~210010:t--Fort-nieuw-Amsterdam-op-de-Manha.

Hartsinck, J. J. *Beschryving van Guiana, op de wilde Kust in Zuid-America*. Amsterdam: Gerrit Tielenburg, 1770.

Hauptman, Laurence M., and James D. Wherry, eds. *The Pequots in Southern New England: The Fall and Rise of an Indian Nation*. Norman: University of Oklahoma Press, 1990.

Hazard, Ebenezer, "Historical Collections: consisting of State Papers and other authentic documents; intended as materials for a history of the United States of America, II." Philadelphia: T. Dobson, 1794.

Heidenreich, Conrad. *Huronia: A History and Geography of the Huron Indians, 1600–1650*. Toronto: McClelland and Stewart, 1971.

Henneton, Lauric. "The House of Hope in the Valley of Discord: Connecticut Geopolitics and 'Anglo-Dutch' Relations (1613–1654)." In *The Worlds of the Seventeenth-Century Hudson Valley*, edited by Jaap Jacobs and L. H. Roper, 169–194. Albany: State University of New York Press, 2014.

Hicks, Benjamin, ed. Records of the Towns of North and South Hempstead, Long Island, New York. 8 vols. Jamaica: Long Island Farmer Print, 1896–1904.

Hoadley, Charles J. *Records of the Colony and Plantation of New-Haven, from 1638 to 1649*. Hartford: Case, Tiffany and Company, 1857.

Hopkins, Rev. Samuel. *Historical Memoirs Relating to the Housatunnuk Indians.* Boston: S. Kneeland, 1753.

Hosmer, James Kendall, ed. *Winthrop's Journal, Vol. I.* New York: Charles Scribner's Sons, 1908.

Huey, Paul R. "The Archaeology of 17th-Century New Netherland since 1985: An Update." *Northeast Historical Archaeology* 34 (1) (2005). Accessed May 10, 2017. http://orb.binghamton.edu/neha/vol34/iss1/6.

Huey, Paul R. "Aspects of Continuity and Change in Colonial Dutch Material Culture at Fort Orange, 1624–1664." PhD diss., University of Pennsylvania, 1988.

Huey, Paul R. "Dutch Colonial Forts in New Netherland." In First Forts: Essays on the Archaeology of Proto-Colonial Fortifications, edited by Eric Klingelhofer, 139–166. Leiden: Brill, 2010.

Hughes, Arthur H., and Morse S. Allen. *Connecticut Place Names.* Hartford: Connecticut Printers, 1976.

Hume, Ivor N. *The Virginia Adventure: Roanoke to Jamestown.* Charlottesville: University of Virginia Press, 1997.

Huntington, Elijah Baldwin. *History of Stamford, Connecticut: From Its Settlement in 1641, to the Present Time, Including Darien, Which Was One of Its Parishes until 1820.* Stamford, CT: Published by the author, 1868.

Intersections International. "Healing Turtle Island." January 7, 2010. Accessed August 31, 2017. http://www.intersections.org/healing-turtle-island-1.

Irving, Washington (aka Diedrich Knickerbocker). *A History of New York, from the Beginning of the World to the End of the Dutch Dynasty.* Rev. ed. New York: Inskeep and Bradford, 1812.

Israel, Jonathan I. *Dutch Primacy in World Trade, 1583–1740.* Oxford: Oxford University Press, 1990.

Israel, Jonathan I. *The Dutch Republic: Its Rise, Greatness, and Fall 1477–1806.* Oxford: Clarendon Press, 1995.

Ives, Timothy H. "Wangunk Ethnohistory: A Case Study of a Connecticut River Indian Community." MA thesis in anthropology, College of William and Mary, Williamsburg, Virginia, 2001.

Jacobs, Jaap. *Dutch Colonial Fortifications in North America 1614–1676.* Amsterdam: New Holland Foundation and Bommelstein Historical Consultancy, 2015.

Jacobs, Jaap. "Dutch Colonial Fortifications in North America 1614–1676." In *The Atlas of Dutch North America,* version 1.0. Dundee, UK: New Holland Foundation and Bommelstein Historical Consultancy, 2015. Accessed January 17, 2018. http://www.newhollandfoundation.nl/wp-content/uploads/2015/11/PDF-Dutch-Colonial-Fortifications-in-North-America.pdf.

Jacobs, Jaap. *Een zegenrijk gewest: Nieuw-Nederland in de zeventiende eeuw.* Amsterdam: Samenwerkende Uitgeverijen Prometheus-Bert Bakker, 1999.

Jacobs, Jaap. *New Netherland: A Dutch Colony in Seventeenth-Century America.* Boston: Brill, 2005.

Jacobs, Jaap, and Louis H. Roper, eds. *The Worlds of the Seventeenth-Century Hudson Valley.* Albany: State University of New York Press, 2014.

Jameson, J. Franklin, ed. *Narratives of New Netherland, 1609–1664.* New York: Charles Scribner's Sons, 1909.

Jameson, J. Franklin. "Wassenaer's Historisch Verhael." In *Narratives of New Netherland, 1609–1664,* 67–96. New York: Charles Scribner's Sons, 1909.

Jennings, Francis. *The Invasion of America: Indians, Colonialism, and the Cant of Conquest.* New York: W. W. Norton, 1975.

Johnson, Charles F. "The Dutch in Hartford." In *Hartford in History: A Series of Papers by Resident Authors,* edited by Willis I. Twitchell, 39–48. Hartford: Plimpton, 1899.

Johnson, Donald S. *Charting the Sea of Darkness, The Four Voyages of Henry Hudson.* Camden, ME: International Marine, 1993.

Johnson, Ellen Terry. *The House of Hope of the First Connecticut Settlers: A Paper Read before the Connecticut Society of the Colonial Dames of America, in Hartford, November 19th, 1895.* New Haven: Tuttle, Morehouse & Taylor Press, 1897.

Jones, Electra F. *Stockbridge, Past and Present; or, Records of an Old Mission Station.* Springfield, MA: Samuel Bowles & Company, 1854.

Judd, Sylvester. "The Dutch House of Good Hope at Hartford." In *New England Historical and Genealogical Register,* vol. 6. Boston: New England Historic, Genealogical Society, 1852.

Karklins, Karlis. "Dutch Trade Beads in North America." *Proceedings of the 1982 Glass Trade Bead Conference* 16 (1983): 111–126.

Keeley, Lawrence H., Marisa Fontana, and Russell Quick. "Baffles and Bastions: The Universal Features of Fortifications." *Journal of Archaeological Research* 15 (1) (2007): 55–95.

Keene, Arthur S. "Biology, Behavior, and Borrowing: A Critical Examination of Optimal Foraging Theory in Archaeology." In *Archaeological Hammer and Theories,* edited by James A. Moore and Arthur S. Keene, 137–155. New York: Academic Press, 1983.

Keener, C. S. "An Ethnohistorical Analysis of Iroquois Assault Tactics Used against Fortified Settlements of the Northeast in the Seventeenth Century." *Ethnohistory* 46 (4) (1999): 777–807.

Kent, Donald H., ed. *Early American Indian Documents, Treaties and Laws, 1607–1789. Volume I: Pennsylvania and Delaware Treaties, 1629–1737,* general editor Alden T. Vaughan. Washington, DC: University Publications of America, 1979.

Kent, Donald H., ed. *Early American Indian Documents, Treaties and Laws, 1607–1789. Volume II: Pennsylvania Treaties, 1737–1756,* general editor Alden T. Vaughan. Washington, DC: University Publications of America, 1981.

Kidd, Kenneth E., and Martha A. Kidd. "A Classification System for Glass Beads for the Use of Field Archaeologists." *Proceedings of the 1982 Glass Trade Bead Conference* 16 (1983): 219–255.

Koenig Alexa, and Jonathan Stein. "Federalism and the State Recognition of Native American Tribes: A Survey of State-Recognized Tribes and State Recognition Processes across the United States." *Santa Clara Law Review* 48 (1) (2007): 1–153.

Koot, Christian J. *Empire at the Periphery: British Colonists, Anglo-Dutch Trade, and the Development of the British Atlantic, 1621–1713.* New York: NYU Press, 2011.

Kraft, Herbert Clemens. *The Lenape-Delaware Indian Heritage: 10,000 BC–AD 2000.* Elizabeth, NJ: Lenape Books, 2001.

Krey, August C. *The First Crusade: The Accounts of Eyewitnesses and Participants.* Princeton: Princeton University Press, 1921.

Krus, A. M. "Refortifying Cahokia, More Efficient Palisade Construction through Redesigned Bastions." *Midcontinental Journal of Archaeology* 36 (2) (2011): 227–44.

Krus, A. M. "The Timing of Precolumbian Militarization in the US Midwest and Southeast." *American Antiquity* 81 (2) (2016): 375–388.

Kupperman, Karen Ordahl. "The Connecticut River: A Magnet for Settlement." *Connecticut History Review* 35 (1) (1994): 50–67.

LaFantasie, Glenn W., ed. *The Correspondence of Roger Williams, Volume I, 1629–1653.* Providence, RI: Brown University Press, 1988.

Lainey, Jonathan. *La "Monnaie des Sauvages": Les colliers de wampum d'hier à aujourd'hui.* Quebec: Septentrion, 2004.

Lambert, Edward R. *History of the Colony of New Haven before and after the Union with Connecticut.* New Haven: Hitchcock & Stafford, 1838. Reprinted, 1976, Rotary Club of Milford, Connecticut.

Largy, Tonya, Lucianne Lavin, Marina Mozzi, and Kathleen Furgerson. "Corncobs and Buttercups: Plant Remains from the Goldkrest Site." In *Current Northeast Paleoethnobotany*, edited by John P. Hart, 69–84. Bulletin 494. Albany: New York State Museum, 1999.

Larner, Kingston. "Field Notes, the Freeman Site." Collection, Paul Huey, 1971.

Lavin, Lucianne. *Connecticut's Indigenous Peoples: What Archaeology, History, and Oral Traditions Teach Us about Their Communities and Cultures.* New Haven: Yale Peabody Museum and Yale University Press, 2013.

Lavin, Lucianne, M. E. Mozzi, J. W. Bouchard, and K. Hartgen. "The Goldkrest Site: An Undisturbed, Multi-Component Woodland Site in the Heart of Mahican Territory." *Journal of Middle Atlantic Archaeology* 12 (1996): 113–129.

Leader, John T. *Life of Sir Robert Dudley Earl of Warwick and Duke of Northumberland.* Florence, UK: G. Barbara, 1895.

Lear, Arnold J. F. van, ed. and trans. *Documents Relating to New Netherland, 1624–1626, in the Henry E. Huntington Library.* Publications Americana, Folio Series, no. 1. San Marino, CA: Henry E. Huntington Library and Art Gallery, 1924.

Lear, Arnold J. F. van, ed. and trans. *New York Historical Manuscripts: Dutch, Vol. II: Register of the Provincial Secretary, 1642–1647.* Baltimore: Genealogical Publishing, 1974.

Lear, Arnold J. F. van, ed. and trans. *New York Historical Manuscripts: Dutch: Volume IV: Council Minutes, 1638–1649.* Baltimore: Genealogical Publishing, 1974.

Lee, Richard. *The Dobe Ju/'Hoansi.* 3rd ed. Toronto: Harcourt Brace, 2002.

Lenig, Donald. "Of Dutchmen, Beaver Hats, and Iroquois." In *Current Perspectives in Northeastern Archaeology: Essays in Honor of William A. Ritchie,* edited by Robert E. Funk and Charles F. Hayes III, 71–84. Researches and Transactions of New York State Archaeological Association 17, no. 1. Rochester: State of New York Archaeological Association, 1977.

L'Honoré Naber, S. P., ed. *Henry Hudson's Reize onder Nederlandsche vlag van Amsterdam naar Nova Zembla, Amerika en terug naar Dartmouth in Engeland, 1609.* 's-Gravenhage: Martinus Nijhoff, 1921. http://www.ianchadwick.com/Hudson.

L'Honoré Naber, S. P., ed. *Reizen van Willem Barents, Jacob van Heemskerck, and Jan Cornelisz: Rijp en anderen naar het noorden, 1594–1597.* 's-Gravenhage: Martinus Nijhoff, 1917.

Lipman, Andrew. *The Saltwater Frontier: Indians and the Contest for the American Coast.* New Haven: Yale University Press, 2015.

Love, William D. *The Colonial History of Hartford Gathered from the Original Records.* Hartford: Rev. William DeLoss Love, 1914.

Mackrael, Kim. 2012. "Quebec Mohawk Turns Freedom Tower Site into New York City's Tallest Skyscraper." *Globe and Mail,* April 30, 2012. Accessed August 31, 2017. https://www.theglobe andmail.com/news/world/quebec-mohawk-turns-freedom-tower-into-new-york-citys-tallest-skyscraper/article 2418629/.

Manack, Richard. *Nijkerk in the New World.* Torrington, CT: New Netherland Nautical, 2013.

Mancini, Jason. "'In Contempt and Oblivion': Censuses, Ethnogeography, and Hidden Indian Histories in Eighteenth-Century Southern New England." *Ethnohistory* 62 (1) (2015): 61–94.

Mandell, Daniel R., ed. *Early American Indian Documents: Treaties and Laws, 1607–1789.* General editor Alden T. Vaughan, vol. 20, New England Treaties, North and West, 1650–1776. Bethesda, MD: University Publications of America, 2003.

Marble Collegiate Church. Website. Accessed 9/4/2017. http://www.marblechurch.org/welcome/history/.

Masthay, Carl, ed. *Johan Schmick's Mahican Dictionary, 1755.* Philadelphia: American Philosophical Society, 1991.

McBride, Kevin A. "Fort Island: Conflict and Trade in Long Island Sound." In *The Native Forts of Long Island Sound Area,* edited by Gaynell Stone, 255–266. Stony Brook, NY: Suffolk County Archaeological Society, 2006.

McBride, Kevin A. "The Historical Archaeology of the Mashantucket Pequots, 1637–1900." In *The Pequots in Southern New England: The Fall and Rise of an American Indian Nation*, edited by Laurence M. Hauptman and James D. Wherry, 96–116. Norman: University of Oklahoma Press, 1990.

McBride, Kevin A. "Prehistory of the Lower Connecticut River Valley." PhD diss., University of Connecticut, 1984.

McBride, Kevin A. "The Source and Mother of the Fur Trade: Dutch Relations in Eastern New Netherland." In *Enduring Traditions: The Native Peoples of New England*, edited by Laurie Lee Weinstein, 31–51, Westport, CT: Bergin and Garvey, 1994.

McBride, Kevin A. "War and Trade in Eastern New Netherland." In *A Beautiful and Fruitful Place*, edited by Margriet Lacy. Albany: New Netherlands Institute, 2013.

McBride, Kevin A. "War and Trade in Eastern New Netherland." Presented at the 11th Annual Native American–Archaeology Round Table, "Early Encounters: Dutch-Indigenous Relations in 17th Century Northeastern North America," October 29, 2016.

McBride, Kevin, David Naumec, Ashley Bissonnette, and Noah Fellman. *Battle of Mistick Fort: English Withdrawal and Pequot Counterattacks.* Report on file with the National Park Service, American Battlefield Protection Program, 2017.

McWeeney, Lucinda. "A Review of Late Pleistocene and Holocene Climatic Changes in Southern New England." *Bulletin of the Archaeological Society of Connecticut* 62 (1999): 3–18.

Mead, Spencer P. *Ye Historie of Ye Town of Greenwich, County of Fairfield and State of Connecticut.* New York: Knickerbocker Press, 1911.

Megapolensis, Johannes. *Een kort Ontwerp vande Mahakuase Indianen, haer landt, tale, stature, Dracht, godes-dienst ende magistrature.* t'Alkmaer: Ijsbrant Jansz. Van Houten, 1644.

Menta, John. *The Quinnipiac: Cultural Conflict in Southern New England.* Yale University Publications in Anthropology 86. New Haven: Peabody Museum of Natural History, Yale University, 2003.

Merrell, James H. " 'I Desire That All I Have Said . . . May Be Taken Down Aright': Revisiting Teedyuscung's 1756 Treaty Council Speeches." *William and Mary Quarterly*, 3rd ser., 63 (4) (2006): 777–826.

Merwick, Donna. *The Shame and the Sorrow: Dutch–Amerindian Encounters in New Netherland.* Philadelphia: University of Pennsylvania Press, 2006.

Meuwese, Mark. *Brothers in Arms, Partners in Trade: Dutch–Indigenous Alliances in the Atlantic World, 1595–1674.* Leiden: Brill Academic, 2011.

Meuwese, Mark. "From Intercolonial Messenger to 'Christian Indian': The Flemish Bastard and the Mohawk Struggle for Independence from New France and Colonial New York in the Eastern Great Lakes Borderland, 1647–1687." In *Lines Drawn upon the Water: First Nations and the Great Lakes Borders and*

Borderlands, edited by Karl Scott Hele, 43–63. Waterloo: Wilfrid Laurier University Press, 2008.

Midtrød, Tom Arne. "The Flemish Bastard and the Former Indians: Métis and Identity in Seventeenth-Century New York." *American Indian Quarterly* 34 (1) (Winter 2010): 83–108.

Midtrød, Tom Arne. *The Memory of All Ancient Customs: Native American Diplomacy in the Colonial Hudson Valley.* Ithaca: Cornell University Press, 2013.

Miles, Lion. *A Life of John Konkapot: The Mohican Chief Who Sold His Berkshire (Massachusetts) Hunting Grounds to Puritan Settlers Hoping That Their Faith and Example Would Benefit His People.* Troy, NY: Troy Bookmakers, 2009.

Miller, Christopher, and George Hamell. "A New Perspective on Indian-White Contact: Cultural Symbols and Colonial Trade." *Journal of American History* 73 (1986): 311–328.

Mills, Lewis S., Jr. "Long Ago in Connecticut: Of the Seizure of the House of Hope." *Lure of the Litchfield Hills* 12 (June 1953).

Milner, George R. "Palisaded Settlements in Prehistoric Eastern North America." In *City Walls: The Urban Enceinte in Global Perspective,* edited by James D. Tracey, 46–70. New York: Cambridge University Press, 2006.

Milner, George R. "Warfare in Prehistoric and Early Historic Eastern North America." *Journal of Archaeological Research* 7 (2) (1999): 105–151.

Moore, Jan A. "Quinnipiac Fishes and Fisheries: History and Modern Perspectives on the Fishes and Fisheries in the Quinnipiac Watershed." *Transactions of the Connecticut Academy of Arts and Sciences* 57 (2001): 1–28.

Morey, Jed. "A Mohawk Ironworker's Widow Remembers 9/11." *Jed Morey: So Far Left, We're Right,* September 12, 2011. Accessed August 31, 2017. http://www.jedmorey.com/2011/a-mohawk-ironworker%E2%80%99s-widow-remembers-911/.

Morgan, Forrest. *Connecticut as a Colony and a State, or One of the Original Thirteen.* Hartford: Publishing Society of Connecticut, 1904.

Nelson, William. "Anthropologic Miscellanea. Indian Words, Personal Names, and Place-Names in New Jersey." *American Anthropologist* 4 (1902): 183–192.

Nelson, William. *The Indians of New Jersey: Their Origin and Development (etc.).* Paterson: Press Printing and Publishing Company, 1894.

Nelson, William. *Personal Names of Indians of New Jersey: Being a List of Six Hundred and Fifty . . .* Paterson: Paterson History Club, 1904.

North Canaan, Town of "Canaan History." Website. Accessed January 19, 2018, http://www.northcanaan.org/nc/history.html.

Norton, Thomas Elliot. *The Fur Trade in Colonial New York, 1686–1776.* Madison: University of Wisconsin Press, 1974.

Norwood, John R. *We Are Still Here: The Tribal Saga of New Jersey's Nanticoke and Lenape Indians.* Bridgeton: Native New Jersey Publications, 2007.

Novak, Robert. "The Dutch in the Housatonic Valley." *Huntington Herald,* July 1998. On the Derby Historical Society website. Accessed January 19, 2018, http://derbyhistorical.org/dutch.htm.

Oakes, Ian. "Kahnawake Mohawk Fastens Milestone Bolt at 'Freedom Tower.'" *Indian Times,* May 3, 2012. Accessed August 31, 2017. http://www.indiantime.net/story/2012/05/03/news/kahnawake-mohawk-fastens-milestone-bolt-at-freedom-tower/050420122028560174118.html.

O'Callaghan, Edmund B. *Documentary History of the State of New York.* Albany: Weed, Parsons & Company, 1850.

O'Callaghan, Edmund, ed. *Documents Relative to the Colonial History of the State of New York.* Albany: Weed, Parsons, 1887.

O'Callaghan, Edmund B. trans. and ed. *Documents Relative to the Colonial History of the State of New York; Procured in Holland, England and France.* Vol. 1. Albany: Weed, Parsons, 1856.

O'Callaghan, Edmund B. *History of New Netherland or New York under the Dutch.* New York. D. Appleton & Company, 1848.

Old Saybrook Historical Society. "Old Saybrook Historical Society." Accessed August 8, 2015. http://www.saybrookhistory.org/web_page.php?id=13.

Olmstead, Earl P. *Blackcoats among the Delaware—David Zeisberger on the Ohio Frontier.* Kent, OH: Kent State University Press, 1991.

OnTheWorldMap. "Connecticut Highway Map." Website. Accessed July 27, 2019. http://ontheworldmap.com/usa/state/connecticut/connecticut-highway-map.jpg.

Orcutt, Samuel, and Ambrose Beardsley. *History of the Old Town of Derby, Connecticut 1642–1880.* Springfield, MA: Press of Springfield Printing Company, 1880.

Otto, Paul. *The Dutch–Munsee Encounter in America: The Struggle for Sovereignty in the Hudson Valley.* New York: Berghahn Books, 2006.

Parker, Geoffrey. *The Dutch Revolt.* Ithaca: Cornell University Press, 1977.

Parker, Geoffrey. *Global Crisis: War, Climate Change, and Catastrophe in the Seventeenth Century.* New Haven: Yale University Press, 2013.

Parker, Geoffrey. *The Thirty Years' War.* London: Routledge, 1997.

Parmenter, Jon W. "Separate Vessels: Hudson, the Dutch, and the Iroquois." In *The Worlds of the Seventeenth Century Hudson Valley,* edited by Jaap Jacobs and Louis Roper, 103–33. Albany: State University of New York Press, 2014.

Paulson, Timothy, and Hubert de Leeuw. *Coming to Terms with Early New Netherland–New York History: 1609, Henry Hudson Revisited.* Albany: New Netherland Company, 2014.

Paulson, Timothy, and Hubert de Leeuw. *Coming to Terms with Early New Netherland–New York History: 1610–1614.* Albany: New Netherland Company, 2013.

Payne-Joyce, David, ed. *Records of the Reformed Dutch Church of Albany NY, 1683–1809.* Wooster, MA, 2000. Accessed January 19, 2018. https://mathcs.clarku.edu/~djoyce/gen/Albany/refchurch.html.

Pearson, Jonathan. *History of the Schenectady Patent in Dutch and English Times.* Albany: Munsell, 1883.

Pettee, Julia. *The Rev. Jonathan Lee and His 18th Century Salisbury Parish: The Early History of the Town of Salisbury, Connecticut.* Salisbury: Salisbury Association, 1957.

Pfeiffer, John. "Preliminary Results: Historical and Archaeological Evidence Demonstrating an Early 17th Century Dutch Presence in Branford Connecticut." *De Nieu Nederlanse Marcurius* 14 (4) (1998).

Pfeiffer, John. "Privateers on the Shoreline." *Newsletter of the Old Lyme Historical Society* 4 (2008): 2.

Pfeiffer, John. "Wood the First Resource." *Lyme Public Hall Newsletter* 15 (2016): 4–6.

Philhower, Charles A. "Indians of the Morris County Area." *New Jersey Historical Society, Proceedings* 54 (4) (1936): 249–267.

Philhower, Charles A. "Ms. A Transcriptions of Indian Deeds." Manuscript copy in the Charles A. Philhower Collection, New Jersey Historical Society, Newark, New Jersey.

Porter, Tom. *Kanatsiohareke—Traditional Mohawk Indians Return to Their Ancestral Homeland.* Greenfield Center, NY: Bowman Books, 2006.

Postma, Johannes, and Victor Enthoven, eds. *Riches from Atlantic Commerce: Dutch Transatlantic Trade and Shipping, 1584–1817.* Leiden: Brill, 2003.

Prezzano, Susan. "Longhouse, Village, and Palisade: Community Patterns at the Iroquois Southern Door." PhD diss., State University of New York at Binghamton, 1992.

Prince, Thomas, ed. *A Brief History of the Pequot War Written by John Mason.* Boston: S. Kneeland and T. Green, 1736.

Proceedings of the New York State Historical Association. New York: New York State Historical Association, 1906.

Public Records of the Colony of Connecticut, 1636–1776. Vol. 1. Hartford: Brown & Parsons, 1850.

Purchas, Samuel. *Purchas His Pilgrimes.* London: Stansby for Fetherstone, 1625; reprinted in facsimile form by Readex Microprint, New Canaan, CT, 1966.

"Records of the Reformed Dutch Church of Albany, New York, 1683–1809." In *Yearbooks from the Holland Society of New York.* New York: Holland Society of New York, 1904.

Report of the Board of Accounts on New Netherland, dated December 15, 1644, in an ms. in the Royal Archives in The Hague, in the *Loketkas* of the States-General, Rubric, West Indische Compagnie, no. 30; 1st Division. In *Documents Relative to the Colonial History of the State of New York*, vol. 1, edited by E. B. O'Callaghan, 149–156. Albany: Weed, Parsons, and Company, 1856.

Richter, Daniel K. "Cultural Brokers and Intercultural Politics: New York–Iroquois Relations, 1664–1701." *Journal of American History* 75 (1988): 40–67.

Richter, Daniel K. *The Ordeal of the Longhouse: The Peoples of the Iroquois League in the Era of European Colonization.* Chapel Hill: University of North Carolina Press for the Institute of Early American History and Culture, 1992.

Rink, Oliver A. *Holland on the Hudson: An Economic and Social History of Dutch New York.* Ithaca: Cornell University Press; Cooperstown: New York State Historical Association, 1986.

Roever, Margriet de. "Merchandises for New Netherland: A Look at Dutch Articles for Barter with the Native American Population." In *Another Man's Trash Is Another Man's Treasure: The Metamorphosis of the European Utensil in the American World*, edited by Alexandra van Dongen, 71–93. Rotterdam: Museum Boymans-van Beuningen, 1996.

Romney, Susannah Shaw. *New Netherland Connections: Intimate Networks and Atlantic Ties in Seventeenth-Century America*. Chapel Hill: University of North Carolina Press for the Institute of Early American History and Culture, 2014.

Rothschild, Nan A. "De sociale aftsand tussen Nederlandse kolonisten en inheemse Amerikanen." In *'One Man's Trash Is Another Man's Treasure': De metamorfose van het Europese gebruiksvoorwerp in de Nieuwe Wereld*, edited by Alexandra van Dongen, 189–201. Exhibit catalog. Rotterdam: Museum Boymans-van Beuningen, 1995.

Rumrill, Donald A. "An Interpretation and Analysis of the Seventeenth-Century Mohawk Nation: Its Chronology and Movements." *Bulletin and Journal of Archaeology for New York State* 90 (1985): 1–39.

Ruttenber, Edward Manning. *History of the Indian Tribes of Hudson's River*. Albany: J. Munsell, 1872.

Salisbury Association. *Salisbury Town Meeting Minutes 1741–1784*. Salisbury, CT: Salisbury Association, 1988.

Salisbury, Neal. *Manitou and Providence: Indians, Europeans, and the Making of New England, 1500–1643*. New York: Oxford University Press, 1982.

Salwen, Bert. "Indians of Southern New England and Long Island." In *Connecticut Archaeology: Past, Present, and Future*, edited by Robert E. Dewar, Kenneth L. Feder, and David A. Poirier, 79–115. Occasional Papers in Anthropology no. 1. Storrs: Department of Anthropology, University of Connecticut, 1983.

Salwen, Bert. "Indians of Southern New England and Long Island." In *Handbook of North American Indians*, vol. 15: *Northeast*, general editor B. Trigger, 160–189. Washington, DC: Smithsonian Institution Press, 1978.

Saville, Foster H. "A Montauk Cemetery at Easthampton, Long Island." *Indian Notes and Monographs* 2 (3) (1920): 65–102.

Schama, Simon. *The Embarrassment of Riches: An Interpretation of Dutch Culture in the Golden Age*. Berkeley: University of California Press, 1988.

Sharaf, A. Torayah. *A Short History of Geographical Discovery*. London: George G. Harrap, 1967.

Shonnard, Frederic, and W. W. Spooner. *History of Westchester County, New York from Its Earliest Settlement to the Year 1900*. New York: New York History Company, 1900.

Shorto, Russell. *The Island at the Center of the World*. New York: Vintage Books, 2005.

Shorto, Russell. *The Island at the Center of the World: The Epic Story of Dutch Manhattan and the Forgotten Colony That Shaped America*. New York: Doubleday, 2004.

Simmons, William S. "Narragansett." In *Northeast*, vol. 15 of *Handbook of North American Indians*, edited by Bruce Trigger, 198–212. Washington, DC: Smithsonian Institution, 1978.

Simpson, Audra. *Mohawk Interruptus: Political Life across the Borders of Settler States*. Durham: Duke University Press, 2014.

Sivertsen, Barbara. *Turtles, Wolves, and Bears: A Mohawk Family History.* Bowie, MD: Heritage Books, 2006.

Smith, Carlyle S. "The Archaeology of Coastal New York." *Anthropological Papers of the American Museum of Natural History* 43, pt. 2 (1950).

Smith, Carlyle S. "A Note on Fort Massapeag." In *Native Forts of the Long Island Sound Area*, edited by Gaynell Stone, 241–242. Stony Brook: Suffolk County Archaeological Association, 2006.

Smith, Philip. *A General History of Dutchess County from 1609 to 1876, Inclusive*. Pawling, NY: Published by the author, 1877.

Smith, Philip E. L. "Land-Use, Settlement Patterns, and Subsistence Agriculture: A Demographic Perspective." In *Man, Settlement and Urbanism*, edited by Peter J. Ucko, Ruth Tringham, and G. W. Dimbleby, 409–425. Cambridge, MA: Schenkman Publishing, 1972.

Smithsonian Institution. *Booming Out: Mohawk Ironworkers Build New York*. Traveling Exhibition Service, 2004. Accessed August 31, 2017. http://sitesarchives.si.edu/exhibitions/exhibits/archived_exhibitions/booming/main.htm.

Snow, Dean R. "Mohawk Demography and the Effects of Exogenous Epidemics on American Indian Populations." *Journal of American Anthropology* 15 (1996): 160–182.

Snow, Dean R. "Mohawk Valley Archaeology: The Sites." *Occasional Paper in Archaeology* no. 23. University Park: Matson Museum of Anthropology, Pennsylvania State University, 1995.

Solecki, Ralph S. "The Archaeology of Fort Neck and Vicinity, Massapequa, Long Island, New York." In *Native Forts of the Long Island Sound Area*, edited by Gaynell Stone, 143–224. Stony Brook: Suffolk County Archaeological Association, 2006.

Solecki, Ralph S. "The Archaeological Position of Historic Fort Corchaug, Long Island, and Its Relation to Contemporary Forts." *Bulletin of the Archaeological Society of Connecticut* 24 (1950): 3–40.

Solecki, Ralph S. "Indian Forts of the Mid-17th Century in the Southern New England–New York Coastal Area." *Northeast Historical Archaeology* 22 (1) (1992–93): 64–78.

Spiess, Mathias, and Hayden Griswold. *Map of the State of Connecticut Showing Indian Trails, Villages and Sachemdoms*. Published by the Colonial Dames of America, 1930. Map and Geographic Information Center, University of Connecticut Libraries, Storrs.

Squier, E. G. "Aboriginal Monuments of the State of New York." *Smithsonian Contributions to Knowledge* 2. Washington: Smithsonian Institution, 1850.

Staffa, Susan J. *Schenectady Genesis.* Fleischmanns, NY: Purple Mountain Press, 2004.

Starna, William A. *From Homeland to New Land: A History of the Mahican Indians, 1600–1830.* Lincoln: University of Nebraska Press, 2013.

Starna, William A. "Indian–Dutch Frontiers." *De Halve Maen* 64 (2) (1991): 21–25.

Steiner, Bernard C. *A History of the Plantation of Menunkatuck.* Baltimore: Steiner, 1897.

Stewart, Frank H. *Indians of Southern New Jersey.* Woodbury, NJ: Gloucester County Historical Society, 1932; repr. 1977.

Stokes, Isaac N. P. "Carta particolare della Nuoua Belgia e parte della Nuoua Anglia." Miriam and Ira D. Wallach Division of Art, Prints and Photographs: Print Collection, New York Public Library, 1930. New York Public Library Digital Collections. Accessed January 1, 2018. http://digitalcollections.nypl.org/items/510d47d9-7c00-a3d9-e040-e00a18064a99.

Stokes, Phelps. *The Iconography of Manhattan Island, Volume 2.* New York: Robert H. Dodd, 1928.

Stone, Gaynell, editor. *Native Forts of the Long Island Sound Area.* Stony Brook: Suffolk County Archaeological Association, 2006.

Strong, John A. *The Algonquian Peoples of Long Island from Earliest Times to the Present.* Interlaken, NY: Heart of the Lakes Publishing, 1997.

Sturtevant, William C. "Two 1761 Wigwams at Niantic, Connecticut." *American Antiquity* 40 (1975): 437–444.

Sylvester, Nathaniel Bartlett. *History of Rensselaer Co., New York.* Philadelphia: Everts & Peck, 1880.

Thomason, Sarah G. "On Interpreting 'The Indian Interpreter.'" *Language in Society* 9 (1980): 182–186.

Thwaits, Reuben, ed. *Jesuit Relations Vol 44, 1656–1658.* Cleveland: Burrow Brothers, 1894.

Thwaits, Ruben Gold, ed. *The Jesuit Relations and Allied Documents; Travels and Explorations of the Jesuit Missionaries in New France, 1610–1791.* 73 vols. Cleveland: Burrow Brothers, 1896–1901.

Trelease, Allen W. *Indian Affairs in Colonial New York: The Seventeenth Century.* Ithaca: Cornell University Press, 1960.

Trelease, Allen W. Indian Affairs in Colonial New York: The Seventeenth Century. Lincoln: University of Nebraska Press, 1997.

Trouillot, Michel-Rolph. *Silencing the Past.* Boston: Beacon Press, 1995.

Trumbull, J. H. *The Memorial History of Hartford County Connecticut, 1633–1884.* Boston: E. L. Osgood, 1886.

Trumbull, J. H., ed. *The Public Records of the Colony of Connecticut Prior to the Union with New Haven Colony.* Hartford: Brown & Press, 1850.

Turgeon, Laurier. "French Fishers, Fur Traders, and Amerindians during the Sixteenth Century: History and Archaeology." *William and Mary Quarterly*, 3rd ser., 55 (1998): 585–610.

Turner, Francis. "Money and Exchange Rates in 1632." *Official 1632 Fan Site.* Accessed August 29, 2015. 1632.org/1632Slush/1632money.rtf.

Underhill, John. *Newes from America.* [1638]. Lincoln: University of Nebraska Digital Texts, 2007.

Van der Donck, Adriaen. *A Description of New Netherland.* Translated by Diederik Willem Goedhuys and edited by Charles T. Gehring and William A. Starna. Lincoln: University of Nebraska Press, 2008.

Van Dusen, Albert E. *Connecticut.* New York: Random House, 1961.

Van Laer, A. J. F., trans. "Council Minutes." *New York Historical Manuscripts Dutch Vol. IV.* Baltimore: Genealogical Publishing, 1974.

Van Laer, A. J. F. "Documents Relating to Arent van Curler's Death." In *The Dutch Settlers Society Yearbook* 3 (1927–28): 30–34.

Van Laer, A. J. F., trans. and ed. *Documents Relating to New Netherland, 1624–1626.* San Marino, CA: Henry E. Huntington Library and Art Gallery, 1924.

Van Laer, A. J. F., trans. and ed. *Minutes of the Court of Fort Orange and Beverwyk.* Albany: State University of New York Press, 1920.

Van Laer, A. J. F., trans. and ed. *Van Rensselaer Bowier Manuscripts.* Albany: State University of New York Press, 1908.

Vaughan, Alden T., general ed. *Early American Indian Documents: Treaties and Laws, 1607–1789.* 20 vols. Frederick, MD: University Publications of America, 1981–2004.

Van Wassenaer, Nicolas. "Historisch Verhael 1624–1630." In *The Narratives of New Netherland, 1609–1664,* edited by J. Franklin Jameson. New York: Charles Scribner's Sons, 1909.

Van Zandt, Cynthia J. Brothers among Nations: The Pursuit of Intercultural Alliances in Early America, 1580–1660. New York: Oxford University Press, 2008.

Venema, Janny. Beverwijck: A Dutch Village on the American Frontier, 1652–1664. Albany: State University of New York Press, 2003.

Venema, Janny. *Kiliaen van Rensselaer (1586–1643): Designing a New World.* New York: State University of New York Press, 2011.

Verhulst, Willem. "Instructions from the Directors of the West India Company, January 1625." In *Documents Relating to New Netherland, 1624–1626,* edited by A. J. F. van Laer. San Marino, CA: Henry E. Huntington Library, 1924.

Vinckeboons, Joan. *Pascaert van Nieuw Nederlandt Virginia, ende Nieuw-Engelandt verthonendt alles wat van die landin by See, oft by land is ondect oft Bekent.* [?1639] Map. https://www.loc.gov/item/2003623405/.

Visscher, Nicolaes. "Novi Belgii Novaeque Angliae Nec Non Partis Virginiae Tabula in locis emendata. Per Nicolaum Visscher." (to accompany) "Atlas minor sive totious orbis terrarum contracta delinea ex conatibus Nico. Visscher." 1690. (half title page) "Atlas Minor sive Geographica Compendiosa, qua Orbis Terrarum (inset) New Amsterdam." Amsterdam: Nicolai Visscher, 1690; 47 x 56 cm. David Rumsey Map Collection. Accessed July 31, 2018. https://www.david rumsey.com/luna/servlet/detail/RUMSEY~8~1~301299~90072256:Novi-Belgii-Novaeque-Angliae-NecNo?sort=pub_list_no_initialsort%2Cpub_date%2Cpub_list_no%2Cseries_no&qvq=w4s:/what%2FAtlas%2BMap%2Fwhere%2FU.S.%2BNorth%2BEast%2F;sort:pub_list_no_initialsort%2Cpub_date%2Cpub_list_no%2Cseries_no; lc:RUMSEY~8~1&mi=38&trs=109.

Visscher, Nicolaes. "Novi Belgii Novaeque Angliae nec non partis Virginiae tabula multis in locis emendate" by Nicolaes Visscher, ?1655 (From the New York Public Library, Image ID 54910, Miriam and Ira D. Wallach Division of Art, Prints and Photographs: Print Collection, NYPL Digital Collections. Accessed July 30, 2019. digitalcollections.nypl.org/items/510d47d9-7a7f-a3d9-e040-e00a18064a99).

Vries, David Pietersz de. Korte Historiael ende Journaels Aenteykeninge van ver-scheyden voyagiens in de vier delen des werelts-ronde, als Europa, Africa, ende America gedaen. Edited by H. T. Colebrander. Werken Uitgegeven door de Linschoten-Vereeniging 3. The Hague: Martinus Nijhoff, 1911.

Wallace, Anthony F. C. King of the Delawares: Teedyuskung, 1700–1763. Philadelphia: University of Pennsylvania Press, 1949.

Warrick, Gary A. "Estimating Ontario Iroquoian Village Duration." Man in the Northeast 36 (1988): 21–60.

Weise, A. J. History of the Seventeen Towns of Rensselaer County. Troy, NY: Francis and Tucker, 1881; repr. 1975.

Weslager, C. A. Dutch Explorers, Traders and Settlers in the Delaware Valley, 1609–1664. Philadelphia: University of Pennsylvania Press, 1961.

Weslager, C. A. "Enrollment List of Chippewa and Delaware-Munsies Living in Franklin County, Kansas, May 31, 1900." Kansas Historical Quarterly 40 (2) (1974): 234–40.

Weslager, C. A. A Man and His Ship: Peter Minuit and the Kalmar Nyckel. Wilmington, DE: Middle Atlantic Press, 1990.

Weslager, C. A. New Sweden on the Delaware 1638–1655. Wilmington, DE: Middle Atlantic Press, 1988.

Whipple, Chandler. First Encounter: The Indian and the White Man in Massachusetts and Rhode Island. Stockbridge, MA: Berkshire Traveler, 1974.

Wholey, Heather A., and Carole L. Nash, eds. Middle Atlantic Prehistory: Foundations and Practice. Lanham, MD: Rowman and Littlefield, 2017.

Wilcoxen, Charlotte. "Arent van Curler's Children." New York Genealogical and Biographical Record 110 (1979): 82–84.

Wilcoxen, Charlotte. Dutch Trade and Ceramics in America in the Seventeenth Century. Albany: Albany Institute of History and Art, 1987.

Wilcoxen, Charlotte. "Dutch Trade with New England." In A Beautiful and Fruitful Place, Selected Rensselaerswijck Seminar Papers, edited by Nancy Anne McClure Zeller, 235–241. Albany: New Netherland Publishing, 1991.

Williams, Kayeneseh Paul. "The Mohawk Valley: Yesterday, Today and Tomorrow." In *Kanatsiohareke—Traditional Mohawk Indians Return to Their Ancestral Homeland*, by Tom Porter, 1–11. Greenfield Center, NY: Bowman Books, 2006.

Williams, Roger. *A Key into the Language of America.* [1643]. Bedford: Applewood Books, 1936.

Wilson, Peter H. *Europe's Tragedy: A New History of the Thirty Years' War.* London: Penguin, 2010.

Winthrop, John. "History of New England." In Winthrop's Journal, 1630–1649. New York: Scribner's, 1908.

Winthrop, John. *Winthrop Papers, Vol. III, 1631–1637.* Boston: Massachusetts Historical Society, 1943.

Witsend. *Sharon's Dutchers Page.* "Connecticut Dutchers." Website. Accessed January 15, 2018. http://www.witsend.org/gen/dutcher/ct.htm.

Woodward, Ashbel. *Wampum.* Albany: J. Munsell, Printer, 1878.

Contributors

Marshall Joseph Becker has been studying the Native peoples of the Delaware River and Delaware Bay for more than forty-five years. He was trained at the University of Pennsylvania in all four fields of anthropology. He now applies archaeology as well as other approaches to gather information about the Lenape ("Delaware Indians") and their neighbors. Becker has published nearly two hundred articles on the Lenape and other Native Americans in scholarly journals as well as popular magazines. He also has published a book and a number of book chapters and monographs on peoples of the Americas. Becker's research has been supported by grants from the National Science Foundation, the National Endowment for the Humanities, the American Philosophical Society, and the National Geographic Society.

Anne-Marie Cantwell is an archaeologist and Professor Emerita at Rutgers University, and Visiting Scholar at New York University. With Diana Wall, she has coauthored the books *Unearthing Gotham* and *Touring Gotham* and many articles on New Netherland. They are currently working on a book on the archaeology of New Netherland. She is coeditor of *Ethics in Anthropology*, *Aboriginal Economy and Ritual in the Eastern Woodlands*, *Copper in Late Prehistoric North America*, and *Research Potential of Anthropological Museum Collections* and has written numerous articles on the politics of the past, colonialism, and pre-Contact trade and ritual. Her archaeological field work is in the Midwest and Northeast at both pre-Contact and historic sites.

Shirley Wiltse Dunn is the holder of Master's degrees in English and History from Albany State Teachers College (now SUNYA), and she has worked as a teacher, museum interpreter, editor, and historic preservation consultant. Dunn is the well-known author of books about the Mohican

Indians, including *The Mohicans and Their Land*, *The Mohican World*, and *The River Indians—Mohicans Making History*. She also edited three books of conference papers on Native Americans for the New York State Museum. Today's Mohican Nation, now headquartered in Wisconsin, recently honored her with a proclamation of appreciation. She received recognition from the New Netherland Project in Albany for initiating the Dutch Barn Preservation Society, and she has been honored as a Fellow by the Holland Society of New York for Dutch studies. With coauthor Allison Bennett, she published a book of unique photos titled *Dutch Architecture Near Albany*. She earlier edited a book of family stories titled *Pioneer Days in the Catskill High Peaks*, and did a series of yearly calendars for the Historical Society of Esquatak. She worked at Fort Crailo for three years as the Assistant Manager.

Charles Gehring was born in Fort Plain, an old Revolutionary War and Erie Canal village in New York State's Mohawk Valley. After completing his undergraduate and graduate studies at Virginia Military Institute and West Virginia University he continued postgraduate work with the assistance of a Fulbright grant at Albert-Ludwigs-Universität in Freiburg, Germany. There he began his study of the Dutch language and first realized that his future research lay much closer to home. In 1973 he received a PhD in Germanic Linguistics from Indiana University with a concentration in Netherlandic Studies. His dissertation was a linguistic investigation of the survival of the Dutch language in colonial New York. He is presently director of the New Netherland Research Center (sponsored by the New York State Library). The Center is responsible for translating the official records of the Dutch colony, promoting awareness of the Dutch role in American history, and providing a center for research in New Netherlandic studies. He has been a fellow of the Holland Society of New York since 1979. In 1994 Her Majesty Queen Beatrix of the Netherlands conferred on him a knighthood as officer in the Order of Orange-Nassau. He has received gold medals from the Netherlands Society of Philadelphia, the Holland Society of New York, and the St. Nicholas Society of New York. Most recently he has become a board member of the Dutch Museum on the island of Saba in the Netherlands Antilles.

Paul Gorgen is a member of the Board of Directors of the Kanatsiohareke Mohawk Community, a writer and researcher from the Mohawk Valley, and enrolled in Kanatsiohareke's Mohawk language program. Recent publications include articles on the Mohawks and the Palatine Germans in the *Yorker*

Palatine, the *Fort Hunter NYS Park Journal,* and in *Plotzlich Da,* a book on German emigration published by the Deutsches Auswanderhaus Museum, Bremerhaven, Germany, in 2015. His article on Clarissa Putman and Molly Brant appeared in the journal *Iroquoia* in 2017. He is retired from IBM and resides in Poughkeepsie, New York.

Lucianne Lavin is the Director of Research and Collections at the Institute for American Indian Studies in Washington, Connecticut. She is a founding member of the state's Native American Heritage Advisory Council, Editor of the journal of the Archaeological Society of Connecticut, and a Fellow of the New York State Archaeological Association. Lavin is an anthropologist and archaeologist who has over forty-five years of research and field experience in Northeastern archaeology and anthropology, including teaching, museum exhibits and curatorial work, cultural resource management, editorial work, and public relations. She received her MA and PhD in anthropology from New York University and her BA from Indiana University. She has written over 200 publications and technical reports on Northeastern archaeology and ethnohistory. Her award-winning book, *Connecticut's Indigenous Peoples: What Archaeology, History, and Oral Traditions Teach Us about Their Communities and Cultures,* was published by Yale University Press in 2013. She is a Connecticut-born resident, having lived much of her life in the lower Housatonic Valley.

Richard Manack is an award-winning public access film producer on the history of the Dutch in Connecticut. He lived in Holland for many years, including a ten-year residency in the Pricen Island section of Amsterdam, which was home to the famous Dutch West Indies Company. Richard is also the owner and captain of a historic Dutch sailing barge, the *Golden Re'al.*

Kevin McBride is an Associate Professor of Anthropology at the University of Connecticut and the Director of Research at the Mashantucket Pequot Museum and Research Center. He has conducted archaeological and historical research in Connecticut, Massachusetts, and Block Island as well as in Baja Mexico, the Caribbean, and Portugal. His research interests include cultural and historical landscapes, maritime adaptations, historical archaeology, underwater archaeology, and battlefield archaeology. McBride is a member of the Society for American Archaeology, the American Anthropological Association, the Society for Historic Archaeology, and the Society for American Ethnohistory and is Adjunct Faculty of the Institute for Exploration. He is a former member of the Board of Directors of the Connecticut Museum of Natural History and of the Governor's Task Force on Indian Affairs. He has written numerous articles on Native American and Colonial archaeology, ethnohistory, archaeobotany, underwater archaeology, and battlefield archaeology.

John Pfeiffer is a graduate of SUNY Albany, receiving his doctorate in 1992. Since the early 1970s he has led many archaeological excavations throughout the Northeast that focused upon both prehistoric Native American as well as historic sites. He is a past president of the Archaeological Society of Connecticut and taught for seventeen years at Wesleyan University's Graduate Liberal Studies Program. The excavations at Branford in the mid-1990s were sponsored by the Branford Historical Society and Wesleyan University's Graduate Liberal Studies Program. He is presently Chair of the Old Lyme Historic District Commission and the Old Lyme Town Historian.

Stephen T. Staggs is on the teaching staff of Calvin College. He received a BA in history from Calvin College, and an MA and PhD in Colonial North America and Early Modern Europe from Western Michigan University. Professor Staggs's interests include the history of early modern Europe and colonial North America, Native-Dutch relations in New Netherland, and pedagogical studies. In 2010–11, he was a Fulbright fellow affiliated with the Vrije Universiteit in Amsterdam, where he researched Protestant conceptualizations of Native Americans made by early modern Dutch theologians. This became a central aspect of his dissertation, which he defended in 2014. Professor Staggs recently became an editor of the H-Low Countries website, which is a part of the H-Net organization of scholars and teachers who advance the educational potential of the internet.

Diana diZerega Wall is an archaeologist who specializes in the study of New York City, from the Dutch period through the nineteenth century. Her interests include colonialism and the construction of class, race, and gender. Professor Emerita at City College and the CUNY Graduate Center, she holds a PhD from New York University. Her books include *The Archaeology of American Cities* (with Nan Rothschild; University Press of Florida, 2014) and the award-winning *Unearthing Gotham* (with Anne-Marie Cantwell; Yale, 2001). She is currently working on a book on the archaeology of New Netherland (with Anne-Marie Cantwell).

Index